The Best of

CHICAGO

Editor
Colleen Dunn Bates

Contributing Editors
Pat Bruno, Dan Kening, Sondra Rosenberg, Stuart Silverman,
David Standish, Jennifer Wolff

Assistant Editors
Pamela Mosher, Connie Ridge, Margery L. Schwartz, Karre Slafkin

Operations
Alain Gayot

Directed by
André Gayot

PRENTICE HALL ▪ NEW YORK

Other Gault Millau Guides Available
from Prentice Hall Trade Division
The Best of France
The Best of Italy
The Best of Los Angeles
The Best of New England
The Best of New York
The Best of San Francisco
The Best of Washington, D.C.

Published by Prentice Hall Trade Division
A Division of Simon & Schuster Inc.
Gulf + Western Building
One Gulf + Western Plaza
New York, New York 10023

Please address all comments regarding The Best of Chicago to:
Gault Millau Inc.
P.O. Box 36114
Los Angeles, CA 90036

Library of Congress Cataloging-in-Publication Data
The Best of Chicago

Includes index.
1. Chicago–Description–1981—Guide-books.
I. Bates, Colleen Dunn.
F548.18.B47 1989 917.73'110443 89-3536

ISBN 0-13-072836-5

Thanks to the staff of Prentice Hall Travel for their invaluable
aid in producing these Gault Millau guides.

CONTENTS

SIGHTS

A tour of the city's must-sees. Gaze across the Midwest from atop Sears Tower, admire Frank Lloyd Wright's creations or just stake out a spot at the beach.

ARTS

The heartland of America is in love with the arts, as you'll discover in these pages. Art museums, cultural museums, science museums, art galleries, classical music, live theater—there's enough to keep the most dedicated culture vulture busy forever.

BASICS

Everything you need to know about getting around in Chicago like a true native. Includes public transportation, late-night services, helpful telephone numbers and a calendar of noteworthy and offbeat events.

MAPS

Orientation maps for finding your way around Chicago.

INDEX

CHICAGO

AMERICA'S BIGGEST SMALL TOWN

S ure, sure, they're calling it the "Third City" these days, since it lost out to Los Angeles in the last census. But Chicago is arguably the biggest truly American city in the United States, since New York belongs to the world and L.A. to the Martians. Or, at any rate, New York attracts all the would-be power brokers in search of megabucks, and in L.A. everyone's writing screenplays, or about to star in one. You'll find some from both camps in Chicago, but there's a home-grown quality as well. Its many ethnic neighborhoods are more like villages than sections of a huge city—everybody knows everybody, and everybody's business. In some ways Chicago is the country's biggest small town—but one with some of the best museums, restaurants and nightlife to be found any-where. A common comparison, not entirely accurate, is that it's the *easier* version of New York, with only ten or so, say, truly *oh là là!* French restaurants to New York's 50 or so. It's a proportion that remains fairly constant in a number of ways—and, generally speaking, it's plenty, whether your passion is avant-garde theater or birdwatching (actually, more species of birds have been spotted in Chicago's lakefront Lincoln Park than in New York's Central Park). There is always so much going on that one never has the time, energy or money to do it all. And Chicago, being Midwestern, is a friendlier place than big cities tend to be: Strangers sometimes actually *smile and say hello* to each other when passing on the street.

For a good part of the year the weather is basically unfit for anything except misery. It turns gray and rotten in late November and pretty much stays that way until April. Chicago is one of the few places in the world where the winter wind has a name. Writer Amiri Baraka described it as the home of the African god Oba, who was transformed into "an icy, death-cold wind" called the Hawk. There are standing arguments about which corner is coldest when the Hawk is out, and every January the city's evening news teams have some poor shivering bastard standing at one of them, wind-chill thermometer in hand, on the 10 o'clock news. Just like on rough North Atlantic crossings, hand ropes are installed along the sidewalks around the Hancock Building and others, so that 92-pound little old ladies won't be blown into the street. Nevertheless, residents rarely call it "The Windy City." That's not cool.

July and August aren't much fun either, thanks to fearsome heat waves and mind-numbing humidity. But for at least four months—May, June, September and October—Chicago is a great place to be. The presence of Lake Michigan is the main reason, a 300-plus-mile-long (and 60 or so across) freshwater miniature ocean left over from the melting of the last glacier 12,000 years ago. The lake makes water a major presence—the lakefront is 22 miles long within city limits. And thanks to the nine-teenth-century engineering feat of reversing the flow of the Chicago River so that it sends its gunk west to the Illinois and eventually the Mississippi rivers, Lake Michigan's water is clean and fit to swim in—at least when it finally warms up in late June.

Chicago has a sort of stage-set quality: Like a frontier Main Street in the Old West, it has a splendid facade along the lake—beaches, parks, museums, innovative high-rises, elegant old buildings. One reason summer lake cruises are so popular is that the city was practically built to be viewed from that perspective. But it's behind the facade, beyond the carpetbagger strip along the Gold Coast, back in neighborhoods of every imaginable ethnic persuasion, that the city that works—in former Mayor Daley's phrase—works. On the North Side, for instance, you don't have to go very far west of Clark Street before the local taverns are populated with mailmen and furnace repairmen and plumbers, not commodities brokers and ad men and young financial wizards. But it's behind the facade, too, that most of the city's problems are hidden. Chicago, with not one but three different black ghettos, has been called, with a certain justification, America's most racially divided city. That's gradually chang-ing, but only gradually. And there is a North Side neighborhood called Uptown that most visitors never see, which is one of the most integrated on Earth—but for the wrong reason. Thais, Vietnamese, blacks, South-ern whites, Native Americans, Mexicans, Puerto Ricans, Filipinos, Kore-ans, you name it—and they all have only one thing in common: that they are poor—populate a neighborhood that Studs Terkel described as "the U.N. of the disadvantaged." But there are happier sides to the city.

Chicago—the name is a Potawatami word for "wild onion," after the abundance of the bulbs found growing along the banks of the river—was an occasional settlement during Indian times, largely because a sandbar across the mouth of the Chicago River provided a rare safe harbor, and later because it proved to be a good stepping stone to the Mississippi and to the West. Sitting smack in the middle of the country-to-be, the place was born to be a nexus, a heartland crossroads. And it's still so—O'Hare remains one of the busiest airports in the world.

The first official non-Indian resident was Jean Pointe du Sable, a Haitian of mixed European and African parentage who set up a trading post at the mouth of the Chicago River in the 1790s. Chicago was incorporated as a city in 1833, but the national financial collapse of 1837 kept the settlement down until the 1840s—when the coming of the railroad put Chicago on the map. Before 1850, such Illinois river towns as Galena, Quincy and Cairo were all bigger and more important than Chicago. But by the 1880s, when the railroads had killed off the river trade celebrated in Mark Twain's *Life on the Mississippi*, these towns had become backwaters while Chicago boomed as the new metropolis of the prairies.

You can measure its flush-times atmosphere back then by what happened after the city burned down that infamous day in October 1871, when Mrs. O'Leary's cow probably *didn't* kick over the lantern that started the blaze. The weather had been bone dry for weeks, and a strong, hot wind was blowing off the prairies. In 24 hours all of downtown and most of the West and North sides were smoldering rubble, with little standing but the new sandstone water tower. But hardly two years later, the city had been rebuilt, bigger and better than before, using innovative building techniques, something that's been a trademark of Chicago architecture since before the Great Fire. Then in the 1880s and '90s, the modern high-rise was invented in Chicago. Figuring out how to float them on vast concrete rafts in the sandy soil was another technique the late nineteenth-century Chicago architects developed. And it didn't stop there. Bauhaus architect Ludwig Mies van der Rohe landed in Chicago in flight from the Nazis, eventually to design the first-ever high-rise, glass-box apartment house, which is still standing near the curve of Lake Shore Drive, all windows and girders—for better or worse.

In the early part of this century, as the steel mills of Gary and Hammond and East Chicago began smoking in earnest, Chicago began to attract its now-majority black population, many from the Mississippi delta. It's a community that has contributed greatly to the city's special flavor—just for starters, the best barbecued ribs in existence (no matter *what* Calvin Trillin says about Kansas City) and the creation of the electric urban blues by Muddy Waters, Little Walter, B. B. King, Willie Dixon, Elmore James, Howlin' Wolf and others—music that provided rock 'n roll with its heartbeat. An early Rolling Stones' song is titled

"2120 S. Michigan Avenue," the address of Chess Records, a nondescript building where most of these blues players recorded. And the blues is still alive and well in Chicago.

Chicagoans have a lot more than the blues to keep them amused. From the mobster-ridden days of Prohibition to the politically scandalous '80s, crime has always had considerable entertainment value in Chicago, even a certain approval, stemming from a shared conviction that only the odd man out isn't a crook. (Mike Royko is not an iconoclast in Chicago; he's giving the majority report.) There's a sort of cheery cynicism about it all—and plenty to be cynical about. Chicago has the most amusing local politics of any city in the country, hands down (or should that be hands up?). Aldermen indicted on felonies and locked up in jail win reelection in their wards. Ballots from various precincts mysteriously appear and disappear depending on who needs the votes. Building inspectors found *not* to be taking bribes are singled out for great praise. Visitors are almost guaranteed one or two criminal indictments of public officials during even a short stay. It's really a lot of fun.

But above all, Chicago is *cool*. Doesn't the Chairman of the Board himself call it "my kinda town"? It has been the setting for some of the most powerful novels in American literature: Theodore Dreiser's *Sister Carrie*, Upton Sinclair's *The Jungle* and James T. Farrell's *Studs Lonigan*, probably the best Chicago novel of them all. These books share a grittiness, a literary populism that's a correlative for the city itself. The Chicago Symphony Orchestra, conducted by Sir George Solti, is year after year the country's best. If we were to create a short list of the world's best museums, The Art Institute and the Museum of Science and Industry would be up near the top. The Chicago Bears, of course, are the coolest team in the NFL, like the old Oakland Raiders used to be, more like a lovable motorcycle gang than a football team. Michael Jordan of the Chicago Bulls has added a level of grace and skill to the game of basketball that's never been seen before. And even the perennially abject Cubs are cool in a weird existential way. They haven't won a World Series since 1945 and they finished the 1987 season in last place, over 30 games out, but still Wrigley Field is packed every afternoon (and now night) that they're in town. Going to the park to drink a little beer and watch the Cubs lose is an essential Chicago summer ritual.

We agree with Frank. It's *our* kinda town, too.

RESTAURANTS

THE WINDS OF CHANGE

The 1980s will go down in Chicago's culinary history as the decade of dining delirium. Just as mushrooms pop magically from the earth after a long spell of rain, so it has been in Chicago with restaurants: For almost ten years they have been springing up·out of nowhere, and still they keep coming. It has simply been a case of restaurateurs and entrepreneurs—spurred by the riches that restaurants can bring and by rampant egomania—discovering that they were standing on fertile ground for restaurant planting. And plant they did—furiously.

To understand how all this came about—this great Tour de Restaurants of the '80s—we must look back to the '70s, a time when Chicago restaurants were suffering from a bad case of lethargy. When we think of Chicago's restaurant food of the early '70s, we are reminded of a quote attributed to Joan Crawford: "If you throw a lamb chop in the oven, what's to keep it from getting done?" The central city of the heartland was dangerously close to going into culinary arrest, and it seemed that no one wanted to come forward to save the patient. So instead of eating out, and being bored to death, Chicagoans started wandering into their own kitchens.

Suddenly everybody was cooking at home. Eating out wasn't exactly a dead issue, but you could count the number of good restaurants around town without using all available fingers. And there weren't many between *un* and *huit* that weren't French. (Nor was there anything close to the conceptual and creative excitement found in the restaurants that have come along in the past eight years or so.) Suddenly, not only was everyone cooking at home, but they were learning how to do it better by attending cooking classes and schools here and abroad. A burning desire filled the hearts and minds of many Chicagoans: to learn more about cooking and food; they were sharpening their taste buds and beginning to appreciate good food a lot more.

Julia Child spurred the revolution via her weekly cooking shows on public television. She made it look easy to prepare difficult (and, to many Chicagoans, heretofore unpronounceable) dishes. "Whip," said the culinary queen, and the sound of beaters clanging against bowls could be heard across the land. The kitchen was the theater for food, and everybody was playing the role of chef. But many of the shows were about to close.

Toward the end of 1981, the kitchen and gourmet home cooking began to lose some of their appeal. Cooks were tiring of cooking. It was a bit much to work all day and come home and cook a gourmet meal. But that was only part of the reason people started to emerge from their kitchens and once again declare the real truth—that they enjoyed cooking once in a while, but it was a lot more fun (and a lot easier) to eat out.

As the era of the gourmet home chef waned, so did the popularity of the cuisine that everyone could pronounce but no one could figure out. Nouvelle cuisine, or at least its plentiful misinterpretations, probably did more damage to French cooking, and America's perception of it, than anything else before or since. Haute went healthy, and people went ho hum. But the very idea of nouvelle made people more aware of a particular style of cooking. And, more importantly, the underlying principles of nouvelle cuisine gave us a better understanding of classic cooking concepts. It also gave chefs—young and old alike—the impetus to be more daring and to explore new ideas, to push the envelope beyond the tried and traditional.

While Chicagoans were honing their culinary skills and coming to a broader understanding of food of all kinds, the foundation for the great Chicago restaurant boom of the '80s was being laid. Richard Melman began stimulating the taste buds of Chicago eaters as early as 1971, when he opened a place called R. J. Grunt's. About a year later, Arnie Morton opened Arnie's, probably the first restaurant-as-theater concept in the Midwest, if not the United States. Neither of these restaurants was exactly the epitome of fine dining, but they helped launch Chicago's culinary revolution and evolution. They also prompted others—entrepreneurs, investors and other restaurateurs—to look at restaurants and the business of feeding people in an entirely different way.

Suddenly the race was on to open restaurants, to create new food ideas, to rethink and remodel, to delve deeper into American cooking and to explore ethnic cooking in greater depths. The winds of change were sweeping across the Windy City, and dining in the city hasn't been the same since.

Chicago, the culinary wasteland of the '70s, became a culinary wonderland. The old-line, seasoned French restaurants are, for the most part, still in business and seem to be reasonably healthy (though, of course, the health of any restaurant is measured in finite degrees and day by day). Mainstream ethnic restaurants—Italian, Greek, Polish, German, Mexican—are faring quite well. And the newcomers—the oh-so-trendy neo-American, Southwestern, California, hip Italian—are packing them in.

(Pockets of ethnicity run deep in this city, and there are few holes, but Midwesterners are not quick to turn themselves inside out when it comes to anything *too* exotic. True, Chicago went crazy for Thai food for a time, but it's no longer such a hot cuisine. Japanese restaurants, with the exception of a few excellent sushi houses, are struggling. Such fringe cuisines as Afghan, Peruvian, Ethiopian and Vietnamese do all right only because they are few in number.)

Chicagoans have often been accused of being fickle when it comes to restaurants. Yesterday's hot restaurant can become ice cold practically overnight. To wit: The Cajun rage, which was burning like a bonfire less than two years ago, is only a flickering flame today. And if you're going to open a seafood restaurant in Chicago, it had better be good, or it'll get the hook real fast. The newest restaurant to open is most often the hottest—for a time. But we don't think it's so much the case that Chicagoans are fickle about restaurants (they certainly are no more fickle than the residents of any other city), it's simply that restaurateurs have changed their modus operandi, switching from restaurant-as-theater to restaurant-as-novelty. Sports bars, micro-breweries, diners, personality-named places, wild-and-crazy ethnic eateries, warehouse wacky, loft-conversion lunacy, comedy-club cuisine. Many of these establishments are not exactly chef d'oeuvres, but if that's what the people want, then that's exactly what the trendsetters—the Levy Brothers, Richard Melman and other monied groups—will give them. And when the novelty wears off and the restless herd moves on to graze new pastures, no one but the owner is to blame.

By any measure of comparison, Chicago is still a bargain-restaurant city. You can eat better here for less money than in any other major American city. We will not notarize the concept that more is better, but in Chicago it is possible to eat hearty and not get heartburn when it comes time to settle the check.

And by any standard of evaluation, Chicago is certainly home to a wealth of culinary talent. With but a few exceptions, Chicago chefs do not receive the national publicity or recognition they justly deserve or that their bicoastal peers elicit, but that slight doesn't deter them from doing their best. We have experienced exquisite pleasure at Chicago's tables, and we expect to experience plenty more, because the talent abounds.

We'd like to see two things happen. The first is an increase in the number of civilized dining retreats: quiet, sensibly sized restaurants where the pleasures of the plate take precedence over all else. The restaurants-as-theater or restaurants-as-novelty have their place, but it is folly to think that any play will run forever. The second is better training for Chicago's budding chefs. In France, the stove is often referred to as the "piano." It would be wise to have the city's young, aspiring chefs spend more time learning how to play this "piano" before they are called upon to perform before an audience.

We, as restaurant critics, are not the final arbiters of good taste in food—the ultimate judge in that regard is the public—but we do possess a few special talents, the most important being the ability to recognize and applaud restaurants that possess a certain degree of quality. At the same time, we are also quick to point out the restaurants that are lacking. In this sampling of Chicago's best and best-known restaurants, we give you our humble opinions and unbiased evaluations. Some are critical, some are complimentary, and all are as accurate as possible, given the uncertainty and mercurial nature of restaurants. And nowhere do the winds of change blow more forcibly than in Chicago.

Pat Bruno

ABOUT THE REVIEWS

Restaurants are ranked in the same manner that French students are graded: on a scale of one to twenty, twenty being unattainable perfection. The rankings reflect *only* the quality of the cooking; decor, service, welcome and atmosphere are explicitly commented on within the reviews. Restaurants ranked thirteen and above are distinguished with toques (chef's hats), according to the following table:

4 toques, for 19/20, exceptional

3 toques, for 17/20 and 18/20, excellent

2 toques, for 15/20 and 16/20, very good

1 toque, for 13/20 and 14/20, good

Keep in mind that we are comparing Chicago's restaurants to the finest in the world—just because the city's best restaurants don't get four toques doesn't mean they aren't exceptionally good. Also, these ranks are *relative*. One toque for 13/20 is not a very good ranking for a highly reputed (and very expensive) temple of fine dining, but it is quite complimentary for a small place without much pretension.

Unless otherwise noted, the prices given are for a complete dinner for two, including an appetizer, main course and dessert per person, along with tax, fifteen-percent tip and a bottle of wine. It is, naturally, hard to estimate the cost of wine; for our purposes we've assumed a modest bottle at a modest restaurant and a good California wine (usually $20 to $30) at a more serious place. Lovers of the great Burgundies, Bordeaux or Champagnes will find their tabs higher than our estimates; conversely, those who like to eat lightly, sharing appetizers and desserts, will spend less. Prices, however, continue to creep up, so some restaurants may have become more expensive than our estimates by the time you visit.

As we've said, Chicago's restaurants are subject to the winds of change, making it difficult for us to predict if the same chef, menu and/or management will be in place by the time of your visit. We ask your forgiveness in advance if a restaurant is somewhat different when you visit—we've done everything we can to keep up with the always-changing Chicago dining scene.

TOQUE TALLY

17/20

Ambria
Le Français

The Everest Room
Jimmy's Place

16/20

Avalon
Café Provençal
Carlos'
Foley's

Jackie's Restaurant
Le Prince
Yoshi's Café

15/20

Coppi
L'Escargot on Halsted
Gordon
Nick's Fishmarket
Les Plumes

Printer's Row
Shaw's Crab House
Sole Mio
Spiaggia

14/20

Arun's Thai
Cafe 21
The Chestnut Street Grill
The Cottage
Eurasia
Froggy's French Café
Frontera Grill
Un Grand Café
J. P.'s Eating Place
Le Mikado
Morton's

Le Perroquet
Ritz-Carlton Hotel/
    The Dining Room
Scoozi!
StreetSide Restaurant and Bar
Topo Gigio
Toulouse
La Tour
Trattoria Bellavia
Le Vichyssois
Yvette

13/20

Army & Lou's
Avanzare
Bistro 110
La Bohème
Buckingham's
Cafe Angelo
Cafe Ba-Ba-Reeba!
Cafe Royal
Cap Cod Room
Carlucci
The Chardonnay
Chez Jenny
Club Gene and Georgetti
Cricket's
Dong Hung Vien Restaurant
Emilio's Tapas Bar and
    Restaurant

L'Escargot on Michigan
Francesco's Hole in the Wall
Hat Dance
House of Hunan
Italian Village: Florentine Room
Jun Japanese Restaurant
Lawry's The Prime Rib
Maple Tree Inn
Mélange
La Même Chose
Moti Mahal
The 95th
P.S. Bangkok
Palm Restaurant
Prairie
Rosebud Cafe
Sabrina Cafe Club

Steven B's
La Strada
Three Happiness Restaurant
Le Titi de Paris

Charlie Trotter's
Tucci Benucch
The Winnetka Grill

12/20

Alexander's
The Bakery
Bay Street
The Berghoff Restaurant
Biggs
Bigsby's Bar & Grill
Billy and Company
Capri Ristorante Italiano
Chez Paul
Cocorico
Courtyards of Plaka
Eli's the Place for Steaks
Galáns
Hatsuhana
The Helmand
Jerome's
Mareva's
Memere's
Memories of China
The Winnetka Grill

Middle East Restaurant and
   Cocktails
Pars Cove
The Parthenon
Pattaya
Pronto Ristorante
The Pump Room
Rico's
Rinconcito Sundamericano
Sayat Nova
Shiroi Hana Restaurant
Standard India Restaurant
Michael Stuart's
Su Casa
Superior Street Cafe
Tijuana Yacht Club
Trattoria Gianni
The Waterfront
Yugo Inn

11/20

Ananda
Bombay Palace
The Canoe Club
Cantonese Chef
Ditka's
Dragon Palace
Fernando's
Green Door Tavern
Heidelberger Fass
Honda
Italian Village: The Village

Kampai Chicago
Orly's
Perinos
Philander's Oak Park
Pine Yard
Pronto Ristorante
Restaurant Suntory Chicago
Rio's Casa Iberia
Samavar
Phil Smidt & Son
Song Huong

Sulo
Tehran Restaurant
Thunderbird Bar and Grill

Uncle Tannous
Zaven's
Zofia's

10/20

At The Tracks
Barney's Market Club
California Pizza Kitchen
Club Lago
Como Inn

George's Restaurant
Italian Village: La Cantina
Moulibet
Tap & Growler

9/20

Annabelle's
Binyon's
Convito Italiano

Hopper's Dining Car
N.E.W. Cuisine
Sieben's River North Brewery

8/20

Genesee Depot

Trattoria Pizzeria Roma

NO RANKING

Wrigley Building Restaurant

THE WORLD'S CUISINES

AFGHAN

The Helmand

AMERICAN

Alexander's
At The Tracks

Barney's Market Club
Bay Street

The Berghoff Restaurant
Bigsby's Bar & Grill
Binyon's
Buckingham's
Cafe 21
The Canoe Club
The Chestnut Street Grill
The Cottage
Cricket's
Ditka's
Foley's
Genesee Depot
Gordon
Green Door Tavern

Hopper's Dining Car
Jerome's
Lawry's The Prime Rib
The 95th
Orly's
Prairie
Printer's Row
The Pump Room
Sieben's River North Brewery
StreetSide Restaurant and Bar
Superior Street Cafe
Tap & Growler
Charlie Trotter's
The Winnetka Grill

ARMENIAN

Sayat Nova

ASIAN-AMERICAN

Eurasia

BRAZILIAN

Rio's Casa Iberia

CAJUN/CREOLE

Maple Tree Inn   Memere's

CALIFORNIA

Avalon
California Pizza Kitchen
Mélange
La Même Chose

N.E.W. Cuisine
Sabrina Cafe Club
Steven B's

CHINESE

Cantonese Chef
Dong Hung Vien Restaurant
Dragon Palace
House of Hunan

Memories of China
Pine Yard
Three Happiness Restaurant

CONTINENTAL

The Bakery
Biggs
Eli's the Place for Steaks
Genesee Depot

Mareva's
Wrigley Building Restaurant
Zaven's

ETHIOPIAN

Moulibet

ENGLISH

Cafe Royal

FRENCH

Ambria
Avalon
Bistro 110
La Bohème
Café Provençal
Carlos'
The Chardonnay
Chez Jenny
Chez Paul
Cocorico
L'Escargot on Halsted
L'Escargot on Michigan
The Everest Room
Le Français
Froggy's French Café

Un Grand Café
Jimmy's Place
La Même Chose
Le Perroquet
Les Plumes
Le Prince
Ritz-Carlton Hotel/
    The Dining Room
Michael Stuart's
Le Titi de Paris
Toulouse
La Tour
Le Vichyssois
Yoshi's Café
Yvette

FRENCH-ASIAN

Jackie's Restaurant

FRENCH-JAPANESE

Le Mikado

GERMAN

The Berghoff Restaurant Heidelberger Fass

GREEK

Courtyards of Plaka

HUNGARIAN

The Bakery The Parthenon

INDIAN

Bombay Palace Samavar
Moti Mahal Standard India Restaurant

INTERNATIONAL

Orly's

ITALIAN

Avanzare Club Gene and Georgetti
Cafe Angelo Club Lago
California Pizza Kitchen Como Inn
Capri Ristorante Italiano Convito Italiano
Carlucci Coppi

Francesco's Hole in the Wall
George's Restaurant
Italian Village
Perinos
Pronto Ristorante
Rico's
Rosebud Café
Scoozi!
Sole Mio

Spiaggia
Steven B's
La Strada
Topo Gigio
Trattoria Bellavia
Trattoria Gianni
Trattoria Pizzeria Roma
Tucci Benucch

JAPANESE

Hatsuhana
Honda
Jun Japanese Restaurant

Kampai Chicago
Restaurant Suntory Chicago
Shiroi Hana Restaurant

LEBANESE

Middle East Restaurant and
    Cocktails

Uncle Tannous

MEXICAN

Fernando's
Frontera Grill
Hat Dance

Su Casa
Tijuana Yacht Club

PERSIAN

Pars Cove

Tehran Restaurant

PERUVIAN

Rinconcito Sudamericano

PHILIPPINE

Sulo

POLISH

Mareva's   Zofia's

SEAFOOD

Annabelle's   Pars Cove
Bay Street   Philander's Oak Park
Cap Cod Room   Shaw's Crab House
The Chestnut Street Grill   Phil Smidt & Son
J. P.'s Eating Place   The Waterfront
Nick's Fishmarket

SOUL FOOD

Army & Lou's

SOUTHWESTERN

Mélange   Tijuana Yacht Club
Thunderbird Bar & Grill

SPANISH

Cafe Ba-Ba-Reeba!   Rio's Casa Iberia
Emilio's Tapas Bar and
    Restaurant

STEAKHOUSE

Barney's Market Club   Eli's the Place for Steaks
Billy and Company   Morton's
Club Gene and Georgetti   Palm Restaurant
Ditka's

THAI

Ananda

Arun's Thai

P.S. Bangkok

Pattaya

UKRAINIAN

Galáns

VEGETARIAN

N.E.W. Cuisine

VIETNAMESE

Song Huong

YUGOSLAVIAN

Yugo Inn

RESTAURANTS

Alexander's

217 W. Huron St.
951-6000
AMERICAN
*Open Mon.-Thurs. 5 p.m.-
1 a.m., Fri. 5 p.m.-2 a.m.,
Sat. 6 p.m.-2 a.m., Sun.
5 p.m.-11 p.m.
All major cards.*

12/20

Alexander's has a certain romantic panache that's missing in restaurants coming onto the feeding line these days. Zebra motif notwithstanding, Alexander's has been designed with an eye toward putting some romance back into dining out. The properly dim lighting has a flattering effect— everybody looks good. And to maximize the effect, banquettes are strategically placed for maximum viewer and viewee interchange. The zebra-fabric-covered, ultra-high-back booths are cradles of comfort that come up just short of fully encapsulating diners. The dark, high ceiling drips with black, gauzy drapes. The food is quite good, the prices are right, and the service staff is fine-tuned. Appetizers such as shrimp Denise and fried calamari are nicely prepared, and the Caesar salad is one of the best around. The whole roasted chicken, which is exactly that—the whole bloomin' chicken, eight golden-brown pieces glistening with olive oil and peppered with tatters of parsley—is moist and aromatic. T-bone steak is great when it's not overcooked, and the same goes for the fish. Desserts, however, are mundane at best. Adjoining the restaurant is Cristal, a darkly lit club/bar (same owner) that's a great place to visit if you really want to end the evening on a romantic note. Dinner for two, with wine, runs about $65.

Ambria

2300 N. Lincoln Park West
472-5959
FRENCH
*Open Mon.-Thurs. 6 p.m.-
9:30 p.m., Fri.-Sat. 6 p.m.-
10:30 p.m.
All major cards.*

Ambria's creative offerings are the product of the imaginative mind of chef/proprietor Gabino Sotelino, one of the most gifted chefs in town—and a lot of other towns as well. Sotelino's cuisine is always on the leading edge of originality—but not wild, foolish invention. His intrinsically good judgment, coupled with two decades of kitchen experience and an innate flair with food, make Ambria's cuisine unique by design and perfectly realized. This is a restaurant that inspires confidence: sedate but not sanctimonious, lively but not loud, precise but not prissy. From its polished-to-a-warm-glow hardwood floors to its dark-wood walls, from its immaculate table service to its beautiful flower displays, Ambria is high-level luxe of the most pleasant kind. Les hors d'oeuvres classique include an impeccable Scottish smoked salmon and, for example, foie gras aux pommes: The delicate slices of duck liver are quickly sautéed until just set, then glossed with a light sauce made from deglazing the pan with sherry; these exquisite gems are enhanced by thin slices of lightly sautéed apples, slender sheaves of Belgian endive and radicchio leaves covered with shredded mâche. Fresh-fish specials might include a creation like loup de mer "Alvadera," in which the fish is sautéed to perfection and wreathed by a brunoise to which have been added pearl-size Champagne grapes. The rack of veal and stuffed leg of capon is a masterpiece on a plate, the capon stuffed with a morel mushroom mousse, the succulent veal touched with luxurious shavings of black truffles. In addition to the à la carte offerings is a petit menu dégustation prepared for parties of two, as well as a grand menu dégustation, which requires one-day advance notice. Desserts are passionately conceived and dedicated to the proposition that the meal isn't over until it's over. Marvelous fresh-fruit soufflés, fig napoleon with caramel sauce, almond génoise butter cake covered with chocolate praline, ethereal white-chocolate mousse laid into a pool of rich chocolate... the excitement goes on. The wine list has outstanding range: One can enjoy the luxury of a 1966 Romanée St. Vivant at $235 a bottle or the simple pleasures of one of the California red varietals, which start at $13. About $120 for dinner for two, with a moderately priced wine.

Ananda
941 N. State St.
944-7440
THAI
Open Tues.-Thurs.
11:30 a.m.-2 p.m. &
5 p.m.-10 p.m., Fri.- Sat.
11:30 a.m.-2 p.m. &
5 p.m.-10:30 p.m., Sun.
5 p.m.-10 p.m.
Cards: MC, V.

11/20

As our bookkeeper once said, there's no accounting for taste. The popularity of this gentrified storefront has always puzzled us. Though its high ceilings, handsome table settings and walls festooned with Chinese, Burmese and Thai art combine to create an attractive dining room, the ambience still stops short of comfort: Tables are too close together, chairs too unyielding, and, on busy nights, the decibel count is daunting. Prices, too, are high considering the diminutive portions. But the food can be delicious, especially the larb Chiengmai, excellent beef tartare generously seasoned with mint and chili or the tom yum goong, two shrimp afloat in a minibowl of lemon-grass broth. There's even better-than-acceptable eggplant, first grilled then puréed with chili and mint, and minced chicken, stir-fried with seasonal bai kaprow leaves and peppers. Beyond these few exceptions, a hesitancy about seasoning prevails, resulting in wimpy, unfocused dishes. Good Thai food can be subtle and complex; timid or anemic, never. Too many dishes at Ananda turn out to be westernized, watered-down versions of Thai classics. Desserts, especially the tough, cloyingly sweet custard and the coconut pies, are downright nasty. Wines and beers are available. A meager three-course dinner for two, with wine, will come to about $50.

> *The prices listed in this guide reflect what restaurants and hotels have informed us they plan to charge at press time. Please don't blame us if they don't coincide exactly with reality.*

Annabelle's

240 E. Ontario St.
944-3170
SEAFOOD
Open Mon.-Fri.
11:30 a.m.-2:30 p.m. &
4:30 p.m.-10 p.m., Sat.
4:30 p.m.-11 p.m., Sun.
4:30 p.m.-9 p.m.
All major cards.

9/20

Inside is a typical seafood-house decor: lots of wood and more wood, from booths to tables to bar. And on the menu are plenty of seafood choices, from shrimp to scrod, from clams to catfish and a few fathoms beyond. What we can't fathom, however, is why a seafood house in heavy competition with places like Shaw's Crab House, Chestnut Street Grill, Nick's Fishmarket and others doesn't clean up its act. Location counts for a lot, so we suspect that Annabelle's traps a great deal of unsuspecting tourists and suburbanites. Whether it gets them back is another matter. We don't question the fact that the fish arrives at the restaurant fresh. We do question what the kitchen does with it from that point on. As many times as we've tried this place, not once has a meal come together the way it should. Something is always off—the appetizer, the entrée, the salad, the dessert. Even the coffee goes from good to bad. Consistency is not something this restaurant understands. About $70 for dinner for two, with wine.

Army & Lou's

420 E. 75th St.
483-6550
SOUL FOOD
Open Wed.-Sat. 11 a.m.-
10 p.m., Sun. 9 a.m.-
10 p.m.
All major cards.

We've never met a meal we didn't like at this stellar, long-standing soul food restaurant. Some we've liked more than others—a lot more—but there's honest-to-goodness goodness in the home cooking served here. Anything tagged gumbo is a good bet: Chicken gumbo and seafood gumbo are especially fine dishes. Smoked ham hock with fresh mixed greens is not the prettiest sight to behold, but it eats like a dream: the hock lean, the meat tender and falling away from the bone. The mustard and turnip greens, a composition in shades of green, are moist and delectable. The fried chicken is nothing short of heavenly, the seasoned batter a real lip-smacker. Baby-back ribs occasionally come up on the dry side, but such side dishes as candied sweet potatoes and cornbread dressing with giblet gravy are perfect accompaniments to the meaty short ribs. Lunch specials are standouts: baked turkey leg, black-eyed peas and neck bones and chopped beefsteak with grilled onions, to name a few. Desserts are a must, even if your diet says you shouldn't. Peach cobbler wraps peach slices around a rich homemade sweet biscuit. Raisin-studded bread pudding, served by the scoop, is dense yet moist, flavored with nutmeg and draped with a properly tart lemon sauce. To make matters even better, the setting is both handsome and comfortable, with booths, wood paneling, white linens and a spirited, lively atmosphere, particularly on Sunday morning following church services. About $35 to $40 for dinner for two, with beer.

Arun's Thai

4156 N. Kedzie Ave.
539-1909
THAI
Open Tues.-Sun. 5 p.m.-
10 p.m.
All major cards.

Arun Sampanthanivat, being a perfectionist, spent nearly a year preparing for a half-mile move. His new restaurant belies the labor, as it should. It is an oasis of calm saved from narcissistic detachment by harmonious proportions and a scattering of art. A rectangular box cut lengthwise, the restaurant is made up of a raised alcove holding four tables and, below, an area with banquettes on either side and tables between. A woven cream fabric threaded by tan stripes lines the walls. Scenes from the life of Buddha in oxblood and acid green, ultramarine and jet, designed by Arun and executed by his brother Anawat, intersperse the walls at regular intervals. The effect is of a quiet presence, yet nothing distracts you from savoring the food or drifting into companionable conversation. The menu starts with a list of standard dishes, goes on to daily specials and is supplemented orally by three or four extra-specials, which are often determined by the availability of short-lived seasonal products. Kang liang, a moderately piquant shrimp-and-vegetable soup, held the place of honor for less than a week, only as long as the restaurant could obtain fresh bai mang luk, a leaf suggestive of basil and mint touched by oil of lemon. Normally we hesitate to recommend shrimp fried rice, a dish that tends to be pathetic beyond redemption. But Arun's version is a triumph: golden and nutty sweet, blessed with a generous breath of garlic and resplendent with a handful of tenderly fibrous and mildly briny crustaceans. Diners who have visited the "land of smiles" will appreciate the visual presentations: Red peppers sliced from crown to base lie open like blown roses, and a mass of shredded daikon becomes a mat on which a fan of cucumber reposes. Two of the staff of six in the kitchen make a specialty of these gracious contrivances. Among the dishes we particularly like are larb, sautéed ground chicken with lemon grass, lime and a half dozen other condiments; a suavely incendiary tom yum goong, hot-and-sour shrimp soup; garlic pork, long on black pepper; a mélange of wild and cultivated mushrooms that's loud with garlic and pepper; yum nau, grilled beef medallions dressed with lime, mint, chili and so on; and prawns, shrimp, mushrooms and snow peas tossed with lemon grass, paprika and garlic and served under a dusting of ground peanuts and diced scallions. For dessert, try the sticky rice cooked in coconut milk and topped with Thai egg-and-coconut custard. Red wines go surprisingly well with Thai food—a California Zinfandel, for example, is dry and spicy, picking up the flowery fragrances and fiery seasonings. A couple may expect to pay $70 for dinner with wine—high for Thai food, but commensurate with the high standards Arun sets for himself.

At The Tracks
325 N. Jefferson St.
332-1124
AMERICAN
Open Mon.-Thurs.
11 a.m.-10 p.m., Fri.
11 a.m.-11 p.m., Sat.
5 p.m.-11 p.m.
Cards: AE, MC, V.

10/20

The gumbos and jambalayas so beloved in New Orleans have made their way north, introducing palates shaped by cheeseburgers and catsup-topped french fries to the pleasurable bite of wood-aged chili sauce, mouth-puckering filé powder and mucilaginous okra. At The Tracks hedges its bets, offering a smattering of Creole and Cajun along with its fashionable American fare, starting with Tabasco and Pickapeppa sauces at the table. But it goes on to diverse, seasonally varied American grub: quilcene oysters from Washington state, pork tenderloin napped with a Cabernet sauce and good, old-fashioned upside-down apple pie. There are also forays into what we used to call Continental food— veal with a Champagne cream sauce, for example. The results can be imaginatively winning, as with the pork- and shrimp-topped Mason Dixon pasta; or misconceived, as with the mushroom-stuffed chicken rolls, which are overpowered by rosemary and a disgustingly thick orange sauce— something like a Thai spring roll made in a high school home ec class. Downstairs, an aqua ceiling beam is laid crosswise against unfinished wood; concrete facings and changing art exhibits (usually photographic) are undercut by boxy tables and homey service—high-tech and "hi y'all" in amiable conflict. The upstairs room often houses a music combo and bar for parties and is worth a glance for its wedge-shape windows set in massive concrete walls. Two people will leave about $50 lighter after dinner with wine.

Avalon
(Stouffer Hamilton Hotel), 400 Park Blvd.
Itasca
773-4000
FRENCH/CALIFORNIA
Open Mon.-Sat. 6 p.m.-
9 p.m.
All major cards.

Swatches of velvety-plum walls glowing faintly in the light of a dramatically stepped ceiling. Etched panels making an asymmetrical sculpture of glass where the foyer spills into the dining room. The gilt-framed pier glass and two impressionist oils cutting a scalene triangle out of the interior space. The two-tiered floor thick with carpeting. The gleam of crystal against linen, the muffled sound of nearby tables... Welcome to Avalon. If the soaring atrium lobby, like a clad Eiffel Tower, hasn't made an impression, the quiet splendor of the dining room will. And the food, now under the aegis of Michael Folz, does a credible job of complementing this splendor. Though devotees of neither crayfish (except in étouffée) nor spinach pasta, we were pleasantly disarmed by chunks of the former tucked into tender spinach ravioli that was bathed in a glistening Nantua (crayfish) sauce. A slice of New York state foie gras—goose, not duck liver—marinated in Madeira and baked whole, makes a kind of poetry, despite a faintly bitter edge; the various garnishes are mere superfluity. Folz smokes the Maine lobster that mingles provocatively with papaya and avocado in the Avalon Salad, an enjoyably vulgar conception. Soups range from such well-made standards as sherry-touched lobster bisque to such once-in-a-while fantasies as chilled cream of passion fruit and prickly pear. Fully half the entrées are fish, often imported brill or John Dory; a favorite is salmon shrouded in a scallop mousse and baked in puff pastry. Each texture and flavor distinct, the orchestration makes for a whole greater than the sum of its parts. Venison and pheasant have been seconded by an original and striking red-chile crêpe. Rock shrimp and squab, game pâté en croûte, sirloin with a mushroom duxelle, salmon rings stuffed with Brie, and sea scallops in fennel cream suggest the style and variety available. Desserts are often limited to such things as individual cheesecakes and fruit tarts or chocolaty variations on mille feuille and pâté à choux pastries. From 6 p.m. to 8:30 p.m., a rolling cart dispenses three kinds of Petrossian caviar and at least one American variety, any of which may be ordered by itself or with flavored Russian vodka as an appetizer. After 8:30 p.m., the cart holds a variety of teas and coffees, the latter decidedly not to our taste. The wine list ranges from modest $20 bottles of American whites to French Burgundies well into three figures, and the list of Cognacs, Armagnacs and liqueurs is delightfully daunting. Bottled water is poured automatically, and both service and busing are enthusiastic, if occasionally fallible. A couple having dinner with wine will spend about $125 and not begrudge a penny of it.

Avanzare

161 E. Huron St.
337-8056
ITALIAN
Open Mon.-Thurs.
11:30 a.m.-2 p.m. &
5:30 p.m.-9:30 p.m., Fri.
11:30 a.m.-2 p.m. &
5:30 p.m.-10:30 p.m., Sat.
5:30 p.m.-10:30 p.m., Sun.
5:30 p.m.-9:30 p.m.
All major cards.

Considering the number of head chefs that have passed through this kitchen over the past few years, it's amazing that it still produces any semblance of good food, but it does—not as good as it once was, but then it was frightfully good early on. Today one finds but little pleasure in most of the pasta dishes. Stay away from those that are complex combinations, and order something simple like the penne rigate or spaghettini with olive oil and basil. Fresh seafood dishes are not given to overcomplex treatments, so they fare well, as does sautéed breast of chicken with mushrooms and pancetta. We never did like the grilled pork chops that come with stuffed prunes, but the grilled veal chop is most appealing and highly recommended. Many Italian restaurants don't put enough effort into desserts, but happily that's not the case at Avanzare. The homemade ice creams are some of the best this side of Milan; we have fallen in love with the raspberry, the pistachio and the cappuccino chocolate as they appear (and, horror of horrors, disappear now and again). Still one of the most stylish (high ceilings, huge windows, handsome bar) and comfortable Italian restaurants in the city, Avanzare has a way to go to recapture its glory (and glorious) days, but we believe it's just a matter of time. About $40 a person for dinner with wine.

The Bakery

2218 N. Lincoln Ave.
472-6942
CONTINENTAL/HUNGARIAN
Open Tues.-Fri. 5 p.m.-
11 p.m., Sat. 5 p.m.-
midnight.
All major cards.

12/20

Like a well-oiled machine, The Bakery churns out faux haute cuisine night after night for a gross or so of primed-to-enjoy patrons. People return after ten years with besotted smiles and order their umpteenth beef Wellington, which in due course is drenched with Cumberland sauce. Or they muse fatuously over the "incredible liver pâté that hasn't changed in all these years," though, in fact, the boiled beef introduced into the pâté (as identified by our waiter) long ago ruined the original silken texture and now unpleasantly films the palate. They simper with Louis Szathmary, owner and—so it's claimed—still the chef, who table-hops, in a manner of speaking, to thank each client and chat with the regulars. We've returned at intervals and found the food ranging from adequate to good, though the same blatantly uncomfortable bentwood chairs and overly close tables make the experience as much a duty as a pleasure. The loose-textured white bread accompanying the pâté has a glossy, enjoyably chewy crust, but it's followed too quickly by a complimentary course: a smoked-turkey salad, perhaps, or square of pork terrine. Only then is the menu recited, which makes choosing a wine with the opening course needlessly difficult. The "complimentary" appetizer is a silly affectation, since meals are prix-fixe ($23 without wine, $3 to $5 more for specials) and could just as easily be dubbed six-course as five. Promotions, if a recent example is any indication, are hardly remarkable values. A $19.62 "meal" with a glass of wine—to celebrate the restaurant's 1962 opening—consisted of, our waiter was quick to point out, "just the beef Wellington and a salad... not a full meal, really." Nonetheless, the sausage-stuffed smoked pork tenderloin, wild boar (at a surcharge), roast goose and bouillabaisse have been satisfying entrées. The salad may be iceberg lettuce with a saccharine boiled dressing, as was ours on our last visit; soups, served from a black minicauldron, have been pleasant but cloying: cauliflower and sour cream one time, tomato bisque another. We've had Linzertorte that was dry and stale and Linzertorte that was moist and delectable; mocha torte and apple Strudel are safer bets. Coffee is included; cappuccino, however, will cost you $2 extra. Service is less pushy than in years past, and the wine list offers some excellent possibilities—for example, the 1984 Willow Creek Zinfandel at a mere $12. Two people will spend about $75 for dinner with wine.

Some establishments change their closing times without warning. It is always wise to call ahead.

Barney's Market Club

341 W. Randolph St.
372-6466
STEAKHOUSE/AMERICAN
*Open Mon.-Fri. 11 a.m.-
11 p.m., Sat. 4 p.m.-
11 p.m.*
All major cards.

10/20

Sporting a face-lift as thorough as Phyllis Diller's (and, on a square-inch basis, about as costly), this shrine to beef, spuds and New York cheesecake appears ready to go another five decades, subject to the same ups and downs that characterized the first five. Actually, 48 years have elapsed since the original Barney Kessel brought his "five-cent beer and free sandwiches" emporium to Halsted Street and began to greet politicians and cronies with "Yes sir! Senator," a phrase that is now Chicago history. Exposed brick walls, vintage photographs, dark wood and a newly installed set of floor-to-ceiling windows provide the ambience in this oasis of macho dining within a desert of commercial streets. Inside, a small but nicely varied salad bar offers spinach and lettuce with tubs of blue cheese for the cream dressing. Several other possibilities include herring in wine, marinated beets, fresh mushrooms, coleslaw and bean sprouts. Unfortunately, we've also found our plates home to gristly, fatty beef that tasted like it was choice rather than prime and Cryovac-packaged rather than dry-aged. Shoestring potatoes may be greaseless and perfectly crisp one time, overdone and greasy another. The two-and-a-half-pound lobsters pulled from a tank in the dining room vary from tender and succulent to tough and chewy. Besides beef and lobster, you'll find pork and lamb chops, excellent ribs and such daily specials as charbroiled swordfish and duckling with raspberry sauce. Patrons divide neatly into the regulars (for whom Barney's long ago achieved landmark status) and visitors (often conventioneers) looking for the Chicago beef of stockyard fame. What they find may be the diminished scion of a great old man, but having no basis of comparison they leave pleased. Quick service from friendly waitresses helps, as do some good, inexpensive wines—Silver Oaks Cabernet Sauvignon for one and Clos du Bois Chardonnay for another. Two should expect to pay upward of $95 for dinner with wine.

Bay Street

1024 N. Rush St.
226-7707
SEAFOOD/AMERICAN
*Open Sun.-Thurs. 11 a.m.-
10 p.m., Fri.-Sat. 11 a.m.-
midnight.*
All major cards.

12/20

At Bay Street we've gorged ourselves on the best steamed littlenecks in recent memory—a dozen tender, briny-sweet morsels, fresh and moist from their garlicky white-wine bath. The blackened sampler, bite-size pieces of fish and chicken, has also started our meal out happily, as has the soup sampler, which on one of our visits consisted of three half-cup tastes of gumbo, shrimp Creole and New England chowder. The regular menu is augmented daily by fresh-fish specials, sometimes as many as a dozen varieties, served baked, blackened, charbroiled or sautéed. We've had wonderful charbroiled tuna, rosy-pink at the center, tangy and meaty throughout, and golden, flaky lemon sole that has been kissed lightly with paprika. These dishes hold their own with the best. Stick to seafood or chicken. Meats—veal

Chesapeake, for example, blanketed with a dismal cheese sauce—usually can't compete with either the finny fare or fowl. Entrées include soup or salad, crunchy steamed veggies, a choice of potato (we like steamed red-skin best) and crusty San Francisco sourdough bread. Desserts run to the likes of cheesecake and ice cream. A modest list of wines, predominantly from California, includes several available by the glass and is supplemented by fifteen imported beers. Ask to sit in the no-smoking section if you have any hopes of carrying on a conversation: The large, block-long dining room is bisected by a piano bar that, at full volume, rivals a discotheque. White walls rising above dark-wood trim sport nautical hangings here and there. Comfortable booths and tables, dim lighting and exposed pipes crisscrossing a dark-green ceiling complete the decor. Service is enthusiastic. Two will spend about $65 for dinner with wine.

The Berghoff Restaurant
17 W. Adams St.
427-3170
GERMAN/AMERICAN
Open Mon.-Thurs. 11 a.m.-9:30 p.m., Fri.- Sat. 11 a.m.-10 p.m. Cards: AE, MC, V.

12/20

Not saying something nice about a restaurant—a Chicago tradition, really—that has been around for so many years wouldn't be kind. And we do like the crusty spirit, the sometimes-crusty waiters, the oak-paneled walls, the often-frenzied pace and the old-world atmosphere, and sometimes we even like the food—especially the schnitzels, the German pot roast and the broiled whitefish. And we like the things that accompany those entrées: creamed spinach or red cabbage or buttered egg noodles or German fried potatoes. And the things we don't like—rack of lamb, seafood platter and a miss or two on the daily specials list—we won't get into. The Berghoff Beer is a fine brew, and there is an in-depth selection of imported and domestic bottled beer. About $20 a person with a stein of beer.

Biggs
1150 N. Dearborn St.
787-0900
CONTINENTAL
Open nightly 5 p.m.- 10 p.m. All major cards.

12/20

Biggs, located in the historic DeKoven mansion, is in direct contrast to the type of places in which the restless herd mills these days. This is relaxed and pleasant dining in the old-world tradition. The appointments are splendid, from the richly paneled foyer to the eighteen-foot elaborately scrolled ceilings. Three of the seven intimate dining rooms have fireplaces, and crystal chandeliers throughout lend more than a touch of luxe. The appetizer selections comprise a dazzling mix of the au courant and the expected, with the former much more exciting—to wit: the fine ravioli stuffed with salmon mousse in a cilantro-touched oyster sauce. So, too, is the salmon tartare and sliced sashimi tuna. Particularly good entrées include the grilled salmon Oriental and the roasted rack of lamb. The fish selection of the day can be impressive at times; then again, we have been disappointed in the way the fish is cooked and sauced. Desserts, however, are consistently impressive. Chocolate fettuccine with a Grand Marnier crème anglaise is a showstopper. Chilled fruit soufflé served with fresh-fruit purée is almost as good. And the divine Miss Chocolate Mousse with three sauces is a chocolate-lover's paradise found. The wine list is appropriate, with some of the vintage Margaux and Pauillacs hovering in the $400 range, though there are more selections at much lower prices as well. About $110 for two, with a reasonably priced California Chardonnay.

Bigsby's Bar & Grill

1750 N. Clark St.
642-5200
AMERICAN
Open daily 11 a.m.-
10:30 p.m.
All major cards.

12/20

Ten or so steps down is a brick-flagged patio for those rare spring and fall days that separate subzero from 90-plus-degree weather. It's also relatively free of Clark Street's traffic noise and pollution. In all weathers, the interior, the lower level of an atrium soaring up past four floors of offices, is a pleasant, button-down spot for good American standards. The chili may need a bracing dash of Tabasco, but it's loaded with chunks of lean beef. Steaks, prime and dry-aged, and ribs are generously portioned and accompanied by crispy shoestring fries. Fresh scrod comes out of the kitchen in fish-and-chips or baked versions, and it's sweetly flaky and moist in both cases. Burgers, salads and vegetable-thick minestrone soup round out the brief menu, which concludes with an ice cream shake aptly, though inadequately, described as "Thick, Rich and Creamy." The ice cream used is Häagen Dazs, and the result is sybaritic. A small, reasonably priced wine list, velvety smooth piña coladas and a 24-ounce daiquiri keep the easygoing, late-night crowd happy. Two will spend about $50 for dinner with wine.

Billy and Company

124 S. Milwaukee Ave.,
Wheeling
541-6160
STEAKHOUSE
Open Mon.-Fri.
11:30 a.m.-12:30 a.m.,
Sat. 5:30 p.m.-1:30 a.m.,
Sun. 4:30 p.m.-12:30 a.m.
All major cards.

12/20

Urban skeptics notwithstanding, there's more to the suburbs than Big Macs, Tastee-Freeze and Joe's Diner. Good restaurants do exist, and probably in equal ratio to the duds as in the city, but locating them requires patience, luck and a strong stomach. So we've located Billy and Company for you—it's just the place when you've a hankering for chunks of beef or a whole duck, rather than the haute cuisine found down the road a piece at Le Français. The interior reeks of suburban chic—velveteen and damask, pink lights peeking out of enamel-smooth black tile, brass and dark wood and similar razzle-dazzle. But friendly, efficient service and a sporty crowd prevent the decor from becoming intrusive. Complimentary relishes arrive in waves: first, pickled red pepper, carrot sticks and cucumber, then dips, both anchovy in sour cream and creamy garlic, then chopped chicken liver. A basket heavy with crackers and rolls (unfortunately unheated) also makes an appearance. Barbecued ribs, which may be ordered as an appetizer or a main course, are meaty, chewy and tangy, just the way we like them. Steaks range from good to very good, but the onions that blanket Billy's

New York sirloin are better on a baked potato. The entrée list goes from Romanian skirt steak and Grecian chicken with roasted potatoes to a handful of veal dishes, winding up with fifteen seafood selections; to each a salad and pasta or potato is appended. Despite so extensive a selection, the food is fresh and deftly prepared. To cap an old-fashioned pig-out, end with Billy's Hot Fudge Cake, a cheerily gross confection of dense chocolate cake, oodles of real whipped cream, chopped peanuts and glossy fudge sauce. Surprisingly, the brief wine list sports such bottlings as Château Coufran and Jordan Cabernet Sauvignon. Dinner for two, with wine, should run about $85.

Binyon's

327 S. Plymouth St.
341-1155
AMERICAN
Open Mon.-Fri.
11:30 a.m.-10 p.m.
All major cards.

9/20

Need a judge, an attorney, an alderman or a city hall zoning clerk? Then head for Binyon's, particularly at lunchtime. Binyon's has been around so long you could squeeze cigar smoke out of the woodwork. And some of the waiters have been around so long they could have come with the foundation (not to mention that some of them move as if they're wearing concrete boots). The food is just as carefree, moving erratically from an outstandingly rich, thick and slick turtle soup to some of the most mundane and uninteresting desserts ever made. In between, though, are some winners, like the prime rib and Irish lamb stew with dumplings, and some losers, like the braised lamb shank and sautéed veal kidneys. The frenzy hour is from noon to 1 p.m., but the front man keeps things moving quite nicely, and if he says the wait is fifteen minutes, it won't be too far off the mark. Dinner, with wine, runs about $22 per person.

Bistro 110

110 E. Pearson St.
266-3110
FRENCH
Open Mon.-Thurs.
11:30 a.m.-midnight,
Fri.-Sat. 11:30 a.m.-1 a.m.,
Sun. 11:30 a.m.-11 p.m.
All major cards.

Modeled after L'Ami Louis, the estimable Paris bistro, Bistro 110, though quite large by bistro standards, has captured the spirit and essence of *le bistrot classique*. To the front of the semicircular bar is the café-atrium dining area with windows facing the street. The larger dining room to the rear has a mix of tables, booths and banquettes. Old plank flooring, burnished to a golden glow, flows into wainscoting. Fanciful murals grace the walls. Less than a one-carat-diamond throw from fashionable N. Michigan Avenue, Bistro 110 attracts a swell mix of swell people from the neighborhood, along with tourists and conventioneers. The ambitious menu is bistro all the way, from French onion soup, fresh foie gras and oven-roasted chicken and steak to apple tart and a selection of French cheeses. The first of the good stuff arrives shortly after you've been seated. An amuse-gueule—a whole roasted head of elephant garlic—is perfect for slathering across a slice of crusty French bread. Woodburning-oven-roasted mushrooms, seasoned with garlic, rosemary and thyme, are tender and pleasant.

The fresh foie gras, marinated in port wine and Cognac and baked gently, is rich, silky and delicate. The oven-roasted chicken, a house specialty, is moist, succulent and seasoned wonderfully with a mixture of herbs. Daily specials like pot-au-feu, cassoulet, roasted rabbit and boudin blanc are generally handled quite nicely. For dessert, the freshly baked apple tart with crème fraîche is truly outstanding, but the chocolate mousse trio is nothing to get whipped up about. Dinner with wine will run about $55 for two.

La Bohème

566 Chestnut St.
(Laundry Mall), Winnetka
446-4600
FRENCH
*Open Tues.-Sat. 11:30
a.m.-2:30 p.m. & 6 p.m.-
10 p.m.*
All major cards.

Suburban shopping malls seldom cut to the gastronomical quick, and the Laundry Mall is an incongruous home for nouvelle-slanted French fare. Still, Chef Didier Durand has won a steady following with his basil-scented duck-and-chicken carpaccio; savory lobster bisque; tautog (Atlantic blackfish) sautéed and served on a bed of fresh pasta; and such deftly managed standards as rack of lamb highlighted by a tartly pungent Provençal sauce or duck breast napped with Riesling. A reasonable ($19.50) prix-fixe menu allows diners to select from six appetizers (like a seafood mosaic and assorted pâtés), five entrées (including veal medallions and a combination of grilled salmon and whitefish) and four desserts. The eight regular desserts range from grainy, overly sweet chocolate mousse, both dark and white, to Grand Marnier cheesecake. Wines are reasonable, and several are available by the glass. Subdued lighting, exposed brick polka-dotted with objets d'artsy-craftsy, and an old-fashioned open fireplace create a romantically hokey interior for getting acquainted or reacquainted. Dinner for two from the à la carte menu, with a modest wine, will total approximately $75.

Bombay Palace

50 E. Walton St.
664-9323
INDIAN
*Open Mon.-Thurs.
11:30 a.m.-2:30 p.m. &
5:30 p.m.-10 p.m., Fri.
11:30 a.m.-2:30 p.m. &
5:30 p.m.-10:30 p.m.,
Sat. 11:30 a.m.-3 p.m. &
5:30 p.m.-10:30 p.m.,
Sun. 11:30 a.m.-3 p.m. &
5:30 p.m.-10 p.m.
All major cards.*

11/20

A remodeling last year spruced up things around the palace, which was starting to look old and tired. The first-floor dining room is a soft, appealing room with carpeting, chairs and walls in a palette of shades of rose. Pastel sea-green banquettes stretch along the left side of the room. On the right side, floor-to-ceiling dividers create a series of intimate dining nooks. The new second-floor dining room uses a similar color scheme and has the same soft appeal as the downstairs room. The Indian breads, cooked in the tandoor clay oven, are excellent. Tandoori roti comes out deep brown and slightly puffed; another flat bread, onion kulcha, has a touch of onions and dry mango stuffing, which adds a great deal of flavor. Pakora, a fritter made from chickpea flour, has the right balance of turmeric, yogurt and garam masala. Mulligatawny soup is too tame and bland for our taste. Tandoori chicken gets the usual garlic, ginger and yogurt marinade, so the essential flavors, as well as the moistness and smoky flavor, are present. Rogan josh—red lamb stew—is powerfully good and spicy. Vegetarians have an ample amount of dishes from which to choose. We have never been able to come to terms with Indian desserts, which for the most part are either bland or cloyingly sweet. Dinner, with wine, costs about $25 per person.

Buckingham's
(Chicago Hilton
and Towers),
720 S. Michigan Ave.
922-4400
AMERICAN
*Open Mon.-Fri.
11:30 a.m.-2 p.m. &
5:30 p.m.-10 p.m., Sat.-
Sun. 5:30 p.m.-10 p.m.
All major cards.*

You may think you've walked into a private club rather than a hotel dining room. Gray and white marble, highly polished mahogany trim, cherrywood pillars, beveled mirrors, dark-red upholstery, gray textured walls highlighted by both bold black-and-white prints and quiet pastels, and well-spaced tables add up to a solid sense of order and comfort. A harpist alternates light classics with familiar pops. The serving staff remains on alert throughout the meal, but at a discreet distance. Empty plates are whisked away, wine is poured, and water and butter are replenished with minimum wait or fuss. It's all terribly civilized. In the past, the food, happily, has lived up to the setting; previous chef Hubert Henri's cooking had earned Buckingham's a rating of 15/20 when we first assembled this guide. But then, not long before press time, a new chef took over. Deadlines allowed us just one quick visit, which neither greatly impressed nor disappointed us; it's too early to say if the newcomer can live up to Henri's high standards. We can only hope that we'll still be able to enjoy dishes as wonderful as Henri's mildly plump California escargots pouched in flaky pastry and set in a pool of sweet red-pepper coulis; scallops napped by a light-as-a-breeze Champagne butter sauce and dotted with lobster roe and caviar; seasonal salads (perhaps mâche, yellow nasturtiums and radicchio with chunks of lobster in a light, tangy olive oil dressing); and such entrées as breast of pheasant stuffed with crab and spinach, or grilled Maine lobster served on perfectly cooked saffron linguine with lobster butter sauce. Desserts are still as good as ever—cheesecake mousse with Grand Marnier, white-chocolate mousse–filled meringue on a puddle of raspberry coulis, layers of chocolate and strawberry mousse on a bed of almond meringue and similar examples of culinary insouciance. The wine list contains some surprisingly reasonable selections. Expect to spend about $115 for dinner for two, with wine.

> *Remember to phone ahead to reserve your table or your room and please, if you cannot honor your reservation, be courteous and let the restaurant or the hotel know.*

Cafe Angelo

225 N. Wabash Ave.
332-3370
ITALIAN
Open Mon.-Fri. 7 a.m.-
10 a.m., 11:30 a.m.-2 p.m.
& 5 p.m.-11 p.m., Sat.-
Sun. 5 p.m.-11 p.m.
All major cards.

For nearly two decades Cafe Angelo has reigned quietly in the north end of the Loop. Though its emergence on the gastronomic horizon created an initial flurry of excitement among the culinary cognoscenti, critics and their faithful followers have long since decamped in search of newer pastures. Cafe Angelo, in the meantime, settled down to feeding a steady stream of theater-goers (from 5 to 6:30 p.m., $12.50 will buy a cup of soup or fresh fruit, one of nine entrées with accoutrements, coffee and a glass of wine) and its core of regulars.

Cafe Angelo deserves to be noticed again. The large bilevel room paneled in dark wood, its walls bearing sconces of electrified candles, sprays of dried grasses and a handful of nineteenth-century European genre paintings, feels comfortable and clubby. Add to that well-spaced tables, fresh flowers on bright-yellow linen and more-than-average competence in the kitchen. The menu boasts a dozen appetizers, nine pastas and eighteen entrées, along with a smattering of daily specials. Among the more interesting starters are spinach crêpes in a pool of Nantua sauce, zesty olive-oil-and-lemon-sparked seafood salad and homemade mozzarella with tomato and basil. Escarole and white-bean soup is rich and earthy, and cappelletti al brodo, tiny meat-filled pasta swimming in spinach-laden chicken broth, is hearty and satisfying. We didn't know red snapper could be as tough as the oversized slab that graced our plate one night, but fortunately first-rate trout stuffed with shrimp and crab proved that the kitchen can turn out admirable fish. Admirable, too, is a mixed grill of chicken, homemade sausage, and pork tenderloin. But the pastas, though fresh, aren't noticeably better than the good, commercial varieties. Tiramisù is the best we've come across in Chicago, sponge cake moistened with grappa and espresso, then topped with cream-whipped Mascarpone and dusted with chocolate. The small wine list is heavy on Italians and moderately priced. Two people ordering à la carte will spend about $70 for dinner, with wine.

Cafe Ba-Ba-Reeba!

2024 N. Halsted St.
935-5000
SPANISH
Open Mon. 5 p.m.-11 p.m.,
Tues.-Thurs. 11:30 a.m.-
2 p.m. & 5 p.m.-11 p.m.,
Fri.-Sat. 11:30 a.m.-2 p.m.
& 5 p.m.-midnight, Sun.
5 p.m.-10:30 p.m.
All major cards.

Cafe-Ba-Ba-Reeba!, a Spanish tapas-bar-cum-restaurant, is one of a kind in Chicago. Tapas, those Spanish appetizers—nibbles or side dishes—are the main attraction, but the young and the lovely, standing three deep at the bar, are definitely a co-feature on weekend evenings. The decor is unquestionably Ba-Ba-Reeba! Hanging over open kitchens are bay wreaths, garlic braids, strings of chiles and de-scented dried cod. Murals of eclectic nonsense are displayed on pastel-hued stucco walls. Picasso might approve. The range of tapas frias (cold tapas) and tapas calientes (hot tapas) is excellent and changes frequently. Pisto manchego is essentially a Spanish ratatouille—zucchini, peppers, olives, eggplant and onion combined in a delectable tomato sauce. Gazpacho and black-bean soup are excellent. Paella is a classic and true to style, with rice, chicken, pork, shrimp, mussels and saffron, all mingling and blending to create a dish of unquestionable pleasure. The kitchen does an outstanding job with seafood, but some of the meat and fowl dishes are not treated with the same respect. And desserts are not very imaginative. The best way to sample the menu is to go with at least four people; six would be even better. There's a good selection of Spanish wines, but the white sangria is a cool and refreshing alternative. Dinner will cost anywhere from $10 to $20 per person, with wine or sangria.

Café Provençal

1625 Hinman Ave.,
Evanston
475-2233
FRENCH
Open Mon.-Fri. 6 p.m.-
10 p.m., Sat. 6 p.m.-
10 p.m. (June 15- Aug. 30:
also open Mon.-Fri. 11:30
a.m.-2 p.m.).
All major cards.

Café Provençal is a restaurant with style. Style comes, first of all, in the ambience. In the main dining room, dark wood lines the wall around the country-French brick fireplace. On the opposite wall, shirred fabric rises from the wainscoting to the beamed ceiling. Porcelain plates and figurines brought from France by owner Leslee Reis adorn the walls, adding a homey touch. Tablecloths, tiny oil lamps and fresh flowers complete the pretty picture. To the rear of the main dining room, separated by café windows, is the garden room, which overlooks the garden where many of the herbs used in the kitchen are grown. And fortunately, there's an equal amount of style in the cuisine, which is done consistently well.

Daily specials are most creative and reflect Reis's passionate relationship with food, and the dishes on the printed menu are no less inspired. Fresh New York foie gras, which gets just a light sautéing and a veneer of duck glaze and balsamic vinaigrette, is silky and luxuriously rich. Soupe de poissons Marseillaise—a tasty mélange of fresh seafood—is deftly seasoned with tomato, garlic and fennel. Fish specials may be of the common sea variety, such as red snapper; then again, they may be fish not so ubiquitous, such as plaice served with a fennel-tarragon butter sauce. Roast rack of lamb never misses being perfectly pink and perfectly delicious. Simple fowl, like chicken, turns into glorious fare when infused with black truffles and sauced with a truffle jus. Desserts would qualify for citizenship in France: charlotte aux pommes with two sauces, trio de tartelettes, seasonal fruits with sorbet, homemade ice creams, pâtisseries maison, all of which are delicious. The wine list is most complete, mostly French and most appropriate, right down to a fine selection of dessert wines. And there are some dazzling Armagnac and Calvados choices. About $120 for dinner for two, with wine.

Cafe Royal

1633 N. Halsted St.
266-3394
ENGLISH
*Open Mon. 11:30 a.m.-
2:30 p.m., Tues.-Thurs.
11:30 a.m.-2:30 p.m. &
5 p.m.-10 p.m., Fri.
11:30 a.m.-2:30 p.m. &
5 p.m.-10:30 p.m., Sat.
4 p.m.-11 p.m., Sun.
11 a.m.-2:30 p.m. &
5 p.m.-9:30 p.m. (tea daily
4 p.m.-6 p.m.).
All major cards.*

Those for whom "English cuisine" is an oxymoron are in for a pleasant surprise. Chef Alan Percival, solidly grounded in classical French cuisine and trained in England, dishes up the likes of cock-a-leekie (chicken soup with leeks and prunes), Melton Mowbray pie (cold pork pie served with chutney), priddy oggy (ham-filled pastie with an apple-cider sauce) and tiddy oggy (potato-onion pastie with a cheese sauce) with finesse and aplomb. There's even a chicken mousse infused with honey and spices and dotted with currants, whose legendary progenitor—so the menu claims—was served at Henry IV's coronation in 1399. Roast beef with Yorkshire pudding is among the best we've had, tender and full-flavored meat seconded by a crispy, eggy popover-like pudding. For starters, we recommend the perfectly browned crab cakes, served with a small dish of delicate mustard cream on the side. Among soups, cock-a-leekie, a heady brew of chicken, leeks and prunes, has few peers. The regular menu is supplemented by a small list of specials; we can vouch for the quail stuffed with savory veal. Those who prefer the piscatorial can choose from brook trout in pastry moistened with apples and cider, honey-glazed salmon or flown-in-fresh Dover sole. Desserts include first-rate trifle (*that* may be the real oxymoron), syllabub, burnt-cream-and-bread pudding. The setting for this culinary Anglo-amble is a former candle factory, half of which is now the Royal George Theatre. The half given over to the restaurant—a series of small rooms, a Victorian snuggery adjacent to the wine cellar and a plethora of nooks and crannies—suggests the labyrinthine intricacies of a Dickensian world. A small, separate room, complete with couch, offers couples so inclined a fine and private place in which to dally with their dinner. Wines are well chosen but expensive, and service is exemplary. Dinner for two, with wine, will lighten the exchequer by about $100.

Cafe 21

(Hotel 21 East),
21 E. Bellevue Pl.
266-2100
AMERICAN
*Open daily 7 a.m.-10 p.m.
All major cards.*

At Cafe 21, the ceiling is polished aluminum—a chic metal that is tech but not high—the floors are cool black-and-white marble and smooth low-pile carpeting, two of the walls are floor-to-ceiling glass, and another wall is mirrored. Sprays of flower are fresh and fluffed, and table settings are elegant and constantly replenished. Make no mistake: This is a classy hotel dining room. But all is not perfection. On several occasions we've seen three people squeezed into banquettes that look like they were designed for two, which is one squeeze play that doesn't work. The food, an innovative mix of American, French and Italian, is high quality, high interest and high priced. The tomato soup, to stretch it a bit, is more like a liquid sandwich—a BLT—than soup; added to the rich and mellow tomato broth are snippets of bacon and shreds of lettuce, simple additions that carry the soup beyond the ordinary. The corn blini sandwich is light and grease free, stacked with smoked salmon and served with the requisite dollop of crème fraîche. Black ravioli stuffed with finely chopped lobster meat in a sprightly basil cream sauce is excellent, but pike in candy-wrapper pasta— tricolored pasta stuffed with a pike mousse—is more contrivance than good taste. Seafood dishes are generally first-rate, particularly those on the daily specials list. The two best desserts in the house are the chocolate crème brûlée and the quadruple-chocolate cake. Dinner for two, with wine, runs about $120.

California Pizza Kitchen

414 N. Orleans St.
222-9030
California/Italian
Open Mon.-Thurs.
11:30 a.m.-11 p.m., Fri.-
Sat. 11:30 a.m.- midnight,
Sun. 11:30 a.m.-10 p.m.
Cards: AE, MC, V.

10/20

It takes more moxie than mozzarella to open a pizza place in the city that practically invented sit-down pizza service, deep-dish pizza and stuffed pizza—a city, in fact, that has more pizza places than any other city in the United States. The California Pizza Kitchen, however, is no run-of-the-mozzarella pizza joint. This is designer pizza, sprung from the freewheeling mind of a La-La Land chef (so they say, but it's not true), born out of the fire of a West Hollywood wood-burning oven (so they also say, but it's also not true). This is designer pizza served in a designer setting: Black tile merges with white tile, an eating counter with high stools sweeps around in front of the pizza builders and cooks, the ceilings are high, and the seating is a combination of banquettes and black, high-tech tables, which are crammed so close together that they invite total and immediate assessment of thy neighbors' eats. And this is designer pizza (read: expensive) made with exotic, complicated, outlandish, dream-created toppings dropped onto a fashionably thin crust. Barbecued chicken pizza, blackened shrimp and smoked pork loin (surf and turf pizza?), chicken-burrito pizza, Peking duck pizza, Thai chicken pizza... it's too much for us to deal with. Sometimes the pizza is decent, but most of the time it's more show than go. Forget about the pizza, if you can, and try some of the pasta dishes, which generally fare much better, as do some of the salads. Desserts, on the other hand, are forgettable. Dinner for two runs about $30, with wine by the glass.

DON'T FORGET: Gault Millau introduces you to the Best of New York, the Best of Washington D.C., the Best of Los Angeles, the Best of San Francisco, the Best of New England, the Best of France, the Best of Paris, the Best of Italy, the Best of London.

The Canoe Club

2843 N. Halsted St.
348-3800
AMERICAN
Open Mon.-Thurs.
5:30 p.m.-11 p.m., Fri.
5:30 p.m.-midnight, Sat.
8 a.m.-2 p.m. & 5:30 p.m.-
midnight, Sun. 8 a.m.-
2 p.m. & 5 p.m.-10 p.m.
Cards: AE, MC, V.

11/20

Eating at The Canoe Club is like eating in the mess hall back at summer camp, but the food and service are better. There's just enough kitsch mixed in with a kaboodle of stuff to pull off the theme. A large canoe is suspended from the ceiling in the big, open dining room. Brick walls are adorned with a moose head, snowshoes and old farm implements—part North Woods and part Wisconsin supper-club trappings.

The food is straightforward American, as in steaks, seafood, hamburgers, meatloaf, stuffed pork chops—ungussied-up vittles that are hearty, refreshing and anything but haute. Thin, crispy onion strings, as fine as vermicelli, are flavorful and free of grease. Steamed-in-beer Bratwurst comes two to an order, plump and juicy, with heavy-on-the-sour Sauerkraut. Baked meatloaf comes with a mushroom gravy and tastes like the kind mom made.

The best deal is the all-you-can-eat Friday-night fish fry, which features tasty beer-battered and deep-fried lake trout. The stuffed pork chop is good or bad, depending on who's cooking, but the mashed potatoes are the real thing—lumps and all. Apple-walnut cobbler is a wedge of wonder, chunks of properly tart apples mixed with pieces of walnuts. About $15 per person, for dinner, with beer.

Cantonese Chef

2342 S. Wentworth St.
225-3232
CHINESE
Open Sun.-Thurs. 11 a.m.-
midnight, Fri.-Sat.
11 a.m.-1 a.m.
All major cards.

11/20

Black leatherette booths and orange lanterns at the entrance, a scattering of landscape scenes and a wall-size relief panel of a pagoda and courtyard in the adjoining room set the tone. Cloth napkins come with the territory, and chopsticks come on request. You'll do well in selecting the likes of Maine lobster Cantonese style, hot-and-sour soup or hong sue shrimp (breaded, deep-fat-fried shrimp served with stir-fried vegetables)—culinary clichés, perhaps, but satisfying nonetheless. Happily, one can do better. The last two pages of the formidable menu offer steamed chicken redolent of fresh ginger teamed up with chunky Chinese sausage; beef braised in bitter melon; broad, chewy rice noodles studded with slithery sea cucumber, fresh scallops and squid and some ragtag shrimp along with straw mushrooms, pea pods and bok choy; lobster stuffed with anise-scented minced pork; and roast duckling with cellophane rice noodles. While beer, both domestic and imported, occupies a small niche amid the list of cocktails, tropical drinks sporting the usual off-putting names and cutesy umbrellas get top billing. Though communication may falter, service tends to be warm and courteous, especially for diners bent on exploration. Dinner for two from the back pages, with a cocktail, should cost about $45.

Cape Cod Room

(The Drake)
140 E. Walton Pl.
787 2200
SEAFOOD
*Open Mon.-Sun. noon-
11 p.m.
All major cards.*

The Drake is home to one of the best seafood restaurants in town, the Cape Cod Room. Léo Waldemeier, a genial Helvetian, presides over a kitchen as big as a baseball field and a brigade of 90. With characteristic Swiss precision, he scrutinizes the fish that he has flown in regularly from Amsterdam, verifying their impeccable freshness and quality. Léo, you see, prefers North-Sea sole and Norwegian salmon to red snappers and other fish native to American waters. One local product, however, receives his full approval: real, honest-to-god caviar from Great-Lakes sturgeon. While it may not rival the finest Iranian roes, it's very good stuff indeed, and a bargain at about a tenth of the price. Patrons of the Cape Cod Room also go for Waldemeier's flavorful version of that American favorite, snapper soup, and his rendition of the classic lobster Thermidor.

Léo Waldemeier is a master craftsman who has carried off medals from culinary competitions all over the planet. He is particularly proud of an award bestowed on him in Singapore by Paul Bocuse for his shrimp Creole and his imaginative hors d'oeuvres. He remains modest, despite the honors: "A chef never stops learning," he declares, as he prepares to set off for a stint at one of the finest seafood restaurants anywhere: Le Divellec, in Paris. Dinner for two is about $110.

Capri Ristorante Italiano

3126 Oak Park Ave.,
Berwyn
484-6313
ITALIAN
*Open Mon.-Thurs. 11 a.m.-
11 p.m., Fri. 11 a.m.-mid-
night, Sat. 4 p.m.-midnight.
No cards.*

12/20

This is a ton of restaurant squeezed into a pint-size space. You'll find but ten tables, and when they are all occupied the atmosphere is that of an Italian festa: elbow-to-elbow eaters, taped Italian music, food flying out of the kitchen, spirited conversation—it's Italian to the core. The decor is best described as "neighborhood Italian": Wine bottles hang from the ceiling; walls are faux brick with faux white arches highlighted with gold glitter; chalet-like wood beams cross the ceiling. No high-priced decorator was engaged to do this place, but we think it's charming and comfortable. The food is wonderful—homemade wonderful. Soups are well crafted, rich and luscious. Calamari fritti is a model of the genre, lightly battered tender rings of gold. Pastas are exquisite: Gnocchi is chewy-tender and gently coated with a fragrant red sauce; baked lasagne is a hefty but delicate and delicious piece of work; and linguine with clams is a masterwork. The littleneck clams, plump and fresh, ring the plate, an essence of garlic wafts up, and the pasta is perfectly cooked. Veal and chicken dishes are just as exciting. Cannoli is the only decent dessert on the menu. Nice selection of Italian wines at moderate prices. Dinner for two, with wine, runs about $50.

Carlos'

**429 Temple Ave.,
Highland Park
432-0770**
FRENCH
*Seatings Sun.-Mon. &
Wed.-Thurs. 5 p.m.,
6:30 p.m., 8 p.m. &
8:30 p.m., Fri.-Sat. 5 p.m.,
6:30 p.m., 9 p.m. &
9:30 p.m.
All major cards.*

Slick and chic, this North Shore boîte has made the move into the vanguard of Chicago's culinary legions. Its success springs in part from a refined and modestly recherché kitchen, but in equal part from a style reminiscent of a genteel European hostelry. Co-owner Carlos Nieto patrols the front, greeting guests, suggesting dishes, discussing the menu with patrons, leaving them flattered at having been found personally worthy of the place. And the place itself, we must admit, emits no false note. An etched-glass panel just past the door creates an entranceway too slight to be a foyer. The bar stands darkly inviting to the left, a casual foil to the dining room's spotless napery, art deco wall sconces, simple bentwood chairs and handful of prints and paintings as severely modern as their narrow frames. Mere moments before we went to press, we learned that chef Roland Liccioni and his pastry-chef wife, Beth, were leaving Carlos' to purchase Le Français. All we know of the new chef is that he came directly from the ovens of Paris's great Taillevent. We have not been able to try his cooking, but we expect Carlos' to stay as good as ever, perhaps even climbing to the three-toque level. In the past, we have enjoyed such dishes as white asparagus and spinach with a seafood medley of impeccable freshness, grilled foie gras with balsamic vinaigrette, squab ravioli perfumed by garlic, duck carpaccio, a pairing of halibut and salmon (sautéed and grilled, respectively), garnishes of zucchini blossoms, mesclun lettuce and baby vegetables, and sorbets that run to passion fruit and green apple. Berry-strewn crème brûlée and an elegant marquise usually win out over the formidable competition on the dessert cart. Wines by the glass help keep the tab within bounds, but an extensive list of notable bottles will challenge your pocketbook's will to resist. A couple that gives in will spend about $125 for dinner with a good wine.

Carlucci

**2215 N. Halsted St.
281-1220**
ITALIAN
*Open Mon.-Fri. 11:30 a.m.-
3:00 p.m. & 5:30 p.m.-
11 p.m., Sat. 5:30 p.m.-
11 p.m., Sun. 5 p.m.-
10 p.m.
All major cards.*

Carlucci is the kind of restaurant in which you can settle in and feel comfortable—all the more so now that it has matured and become comfortable with itself. One big sweep of the room allows patrons to view one another, but clever placement of dividers and tall plants ensures as much privacy as one really wants when dining out. The restaurant is much in the style of a luxe-but-not-plush ristorante that one would find in Milan or Florence. And recently, Carlucci's menu has become more aggressively regional; specialties of many regions of Italy are featured at a reasonable price and are amply but not excessively portioned, allowing you to sample a number of courses. Minestrone di Bologna is not your basic vegetable soup—it's light and elegant, with a rich taste that's enhanced by tortellini. Cannelloni dell catania by any other name are those wonderful tubes of pasta stuffed with ricotta and beef and covered with a lusty tomato sauce. Second-course selections are a varied lot ranging from stuffed beef rolls to grilled baby lamb chops to osso buco. The regional menu is supplemented by The Best of Carlucci menu, which features such house basics as fried calamari, paglia e fieno (sausages with noodles), zuppa di pesce (fish soup) and an assortment of seafood dishes. A lovely outdoor garden houses al fresco diners in season, and a café serves light meals, exceptionally good pizza, ice cream and take-out. The notable wine list is most attractively priced. Dinner for two, with wine, runs about $70 a person.

The Chardonnay

2635 N. Halsted St.
477-5130
FRENCH
Open Sun. & Tues.-Thurs.
5 p.m.-10 p.m., Fri.-Sat.
5 p.m.-11 p.m.
Cards: AE, MC, V.

Dine on marble-topped tables and choose from about 25 wines by the glass or 1,500 by the bottle. One of these side-by-side storefronts is a wine shop and bar, the other a long, narrow dining room with bentwood chairs, dark-green carpeting and wine racks lining the walls. Three trompe l'oeil windows, each bearing a huge splash of flowers against a backdrop of blue sky and fleecy clouds, bring a touch of airiness to the space. Chef Jean-Marc Poulin changes his menu every two to three weeks, and owner/wine maven Mitchell Dulin is always on hand with suggestions for complementary vintages. Select the right dishes from the limited offerings and you're in for a marvelous meal. Unfortunately, not everything is equally good, and we've come away dissatisfied on occasion. Our favorite starters are just-barely steamed asparagus with a buttery mustard sauce flanked by two perfect pastry puffs; a duck confit alternating with Belgian endive leaves; and wheels made from crêpes rolled around a rich mince of soft-shell crab. The chicken-filled tomato ravioli is also worth considering, but the chicken curry salad and artichokes and mushrooms à la grecque are pretty dismal, redeemed only partially by accompanying crunchy lentil and sunflower sprouts in a tangy mayonnaise. The duck-liver mousse is robust and smooth. For entrées we recommend the rosy breast of duck with spiced apple napped by a fruity but not-too-sweet blueberry sauce, or the grilled fish, especially tuna or salmon. Skip the tough, tasteless breast of veal. Desserts have likewise delighted and disappointed. Among the delights are a chocolate marquise, caramel mousse and rich, crumbly blueberry tart. On the other hand, strawberry-mousse cake has been dismally gelatinous, and Grand Marnier ice cream, creamy but otherwise nondescript. Coffee is excellent. A meal for two, with wine, will be about $85.

The Chestnut Street Grill

845 N. Michigan Ave.
(Water Tower Place,
mezzanine level)
280-2720
SEAFOOD/AMERICAN
*Open Mon.-Thurs.
11:30 a.m.-10:30 p.m.,
Fri.-Sat. 11:30 a.m.-
11:30 p.m., Sun. 11 a.m.-
2:30 p.m. & 4:30 p.m.-
9:30 p.m.
All major cards.*

There is much to like about this (mostly) seafood restaurant. The service staff is as familiar with the fish it serves as a fishing boat's crew is about the catch it brings in. There is a definite seafood-grill atmosphere—white-tile flooring, wood-paneled walls, brass accents, seashell wall lights—and the open kitchen in the center of the room where the grilling takes places adds further taste to the cool-but-not-swank visual feast. Fresh fish and the list of daily specials are the mainstay. Some names you will recognize, but some you may not, for this restaurant (which is fast becoming venerable) covers a lot of water to bring in all kinds of swimmers. The fried calamari is the best around: tender, lightly battered, delicately crisp rings of gold that are like peanuts—you can't stop eating them. Swordfish steak is grilled with restraint so it arrives glistening with its natural juices. Grilled sea scallops are handled masterfully, the surfaces of the plump nuggets delicately brown, the insides juicy and moist. A la carte grilled vegetables are delicious, as is the New England clam chowder and the sourdough bread. A dessert not to miss is the cappuccino ice cream—the fantasy lives on for days after the fact. Spa-menu selections are available for conscientious types who wish to avoid butter and salt, and those who don't eat fish will find several meat dishes. The wine list is all California, nearly all whites and quite extensive. Dinner will run about $85 for two, with wine.

Chez Jenny

900 N. Franklin St.
951-5858
FRENCH
*Open Mon.-Sat. 5 p.m.-
11 p.m., Sun. 5 p.m.-
10 p.m.
All major cards.*

It didn't work as Amerique, when the chef/owner was Jennifer Newbury and the food was Franco-American. It didn't work when Newbury lost her heart and most of the kitchen chores to Dennis Terczak, who abandoned his high-profile chef's role at Avanzare to play kitchen doctor at Amerique, installing a new Franco-Italo-American menu. Everybody got confused, including the customers, so the place closed and went through a retrofitting and renaming: Chez Jenny.

Now everybody understands: Chez Jenny is a French bistro. The cold, stark, warehousey interior has been transformed into a warm, wood-rich, comfortable, charmingly reasonable facsimile of a real French bistro. The food is not as close to being authentic as the decor, but if you pick your way around the menu carefully, there's more than enough to enjoy. The terrine de lapereau is not the best dish to hop onto for an opener—the aspic that coats the studs of rabbit and vegetables should go the way of all aspics: banished forever from all menus. Much better is the duck pâté with cabbage and onion and a pear-caramel sauce, a highly flavorful way to start your meal. Another hors d'oeuvre not to be overlooked is the homemade pan-fried sausage with duchesse potatoes. Salads, as it generally goes with Americanized French restaurants, are served before the entrées;

our choice is always the frisée au fromage de chèvre frit (frisée greens with sautéed goat cheese), a fresh, flavorful dish. Roast leg of lamb with white beans and grilled rib-eye steak with bordelaise sauce are two main courses that do taste-justice to bistro cooking, and the roasted chicken is an inspired piece of kitchen witchery. On the other hand, the whole duck breast with a prune and port sauce is an ugly duckling that gets caught in a sauce fight—too much sauce for too little duck. Fresh-fish specials are always quite nice. Try to save room for dessert: homemade ice cream, great sorbets, perfect crème brûlée. Dinner for two, with wine, runs about $65.

Chez Paul

600 N. Rush St.
944-6680
FRENCH
Open Mon.-Thurs.
11:30 a.m.-2:30 p.m. &
5:30 p.m.-10 p.m., Fri.
11:30 a.m.-2:30 p.m. &
5:30 p.m.-10:30 p.m., Sat.
5:30 p.m.-10:30 p.m., Sun.
5:30 p.m.-10 p.m.
All major cards.

12/20

Another Chicago institution, Chez Paul is long on kitsch and glitz, if in need of a scrub behind the ears. Still, where else can one get authentic tripe à la mode de Caen, the meat chewy-savory, the sauce fragrant with herbs and tomato? An amiable throwback to the Neanderthal days of "fine" dining, Chez Paul serves the seafood crêpes we cut our teeth on way back when no self-respecting shellfish would be caught dead without its gruel-thick cheese sauce. Lobster cardinal, Maine-fresh to the palate, bears up well under *its* cheesy mantle. Those bent on the ultimate stroll down memory lane may opt for cherry- or orange-glazed duck or a pepper-studded, Armagnac-flamed beef filet, both pleasant enough, though, gastronomically speaking, antediluvian. Country pâté, seafood cocktails, chops and steaks and the like make up the bulk of the offerings. The walls bristle with paintings that look like they were painted-by-number, and neither the elegant ceiling-high windows nor the romantic old-world chandeliers·have, in the past, been enough to make us overlook occasional evidence of sloppy housekeeping. Dinner for two, with wine, should come to about $90.

Club Gene and Georgetti

500 N. Franklin St.
527-3718
STEAKHOUSE/ITALIAN
Open Mon.-Sat.
11:30 a.m.-midnight.
Cards: AE, DC.

Food trends come and go. But through it all Gene and Georgetti holds fast to the basic fare that has made it popular for so many years, defiant proof that you don't need to be new, slick or trendy to make it in the restaurant business. It's an Italian restaurant and a steakhouse all rolled into a three-flat (which is starting to lean to the right) that is caught in a time warp, circa 1920. Regulars get the best tables, hence the best waiters; if you're not a regular, don't expect too much, except maybe the best steaks in town. Filet mignon is a high, handsome cut of meat the size of, say, two hockey pucks stacked atop one another. T-bone steaks border on mammoth—the tenderloin of the steak is a meal in itself. Sirloins are seared so nicely that when you cut through the charred surface, the juices run free. This is quality aged beef through and through. Unfortunately, the Italian side of the menu doesn't fare as well. Pasta is often overcooked; sauces are harsh tasting and heavy. And the seafood dishes pale mightily in comparison to steaks. But the spinach sautéed in olive oil and garlic is terrific, and calves' liver and bacon is a tasty alternative to the steak. Desserts can be skipped. About $60 for two, with wine.

Club Lago

331 W. Superior St.
337-9444
ITALIAN
Open Mon.-Fri. 11 a.m.-
8 p.m., Sat. 11 a.m.-
3:30 p.m.
No cards.

10/20

This tavern/restaurant is smack in the middle of the now-restaurant-fashionable part of the city known as River North. Open since 1952, Club Lago in the past three years has seen a number of new places move onto its turf, but loyal fans have not had their heads turned by all those beautiful-looking newcomers. As you enter, there's a thirteen-stool bar on the left with gallon jugs of Gallo wine proudly on display. A fifteen-table dining room starts where the booths leave off. For the class it's in, Club Lago has a lot of class. The food is mainly Italian—though not the kind of Italian served a few blocks to the west at Scoozi. This is old-fashioned Italian: spaghetti or mostaccioli (small mustache-shape pasta) with meatballs or sausage, green noodles with meat sauce, baked lasagne, chicken Vesuvio, calamari and a lot more. For a small place, the menu is ambitious: twelve veal dishes and chicken prepared ten different ways. We highly recommend the calamari, braciola and the baked cod, as well as the spaghetti and meatballs, which we believe is fast becoming quite alla moda. Great lunch spot. About $15 per person for dinner with wine.

Cocorico

1960 N. Clybourn Ave.
248-0700
FRENCH
Open Mon.-Thurs. 5 p.m.-
10 p.m., Fri.-Sat. 5 p.m.-
11 p.m.
All major cards.

12/20

The menu explains that "cocorico" is the sound a rooster makes, and that the rooster is the most treasured bird in France. The menu also provides an explanation of what a brasserie is all about: a relaxing place to eat, drink and unwind, a place to enjoy wine with a full-course dinner or just some frites. Cocorico fits its self-proclaimed profile. Located in a reconstituted factory building from the twenties, Cocorico is a multilevel affair with nicely spaced tables, cozy booths, some brick walls and a wood-beam ceiling. The rooster theme is carried throughout—breadbaskets, ceramic roosters, rooster art. We like the low-key casualness of the place. We also hope that the service staff increases its understanding of food in general and what the kitchen is cooking in particular. Cassoulet toulousain is quite good, even though it is not true to its roots (no goose). The onion soup is nothing short of sensational. Paillard maître d'hôtel, or minute steak, is a nice piece of meat most of the time, and the accompanying frites are great all of the time, but grilled chicken sometimes spends too much time on the grill. A dessert to seek out is the baked Alaska, but we suggest sidestepping the profiteroles filled with a chocolate- and-Kahlúa pastry cream. Dinner for two, with wine, runs about $50.

Como Inn

546 N. Milwaukee Ave.
421-5222
ITALIAN
Open Mon.-Thurs. & Sun.
11:30 a.m.-11:30 p.m.,
Fri.-Sat. 11:30 a.m.-
12:30 a.m.
All major cards.

10/20

It is sad to see what's happening to this venerable Chicago restaurant, which has been in operation since 1924. The decor in the labyrinthine leviathan is wonderful: Cozy dining nooks, marble floors, huge art posters, massive sprays of flowers and objets d'art present diners with a composed and attractive setting, and each year the decor is improved. Would that the food were fussed over in the same way. It seems that the Como Inn is more interested in a visual feast than the feast itself. Why, for example, would a onetime bastion of Italian cuisine serve a side dish of boiled carrots that tasted as if they had started off frozen? Why serve with the carrots a naked boiled potato? Why does it cost so much for a dish of eggplant parmigiana that is but three slices of eggplant topped with cheese and tomato? More miscues: When asked if the clams on the spaghetti con vongole were whole baby clams, the waitress responded, "Of course!" She wasn't even close—the clams were chopped so finely they could have been put through a sieve. A half bottle of Soave wine was ordered; it was brought in a carafe; we didn't see the bottle; and we don't believe it was Soave. But there is value here, which must be why it remains one of the most popular Italian restaurants in the city. The food, however, has slid immeasurably. Veal can be dry and stringy; the same is true for chicken. Pasta dishes were always good, but now they are a hit-or-miss affair. The decor is dazzling, but the food is a dud. About $40 for dinner for two, with wine.

Convito Italiano

11 E. Chestnut St.
943-2984
ITALIAN
Open Mon.-Thurs.
11:30 a.m.-2:30 p.m. &
6 p.m.- 10 p.m., Fri.-Sat.
11:30 a.m.-2:30 p.m. &
6 p.m.-11 p.m., Sun.
5 p.m.-9 p.m.
Cards: AE, MC, V.

9/20

This restaurant has delusions of grandeur. The waiters have delusions, too. On our last visit, they gave the impression that they were working in the only, and the best, Italian restaurant in the world (sorry to bust your bubble, gang, but you aren't). There was one gentleman up front—host would be a misnomer—who, it seemed, is a maître d'-in-training for Chez Snob. Loosen up, people! This combination restaurant (upper level)/Italian deli (first level) never seems to want to be friendly to its paying guests, and yet it remains quite popular. We can't figure it out. Well, maybe we can. Sometimes the place does serve decent food, but you can't count on it being cooked the same way twice—it's a roller-coaster ride. When the kitchen hits a pasta or chicken dish right, it's nothing short of sensational. The same goes for desserts and ice creams. But when they're bad, they're very, very bad, and they charge more than they should for what you get. Dinner runs about $30 a person, with wine.

*ime was when life's finer things such as Hine Cognac were the preserve of a privileged few.

Today, it is still the true connoisseur who appreciates the mature, mellow flavour of Hine.

The dictionary defines a connoisseur as "one who is an expert judge in matters of taste".

And who are we to argue.

BRASH, BOLD GUIDES
TO THE BEST OF THE VERY BEST

Also available:

THE BEST OF CHICAGO

THE BEST OF NEW ENGLAND

THE BEST OF FRANCE

THE BEST OF PARIS

THE BEST OF LONDON

THE BEST OF ITALY

Coppi

1212 N. State St.
944-1313
ITALIC
*Open Mon.-Sat. 4:30 p.m.-
11 p.m.*
Cards: AE, MC, V.

This may be the restaurant Chicago has been waiting for, a haven for those like us who have yearned for the intense flavors and straightforward presentations that are the essence of Italian food. The front rooms boast sky-blue ceilings crossed by flotillas of trompe l'oeil clouds. The inner rooms, one home to a wood-rich bar, reign darkly around a fireplace stove big enough for the proverbial fatted calf. And a baby grand of no-less-imposing dimensions fills a corner of the innermost room, which is usually reserved for private parties. Order antipasto misto and watch your waiter spoon sweet melrose peppers and herbed Italian sausage onto a plate, add leeks sautéed in chicken broth or eggplant parmigiana barely kissed by heady Tuscan olive oil, and pile white beans or lentils in a homemade tomato sauce next to seafood salad or fresh sautéed sardines. These, of course, are mere examples—the selection changes daily; only the quality remains constant. Sautéed tomatoes, toasted French bread with olive oil, and smoked mozzarella with basil and roasted peppers are among the other seductive openers. Entrées are heavy on the pasta—bucatini (thick spaghetti) dressed with a zesty tomato-pancetta sauce spiked with hot peppers is one such representative—but always include the likes of rare lamb with dark lentils, red snapper roasted with olive oil and rosemary, and chicken under layers of prosciutto and provolone. Though good, such desserts as tiramisù (sponge cake moistened with grappa and espresso and topped with Mascarpone) don't always reach the heights of the rest of the meal. Dinner for two, with wine, will set you back about $70.

The Cottage

525 Torrence Ave.,
Calumet City
891-3900
AMERICAN
*Open Tues.-Thurs.
11:30 a.m.-2 p.m. &
6 p.m.-10 p.m., Fri.
11:30 a.m.-2 p.m. &
6 p.m.-11 p.m., Sat.
5 p.m.-11 p.m.*
Cards: MC, V.

It's about twenty miles from downtown Chicago to The Cottage in Calumet City. The area surrounding this restaurant is not exactly an Elysian delight, but there it sits, a pleasant imitation of a French country cottage. Some of the decor suggests more early American than country French, but the plaster walls, wood-beam ceilings and entry-area fireplace create the proper illusion. Carolyn Buster tends the kitchen chores, and her husband, Jerry, handles the front of the house. These two able restaurateurs for thirteen years now have cultivated a loyal following with their special kind of hospitality and excellent food. One of the best ways to sample The Cottage's menu is the table d'hôte menu, which includes appetizer, soup, salad, entrée, dessert and coffee. The list of appetizers comprises far-from-listless creations: The smoked Petrossian salmon with a lake trout pâté is exquisite; the lamb sausages with peppers and a fragrant white-bean salad are no less interesting or tasty; and the grilled spiced quail with a cherry cider sauce is a fascinating dish. Check the blackboard listings for the nightly entrées, which range from a duck-and-quail combination to grilled swordfish to smoked baby pheasant to Cottage schnitzel. Desserts are choice creations all, but the raspberry cake and the divine strawberries cardinal (vanilla mousse, fresh strawberries, raspberry coulis and whipped cream) are downright astounding. The wine list isn't long, but it is exceptionally well thought out; the best values are in the California Chardonnays and Cabernet Sauvignons, of which there is a fine selection. Dinner for two, with wine, runs about $100.

Courtyards of Plaka

340 S. Halsted St.
263-0767
GREEK
Open Sun.-Thurs. 11 a.m.-
midnight, Fri.-Sat.
11 a.m.-1 a.m.
All major cards.

12/20

This place is refreshingly free of the standard Greek restaurant hokum: no shouts of *oopaa* every two minutes, no bouzouki music, and no one leaps from his seat to do a Greek dance in a spontaneous moment of uncontrollable passion. Do not be dismayed, however. The pyromaniac waiters are hard at work raising towers of flame, almost to the ceiling, for the saganaki cult of flaming-cheese worshipers. And the noise level is exactly what you would expect from a busy, bustling Greek restaurant. Taramosalata, that cool and delicate whipped fish roe, spreads nicely over good Greek bread. If there were one salad left on Earth, let it be a Greek salad, and let it come from this restaurant. Fish specialties are exceptionally good, especially when sea bass is on the menu. The bass arrives whole, still sizzling from the broiler, all parts intact. The waiter deftly bones it and delivers the delicious fish in no time flat. And you won't go wrong with the cod either, but unless you *really* like garlic, watch out for the puréed potatoes served with it. Almost every Greek specialty (most of which you will never learn to pronounce) is on the menu, including galaktobourikol, that weighty but wonderful dessert of custard between layers of phyllo. About $40 for dinner for two, with a bottle of decent Greek wine.

Cricket's

100 E. Chestnut St.
280-2100
AMERICAN
Open Mon.-Thurs. 7 a.m.-
11 a.m., noon-2:30 p.m. &
6 p.m.-10:30 p.m., Fri.-
Sat. 7 a.m.-11 a.m., noon-
2:30 p.m. & 6 p.m.-
11:30 p.m., Sun. 11 a.m.-
2:30 p.m. & 6 p.m.-
10:30 p.m.
All major cards.

The power lunch and power dinner set are really wired into Cricket's. Lunchtime brings out the best of the breed, though, when socialites of some standing are lavished with all the care and attention their precious pelts so richly deserve. Cricket's club-like setting invites this brand of social bonhomie: pegged oak floors, wood beams overhead, dark-wood paneling and checkered tablecloths create the effect of a private domain. Power is further enhanced by corporate toys: Model trucks, planes and trains hang from the ceiling. Important magazine covers featuring important people are framed and hung on the walls. Sadly, things haven't been the same in the kitchen since chef Guy Petit left to start his own place. Not that there's been a compromise on the quality of the ingredients—it's just that Petit's deft touch and precision are missing. Still, one can dine well on the grilled salmon with Pommery mustard sauce, the chicken hash Mornay with wild rice, and the rack of lamb. The best of the dessert bunch are Cricket's original cheesecake and crème brûlée. The New Orleans brunch on Saturday and Sunday has some excellent, if not authentic, offerings. About $50 per person for dinner with wine.

Ditka's

223 W. Ontario St.
280-7660
AMERICAN/STEAKHOUSE
Open daily 11 a.m.-3 p.m.
and 5 p.m.-midnight.
All major cards.

11/20

Though it doesn't like to be called a sports bar, Ditka's is a sports bar—in more ways than one. *Sports* as in athletes who sit around and compare neck sizes. *Sports* as in umpteen TV sets that flick away at the eyes and ears with enough sports action to bowl you over. *Sports* as in dandy, when the men-about-town train their sights on, and flex their pecs for, the ladies-about-town who go gaga over that sort of thing. *Sports* as in dishes (as in food) named after sports luminaries, like Tommy Lasorda (linguine with clam sauce), Vinny Testaverde (paglia e fieno), Harry Caray (fried calamari) and, of course, Mike Ditka (pork chops). We now take our tongue out of our cheek and let it deal with the food at hand, which, like athletes, has its good days and its bad. The Bear Burger (lunch only) is an awesomely good mound of ground beef. The steaks are, believe it or not, not bad. The Tommy Lasorda isn't a grand-clam sensation, but it has its moments. But the snails in the escargots en croûte should never have crawled into that piece of dough, and Jerry Vanisi's veal chop can be unbearably overcooked. Desserts are nothing to scream about. About $30 to $35 a person for dinner with a couple of beers.

Dong Hung Vien Restaurant

7136 N. Milwaukee Ave., Niles
647-8419
CHINESE
Open Mon.-Fri. 11:30 a.m.-
10:30 p.m., Sat.-Sun.
2 p.m.-10:30 p.m.
Cards: MC, DC, V.

Cantonese food, once synonymous with Chinese food, fell into disfavor when Szechwan and other styles burst onto the scene in the mid-'70s; sophisticated diners dismissed chow mein–egg foo yung fare with disdain. Unfortunately, they threw out the baby with the bath water; Cantonese food, at its best, remains one of the joys of Chinese cooking. One of the finest exponents of this style is Dong Hung Vien, whose comfortable tables and booths are usually crowded with Asian business people and exuberant families ordering six to eight courses that most emphatically do not include the old one-from-column-A and one-from-column-B standbys.

Our favorites are succulent roast duck stuffed with mashed taro, a rich, hearty, stick-to-the-ribs dish, and boned squab slivered and sautéed with similarly cut vegetables, then wrapped in lettuce leaves at the table. Steamed whole pike, redolent of ginger and anise and lovingly garnished with carrots, scallions and mushrooms, tastes as good as it looks; and shredded beef stir-fried with Chinese vegetables and served in a nest of crisp julienned potatoes is both elegant and delicious. When abalone is fresh, order it sizzling, as good a way to have it as any we've tried. Fresh Maine lobster at $12 is a frequent special and will be prepared in a variety of ways—the traditional Cantonese black-bean sauce is appropriate and particularly good. For starters, we gravitate toward a special egg roll stuffed to bursting with liver and vegetables, juicy shrimp-and-pork-filled dumplings called shu mai and the oddly named Charlie's Angel Treat—eight lightly battered, deep-fat-fried bean-curd cubes, their partially melted centers custardy sweet. Such sugary, gelatinous desserts as sweet bird's-nest broth or almond cream clearly are acquired tastes, which we have yet to acquire. Since wines are limited to Lancers and Paul Masson, beer best suits this fine cooking. Two dinners including beer will cost about $44.

Dragon Palace

3357 W. Peterson St.
588-2726
CHINESE
Open Sun. noon-10 p.m.,
Tues.-Thurs. 11:30 a.m.-
10 p.m., Fri.-Sat. noon-
midnight.
Cards: DC, MC, V.

11/20

We've had wonderful meals at Dragon Palace, Chicago's only Taiwanese restaurant, and we've had clunkers, but fortunately most have been good. When Jason Lai, proprietor and weekend singer, is around, the quality is high; when he isn't, as often as not, it isn't. Ask for the hakka and dim sum menu, and try the likes of cold stewed sinew: translucent, almost flavorless, rubbery strips that all but successfully resist mastication, a dish that emphasizes texture rather than flavor. Hot-and-sour jellyfish verges on incandescent, while red-cooked pigs' feet is sweet and gelatinous. Pan-fried oysters, on the other hand, are slippery, difficult to manage with chopsticks and drowned in a gooey tomato sauce. Our favorites are turnip cake and taro cake, each to be dipped in a wonderfully piquant homemade garlic soy sauce, and resilient water crystal dumplings that come to life with a dab of sinus-clearing chili sauce. Whole, deep-fried fluke has been superb—crisp and dry on the outside, moist and white within—but it also has been second-rate. When it's on, even the crisp-fried fins should be eaten. Tiny clams sautéed with black-bean sauce, stir-fried tripe and sautéed spinach with garlic are the most reliable entrées. The large, comfortable room is frequently reserved in whole or part for parties. Lai's daughter and niece perform folk dances most weekends. Approximately $45 should cover dinner for two, with beer.

Eli's the Place for Steaks

215 E. Chicago Ave.
642-1393
CONTINENTAL/STEAKHOUSE
Open Mon.-Fri. 11 a.m.-
2:30 p.m. & 4 p.m.-
11 p.m., Sat.-Sun.
4 p.m.-11 p.m.
Cards: AE, MC, V.

12/20

Everything about this restaurant is old—the furniture, the service staff, the decor (when was the last time you saw stained glass in a restaurant?), the style of the food. And you can tell by looking at the menu (large type) that Eli's caters to the older-but-wiser quiet-money set. We write these words with a smile, though, for there is something special about this place; Eli's is like a time capsule that just keeps ticking and pleasing the pols and the pepper shakers (Frank Sinatra has eaten here a lot over the years). It is first and foremost a meat house; of the 25 entrées on the dinner menu, only 4 are from the fish family. No, the best dish in the house is not the prime steaks or prime rib—it's the calves' liver with onions, peppers and mushrooms (it's also one of the lowest-priced entrées). If it makes any sense to call liver "stunning," then the word is appropriate. Those who cling to old dishes and refuse to let them go can have châteaubriand (for two) bouquetière with béarnaise sauce, broiled chopped steak (it's terrific) and shrimp de Jonghe. Eli's made cheesecake famous around these parts, and just as a hot dog tastes better at the ballpark, the rich, creamy and delicious cheesecake definitely tastes better here. Dinner for two, with a cocktail, runs about $60.

Emilio's Tapas Bar and Restaurant

4100 W. Roosevelt Rd., Hillside
547-7177
SPANISH
Open Mon.-Thurs. 11:30 a.m.-10 p.m., Fri. 11:30 a.m.-11 p.m., Sat. 5 p.m.-11 p.m., Sun. 5 p.m.-10 p.m.
Cards: AE, MC, V.

• The low-slung, mansard-roofed building that houses Emilio's was a fast-food operation in a former life. From the outside the building is not very possessing, but the picture inside is a different story. Emilio's has the look and feel of a taberna/tapas bar/restaurant in a small town along the Costa Brava or in a hamlet in the foothills of the Pyrénées. White lace curtains are used to divide the large dining room into two sections, and café-curtained windows break up the simulated plaster walls. To the right, as you enter, a glass display case showcases platters of the various tapas dishes; on the floor is a colorful mosaic of an octopus. We don't mean to suggest that this is an imperious place—it's actually small, quite homey and, in the spirit of tapas, a great little restaurant. Don't miss the pan con tomate, jamon y queso (Manchego cheese, ham and coarsely chopped fresh tomatoes on grilled bread). The grilled squid with garlic and lemon or any of the other many excellent tapas selections. However, if we were able to have only one dish at Emilio's, it would be the paella, a jubilant feast that includes golden, saffron-tinted rice, tiny green peas, glowing red lobster claws, black mussels in their shells, tiny littleneck clams, chunks of chorizo and pieces of fresh tomato... a magnificent, aromatic, delicious banquet. If we had to pick but one dessert, it would be the profiteroles. Dinner with a pitcher of sangría should cost two about $40.

L'Escargot on Halsted

2925 N. Halsted St.
525-5522
FRENCH
Open Mon.-Sat. 5 p.m.-10:30 p.m.
All major cards.

A little chronology may be in order here. First, there was plain old L'Escargot. From October 1968 until October 1979, a core of loyalists did not willingly allow a week to go by without enjoying Lucien Vergé's coq au vin or cassoulet at the low-key, darkly reserved Halsted Street bistro. Fire ended that chapter of the restaurant's history. Chapter two, L'Escargot on Michigan, began in 1980 when co-owner Alan Tutzer revived the name and much of the menu in the Allerton Hotel downtown. To complete the saga, in 1984 a L'Escargot bearing the qualifier "on Halsted" took up residence at the old New Town address. Curiously, there's not much sense of déjà vu. The interior has a sparkle quite unlike the petit bourgeois rusticity of the original. Wooden, wainscotted walls, painted a cream color three-quarters of the way up, then a cool blue touched by green to the ceiling, form an elegant background for the occasional French street sign and movie poster, framed prints of landscapes and figure studies in charcoal.

Chef Domenico Lopez creates a bourgeois cuisine of considerable refinement. Pâtés range from satisfyingly coarse, peppercorn-studded pork terrines and mildly gamey rabbit to vibrant chicken and duck liver. Cold cream-of-zucchini soup, too rich to finish, captures the elusive flavor of the vegetable admirably. Onion tart suffers only from a bottom crust that can be too soft. Entrées include soup or an appetizer; snails, shrimp and baked onion soup cost a little more. Salmon straddling pools of lobster and Champagne sabayon sauces starts out good but ends up superb, the subtle flavors growing bite by bite. Duck, lamb and pork mingle with white pea beans in the Toulouse-style cassoulet, which is presented in its pot before being served with a spoonful of light-yellow mustard. Lighter appetites might prefer seasonal vegetables steamed and dressed with a beurre blanc or the sautéed chicken breast with wild mushrooms; but we, being heartier of appetite than some, prefer the casserole of snails baked under puff pastry, filet in port wine sauce laced with truffles, or rack of lamb. A simple house salad with a mustardy cream dressing is served before or after your entrée, as preferred. Desserts measure up to the rest. An almond-sheathed, fresh-fruit napoleon ended our last meal here on a particularly agreeable note, accompanied by an intense, smoky cappuccino, its foam unsullied by nutmeg or cinnamon. An exquisite and remarkably reasonable wine list (the Aloxe-Corton Grande Reserve is incomparable at $21.50) and some lovely Armagnacs complement the food, and service errs only, if at all, in the direction of excess enthusiasm. Two people will spend about $95 for dinner with wine.

L'Escargot on Michigan

(Allerton Hotel)
701 N. Michigan Ave.
337-1717
FRENCH
Open daily 7 a.m.-10 a.m.,
11:30 a.m.-2:30 p.m. &
5 p.m.- 10:30 p.m.
All major cards.

Dining at this Streeterville sibling of the Halsted operation has been problematic. While venison has been beautifully complemented by grillotines (Cognac-infused French cherries), or almost as well by a trio of puréed chestnuts, split peas and potato, and while we confess encountering veal of a miraculously delicate lushness, glitches do plague some of the food. The potato basket holding wild mushrooms has been greasy and the fungi have varied from robust and unusual lobster mushrooms (oddly suggestive of apple) to dry, unappealing morels and oyster mushrooms. A stridently acidic beet borscht has followed a timbale of spinach not much different from a hotel dining room's creamed spinach. But then we always wind up forgiving these sins after enjoying such dishes as the full-flavored veal-and-pork pâté bristling with chopped pistachios and truffles, the superior warm leek tart and the Russian cream—crème fraîche dotted with globes of golden, red and black American caviar; we forgive *and* forget after the tuna paillard, which rivals Hawaii's best. We usually opt for the lemon tart or pistachio soufflé, but the other desserts don't lag far behind. The wine list duplicates Halsted's. A brasserie interior—street signs, movie posters, muddy-blond slatted woodwork and dividers—creates a comfortable space; at times, service passes over from attentive to zealous, with wine being topped off almost sip by sip. Two people will leave about $85 lighter after dinner with wine.

Eurasia
200 E. Chestnut St.
387-2742
ASIAN-AMERICAN
*Open Mon.-Thurs. 5 p.m.-
11 p.m., Fri.-Sat. 5 p.m.-
midnight, Sun. 5 p.m.-
10 p.m.
All major cards.*

The menu has an introductory statement: "At Eurasia, East meets West in a mythical setting. Here you'll taste the flavors and cuisines of Asia, married with the cooking techniques and foods of Europe and the states." Yet another Levy Brothers restaurant, Eurasia is a sleek, modern dining venue with an ambience that, like the menu, reflects cultural intermingling. Everything is visually exciting: the black-lacquer tables and chairs, the colorful cloth wall hangings, the custom-decorated dishes and platters. And the place is as spirited as the teas are gentle. The menu gets pretty enthusiastic describing the dishes—justifiably so, since the flavor combinations are exotic and lustful. Stir-fried squid with roasted red peppers and a pine-nut nori (dried seaweed) butter is a standout appetizer, rich with one taste sensation after another. Ditto for the Peking chicken salad. Potstickers with a lamb-and-cabbage filling are tough around the edges but flavorful. Such entrées as wok-charred tuna and sesame-grilled lamb chops draw deeply from the flavors found in the Pacific Basin countries. The former uses shichimi togarashi spice mix, with good results; the lamb chops are glazed with caramelized shallots and come with a sweet sesame barbecue sauce. The crispy scallion crêpes that come with the Peking duck are sensational. Desserts don't measure up to the rest of the menu—they're overly contrived, especially the ice kacange, which is nothing more than a mound of finely shaved ice flavored (weakly) with fruit purées. Nice selection of wines and Oriental beers. Dinner for two costs about $90, including wine.

DON'T FORGET: Gault Millau introduces you to the Best of New York, the Best of Washington D.C., the Best of Los Angeles, the Best of San Francisco, the Best of New England, the Best of France, the Best of Paris, the Best of Italy, the Best of London.

The Everest Room

440 S. LaSalle St.
(1 Financial Plaza),
40th Fl.
663-8920
FRENCH
*Open Mon. 11:30 a.m.-
2 p.m., Tues.-Fri.
5:30 p.m.-8:30 p.m., Sat.
6 p.m.-9:30 p.m.
Cards: AE, MC, V.*

Getting to The Everest Room from the private parking garage in the lower level of the building is not unlike scaling a mountain, as it requires three elevator changes and a trek down a narrow, stark-white corridor. But the rewards that await at the top are worth it. The room itself has been called "tacky" by some restaurant critics, but we disagree. We like the unusual decor. The leopard-print carpeting and the wild-animal murals at either end of the dining room are there, we suppose, to work in concert with the name of the restaurant, though that's as far as the wilderness concept goes. And though plush touches abound—crisp napery, elegant place settings, spacious tables, comfortable chairs, a tuxedoed staff—there is nothing sanctimonious about the place. In fact, it is quite spirited. "Polished" is the best word to describe the service: The staff members, and they number many, are well aware of the fine nuances and ingredients that go into the meticulously prepared dishes conceived and created by chef Jean Joho, who had a bit of a rocky start when The Everest Room first opened but is now displaying a remarkable level of kitchen mastery.

First-course elegance could come in the form of a mosaic of leeks, foie gras and mushrooms or a pot-au-feu of lobster. As good as these dishes are, though, it would be hard to pass up the simply outstanding black squid risotto. The perfectly creamy rice is studded with small pieces of tender squid and perfumed with an aromatic blend of basil, oregano, thyme and a hint of garlic—a ravishing risotto. Entrées surpass excellence. John Dory, a fish whose taste rivals that of turbot, is sautéed, wrapped in a thyme-flavored julienne of potatoes and then roasted to perfection. Le suprême de saumon soufflé Paul Haeberlin is sublime elegance on a plate: a pike mousse layered over thin scallops of salmon, which are then poached in fish stock and wine. The sauce is a reduction of pan juices, to which cream, butter and lemon juice are added. This celebrated dish of L'Auberge de l'Ill in Illhaeusern, France, is captured faithfully in all respects by Joho, who apprenticed there with the great Haeberlin. Tournedos cut from the saddle of venison are roasted, thinly sliced, fanned out on the plate and served with a natural sauce flavored with fresh elderberries. No fewer than eleven desserts are offered each evening, an ever-changing, enticing rhapsody of enjoyment: a fantasy of chocolate (white- and dark-chocolate mousse, chocolate cake, chocolate ice cream and two chocolate sauces); a symphony of pears (whole poached pear, pear bavarois, pear sorbet, white and dark caramel sauce); a raspberry-and-chocolate terrine; a triple-chocolate fondant with pistachio sauce... the delicious list goes on and on. Be prepared to pay about $150 for dinner for two, with wine.

Fernando's

3435 N. Lincoln Ave.
477-6930
MEXICAN
Open Mon.-Thurs.
3:30 p.m.-10:30 p.m., Fri.-
Sat. 3:30 p.m.- 11:30 p.m.,
Sun. 3:30 p.m.-10 p.m.
All major cards.

11/20

Beach umbrellas suspended from the ceiling and tall potted plants scattered around the large room fronting Lincoln Avenue create the illusion of dining in a patio. There is a small one out in back for those who demand the genuine article, but on a typical Chicago summer evening (that is, hot and muggy), we prefer imaginary gardens with real air conditioning. The menu, which reflects several regions of Mexico, is not extensive. The ubiquitous tacos, enchiladas and fajitas appear along with a few specialties from Chihuahua, Mazatlán, Puebla, Veracruz and the Yucatán. Warm tortilla chips, a trifle greasy, and exuberant salsa begin the meal on a promising note. The promise continues with sopa de ajo that is unstinting with fresh garlic, a concoction that would have any vampire in a ten-block radius begging for mercy. Sopa del dia is a generous bowl of chicken soup, its clear broth loaded with chunks of sweet chicken, avocado, onion and red peppers, savory with cilantro and flat-out wonderful. Red snapper Veracruz, baked with tomatoes, wine, capers and olives, is competently prepared, though the fish can be less than pristine, a failing shared by the sautéed brook trout. Though nicely flavored, steak ranchero has been known to be tough. Pollo estilo Oaxaca, parchment-wrapped chicken breast and mushrooms baked in a sauce of tequila and fiery red peppers, can be bracing or overwhelming depending on your mood and the mood of the chef, who varies the amount of hot stuff he throws in on any given evening. Excellent flour tortillas provide much-needed relief and make mopping up fun, but you may have to ask for them, since the harried waiters get forgetful on busy nights. Creamy flan and crisp sopapillas end the meal on a satisfying note. About $40 should cover dinner for two, with beer or sangría.

Foley's

215 E. Ohio St.
645-1261
AMERICAN
Open Mon.-Thurs.
11:30 a.m.-2:30 p.m. &
5:30 p.m.-10:30 p.m., Fri.
11:30 a.m.-2:30 p.m. &
5:30 p.m.-11:30 p.m., Sat.
5:30 p.m.- 11:30 p.m.
All major cards.

Some of the most imaginative cooking in Chicago is served in this large, comfortable dining room in the heart of Streeterville. Chef Joe Doppes rules the kitchen for talented owner/chef Michael Foley, whose Printer's Row helped set a new standard for cuisine in the city. Doppes's creations run the gamut from reliably successful standbys to innovative and gratifying combinations. Dilled home-cured salmon on herb toast, juicy-ripe melon with prosciutto and a platter of smoky, traditionally garnished pâtés are offered as appetizers, along with briny-sweet mussels in green curry and cream, sweetbreads pungent with lemon grass and chives, and calamari stir-fried Szechwan-style with peppers, pea pods and eggplant. A salad can be as simple as crisp Belgian endive topped with goat cheese and bacon or as startling as gently smoked sturgeon on a bed of field greens bathed in a sprightly caviar vinaigrette.

Choices among entrées range from perfectly grilled salmon,

grouper or veal medallions to a daring tuna tempura sashimi, lightly battered slabs of tangy-fresh tuna that are quick-fried so the fish remains cool inside. The contrast between the delicate egg coating and the robust meaty center challenges our notion of textural possibilities. While closer to the culinary mainstream, breast of duck, sautéed and served with leg confit on braised cabbage flavored with pancetta, is no less satisfying. Desserts run from excellent to outstanding: espresso mousse, chocolate crêpes folded around fresh fruit, a napoleon of berries and whipped cream. The large, comprehensive wine list features a fair number of moderately priced vintages. A couple will spend around $92 for dinner with wine.

Le Français
269 S. Milwaukee Ave., Wheeling
541-7470
FRENCH
Open Tues.-Sun. 6 p.m.- 10 p.m.
All major cards.

We agree (despite the sexist noun and pronoun) with Browning's "Ah, but a man's reach should exceed his grasp,/ Or what's a heaven for?" We agree in principle, that is; our dreams are haunted by the perfect restaurant, a will o' the wisp, its essence captured, its impalpable spirit made flesh. At times such contemporary masters as Paul Haeberlin and the Troisgros make it seem almost within grasp. One of the few this side of the Atlantic who has been able to work that trick is Jean Banchet. And now, after displaying a remarkable level of talent and technical mastery for seventeen years, and meeting with considerable success in the process, Banchet is leaving Le Français for the less-exhausting life of a restaurant consultant. We learned this important news just three days (literally!) before this book was headed for the printing press, and the changing of the guard had not yet taken place. We'll tell you what we know: The new owners are the skilled husband-and-wife team of Roland and Beth Liccioni, who had been producing outstanding food at Carlos' (he as chef, she as pastry chef). By the time you read these words, they will be firmly insconded in their new kitchen—but don't expect any great changes, at least not immediately. The menu and decor are sure to remain the same for some time: the Liccionis' influence should be noticeable only in a moderate lightening and modernizing of the cooking technics. What the diner sees—away from a high-ceilinged, spacious kitchen festooned with stainless-steel stock pots and copper sauteuse pans—might pass for a French relais gourmand in or near Lyon, perhaps Pierre Orsi. Le Français, however, finds its own way, a haute-bourgeois culinary citadel whose reddish-brown hardwood walls display a potpourri of Quimper porcelain, nineteenth-century French and Italian genre paintings and provincial copperware. Sheer draperies soften the light. Crystal and silverware stand out against stark-white napery.

In the past, the food has, if anything, surpassed its setting. We have witnessed such extravagant combinations as the breasts of duck, quail and squab, a whisper darker than saignant, with rouennaise sauce (a bordelaise thickened by sieved duck liver) and morels; brandade de Morue, smoky and garlicky dried cod that is mashed, topped with a semi-soft quail egg and served in a puff pastry; roast lobster beyond both reproach and description; and sweetbreads "Fernand Point," the curd-soft, nut-pungent meat basking in a cream sauce rife with green beans, chanterelles and the black magic of gastronomy, Périgord truffles. *Foie gras d'oie ou de canard? Bien sûr!* And beluga caviar, if you must. It would be better, though, to sample the pâtés and seafood terrines, which are not available just anywhere, a selection of five or more arranged among glittering diced aspic and mâche; or the sublime mussel soup with saffron and basil; or the vegetable millefeuille stung to vibrancy by truffles vinaigrette. For us, the gratin de fruits, pear tartes, sorbets and ice creams, alternating with madeleines and similar bits of pâtisserie, have been preferable to the soufflés, which are merely very good.

Dinner for two, with wine, will cost upward of $160.

Francesco's Hole in the Wall

254 Skokie Blvd.,
Northbrook
272-0155
ITALIC
Open Mon. & Wed.-Fri.
11:30 a.m.-2:15 p.m. &
5 p.m.-9:30 p.m., Sat.-Sun.
5 p.m.-9:30 p.m.
No cards.

Francesco's Hole in the Wall really is a hole in the wall. This closet-size place offers elbow-to-elbow dining at its intimate best. There is always a wait for a table, and you know and we know that people don't wait unless the wait is worth it. We won't go into the decor; let's just say it's early rec-room Italian. But don't interpret that as harsh criticism, for the spirit of the place and the food are what this place is all about. The blackboard menu on the wall describes what owner/chef Franco is dishing out that particular day, which could be delectable fried calamari, or the perfect example of what baked clams should be, or wonderful roasted peppers, just to mention a sampling of the appetizers. Pasta dishes are wonderful. Capellini puttanesca is fragrant and spicy, and linguine with clams has just the right hit of garlic—the aroma alone is enough to dazzle the senses. And entrées don't often miss the mark. One that does, however, is lobster fra diavolo, which is heavy on the diavolo and light on the lobster. But veal francese is quality and tenderness and good taste from one delicious bite to the next. Francesco does well by fish, too; the red snapper Livornese is a standout creation. The best dessert in the house is the tiramisù, but we think the cannoli cake is just as dreamy.

About $50 for dinner for two, with wine.

> *Some establishments change their closing times without warning. It is always wise to call ahead.*

Froggy's French Café

306 Green Bay Rd.,
Highwood
433-7080
FRENCH
*Open Mon.-Thurs.
11:30 a.m.-2 p.m. &
5 p.m.-10 p.m., Fri.
11:30 a.m.-2 p.m. &
5 p.m.-11 p.m., Sat.
5 p.m.-11 p.m.
Cards: CB, DC, MC, V.*

Froggy's may have a new menu every month, but the value remains the same—top notch. For $20.95, the Gourmet Menu includes six courses—a hot and a cold appetizer followed by a sorbet, entrée, salad and dessert. Cold starters have included such choices as a sausage of bay scallops with two sauces, cold asparagus mousse in a pool of carrot cream, and baby quail stuffed with veal mousse surrounded by onions steeped in raspberry vinaigrette. Hot openers include a snail pâté baked in a pastry shell and made piquant by a sauce of green peppercorns, New Zealand green lip mussels glazed with essence of pimiento, and quenelles of pike and shrimp bathed in saffron cream. The dozen or so entrées that appear regularly include authentic tripe à la mode de Caen; herb-roasted rack of lamb encircled by tomatoes, onions and peppers; pink breast of duck served with a roasted leg in a red-wine sauce; salmon grilled with black peppercorns on a bed of leeks; casserole of Maine lobster braised with white wine and fresh vegetables; and several other reliably imaginative dishes. Our grapefruit sorbet came laced with vodka, a special touch that lifted it out of the ordinary. Desserts live up to the rest of the meal. We have fond memories of golden, flaky puff pastry surrounding dark, rich chocolate mousse, an ethereally delicate mousse of berries and an intensely tart and winey passion-fruit cake. The decor verges on the spartan, redeemed by a smattering of copies of impressionist paintings. Service is professional and the wine list moderately priced. Dinner for two, with wine, will cost about $70.

Frontera Grill

445 N. Clark St.
661-1434
MEXICAN
*Open Tues.-Thurs.
11:30 a.m.-2:30 p.m &
5:30 p.m.-10 p.m., Fri.
11:30 a.m.-2:30 p.m. &
5:30 p.m.-11 p.m., Sat.
10:30 a.m.-2:30 p.m. &
5:30 p.m.-11 p.m.
All major cards.*

Frontera Grill is a pretty restaurant that has been spared the unnecessary froufrou (the rubber reptiles hanging over the front counter could go, though): a tile floor, oak tables and booths, overhead fans, earth-tone wall colors set off by Mexican folk art. It currently is one of the most popular Mexican restaurants in the city. Owner Rick Bayless, after bouncing around Mexico for a few years, wrote an amazingly authentic Mexican cookbook, which was released just about the time he opened his restaurant. And he knows how to cook authentic Mexican food, too. Exceptionally good regional specialties change on a monthly basis and go far beyond the old-hat, boring Mexican food served by most "authentic" Mexican restaurants. To wit: wood-roasted squab with smoky chipotle peppers, roasted tomatillos and roasted potatoes; seared sea scallops in a creamy pumpkin-seed pipián; chile-marinated marlin with avocado-tomatillo sauce; turkey breast in red mole sauce; and the list goes on. A house specialty—tacos al carbon—allows the diner to fold skirt steak, chicken or duck into a homemade tortilla. Served with salsa, frijoles charros and guacamole (an excellent rendition), these are tacos of another kind—the best kind.

Some Mexican basics include quesadillas, queso fundido and garnachas, but we find that Bayless is at his best with the more typically regional dishes, and he is a master at making a mole sauce. Desserts are not quite as interesting as the rest of the menu, but the prickly pear ice cream is a nice end-of-the-meal palate cleanser. About $25 a person for dinner with a Mexican beer or two.

Galáns

2210 W. Chicago Ave.
292-1000
UKRAINIAN
Open Tues.-Thurs.
11:30 a.m.-10 p.m., Fri.-
Sat. 11:30 a.m.-11 p.m.,
Sun. 11:30 a.m.-9 p.m.
Cards: AE, MC, V.

12/20

The decor is toned-down glitz that has been laced with dashes of contemporary and a few sprinkles of downtown suave. Separated from the main dining room by a glass-and-wood divider is a restful bar, the kind where you can sit and stare into your drink and not be disturbed. The prices are refreshingly low, and the food is old-world and hearty. If you like lots (and we mean lots) of food, order the Kozak feast. It starts with a hot, full-flavored borscht; steams on through cabbage rolls (holubtsi), varenyky (dumplings filled with a purée of potato and cheese), Ukrainian sausage with Sauerkraut, chunks of beef tenderloin and pork, and potato pancakes; and finishes strongly with the torte of the day. It's quite a feast. Chicken Kiev is as it should be, right down to the seasoned butter that oozes out when the breast is pierced. Excellent chicken paprika, too. The hot apple Strudel is a model of the genre. This is not the place to go if you're dieting—but it *is* the place if your bank account is slim. About $15 per person for a big meal with wine.

Genesee Depot

3736 N. Broadway
528-6990
AMERICAN/CONTINENTAL
Open Tues.-Thurs.
5:30 p.m.-10:30 p.m., Fri.-
Sat. 5:30 p.m.-11 p.m.,
Sun. 5 p.m.-9 p.m.
Cards: AE, MC, V.

8/20

Popular with couples and small unisex groups, this rustic, gussied-up tea-room version of a traditional North Side joint hasn't improved over the years, despite the stiff competition. Dishes we once found a welcome departure from the greasy meatloaf and glue-like chicken à la king endemic in the days of Chicago's potluck palaces now smack of a cafeteria mind set. Consider, for example, four dishes centered around a chicken breast, varied only in that one has a bread stuffing, red cabbage and spinach noodles filling out the plate, another appears under a Gruyère sauce and, well, you get the picture. Shrimp Creole rises above mediocrity, partly because the shrimp are sizable, plentiful and flavorful, and the accompanying spanking-fresh zucchini helps make up for dull brown rice. Three veal dishes, boiled beef and one or two fish specials fill out a menu that reaches its nadir in an overcooked boneless duck breast under a horribly sugary fruit sauce. There are no appetizers, but the home-made soup is good; and on request an entrée can be split between two to start. On the positive side, the Depot (which doesn't have a liquor license) will serve your beer or wine without levying a corkage charge (no wine buckets, though). Two people will spend about $35, without wine.

George's Restaurant

230 W. Kinzie St.
644-2290
ITALIAN
*Open Mon. 11:30 a.m.-
2 p.m., Tues.-Thurs.
11:30 a.m.-2 p.m. &
5:30 p.m.-8:30 p.m., Fri.-
Sat. 11:30 a.m.-2 p.m. &
5:30 p.m.- midnight, Sun.
5:30 p.m.-8 p.m.
All major cards.*

10/20

Restaurateurs, seeking renown or perhaps notoriety, often name their culinary offspring after themselves (thus, the triumvirate of Gordon, Lexander and Sinclair, which, for its brief existence, exhausted Gordon Sinclair's monikers). George's Restaurant, George Badonsky's baby, began as a swank northern Italian eatery back when "Italian" was synonymous with tomato sauce thick with dried oregano, meatballs big and tough enough to pass for handballs and candle-plugged Chianti bottles on red-checked oilcloth. Since then George's has metamorphosed into a supper club with a $19.50 prix-fixe menu. Such wonderful dishes as salmon tartare have been replaced by seafood lasagne, gustatory clichés of the veal scaloppine and chicken breast- with-provolone-and-artichoke ilk and a handful of slightly more provocative offerings, like beef in Barolo wine sauce and scallops and shrimp with porcini mushrooms. The house salad, romaine dressed with an assertive vinaigrette and a shower of sweet Parmesan grated at the table, has the simple excellence that other dishes at best merely approach. "George's Symphony of Desserts," which changes from time to time, also scores a bull's-eye: intense chocolate sauce swaddling slabs of bread pudding, delicate ricotta cheesecake surrounding more delicate white-chocolate mousse, flourless chocolate cake on velvety crème anglaise. Vegetarian or kosher meals are available with a few days' notice.

Black faux-marble tables, dark-green banquettes, a dropped ceiling and subdued light softly reflected by the beige walls make a comfortable setting for relaxed dining; from 8:30 p.m. on, diners are entertained by a jazz combo, comic, singer or some such act. Dinner with wine will cost a couple about $70; after 8 p.m., you'll have to pay a cover charge, which varies with the acts.

Gordon

500 N. Clark St.
467-9780
AMERICAN
*Open Mon.-Thurs.
11:30 a.m.-2 p.m. &
5:30 p.m.-9:30 p.m., Fri.
11:30 a.m.-2 p.m. &
5:30 p.m.-1 a.m., Sat.
5:30 p.m.-1 a.m., Sun.
11 a.m.-2:30 p.m. &
5:30 p.m.-9:30 p.m.
All major cards.*

You have to admire owner Gordon Sinclair. He finds a talented chef, and as fast as the ink dries on a laudatory review he loses the chef to one of the larger restaurant groups in town. But through it all (four or five chefs over the past twelve years), he has managed to keep Gordon on an even keel. And though this waltz of the chefs has caused a few missteps along the way, the restaurant has never lacked innovation and flair. The chef (as of this writing) is Cory Schreiber, and the way things are going, Sinclair has found another winner to head the kitchen at his white-tableclothed, tongue-in-chic, beautifully decorated restaurant. Schreiber (formerly of Seasons restaurant in the Bostonian Hotel) has at his command an astonishing range of taste combinations. Rack of lamb with honey dates and cumin is a sensational dish. Roasted sweetbreads with peas and morels is so good it could give sweetbreads a good name. What could be simpler than a roasted breast of chicken; what could be more delicious than the chicken basking in its own sublime flavor? An appetizer of parsley tagliatelle is wrapped with the appealing flavors of basil and garlic; seared sea scallops with tomatillos and cilantro is a blissful creation. And Gordon's classic (and original) appetizers—artichoke fritters and egg-plant with duxelles and blue cheese—are capable of happily surprising even the most jaded of taste buds. Desserts could make the sweet-tooth fairy come out of hiding and take up permanent residence. Gordon is the home of the original flourless chocolate cake, and there isn't a better rendition around. Coconut Bavarian cream with strawberries and vanilla sauce is also devastatingly good. Lunch selections are just as appealing, as is the Sunday brunch. Now if Gordon would just do something about making better espresso... Dinner for two, with wine, will set you back about $90.

Un Grand Café

2300 Lincoln Park West
348-8886
FRENCH
Open Mon.-Thurs. 6 p.m.-
11 p.m., Fri.-Sat. 6 p.m.-
midnight.
All major cards.

What a nice restaurant Un Grand Café is—a pleasant, comfortable, handsomely appointed French bistro, an ideal setting in which to enjoy hearty and traditional French fare. Banquettes follow dark-wood walls accented by large and small mirrors and French posters. The tables and chairs are café-style, the table flowers are fresh, and the lighting is as soft as the napery. Diners find a small pot of mustard on the table, along with a slab of sweet butter and crusty bread. We enjoy this bistro if only for the steak frites. A simple steak, but what a steak to savor—lean, quality beef with a rich, succulent flavor. And the fries—no bigger than matchsticks—are crisp outside, soft inside, a little brown along the edges... just wonderful! Classic onion soup is robust and aromatic, the slivered onions thick in the rich broth. Fish is prepared simply, just a light turn on the grill, and grilled calves' liver with mustard sauce is silky and richly satisfying. Pastries, cakes and tarts have their moments, but they don't always seize us with satisfaction; fresh-fruit tarts and sorbets are the safest choices. We like this bistro, but we would like it even more if it expanded on the plats du jour, which are rather limited. About $70 for two, with wine.

Green Door Tavern

678 N. Orleans St.
664-5496
AMERICAN
Open Mon.-Thurs. 11 a.m.-
11 p.m., Fri.-Sat. 11 a.m.-
midnight, Sun. 1 p.m.-
9 p.m.
Cards: AE.

11/20

The Green Door Tavern is housed in a frame building that dates back to 1872, and many of the bar fixtures installed in the twenties still exist in the present bar, a fact that does not go unnoticed by the eager eaters who love this contra-status hangout. Surrounded by four of the hottest new restaurants in the city, this grog-and-grub shop still packs them in, particularly at lunchtime. When it's not blistery cold, the lean-to sun-porch affair on the side of the building is the place to be seated. (We don't know why, since it's nothing fancy, and the only view is of the traffic zipping by.)

The food is basic home cooking—exactly what you would

expect from a tavern. The hamburgers, served on a metal beer tray covered with aluminum foil, are big and juicy and come with corn chips, coleslaw and baked beans. Meatloaf and mashed potatoes are exceptionally good—when available. Soups aren't so great, but the chili is. Ribs, served only at dinnertime, are a slab to behold, with a barbecue sauce that zings with the best of them. Great selection of imported and domestic beers. About $15 a head, with beer or wine.

Hat Dance
325 W. Huron St.
649-0066
MEXICAN
*Open Mon.-Thurs. 5 p.m.-
10:30 p.m., Fri.-Sat.
5 p.m.-11:30 p.m.
All major cards.*

Hat Dance is lively but not rambunctious, the decor fanciful rather than fantastic, the food upbeat and, except for the oddity of sashimi at the ceviche bar, reasonably authentic. This bustling, gentrified taqueria *es muy simpatico*. Stepping down from the front area, which is a hip-to-hip seething mass of humanity after 6 p.m., diners negotiate what could pass for a prom-night ballroom. Cement pillars erupt into palm-leaf sprays on their way to the ceiling, and globe lights cast a glow on pallor-stricken lemony walls. An umbrella dangles here, a Spanish shawl there. Hollywood's idea of pre-Hispanic ideograms catches the bemused eye. It resembles no Mexico that ever was, but it's a mighty amusing arena for drinking lime-tangy margaritas or Carta Blanca beer while glancing over the menu or listening to a recitation of specials. To start, try the geoduck (pronounced *gooeyduck*) cocktail, the mollusk sweet and of a faint, potato-like earthiness, or the vuelve a la vida, a geoduck plus shrimp and oysters, strong rivals for the fresh ceviche. A traditional ancho pepper, when available, gives the chile rellenos an authentic bite, which is soothed by melted chihuahua cheese. Pozole isn't authentic, the pork-and-hominy stew lacking the pig's head needed for gelatin and flavor, but it's a heart-warming substitute on a cold night. Though smoked-chicken-and-wild-mushroom tamales and crab quesadillas might puzzle visiting Oaxaquenos, they do just fine for norteamericanos honed on Tex-Mex and California nouvelle. Among the entrées, the pork chops adobada—hatch-marked from the grill, tender, smoky, lean but not dry—and the wood-roasted chicken clamor for attention, while plank-roasted shrimp, chicken mole and grouper filet murmur in the background. Overdone potatoes and scorched vegetables have been among the occasional, minor lapses. Try champurrado, cornmeal-thickened and coffee-flavored hot chocolate, in lieu of dessert, or try the caramelized pecans, figs with rice pudding or, on the lighter side, the day's sorbet or ice cream. When the pace gets frenetic, the kitchen may fall behind, but seldom for longer than a few minutes. Since reservations aren't accepted, a wait is virtually certain if you arrive after 6 p.m. Two of you will have to ante up about $55 to join in this particular hat dance.

Hatsuhana

160 E. Ontario St.
280-8287
JAPANESE
*Open Mon.-Sat. noon-
2 p.m. & 5:30 p.m.-
10 p.m., Sun. noon-2 p.m.
All major cards.*

12/20

Long the Palais-Royal for local sushi buffs, this sleek café-restaurant looks like it belongs in midtown New York more than in Chicago. It manages to do a credible job despite the defection of one of its most experienced sushi chefs, who took permanent French leave to open his own *coin de Japon* north of Lincoln Park. While no longer Chicago's standard bearer, Hatsuhana still offers fresh to spanking-fresh fluke, tuna, yellowtail and the like, either as bright minislabs of sashimi or laid along vinegar-dosed rice to form sushi. Smoked salmon, a flap of steamed octopus like a lilliputian cape, and butterflied shrimp are other notable dishes. So is raw flounder, a cousin to fluke, but, in our experience, less voluptuously tender. For more complex preparations, we opt for the torame, broiled squid-wrapped smoked salmon, which supposedly mimics a tiger's eye; negimaki, a scallion-beef roll broiled teriyaki fashion; and chawan mushi, steamed egg custard enlivened by bits of seafood and vegetables. Delicately crisp tempura, teriyaki (fish or beef) and fair broiled Maine lobster round out a menu that's narrow in scope compared to the competition's. A few combination plates are also available. One of the most intense miso soups we've ever tasted hides a surprising collection of baby clams, bacon and enoki mushrooms in its murky depths. Prices tend to be high, which is understandable given the location. Ash-blond woodwork and white stucco accent a dramatic zigzag sushi bar that runs along the right-hand wall like a stroke of lightning to the rear of the deep, single room. With beer or saké, dinner for two should come to about $55.

Heidelberger Fass

4300 N. Lincoln Ave.
478-2486
GERMAN
*Open Mon. & Wed.-Sat.
11:30 a.m.-10 p.m., Sun.
noon-10 p.m.
All major cards.*

11/20

One of the few remaining bastions of *gemütlichkeit* in what was once a flourishing German neighborhood, Heidelberger Fass seems stuck in a time warp. The place has changed very little in the last two decades. Sauerbraten, Wiener Schnitzel, beef rouladen and Kasseler Rippschen occupy center stage on the menu, and the dirndl-clad wait-resses, though a bit longer in the tooth these days, dispense Bratwurst and bonhomie as they always have. The decor is vaguely Bavarian: beamed walls and ceilings, beer steins of every conceivable size and shape in every available nook and cranny, and a relic of a Black Forest cuckoo clock, which, like everything else here, no longer notes the passage of time. Choose the standard German offerings and you won't go wrong. Ochsenmaul salad, strips of head cheese with pickled vegetables, and first-rate liver dumpling soup are our favorite openers. Beef rouladen—a thin slab of meat rolled around Sauerkraut, bacon and pickle, covered with a rich, dark gravy—makes a good entrée. Half a roast duck, a frequent special, and the Heidelberger platter, a trio of smoked pork and sausages on a bed of Sauerkraut are also wise choices. But Wiener Schnitzel does not live up to its Austrian progenitor, and the venison is tough and stringy. Eggy spaetzle, on the other hand, makes a satisfying starchy accompaniment. Warm, flaky apple strudel with freshly whipped cream wins out over other desserts. Good German beer and wine help celebrate *gemütlichkeit* in style. The dinner tab for two should be about $60, with wine.

The Helmand
3201 N. Halsted St.
935-2447
AFGHAN
Open Mon.-Thurs. 5 p.m.-
10:30 p.m., Fri.-Sat.
5 p.m.-11:30 p.m.
All major cards.

12/20

Situated in a storefront that once purveyed plants, Chicago's only Afghan restaurant continues the leafy tradition with pots of foliage placed between tables and along its sides; more than a dozen trees at the windows separate diners from the outside world. Walls, covered with brown and silver-gray cloth, are punctuated by brassware, Afghan costumes and framed oil paintings. The food is a highly successful marriage of strong and subtle flavors. Robust chunks of beef lurk among earthy chickpeas, mung beans and black-eyed peas in an otherwise delicate yogurt soup called mashawa. Our favorite appetizers are kaddo borawni, lightly tart pumpkin with garlic-infused yogurt, and bowlawni, a flaky pastry filled with leeks and potato and garnished with mint-flecked yogurt. But we also recommend as an opener the salad of potatoes and chickpeas flavored with cilantro. Only one chicken, three lamb and four beef dishes grace the list of entrées, which is supplemented by occasional specials. We can vouch for the sabzy challow, cubes of beef in puréed spinach, and dwopiaza, tenderloin of lamb sautéed with yellow split peas accompanied by tart, marinated onions. Chicken lovers will do nicely with murgh challow, chicken with yellow split peas on a mound of buttered, baked rice. Traditional cardamom-spiked tea is served here, but regular coffee is also available. Try burfee (sweetened semolina) for dessert. The wine list is small but choice, with several good and inexpensive vintages. Well-spaced tables and competent, slightly laid-back service enhance a pleasant, out-of-the-ordinary dining experience. Dinner for two, with wine, will run around $45.

Honda
540 N. Wells St.
923-1010
JAPANESE
Open Mon.-Thurs.
11:30 a.m.-2 p.m. &
5:30 p.m.-10 p.m., Fri.-
Sat. 5:30 p.m.-11 p.m.
All major cards.

11/20

It's some sort of tribute to Chicago's capacity for sushi, sashimi and assorted yakis that a Japanese firm chose to build a five-story building to house its restaurant at this location, with dining areas on the lower levels, and kitchen and staff upstairs. The gleaming black-pagoda roof with a horizontal thrust produces a dramatic impact among the shabby brick structures of Wells Street. The interior, unfortunately, lacks focus. Dining rooms are bare rather than austere, and filled with distracting sound reflections. Tatami rooms tucked away opposite second- and third-floor corridors are better, but they're reserved for private parties and the intricate ritual of kaiseki dinners (many small courses).

Customers may choose from more than 200 items, which are reasonably priced given the ostentation of tuxedo-clad waiters and Château Latour on the sideboard. Among the more reliable items are sushi and generally excellent sashimi: translucent sea bass, rose-petal pink tuna, white octopus strips with a scallop edge of lavender "skin" and up to a dozen more. Dipped into a puddle of wasabe, explosive green horseradish and soy sauce eaten with petals of fresh ginger, all but the rubbery shrimp have approached perfection. Not so lobster kogane yaki, a three-quarter-pound victim of excessive oven time; tough and dry, it made $18.50 seem like a ripoff. To get away from such familiar dishes as beef sukiyaki, chicken teriyaki and shrimp tempura, all competently prepared, try kushi mirugai, giant clam grilled on a bamboo skewer, or ika masagonye, silver-gray and puckery squid in an orange froth of sweetly pungent crab roe. Kaiso salad consists of four seaweeds—a pastiche of crunchy and noodle-like, hair- thin and leafy—in colors that range from dark coral to celadon green. Saké and Western beer go best with Japanese food, though a variety of fairly expensive wines is available. Dinner with beer will cost a couple about $65.

Hopper's Dining Car

900 N. Michigan Ave.
280-3320
AMERICAN
Open Mon.-Thurs. 11 a.m.-
11 p.m., Fri.-Sat. 11 a.m.-
12:30 a.m., Sun. 9 a.m.-
10:30 p.m.
All major cards.

9/20

The Levy Brothers, experienced restaurateurs with umpteen restaurants under their belt, got sidetracked with this simulated restaurant in a railroad dining car. They got so carried away with the theme that they seem to have forgotten about the food. The fact that this restaurant is located in the ritzy new building that's home to the new Chicago Bloomingdale's helps keep the place busy, and the model train zipping around overhead is great for gawking kids. And though the Levys would like us to believe otherwise, what we've got here is primarily kiddie food made to menu-read like adult food. To wit: homemade Italian sausage with creamy polenta, veal meatloaf with potato pancake, macaroni with four trendy cheeses, chocolate fudge pie, S'mores (graham crackers, milk chocolate and toasted marshmallows). The adult stuff includes things like hamburgers (sometimes they're good; sometimes they're horrid), smoked mozzarella and eggplant (runs hot and cold) and fashionable salads. We wouldn't call this place a dining car named desire. Dinner for two, with drinks, runs from $20 to $30.

> *The prices listed in this guide reflect what restaurants and hotels have informed us they plan to charge at press time. Please don't blame us if they don't coincide exactly with reality.*

House of Hunan

535 N. Michigan Ave.
329-9494
CHINESE
*Open daily 11:30 a.m.-
10:30 p.m.
All major cards.*

One of the largest menus in town—153 appetizers, soups and entrées—offers a comprehensive sampling of geographical styles: Mandarin/Peking, Hunan, Szechwan, Shanghai, Canton, Taiwan and Fukien. It does so in a long, well-lighted, attractively decorated room whose booths and tables are set with white linen. Alongside the room, a dimly lit bar provides a lounge for before-dinner drinks and casual dining. For the most part, dishes here are quite good, albeit refined rather than robust. Peking duck has a faint aromatic smokiness and crisp skin. Tucked inside a chewy pancake with scallions and plum sauce, it creates an unforgettable mélange of textures and flavors. Seafood lovers can do a lot worse than the piquant lobster with ginger sauce kissed by garlic or the whole pike steamed with ginger and ham and dotted with scallions and mushrooms. Among the more unusual appetizers are layers of minced scallops wrapped in seaweed, spinach and egg, fiery beef tripe and mild, crunchy jellyfish. Winter-melon soup comes with still-firm chunks of winter melon in a clear, peppery chicken broth accented by bits of ham. Mock Peking duck, shredded ham and shrimp sandwiched between layers of crisp soybean skin and wrapped in a crêpe, is out of the ordinary, as is beef sautéed with delicate fresh bamboo tips, a seasonal dish from the Fukien province. Tea leaf–smoked pork reminds us of superior Virginia ham, while a vegetable dish of folded leaves of bean curd sautéed with crisp bok choy and pungent mushrooms plays off textures and flavors effectively. Fresh fruit, ice cream or sherbet, and apple or banana fritters make up the dessert list. With wine or beer, a couple will spend about $55 for dinner.

Italian Village

71 E. Monroe St.
332-7005
ITALIAN
*Florentine Room: open
Mon.-Fri. 11:30 a.m.-
2:30 p.m. & 5 p.m.-10 p.m.,
Sat. 5 p.m.-midnight; The
Village: open Mon.-Thurs.
11 a.m.-1 a.m., Fri.-Sat.
11 a.m.-2 a.m., Sun. noon-
midnight; La Cantina: open
Mon.-Fri. 11:30 a.m.-
midnight, Sat. 5 p.m.-
midnight.
All major cards.*

Celebrating more than 60 years in business, the Italian Village consists of three separate restaurants, each with its own kitchen and its own menu. It's not impossible to get lost in this colossus of cuisine, with a dining room on the main floor (the more expensive and more polished Florentine Room), the second floor (The Village, with somewhat lower prices) and the lower level (La Cantina, which throws in some American dishes along with Italian specialties). The food in the Florentine Room is more precise and original than the other two dining venues, since the menu changes with the seasons. Fish and veal dishes are particularly noteworthy, and many of the pastas are original in conception and quite good. But some dishes, such as rabbit in a sweet-and-sour sauce with raisins, are strangely out of place. The tiramisu is decent but not great. And the other desserts, such as caramel custard and banana ice cream with rum, should be banished along with the rabbit. Dinner for two in the Florentine Room, with wine, will run about $80.

Florentine Room:

The Village:

11/20

La Cantina:

10/20

The Village menu has just about every Italian dish you've ever heard about, read about or eaten—close to 200 dishes in all. A replica of an Italian village complete with water mill and twinkling stars above, this room is easy to order in: just close your eyes and stab a finger at the menu. You'll end up with something decent and filling (the 30 pasta dishes alone should keep any pasta lover interested). Veal comes about twelve different ways, but the best of the batch is the veal alla bolognese. Two people can have a swell dinner for less than $50 with wine.

We'd just as soon skip La Cantina, but if there's no room in the other two rooms, the chicken Vesuvio here is good, as is the linguine with squid in tomato sauce. About $50 for two, with wine.

The Italian Village's wine cellar houses close to 1,000 bottles (the wine list has a table of contents), so you'll have little problem finding a fine wine with the right price tag if you have the time to wade through the list.

Jackie's Restaurant
2478 N. Lincoln Ave.
880-0003
FRENCH-ASIAN
Open Tues.-Thurs.
11:30 a.m.-1:30 p.m. &
5:45 p.m.-8:30 p.m., Fri.-
Sat. 11:30 a.m.-1:30 p.m.
& 5:45 p.m.-9:30 p.m.
All major cards.

Small and intimate (about seventeen tables) when measured against the size of restaurants opening these days, Jackie's is a settling and comfortable place. Tablecloths, fresh flowers and varying patterns of Villeroy and Boch china enliven the decor, which otherwise is simply a matter of ceiling fans dropping down from a high, pressed-tin ceiling, touches of oak and brass and a small service bar near the kitchen door. The room is best described as elegantly simple. The cuisine that chef/owner Jackie Shen labors over with love is excitingly original, never banal, conceptually correct and a delicious feast for the palate and eyes. The printed menu has classic dishes, like Dover sole with a scallop mousse, rack of lamb with rosemary sauce and roasted breast of duck with black-peppercorn sauce—any of which would satisfy the most demanding palate. It is the wide range of daily specials, however, that intrigues and tantalizes. Ballotine of rabbit is an inspired, scintillating creation in which the rabbit meat is wrapped with bacon, rolled and stuffed with shiitake mushrooms, sweetbreads, spinach, carrots and Chinese sausage. The phyllo nest is equally exciting: A small basket shaped like a flower is formed from the phyllo dough and filled with tiny, tender bay scallops and thin slices of exotic mushrooms. A coulis of tomatoes enhanced with garlic and basil and topped with a smidgen of beluga caviar rides atop the scallops—a crowning touch of flavor. Chinese bouillabaisse is as tasty as it is original. The same can be said of the fresh tuna, which is marinated in soy and sesame oil prior to sautéing. It is impossible to ignore Jackie's desserts: The most devastating is something called a chocolate bag. The bag, formed out of Callibaut dark chocolate, is filled with cloud-like layers of light, smooth white-chocolate mousse and sliced strawberries. Sitting atop this sweet cloud are fresh raspberries, slices of kiwi and whipped cream—it is at the same time angelic and devilishly good. Dinner for two, with wine, can range anywhere from $60 to $100.

Jerome's
2450 N. Clark St.
327-2207
AMERICAN
Open Mon. 5 p.m.-11 p.m., Tues.-Thurs. 11:30 a.m.-11 p.m., Fri. 11:30 a.m.-midnight, Sat. 8 a.m.-midnight, Sun. 10 a.m.-11 p.m.
Cards: AE, MC, V.

12/20

Jerome's front deck/outdoor café is perfectly positioned to see and be seen, and it's filled with neighborhood types who like to play at European café in the summertime. Inside, there's a bar on one level and, a few steps up, a large, open dining room with cloth-covered tables and peach walls adorned with strange (some say interesting) artwork. There never seems to be enough waiters, so service flags, and it takes a wave or two to get things going. But once the meal happens, it happens. This is good, solid, basic, ungussied-up American fare that has some interesting moments. The Cuban black-bean soup is terrific— dark and murky, loaded with beans and topped with chopped onions—and it goes marvelously well with the glorious homemade bread. Pasta of the day (usually penne) comes with some type of seafood. It may end up being more pasta than seafood, but it's still a dish that eats well. One of the best on the menu is the calves' liver, thinly sliced and sautéed in walnut oil with onions and topped with scallions. Scallops Pernod is a rather nice dish, too. An ample portion of bay scallops—tender morsels all—is wonderfully seasoned with shallots, Pernod and cream; fresh spinach, which weaves through the scallops like seaweed, is an inspired touch. Homemade brownies are gratis at meal's end, but you shouldn't forego trying the magnificent apple Streusel pie (à la mode), the triple-layer carrot cake or the chocolate pecan pie—they're all outstanding. Dinner costs about $25 per person with wine.

Jimmy's Place
3420 N. Elston Ave.
539-2999
FRENCH
Open Mon.-Fri. 11:30 a.m.-2 p.m. & 5 p.m.-9:30 p.m., Sat. 5 p.m.-9:30 p.m.
Cards: CB, DC, MC, V.

Owner Jimmy Rohr is an opera buff: The walls are lined with prints, posters and pictures of opera stars; and recordings of arias, recitatives, choruses and duets swell the rooms with drama. It seems quite appropriate, when you consider that classic dining is, in fact, a series of interesting events. Jimmy's Place is a little larger after the addition, a few years ago, of a pleasant atrium-greenhouse room to the left of the center kitchen. Like slipping into a comfortable old shoe, though, regular patrons prefer the smaller dining room where, ten years ago, in an unlikely part of the city, Jimmy Rohr began to orchestrate a cuisine that had style. Though nourished by its classic French roots, the cooking at Jimmy's pushes the edges of the envelope. Innovation, more than a dash of panache, clever taste combinations and an understanding of good food come together in grand concert. The tickets don't come cheap, but it's an amazing performance that is well worth the price. And to make the matter of dining out even more interesting, the menu changes monthly, so we can give you only a sampling of a meal that was, but was not easily forgotten. The appetizer, tender grilled quail on an inlay of silky duck mousse with a fragrant basil jus, set the perfect tone. Salad is included with the main course, but for a small sum, Jimmy's special salad—spinach, radicchio and endive painted lightly with a winsome anchovy sauce and garnished with croutons, red onions and capers—is something special. Grilled saddle of lamb reposes in splendor on a bed of roasted peppers, an accompaniment of sautéed goat cheese nudging the flavor along nicely. Divine ice cream—almond praline, rich and ravishing—is followed by an exactingly made, foamy-rich espresso. This is a finely tuned restaurant that makes dining a pleasure from start to finish. Dinner for two, with wine, runs about $110.

Jorge's Restaurant y Cantina
1161 N. Dearborn St.
787-5050
MEXICAN
Open Mon.-Thurs. 11 a.m.-
11 p.m., Fri.-Sat. 11 a.m.-
midnight, Sun. 11 a.m.-
10 p.m.
Cards: AE, MC, V.

10/20

Housed in a four-story brownstone on the Near North Side, Jorge's moved into space once occupied by a country French restaurant. But it took only minor cosmetic changes to make it look Mexican. Walls are stucco, Mexican artifacts hang here and there, wood abounds. The dining room on the upper level has a fireplace, and the cantina on the lower level has that casual cantina feeling. The food here is no better than that served at a host of other Mexican restaurants in the city, and no different either. All the Mexican basics, from guacamole and sopes to queso fundido, chile rellenos, enchiladas and so on, make up the predictable menu. One outstanding dish worth mentioning is the camarones con cilantro, in which garlic, lemon and fresh cilantro suffuse the shrimp and elevate it to a taste level that surpasses the other dishes on the menu. Desserts are pedestrian and not worth the calories or the price. About $45 for two, with Mexican beer.

J. P.'s Eating Place
(Claridge Hotel),
1244 N. Dearborn St.
642-2088
SEAFOOD
Open Mon.-Thurs.
6:30 a.m.-10:30 a.m.,
11:30 a.m.-2:30 p.m. &
5 p.m.-10:30 p.m., Fri.-Sat.
6:30 a.m.-10:30 a.m.,
11:30 a.m.- 2:30 p.m. &
5 p.m.-midnight, Sun.
6:30 a.m.-10:30 a.m.,
11 a.m.- 2:30 p.m. &
5 p.m.- 10 p.m.
All major cards.

Shrimp étouffée, bouillabaisse, tuna teriyaki... this is Mexican? No, this is J. P.'s Eating Place, a seafood establishment that has been persistently misclassified as Mexican, partly because a handful of Mexican dishes graces the menu, and partly because owner Jorge Perez hails from south of the border. The menus at both locations are nearly identical, as is the quality—top notch. An amazing 20 to 25 *fresh* seafood selections are offered every day, and the sampling possibilities are almost endless. Have anything as tapas, and pay by weight (75 cents to $1 per ounce for most fish varieties) or by the piece (75 to 85 cents per oyster or clam, $2.95 per soft-shell crab). Or choose one of five threesomes as an entrée, or create your own twosome, threesome or whatever you want. Blackened mako shark is outstanding, as are tuna, salmon and scampi. A pretty good North American version of bouillabaisse based on a saffron-rich stock

1800 N. Halsted St.
664-1801
Open Mon.-Thurs.
11:30 a.m.-2:30 p.m. &
4 p.m.-10:30 p.m., Fri.-Sat.
11:30 a.m.-2:30 p.m. &
4 p.m.-midnight, Sun.
4 p.m.-10 p.m.
All major cards.

Jun Japanese Restaurant
434 W. Diversey Pkwy.
477-5511
JAPANESE
Open Tues.-Thurs.
11:45 a.m.-2:50 p.m. &
5:30 p.m.-10:30 p.m., Fri.-
Sat. 11:45 a.m.-2:50 p.m.
& 5:30 p.m.-11 p.m., Sun.
3:30 p.m.-10 p.m.
All major cards.

made from John Dory and red snapper sparkles with shrimp, crab legs, mussels, tuna and swordfish; a good, garlicky rouille sauce adds a fine Mediterranean touch of authenticity. The cioppino has its devotées, but we find it more an unrelieved tomato sauce than shellfish stew. Paella, on the other hand, is the best we've had outside Valencia, the rice firm, barely moist, aromatic with saffron and loaded with chicken, sausage, shrimp, clams and mussels.

And carnivores need not go hungry, with just under a dozen items to choose from; especially good is the tender veal chop milanese, which is lightly breaded, sautéed to pink at the center and served with a tangy lemon sauce. Bread pudding and flan make for happy endings. The two locations present sharp contrasts in decor: At the Claridge you'll dine in a comfortable hotel or club dining room; on Halsted Street you'll be part of a razzle-dazzle happening, where green plants, biomorphic sculptures and wall hangings bounce the youngish crowd's chatter back and forth. A couple will spend about $78 for dinner with wine at either location.

Once, at 5 a.m. in a fish market on Maui, we sampled some remarkable tuna—the fatty belly strips, the tail, the back—with the chef at the Kapalua Bay Hotel. He had invited us along while he picked the day's fish. Not every piece of sushi and sashimi at Jun's reaches the perfection we discovered that morning, but some do, and many approach it. The sushi bar to the right of the entrance has a limited but choice selection: velvety hamachi (yellowtail), slate-smooth hirame (fluke), chewy, briny mirugai (giant clam), slippery masses of pungent, acrid uni (sea urchin) wrapped in crackly nori (seaweed), pungently salty saba (mackerel) and several others, all commendably fresh. Also served are various makis (rolls), bits of tuna, cucumber and/or avocado surrounded by rice and wrapped in nori. At lunch the sushi/tempura combination is a terrific bargain; for $6.95, you get four superb kinds of sushi and, on a separate wooden tray, two delicately crisp, utterly greaseless tempura shrimp on a heap of tempura-fried vegetables. In the evening, tempura may be ordered as an appetizer, a dinner or as part of Jun's Special, a tour de force that also includes sushi, sashimi, fish teriyaki and half a broiled baby lobster. Beef karashi-ae with mustard sauce is good but takes a back seat to the seafood and such specialties as boiled spinach with sesame-soy sauce and fried bean curd. Dinners include miso soup, an assortment of pickled vegetables and relishes, an eminently forgettable western salad, rice, tea and dessert—perhaps green-tea ice cream, an uneasy, mildly bitter fusion of east and west. The decor is appropriately simple and pleasant, and the service is friendly and helpful, despite a mild language barrier. Dinner for two, with saké or beer, can range anywhere from $30 to $55, depending on the extent of your feast.

Kampai Chicago

414 N. Orleans St.
787-4430
JAPANESE
Open Mon.-Fri. 11:30 a.m.-2:30 p.m. & 5 p.m.-10 p.m., Sat. 5 p.m.-10 p.m.
All major cards.

11/20

When this restaurant realizes that at lunchtime people don't have all day to eat, it might do more lunch business. But, fortunately, sushi eaters don't have a wait (or waiter) problem, since they can sit at the only floating sushi bar in the Midwest. The sushi chefs lay their miniworks of food art on plates, which in turn are placed on small, flat, wooden boats. Joined bow to stern, the boats float in a trough past the diners. See something you like? Lift the plate off the boat and have at it. Tekka and kappa maki and the California roll have always been nicely handled. An extensive selection of nigiri-sushi (those classic morsels of raw fish and vinegared rice) ranges from sweet shrimp to sea urchin, with many denizens of the deep in between. Beef or shrimp kushikatsu (a noodle soup) is a good dinner opener, as is the tempura appetizer. Teriyaki, which comes in chicken, beef and salmon versions, has always hit the mark. Udon (noodles in a pot) is a hit-or-miss affair; we've had good and bad. More consistent is the outstanding grilled king mackerel. Don't waste your money on the desserts. About $17 per person, with beer.

Lawry's The Prime Rib

100 E. Ontario St.
787-5000
AMERICAN
Open Mon.-Thurs.-11:30 a.m.-2 p.m. & 5 p.m.-11 p.m., Fri. 11:30 a.m.-2 p.m. & 5 p.m.-midnight, Sat. 5 p.m.-midnight, Sun. 3 p.m.-10 p.m.
All major cards.

An Edwardian decor, polished-wood floors, crisp napery, gracious paintings and fresh flowers may seem unlikely trappings for a place whose raison d'être is prime rib, but who's beefing? For dinner that's all there is—one entrée: prime rib. (Lunch offers more choices.) Four cuts of beef are listed on the menu: English, extremely thin slices; the Lawry cut, medium thickness; the Chicago cut, an extra-thick portion that includes the rib bone; and the California cut, perfect for lighter appetites. We've tried them all, and each in its own way is a high-quality, flavorful, exceptionally tender cut of beef. The beef is sliced tableside at one of Lawry's specially made "rolling kitchens," so you see what the slicing chef has in store for you. Included with the entrée are a handsome mound of creamy (and real) mashed potatoes, a light, puffy Yorkshire pudding, whipped-cream horseradish for slathering across the beef, and Lawry's famous spinning salad bowl (a mixed green salad with a dash of showmanship). A la carte vegetables, like the baked potato and creamed spinach, are wonderful. The best dessert in the house is the trifle, a spongy, gooey, rich mix of sponge cake, custard and fresh fruit. About $30 per person, with wine.

Maple Tree Inn

10730 S. Western Ave.
239-3688
CAJUN/CREOLE
Open Tues.-Thurs. 5 p.m.-
9:30 p.m., Fri.-Sat. 5 p.m.-
10:30 p.m.
Cards: MC, V.

This place reeks of the flavor of New Orleans. As you walk past the iron gate and enter the private walkway leading to the courtyard in the rear of the brick two-flat that houses the restaurant, you might expect to hear the rambunctious syncopation of hot jazz. The illusion continues as you pass through a massive red door, from which wood stairs lead you into a small bar area. At that point your nose starts to pick up an appetizing mélange: spice boil, hickory, simmering gumbo. A series of dining rooms—some large, some small—has walls that are covered with old-newspaper-type wallpaper, vintage song sheets and framed prints of bottles of Tabasco sauce and other Bayou paraphernalia. The setting is, well, homey. Alligator soup is the real thing—not mock, mind you—the chunks of white alligator meat floating in a clear and satisfying vegetable-studded broth. Andouille sausage is densely textured, lean and spicy-hot. Fried oysters are tender beauties wrapped in a light batter. Gumbo is an exciting mix of flavors—shrimp, sausage, okra, sweet blue crab, rice—in a thick, rich stock that is not too burning-hot. "Boats" of garlic-accented bread are filled with a whole raft of interesting choices: frogs' legs, catfish nuggets, oysters, shrimp. Crawfish étouffée is one of the best renditions around these parts. Save room for the fine pecan pie or the Mississippi mud cake, a high-rising hunk of rich, dark chocolate that's creamy and gooey-good. In summer, the outdoor courtyard eating area is lively and lots of fun. About $25 per person with wine, but a Dixie Beer is the more appropriate choice.

Mareva's

1250 N. Milwaukee Ave.
227-4000
POLISH/CONTINENTAL
Open Mon.-Fri. 11 a.m.-
11 p.m., Sat.-Sun. 4 p.m.-
11 p.m.
All major cards.

12/20

Mareva's is without a doubt one of the most luxe Polish restaurants in the city. The dining room is plush, with dark-green chairs and comfortable booths covered with the same soft fabric. Light-wood wainscoting gives way to moiré wallpaper. Huge brass chandeliers march the length of the room, their light reflecting in the mirrors and off the etched-glass dividers. Crisp, spotless linens and fresh flowers grace the tables. Most evenings there is pleasant dining-type music coming from the baby grand piano in the center of the room. It's all rather swell, right down to the tuxedoed waiters. What could be more dyed-in-the-dough Polish than pirogi? And Mareva's pirogi are precious (and creative) puffs of pleasure. They come stuffed with a duxelle of wild mushrooms or a mousse of chicken or a forcemeat of veal, to mention just a few. Herring in sour cream is exceptionally good. Fish specials are handled well, but have a tendency to be over-nouvelled with, for example, a raspberry sauce and too much fresh dill. Veal Mareva, which is sautéed and laced with a butter and sherry sauce, is excellent. Homemade cheesecake is dense, creamy and delicious. Lunch specials are quite creative; dinner will run about $30 per person, with wine.

Mélange

(Plaza del Lago),
1515 N. Sheridan Rd.,
Wilmette
256-1700
SOUTHWESTERN/CALIFORNIA
Open Sun. 5 p.m.-9 p.m.,
Tues.-Thurs. 11:30 a.m.-
2:45 p.m. & 5 p.m.-
10 p.m., Fri.-Sat.
11:30 a.m.-2:45 p.m. &
5 p.m.- 11 p.m.
All major cards.

Salmon and turquoise walls and hanging plants in an asymmetrical room bring a touch of the West and Southwest to the Plaza del Lago shopping center. The decor complements the food, which changes with the season, though its New Mexico/California roots remain in evidence. David Jarvis is the kitchen genius, and his tortilla soup, redolent of chile and toasted corn, has few peers. Pastas are made fresh daily. The saffron fettuccine with duck confit was our favorite until we tried the tomato ravioli stuffed with salmon mousse. The one time we had calves' liver with pancetta it was pink in the middle, as requested, but marred by a faint touch of bitterness—a fault, we're reliably informed, that seldom occurs. Duck, on the other hand—the breast roasted medium rare, the leg a succulent confit, glazed with honey and garlic—could not have been improved. Desserts run to bread pudding and homemade ice creams and sorbets. Among he latter we wholeheartedly recommend the tamarind, which is mildly tart and astringent, and the white chocolate, which is thick, creamy and rich. Reasonably priced wines, mostly from California, may be ordered by the glass or bottle. A couple can expect to spend about $80 for a meal that includes a bottle of wine.

La Même Chose

5819 W. Dempster St.
965-1645
CALIFORNIA/FRENCH
Open Tues.-Sun. 5 p.m.-
10 p.m.
Cards: AE, MC, V.

What this place is "the same thing as" has never been clear to us, but owner/manager/chef Kim creates such bargain-basement miracles that we consistently forget to ask him. The point, after all, is what the prix-fixe menu affords a budget-beleaguered diner. The answer depends on when you visit and how much you order: orders placed before 6 p.m. command a fifteen-percent discount, so the five-course meal, normally a mere $18.95, drops to an astounding $16.10. Menus change monthly; the five nightly appetizers take such refreshing forms as salmon cake with rémoulade sauce, smoked wild duck with tomato pasta, and shrimp, avocado and papaya bathed in a light brandy sauce. The single salad tends to be greens under a nut-oil vinaigrette, at times with a fruity nouvelle addition sitting awkwardly to one side, and the soup may range from mussel and saffron to an elegant cream of three wild mushrooms. For entrées, we're suckers for the fish combinations, like the poached salmon and halibut with a saffron ginger sauce. But we've felt compelled to have quail on more than one occasion, especially the honey-glazed brace stuffed with veal sausage. As for the decor, the fancified-storefront exterior hasn't much to do with the interior's elegant booths and free-standing tables, with their cool linen and silver and crystal place settings; it all feels like a 1950s New York dining room. After passing through the glassed-in foyer, we are always struck by the *New Yorker*esque pastel washes.

Desserts tend toward restrained extravagance: brandied

fruit tart, flourless chocolate cake in a pool of raspberry purée, almond cup filled with chocolate mousse haunted by Grand Marnier. The wine list is skimpy but reasonable, service hesitant but well intentioned. Diners who forgive an occasional glitch tend to become regulars. Dinner with wine runs $65 per couple.

Memere's

22 Chicago Ave.,
Oak Park
524-2150
CAJUN/CREOLE
Open Mon.-Thurs. noon-
2 p.m. & 5 p.m.-9 p.m.,
Fri.-Sat. 5 p.m.-9:30 p.m.,
Sun. 5 p.m.-9 p.m.
Cards: AE, MC, V.

12/20

This small storefront restaurant is a spirited place with about thirteen tables and enough down-home atmosphere to fill a shrimp boat. Old biscuit tins and baking molds hang from the wall; an old, enameled stove lurks in one corner and a galvanized washtub in another. All that hard stuff is softened by tablecloths and the pleasant smiles of the waiters—some are family—as well as the overall "We're glad you're here" attitude that pervades the place. The menu is simple: about eight or nine entrées, which come with soup or salad and a choice of jambalaya, red beans and rice, black-eyed peas or french fries on the side. Catfish, coated with cornmeal and deep-fried, has just the right, light crunch; underneath that golden exterior the fish holds firm and is moist and flavorful. Crawfish étouffée, served in a large, platter-like bowl, is loaded with crawfish tails, lots of flavor and enough rice to start a paddy. Louisiana-style roast chicken is anointed gently with Cajun spices—maybe too gently, since the full flavor fails to come through. Jambalaya is not the best around, but the blackened redfish is undeniably one of the best dishes in the house. Not much ado about desserts, except for the Louisiana-style fried bananas, which after a serving will make you wish you could pole a boat home to work it off. About $15 a person, with a wine that was bottled last year in California.

Memories of China

1050 N. State St.
642-1800
CHINESE
Open Mon.-Fri. 11:30 a.m.-
2:30 p.m. & 5 p.m.-
10 p.m., Sat. 5 p.m.-
10 p.m., Sun. 5 p.m.-
10 p.m.
All major cards.

12/20

Formerly Hunan Palace, this posh Newberry Plaza establishment sports a new menu along with its new name and management. The decor remains largely the same: opulent. Ceiling-high glass panels look out onto an atrium court. Red-lacquer walls are punctuated by dark-wood trim, and here a painting, there a shelf bearing Chinese porcelain, with alcoves scattered throughout. A multicolor expanse of thick carpet adds to the general sense of plush and lush. The twelve-page menu with its lovingly detailed descriptions may make you wish you had stopped off first for a quickie speed-reading course. The staff, however, is generous with suggestions and explanations, which helps keep the sheer number of choices from becoming overwhelming.

Savory-sweet potstickers make a good beginning, as do crispy shrimp, lightly crunchy on the outside and faintly moist at the center. Zesty escargots on tiny skewers tease the taste buds, and the Guangshow pickled vegetables made us instant addicts. Steamed soup in bamboo cup, a meaty ginger broth surrounding delicate minced pork, is outstanding. Also deserving of mention is stir-fried pike, the mildly earthy fish glistening with sauce and lavishly garnished with straw mushrooms, bamboo shoots and water chestnuts. Beggars' chicken, on the other hand, is baked in lotus leaves and made with rock Cornish hen but is stuffed with minced chicken instead of the traditional pork or pork and ham; it suffers from the substitutions. Minced chicken in lettuce leaves, though good, lacks the succulence of its famous progenitor, which is made with squab. And the meat in Peking lamb is sadly beyond redemption in a much-too-thick and overdone batter. Braised bear's paw and other special dishes not on the menu are sometimes available. Maître d' Alfred, whose enthusiasm is infectious, will happily let you know what departures from the ordinary the chef can provide on any particular day or evening. Around $55 for dinner for two, with beer.

Middle East Restaurant and Cocktails

2701 W. Lawrence Ave.
878-6533
LEBANESE
*Open daily 11 a.m.-2 a.m.
No cards.*

12/20

When he's there, former army cook Simon Kambar presides over this chaotic neighborhood hangout. When he's away, whoever's on hand fills in, with seeming reluctance, making up plates of food to be eaten at Formica tables and preparing orders to go. This takes time, so we wait while the regulars send up a pall of smoke over endless cups of coffee, or we watch them play electronic games with an intensity surprising in 40- to 50-year-old men. On Friday and Saturday nights, lights flood a minuscule podium, and a local group stomps up a storm of Middle Eastern and American rock. The food makes it all worthwhile. Try the chicken kallaie, white meat pan-fried with onions and green pepper, a dash of lemon juice and an authoritative dash of cayenne. Tender cubes of lamb shish kebab are as good as kafta kebab, whose minced beef arrives heady with onions and parsley. The standouts, however, are hummus—a pool of chickpeas, tahini (ground sesame seeds) and olive oil ringed by cayenne pepper—and baba ghanouj, a smoky, creamy amalgamation of baked eggplant, tahini and olive oil. Meat items may be ordered in sandwiches or as plates garnished with onion rings, tomatoes, black olives and pickled peppers, and accompanied by rice. Nothing costs more than $6.75, and that brings a combination plate preceded by a cup of soup. The bar is surprisingly extensive, and specials often supplement the relatively brief menu. Baklava, its phyllo pastry crisp and nut-strewn, demands the excellent Lebanese coffee. Dinner for two, with beer or wine, should cost no more than $30.

Le Mikado

21 W. Goethe St.
280-8611
FRENCH-JAPANESE
*Open nightly 5 p.m.-
11 p.m.*
All major cards.

Enzio's rode the crest of nuova cucina on this corner before spinach-stuffed ravioli and wild boar heaped on arugula trotted off to the kingdom of cliché. After Enzio's wipeout, Bolton's lent a different sort of panache to Goethe and Dearborn, whose sedate fantasy played like a marimba across a burgeoning yuppie population and whose food was a restrained Republican brand of California nouvelle. But Bolton's also failed. A seven-month hiatus ensued, and one of the Gold Coast's hottest properties languished on the vine. Then Jacques Barbier, once the resident genius at Winnetka's La Bohème, decided to provide chef Daniel Kelch with a vehicle for his creative energies. The result is Le Mikado, which offers an often exquisite, only occasionally disappointing fusion of Japanese and French ingredients and culinary techniques.

We're particularly partial to the gyoza, Japanese wheat dumplings filled with a robust pheasant sausage straight out of Escoffier; the three overlapping crescents lie half hidden among a phalanx of asparagus spears and a tangle of sliced shiitake. A frequent special draws upon the West: mildly briny baby shrimp in a light cream sauce and marinated green-lip mussels supporting a glittering sprinkle of diced onion and red pepper. From the East, it takes Manila clams in ginger-touched miso. East and West contribute to a pungent Japanese oyster in mica-fine phyllo pastry. Gently pan-fried skate, resuscitated by lime and tangerine and lulled by pistachio butter, should forever banish from menus the same fish done beurre noir. It is perfect. Composed salads don't measure up to the appetizers and entrées, and one entrée, lamb chops subdued rather than finished by a piquant sauce, left much to be desired. Such desserts as plums in an almond phyllo dough marry East and West successfully; most other desserts favor the West, more or less successfully. Dove-gray walls, commodious booths, Japanese shoji rice-paper panels and floral arrangements create a charmingly civilized setting in which to sample some of Chicago's most inventive cooking. The wine list includes a few lovely, offbeat selections, such as the excellent, grassy-floral white Châteauneuf du Pape. Dinner for two, with a modest wine, carries a $75-to-$80 price tag.

Morton's

1050 N. State St.
266-4820
STEAKHOUSE
*Open Mon.-Sat. 5:30 p.m.-
10:30 p.m.*
All major cards.

Like any real city, Chicago is a bundle of contradictions. Its lakeside skyline marries technology to natural beauty. Its populace ranges from Polish to Vietnamese and visits Wrigley Field and Lyric Opera just about equally. It's a metropolis whose Bulls and Bears make fortunes on the playing field and in the stock market, and it's a haven for gourmets and a mecca for gourmands. But above all, it's the place for steak. Neither the stockyards' demise nor the emergence of cholesterol counting as a national pastime has made much headway among dedicated carnivores. They subscribe to the doctrine that man does not live by bread alone and think carbo-loading is for the birds.

Morton's occupies a special niche in their hearts—and ours too. The low-ceilinged, spacious, downstairs dining room is a shrine to prime, dry-aged beef that's never seen the inside of a Cryovac bag. One wall sports a bas-relief copper cow (a sort of dairy frieze), the others are emblazoned with studio photographs—baseball players, comics, politicos, pop stars. A chalkboard invisible to most diners lists chops, steaks, chicken, lobster and fish, and the waitperson presents examples on a rolling cart with an accompanying bit of patter, not necessarily including prices. Pound-and-a-half porterhouses, crusty-tender and tangy, and decadently tender filet mignons outdo even the magnificent strip steaks and Maine lobsters, split and broiled briefly to succulent splendor. Hash browns, darkly crisp and grease-less, are de rigueur despite their surcharge. Share side dishes of sautéed mushrooms and asparagus, and try ripe beefsteak tomato slices as a refreshing alternative to a tossed salad. For dessert, the lemon soufflé, zesty with fresh fruit, steals top honors from the excellent cheesecake. Wines are limited and expensive, service tends to be rushed, and background noise can mount unpleasantly as people unconsciously raise their voices in an effort to be heard over similarly raised voices. Figure on $110 per couple for dinner with wine.

Moti Mahal
2525 W. Devon Ave.
262-2080
INDIAN
Open Mon.-Sat. noon-3:30 p.m., Mon.-Thurs. 5:30 p.m.-10 p.m., Fri.-Sun. 5:30 p.m.-11 p.m. All major cards.

"How I should like to visit India," exclaims Becky Sharp, Thackeray's disingenuous heroine, who, being misled by the cool sound of the word "chili," comes close to choking on an incandescent chutney. More worldly wise, or at least more chili wise, we enjoy stoking the fire in our chicken jalfrazie by adding hot-hot green chutney to its capsicum-laden tomato sauce. Chana masala, chickpeas bobbing about in a dark curry, gets the sweet-and-sour tamarind pickle chutney, and smoky-hot deep-fat fried banana peppers (mirchi pakoras) receive a dollop of the green stuff and a chastening touch of blessedly mild mango chutney. Tangy rice- and lentil-flour crêpes stuffed with spiced onions and potatoes blossom under dabs of grated coconut sauce. Meats and fish cooked in the tandoor (clay) oven arrive a nicely burnished flame red, and the kitchen puts forth an excellent navratan curry, the vegetables of the day in a light-brown cream-based sauce. Rice dishes—meat-dotted biryanis, Kashmiri pullau yucked up with canned fruit—aren't nearly as worthwhile as the breads: whole-wheat pooris puffed into steamy balloons, flat chapatis, buttery-rich onion naan. Desserts run the gamut from sweet to saccharine, a sign of authenticity. Since nearly half the dishes exclude meat, vegetarians need not go hungry in the midst of committed carnivores. Clean woodwork, café curtains, cloth napkins and window-box planters, taken for granted in a modest bistro or trattoria, are a welcome surprise here, given the grim and greasy interiors usually found at the competition. The bottom line for two happily satiated gourmands shouldn't exceed $42.

Moulibet

3521 N. Clark St.
929-9383
ETHIOPIAN
*Open Sun. & Tues.-Thurs.
5 p.m.-10 p.m., Fri. 5 p.m.-
11 p.m., Sat. 5 p.m.-
midnight.
Cards: AE, MC, V.*

10/20

For most of us, Ethiopian food is not only an acquired taste but one whose acquisition has been, until recently, dependent on guesswork. For too long the only Ethiopian restaurant in town presented diners with a debased version of the tradition, out of indifference, ineptitude, or both. Over the past two years, however, a handful of fair-to-good storefront restaurants has made the cuisine accessible. Though the finest of the lot, the much-lamented Addis, has not survived, several passable successors continue to dish up wats and alichas to admiring patrons. Moulibet is one of the best. Its wats (stews in which garlic and red pepper play prominent roles) are distinctly different from its alichas, which are sweeter dishes based on herbs and aromatic, rather than peppery, spices. The injera one tears off in patches to scoop up meats and vegetables contains teff, an iron-rich grain available only from a farm in Idaho. The result is a tangy, not sour, flatbread that is porous enough to soak up juices yet tough enough to stand up to them. (The wheat-and-millet pretender often served elsewhere adds insult to injera and should be made a federal offense.) Moulibet's weekend special, trout braised in a pungent wat, deserves mention, as do yedoro siga tibs (chicken, green peppers and onions) and an intense chickpea preparation called metin shurp wat. Kitfo, Ethiopian steak tartare laced with cayenne, makes a vivid shared appetizer; ketenya, an appetizer of cheese and mustard greens baked in injera, vaguely re-sembles a spanakopita in phyllo dough.

Since the food is prepared to order, meals are leisurely in this typical Chicago storefront restaurant. Travel posters, Ethiopian prints, artifacts and utensils share wall space; the only other outstanding feature in the rather dark interior is a giant mural of the Queen of Sheba returning home from a visit to King Solomon. When it's available, the tedj, an herb-spiked honey wine, makes an unusual accompaniment to the food. Several desserts are available to placate the American palate. A satisfying and novel meal with beer or wine should cost a couple no more than $35.

*Some establishments change their closing times
without warning. It is always wise to call ahead.*

N.E.W. Cuisine
360 W. Erie St.
642-8885
CALIFORNIA/VEGETARIAN
*Open Tues.-Sat. 5 p.m.-
10 p.m.
Cards: AE.*

9/20

A quiet haven for diet-conscious diners amid River North's boom and bustle seems unlikely, yet Anne Finance has installed one in a walk-up around the corner from Scoozi! and not far from the frenzy of Ed Debevic's. Between the counter (which displays the pastries of the day) and the smallish room (with its exposed beams and pipes and white-paper-covered tables), N.E.W. has a pleasant, tea-room ambience. Without prodding from environmentalists, she also has forbidden smoking. Diners intent on meat-and-potatoes fare had best trundle on over to The Green Door or Harry Caray's; N.E.W.'s entrées are limited to vegetarian dishes and grilled, baked or poached fish. Shellfish, because of their high cholesterol content, fall under the same ban as meat and poultry, but buttery, gooey cakes and wine have strangely yet happily been spared. The result is a mixed bag: strong on good intentions, haphazard in practice. Whole-grain millet bread, earthy and mouth-fillingly good, is baked on the premises. Soups—cabbage, for example, or broccoli, cabbage and onion with diced steamed potatoes—tend to be creamed or puréed, an attempt to restore the flavor a meat stock would normally supply. Nuts appear frequently: cashews coating a cheese-and-pepper terrine that's lapped by red-pepper sauce, or a chestnut dotting the whipped cream center of a rolled banana-nut cake. Excellent ginger-sautéed salmon, sashimi-rare at the core, would be dazzling if something more than pedestrian spinach fettuccine kept it company. A leek-and-chèvre tart alternates with leek and Gruyère. Leeks also show up as an appetizer, a mixture of the tough, dark green and the more tender white. Wines are reasonable, and the decaffeinated coffee beats all but the finest regular brews. For dinner, two people will pay about $60.

Nick's Fishmarket
(1 First National Plaza),
Monroe St. & Dearborn St.
621-0200
SEAFOOD
*Open Mon.-Thurs.
11:30 a.m.-3 p.m. &
5:30 p.m.-11 p.m., Fri.
11:30 a.m.-3 p.m. &
5:30 p.m.-11:30 p.m., Sat.
5:30 p.m.-11:30 p.m.
All major cards.*

Nick's Fishmarket is comfortable. Generously portioned banquettes (some as big as a small bus) run along the walls and down the center of the large main dining room to the left of the captain's stand. The layout gives the diners a feeling of intimacy—each banquette feels like a private little island. Romantic enhancements are heightened (or dimmed) by the rheostat that controls the lighting in each banquette. (Some of the waiters have an Edison complex, dimming or brightening the lights at whim.) It's all rather grand, as in big-time swell, but without any overt stabs at pomposity. And they do know how to handle fish. Oysters and clams are pristine, sweet and delicious. Fried calamari are golden jewels of tenderness and good taste. A platter of cold appetizers, sized according to the size of the party, includes oysters, clams, crab claws and shrimp. All are deliciously fresh, but the presentation is a stunner. Swordfish Stavros is a marvelous dish—grilled to the pink of perfection and enhanced with fresh spinach and feta cheese, the swordfish parrying with the taste buds in the best sort of way. Lobster tail is succulent, sweet and richly satisfying—exactly what lobster should be. If you want more than the tail, try either the two-pound-plus Maine lobster or the lobster thermidor. Calamari steak Ricci is handled with squid gloves: The body of the squid, sautéed in a lemon-butter sauce, evokes the pleasantly mild taste of abalone. Hot-fudge chocolate cake is the best dessert in the house, followed by the cheesecake. The wine list, of course, is composed primarily of whites, with emphasis on California Chardonnays, white burgundies and champagnes. Dinner from $40 to $60 per person, with wine.

The 95th

(John Hancock Center),
875 N. Michigan Ave.
787-9596
AMERICAN
Open Mon.-Thurs.
11:30 a.m.-2 p.m. &
5:30 p.m.-10 p.m., Fri.
11:30 a.m.-2 p.m. &
5:30 p.m.-11 p.m., Sat.
6 p.m.-11 p.m., Sun.
10:30 a.m.-2 p.m. &
5:30 p.m.-10:30 p.m.
All major cards.

If cloud-high dining does not a restaurant make, it doesn't hurt either. Towering 95 stories above the Gold Coast's hurly-burly can provide a stunning backdrop for cocktails and food. When the resident Aeolus ("the Hawk") whistles fog and smog off into the boonies, Lake Michigan's horizon-stretching basin of blue, along with downtown's daytime forest of steel and glass or nighttime net of unwavering lights, catch the breath. Inside, crystal chandeliers kick the light from prism to prism, ocher and sheer-white draperies contrast dramatically, and mirrored columns and dark, paneled wood define the edges of an immense room. Those steel straps cradling the building like a Brobdingnagian Cross-Your-Heart bra cut into the view in places, but the effect is not wholly negative. There's an exciting sense of mass and power in the steel angling upward just beyond the window. The menu varies from season to season. American food, from Santa Fe's adobados to Minnesota's wild rice–pine nut soup and Washington's Dungeness crab to East Coast bluefish, reigns supreme, complemented by crusty sourdough bread and buttermilk-tangy salt-free butter. Wheat sprouts and Laura Chenel's chèvre have given a pungent, nutty cast to paper-thin marinated sirloin. An intense curry-and-lemon-grass-spiked broth has held three crab ravioli, the pasta meltingly sweet, the crab briny and laced with pepper. The simple salads are best before such rich food as rabbit on a potato-turnip pancake and grilled bluefish with artichokes. Desserts may be overly sweet (white-chocolate mousse) or excessively fussy. Clearly the kitchen is trying to make a statement about and through American food, and, just as clearly, the effort too often shows. Ask for the wine list and you'll receive a hefty book in which greater and lesser mingle comfortably. Eyrie Vineyards 1985 Pinot Gris, a wonderful Oregon white that tastes of melon and caramel and leaves an aftertaste of honey and lemon, costs all of $16. A couple should be prepared to spend about $120 for dinner with wine.

Orly's

600 S. Dearborn St.
939-6600
AMERICAN/INTERNATIONAL
*Open Mon. 11 a.m.-3 p.m.
& 5 p.m.-10:30 p.m., Tues.-
Thurs. 11 a.m.-3 p.m. &
5 p.m.-11 p.m., Fri. 11
a.m.-3 p.m. & 5 p.m.-
11:30 p.m., Sat. 8:30 a.m.-
11:30 p.m., Sun. 10:30
a.m.-2:30 p.m. & 4 p.m.-
9 p.m.
Cards: AE, MC, V.*

11/20

The abbreviated entrance hall fills up fast most nights; by 6 p.m. a crowd of parched, Italian-suited office workers from the surrounding concrete canyons lines the bar. Where once a massive aquarium served as a centerpiece, four plaster Indians now oversee patrons scarfing down free Buffalo chicken wings and onion rings from 5 p.m. to 7 p.m. The main dining area, a railroad flat lined with booths, expands near its terminus into a raised alcove. Warm woods and stained glass combine with a friendly staff and lively clientele to produce a convivial atmosphere for putting away generous portions of standardized food. Appetizers are divided into American and international, but whether one chooses Cajun shrimp or Peruvian ceviche, vegetable tempura or beer-batter onion rings, the result suggests formula more than individuality. Still, Portuguese sausage soup, chicken Veracruz and firm, coconut-studded Tahitian shrimp are satisfying forays into exotica. And the steaks, ribs and omelets provide plenty of good down-home eating. Desserts go from sweet to extremely sweet, with pecan pie and carrot cake among the less intense and more successful. For a couple, $52 should cover the tab for dinner with wine.

P. S. Bangkok

3345 N. Clark St.
871-7777

P.S. Bangkok II

2521 N. Halsted St.
348-0072
THAI
*Open Mon.-Thurs.
11:30 a.m.-10 p.m., Fri.-
Sat. 11:30 a.m.-11:30 p.m.,
Sun. 4:30 p.m.-10 p.m.
All major cards.*

A pioneer of the first great incursion of Thai food in Chicago (in the early 1980s), P.S. Bangkok begat P.S. Bangkok II a few years ago; chef Ruckkiat Buraketchakul was sent over to oversee the operation. The menu remains the same in both, an awesome tabulation of 200-plus dishes covering soups, finger-food curries potent enough to cause an esophageal meltdown, rice and rice noodles garnished this way and that way (almost ad infinitum) and the welcome relief of iced fruit compotes and Thai coffee. Sukanya Yongsawai and her husband remain at the original to do the cooking, which strays from the canon just a wee bit at times to accommodate tentative Midwestern palates. Beware, though, of asterisked items, such as kang pa, a green curry marked "verry hot" (sic) on the menu that turns up *very* hot on the plate. Nam sod and yum pla muk, minced pork and squid salads, respectively, can vie with Bangkok's versions, and the lemon-grass-shrimp soup, tom yum goong, is classically rendered. Don't bother to ask for chopsticks, which are not Thai implements (though some restaurateurs accommodatingly supply them to eager-beaver customers). The long, clean, pleasant room lined with Thai travel posters is fairly nondescript—except for the puzzling, phony Thai hut (thatched roof and all) that protrudes out from the side of one wall. Bring your own wine or beer, preferably the latter and plenty of it. A dinner fit for gourmands will set two people back about $38.

Palm Restaurant

(Mayfair Regent Hotel),
181 E. Lake Shore Dr.
944-0135
STEAKHOUSE
Open Mon.-Fri.
11:30 a.m.-10:30 p.m.,
Sat. 5 p.m.-10:30 p.m.
All major cards.

As a veteran of the not-much-lamented stockyards likes to say, "Nouvelle cuisine is to look at. You want to eat, order a steak." In its mythic view of itself, even if not anchored wholly in reality, Chicago remains a steak town. That one of its favorite cuts is the New York strip, and that one of its best steakhouses is a spin-off of the Palm in New York, makes little difference to our trencherpersons. The Palm's bottom line is a slab of meat whose crusty surface encloses grainy, wine-tangy, apparently dry-aged prime beef. The three-inch-thick filet mignon approaches the New York strip in flavor and, as might be expected, surpasses it in tenderness. Portions range from large to immense, and so do the tabs. The famous cottage fries may be tough and the french-fried onions a tad greasy, but mushrooms and asparagus are among the excellent fresh vegetables worth ordering as side dishes to share. Maine lobsters, ranging from three to more than twenty pounds, can easily destroy a budget, and New York cheesecake or excellent chocolate-mousse pie will do equal damage to a diet. Air heavy with smoke that ceiling fans stir but fail to dissipate and walls heavy with caricatures and cartoons of local celebrities, famous names and comic book characters are part of the shtick—as is a noise level that can become unpleasant over the course of an evening. The small wine list includes a few reds suitable to the occasion. Two should plan on at least $95 for dinner with wine.

Pars Cove

435 W. Diversey Pkwy.
549-1515
PERSIAN/SEAFOOD
Open daily 11 a.m.-11 p.m.
All major cards.

12/20

Owner Max Pars has managed to maintain low prices and high quality for more than a decade. One of the first restaurants in the area to serve khorasht fesenjan, ghormeh sabzi and other Persian classics (see below), Pars Cove also features fresh whitefish, trout, salmon, swordfish and snapper, when available. The good news is that ingredients, especially fish, are always fresh; the bad news is that sometimes preparations are heavy-handed and fish overcooked. Meals begin with warm flat bread, dense and chewy, topped with melted butter and sumagh (similar to paprika) superb homemade soups and one or more of a half dozen appetizers: baked eggplant mashed with garlic and yogurt, a bland, mildly bitter spread; aromatic grape leaves stuffed with rice, nuts, prunes and raisins; lemony chicken kebabs; or minty chopped cucumbers in yogurt. The hearty, traditional dishes, such as khorasht fesenjan, boneless chicken simmered in pomegranate juice with walnuts and onions, and ghormeh sabzi, a stew of beef, beans and leeks seasoned with parsley, fenugreek, onions and dried lime, are exotic and appealing. Skewered items abound, our favorites being the savory ground-lamb-and-beef koubideh, and ju jah kebab, juicy marinated chicken. Seafood is served steamed, sautéed, broiled, blackened or kebabed on a bed of pasta, rice or, in the case of lobster, lettuce. A few non-Persian versions of chicken, lamb and beef are also available. An occasional dessert is zolobia, fried yogurt and flour anointed with honey and rosewater, a more interesting ending than the customary flan or ice cream cake. Despite its basement location, there's an airy feeling to the place, to which comfortable chairs, well-placed tables and cheerful lighting all contribute. About $40 should take care of dinner for two, with wine.

The Parthenon
314 S. Halsted St.
726-2407
GREEK
Open Sun.-Thurs. 11 a.m.-
1:30 a.m., Fri.-Sat.
11 a.m.-2 a.m.
All major cards.

12/20

The Parthenon is one of the more spirited restaurants in Greek Town. Its three bright dining rooms are bustling with waiters hard at work and customers hard at their food and drink. And this place dishes out some of the best Greek food around. Saganaki, the famous flaming-cheese appetizer, was created here, and the waiters can raise a tower of flame with the best of them. Taramosalata—whipped fish roe—is silky-smooth, clean tasting and not too powerfully seasoned. Greek salads are a model of the genre. Fried cod filets are always delicious and cooked just right. Skordalia, a mix of puréed potatoes and garlic, is so strong it may force you to slink off into the night. Spanakopita—spinach cheese pie—is a delectable combination of fresh spinach and sharp feta cheese laid between layers of flaky phyllo dough. Broiled fresh red snapper is wonderfully aromatic from its basting with oil, lemon and oregano. Lamb and chicken dishes are especially good. The best of the desserts are the crème caramel and honey-almond cake; the baklava is too stiff and dry for our taste. Choose from an excellent selection of Greek wines served by the bottle, carafe or glass. About $30 for two, with wine.

Pattaya
114 W. Chicago Ave.
944-3753
THAI
Open Mon.-Fri. 11:30 a.m.-
10 p.m., Sat.-Sun.
4:30 p.m.-10 p.m.
All major cards.

12/20

The startling proliferation of Thai restaurants has not produced many better than Pattaya, which occupies a special niche in our hearts. It serves hoi tod, a raggedy rice-flour and scrambled-egg pancake, somewhere between a waffle and a crêpe, that enfolds a mess of smoky-sweet mussels and crunchy bean sprouts. Under the blandishments of a chili-spiked vinegar sauce, the ensemble, like a Southeast Asian hangtown fry, is the stuff of legends. One dish, however, does not a restaurant make, but fortunately Pattaya also serves commendable tom yum goong, its piquant broth studded with shrimp and straw mushrooms; nam sod, ground pork salad laced with lime juice and devastatingly hot chilis; pa nang gai, chicken curry seasoned with red chili, coconut milk and leaves of the wild lime tree; and one of the city's finest squid stuffed with ground pork. Americans who equate Thai food with incandescence may be surprised to find a number of relatively mild dishes, a spectrum of peppers that reflects sophisticated Bangkok—chili sauce and powder may be applied at the table to bring tears of pleasure to the eyes of the most dedicated fire-eater. Thai egg custard, a moistly grainy taro-and-coconut-milk confection, and banana stewed in coconut milk, oddly tart in its hyper-sweet bath, along with iced Thai coffee, help cool down palatal meltdowns. Lime-colored walls set off by a handful of temple rubbings, immaculate linen-set tables and the charm of leisurely ceiling fans make a comfortable ambience for the food and generally attentive service. Beer, domestic or imported, is available, as well as wine and cocktails. Dinner for two, with beer, will cost $35 to $40.

Perinos

1339 N. Wells St.
988-9883
ITALIAN
Open Mon.-Fri.
11:30 a.m.-2:30 p.m. &
5:30 p.m.-11 p.m., Sat.
5:30 p.m.-11:30 p.m., Sun.
5 p.m.-10:30 p.m.
Cards: AE, MC, V.

11/20

There seems to be no end to the proliferation of Italian restaurants in Chicago these days. Perinos, one of the latest in a crowded field, concentrates on northern Italian cuisine with occasional nods toward California. Such dishes as pasta stuffed with duck, zucchini and sun-dried tomatoes in a Champagne sauce; veal sautéed with shallots, Swiss cheese and avocado; and breast of duck broiled with maple syrup, molasses and a creamed date sauce are pronounced departures from traditional cucina Italiana. But the bulk of the offerings remains true to the old country. We suggest beginning with slices of buffalo mozzarella alternating with tomato and fresh basil, the trio bathed in a fruity, pungent olive oil and garnished with excellent roasted peppers. Unfortunately, the meal too often goes downhill from that fine start. Veal tonnato lacks distinction. Pasta e fagioli, made with kidney beans instead of white, which are then left whole rather than puréed, is disappointingly thin and salty. On our last visit, the homemade carrot fettuccine with asparagus tips and pancetta in a cream sauce—basically a good dish—had been allowed to toughen and dry out under a heat lamp. Excellent marinated beef in a rich tomato sauce arrived without the mushrooms promised by the menu. Desserts are only fair, but the decor is bright and cheerful— white linens and fresh flowers against a backdrop of exposed brick walls. A display pantry under a red-and-white-checkered canopy enables patrons to watch the pasta being prepared. Two will spend about $75 for dinner with wine.

Le Perroquet

70 E. Walton St.
944-7990
FRENCH
Open Mon.-Fri. 11:45 a.m.-
2 p.m. & 6 p.m.-10 p.m.,
Sat. 6 p.m.-10 p.m.
Cards: AE, CB, DC.

When you enter the lobby of the old, gray stone building, a gentleman in a dark suit checks your name on the reservations list. He opens the door to the small elevator, and a moment later you arrive on the second floor to exit into a charming, sedate dining room with the ambience of a private club. Comfortable and plush red-velvet banquettes flow along the walls. Huge sprays of fresh flowers fill the center of the room. Mirrored columns reflect and enhance the pleasantly lighted room. Small lamps and fresh flowers add more light and color to decently spaced, generously sized tables. Though this grande dame of French cooking, which opened in 1972, is looking just a bit old, there are still many feasts to explore here—both visually and orally. We have dined at Le Perroquet since year one; and, as always since year one, the moment you are seated the service staff springs quietly into action. Bottled water is poured, drink orders are taken, an amuse-gueule—a small plate of tiny canapés—is set on the table. Time is given to enjoy an apéritif before menus are proffered.

The fixed-price menu selections haven't changed much in recent years, but the choices are solid. Prosciutto with melon is sliced when ordered, the meat a shade thicker than usual, ringed with sweet balls of melon. Salad, served before or after the entrée, is Bibb lettuce—nothing more than that—lightly glossed with a slightly thickened vinaigrette dressing. Tournedos of beef in a shallot reduction sauce are exemplary, the aged beef tender and luscious. Soufflés are ethereal, a classic of the genre, and come in a choice of six flavors. Specials of the day include some exciting choices: A broccoli mousse is ringed with tender sea scallops in a saffron sauce. Grilled Canadian salmon is perfect and perfectly enhanced with a scintillating dill sauce. Lamb chops are rosy pink, succulent and escorted by an exciting basil sauce. Pastries of the day are works of edible art. Le Perroquet is undoubtedly one of the most civilized restaurants in Chicago today. Dinner for two, with wine, costs about $150.

Philander's Oak Park

(Carleton Hotel),
1120 Pleasant St.,
Oak Park
848-4250
SEAFOOD
*Open Mon.-Thurs.
11:30 a.m.-2 p.m. &
5:30 p.m.-10 p.m., Fri.
11:30 a.m.-2 p.m. &
5:30 p.m.-11 p.m., Sat.
5:30 p.m.-11 p.m., Sun.
11 a.m.-3 p.m. &
5 p.m.-9 p.m.
All major cards.*

11/20

The selection of fresh oysters and fresh clams at this restaurant-in-a-hotel is wonderful. Pristine oysters from waters up and down either coast, available by the piece, half dozen or dozen, have never been anything but the best. Once past the oysters, though, get ready for some choppy waters. We have had great seafood here; then again, we have had seafood that was a net loss. Best bets for appetizers are the smoked salmon and the oysters Rockefeller, though you might want to cancel your order when you see the prices. Entrée prices shape up the same way: The quality and selection are there—and we *like* the shrimp de Jonghe and the steamed Dungeness crab—but the value-to-price relationship is askew, which dampens our enthusiasm considerably. On one occasion we had Lake Superior whitefish that was broiled to perfection; a week later it sank to the depths from overcooking. The same has been true with the flounder. Desserts are nothing but sweet nothings, except for Petersen's ice cream, which you can get a lot cheaper if you drive to Petersen's itself, a few blocks west. Dinner for two runs about $90, with wine.

Pine Yard

924 Church St.,
Evanston
475-4940
CHINESE
Open Mon. & Wed.-Thurs.
11:30 a.m.-2 p.m. &
4:30 p.m.-9:30 p.m., Fri.
11:30 a.m.-2 p.m. &
4:30 p.m.-10 p.m., Sat.
4:30 p.m.-10 p.m., Sun.
4:30 p.m.-9 p.m.
Cards: MC, V.

11/20

Located in a brick-and-wood freestanding building just east of the elevated train tracks, Pine Yard is about as nondescript as a building can be and, as restaurants these days go, is nothing fancy. The two dining rooms have wood-lath-decorated walls, on which hang Chinese art prints and paintings. This is no-frills, unpretentious dining, and the service staff is a model of business-like efficiency. Some of them won't win any awards for congeniality, but they bring the right food at the right time. The menu is a mix of Mandarin, Cantonese and Szechwán, with ample choices from each of those provinces. The all-time favorite Chinese appetizer—potstickers—is exceptionally good. Steamed and pan-fried, these plump beauties are crisp on the bottom and soft on top, with a moist and fragrant pork filling. Mongolian beef comes with a perfect balance of flavorings—the thin strips of lean and tender beef, fragrant with sesame oil and flavor-enhanced with shreds of scallions, are marvelous. Moo shu dishes, especially the pork version, are quite good. The specialty of the house, crispy duck, really is special. The whole duck, cut into umpteen pieces, is as crisp as promised and delectable, too. Unfortunately, seafood dishes don't always fare as well. Sea scallops will be dry, shrimp mushy and barbecued pork not the best we've had. Fried rice needs more moisture and more of the designated food, as in more pork in the pork-fried rice. Don't bother with dessert. Dinner is about $25 a person with wine.

Les Plumes

2044 N. Halsted St.
525-0121
FRENCH
Open Mon.-Thurs.
5:30 p.m.-9:30 p.m., Fri.-
Sat. 5:30 p.m.-10 p.m.
Cards: AE, MC, V.

Relaxed plush is the best way to describe the intimate, informal elegance of this small—60 seats, give or take a few—and pleasant place that sits smack in the middle of Halsted Street's restaurant row. Forest-green banquettes sweep around one wall in the raised-floor dining area. Peacock feathers float outward from large vases that cap warm, blond-wood columns rising toward the skylight of the vaulted ceiling. A small bar to the right, as you enter, is a warm invitation to sample a glass of wine from the open-bottle selection. Owners Greg Mulcahy and Tom Culleeney each spent six years under the tutelage of Jean Banchet at the esteemed Le Français restaurant in Wheeling—Mulcahy as sous chef and Culleeney as pastry chef. You can't ask for better credentials. Early in its career, this three-year-old restaurant suffered from service lapses, but time has healed that affliction.

There is much to enjoy at Les Plumes; in fact, it may well be one of the most underrated restaurants in Chicago. The cooking has true finesse. Consider an appetizer of quail with truffles and goose liver in puff pastry or fettuccine with smoked duck. Or consider the state-of-the-art pâtés. Salad creations should turn other restaurants green with envy. Lightly breaded morsels of goat cheese sautéed with brioche crumbs fall gracefully over curly endive misted with a mustard vinaigrette. Smoked breast of duck adorns Belgian endive and radicchio, all of which is dressed with a winsome hazelnut vinaigrette. That's but a taste of two out of four wonderful salads. Entrées are stunning in their presentation—even a simple dish like roast chicken with cabbage looks enticing. Quail stuffed with wild mushrooms glistens with goodness within its ring of fanned slices of sautéed duck. A trilogy of fish might be composed of such swimmers as salmon, tuna and swordfish filets, each with a distinctive and well-crafted sauce. Daily specials are no less interesting or appealing, and desserts are spectacular. White-and dark-chocolate mousse with white-chocolate ice cream and chocolate sauce is a work of art that will send you into a state of bliss. The hot apple tart with cinnamon ice cream and caramel sauce is so luxurious it sings with the delights of calorie sinning. The dacquoise is a classic, the hazelnut and almond meringue disc filled with an enchantingly delicious walnut and almond cream. The wine list is as ambitious as the menu, with appropriate choices at several price levels. Dinner for two, with wine, is about $100.

Prairie
500 S. Dearborn St.
663-1143
AMERICAN
Open Mon.-Thurs.
6:30 a.m.-10:30 a.m.,
11:30 a.m.-2 p.m. &
5:30 p.m.-10 p.m., Fri.
6:30 a.m.-10:30 a.m.,
11:30 a.m.-2 p.m. &
5:30 p.m.-11 p.m., Sat.
6:30 a.m.-2 p.m. &
5:30 p.m.-11 p.m., Sun.
6:30 a.m.-2 p.m. &
5 p.m.-10 p.m.
All major cards.

Despite the best efforts of chef Stephen Langlois and general manager Deborah Pagels, "Midwestern cuisine" is an oxymoron; it is kinder and more accurate to label the provender dished up here "Midwestern food." It is a worthwhile distinction. Smoked-trout terrine with a horseradish-spiked dill mayonnaise and pan-fried lake perch with glazed yam sauce, to name two items, do not suggest a unified vision, nor do they describe dishes with a regional identity— as does boeuf en daube provençal or Peking duck. Sirloin of buffalo on the other hand, does specify something indigenous and is worth trying. The meat is lean, tenderly grainy and milder than beef, but equally receptive to a crusty surface and a medium-rare treatment. Langlois favors local produce, so you can expect corn, rutabagas, wild rice, cranberries, blueberries and pecans to support sadly characterless farm-bred Iowa pheasant, smoked turkey breast and broiled Lake Superior whitefish. Baked walleye pike, made with a wild-rice-and-spinach stuffing and a cream sauce threaded by parsley, proves complex and subtle. And delicately moist roast chicken on a bed of corn-and-sage stuffing reaffirms our belief that fried and stewed chicken often testify to an inadequacy on the part of either bird or chef.

Success and failure may rub shoulders on the plate, as when sautéed wild mushrooms lacked intensity and pungency, but a chive popover alongside had a tangy edge and firmly porous texture makes it a joy to bite into. The brandied loaf of duck, pheasant, rabbit sausage and turkey is a hit, as is Prairie Berry ice cream, butterscotch-smooth and rife with strawberry, raspberry and blueberry flavors. The interior is said to be a chip off the Frank Lloyd Wright block. But the chip has flown wide, which is good, given Wright's proclivity for expecting people to remold the human frame to fit his unyielding imagination. Two people should plan on about $80 for dinner with wine.

Le Prince

Swiss Grand Hotel
323 E. Wacker Dr.
565-0565
FRENCH
Open Mon.-Sat.
6 p.m.-10 p.m.
All major cards.

Louis Outhier, the great French chef and restaurateur turned consultant, has a Midas touch. He built the Marquis de Lafayette into Boston's finest and struck gold again in New York with Lafayette in the Drake Hotel. The French have a saying, "never two without three," and his third American venture, Le Prince, opened recently to rave reviews. Relatively classic French cuisine with a nod towards lightness and a step away from heavy sauces is served up in the dark-wood dining room with its Louis XIV chairs and Burgundy red patterned carpeting. You can eat consistently well here, though with a greater emphasis on formality than fireworks on the plate. The French and American wine list is young and needs some depth and age. Given its artisocratic bloodlines, we're betting this hotel restaurant will show its class as one of Chicago's tops and fully merit our rating. Figure $150 for two with wine.

Printer's Row

550 S. Dearborn St.
461-0780
AMERICAN
Open Mon.-Thurs.
11:30 a.m.-2:30 p.m. &
5:30 p.m.-10 p.m., Fri.
11:30 a.m.-2:30 p.m. &
5:30 p.m.-11 p.m., Sat.
5:30 p.m.-11 p.m.
All major cards.

Printer's Row was much ado about food in its early days, but the ado has slipped a bit since owner/chef Michael Foley's attention was diverted when he opened another restaurant (Foley's on E. Ohio Street) a few years ago. When Printer's Row first opened, it was a model for the then-emerging cuisine known as New American, and Foley's imagination and flair for culinary creativeness were evident in every dish. Today, Foley still has his hand in things, but his grasp seems weakened just a little. We still like the rich, clubby atmosphere of the place, but little things like chipped dishes and dime-store serving pieces (sugar packets thrown onto a glass saucer with the espresso service) are definitely out of place. And some of the waiters have an attitude problem. But make no mistake about it—the food is still excellent, and the presentations are handsome. Outstanding appetizers include the venison ravioli with endive and duck liver and the carpaccio. Game and fish entrées (such as grilled venison with timbale of wild rice and a particularly fine buffalo carpaccio) consistently fare well, but pasta dishes (we were recently served an almond pasta with vanilla sauce that would have made a better dessert than entrée) can offer more fantasy than finesse. Entrée salads on the lunch menu are excellent. The chocolate cake roll is a divine chocolate dessert, but the sorbets, which at one time burst with flavor, are sometimes lifeless. Dinner with wine will cost two about $90.

Pronto Ristorante

200 E. Chestnut St.
664-6181
ITALIAN
Open Mon.-Thurs.
11:30 a.m.-11:30 p.m.,
Fri.-Sat. 11:30 a.m.-
midnight, Sun. 4 p.m.-
10:30 p.m.
All major cards.

11/20

Still a popular Italian restaurant (due in part, we suspect, to its proximity to Water Tower Place, Michigan Avenue and a host of hotels), Pronto's strength lies in its pasta dishes. On display in the front of this modern (though old-looking), table-tight, brass-and-glass ristorante is the pasta maker, who rolls, cuts and hangs the freshly made pasta that goes into most of the pasta dishes. Choose from about fifteen pasta dishes in all; all the ones we've sampled over the years have fared well. Spaghetti alla carbonara is laced with the smoky taste of bacon and rich with cream. Capellini with pesto sauce is fragrant with basil and garlic, the green sauce clinging to the perfectly cooked pasta. The lasagne, however, has not always thrilled us, the pasta too mushy, the red sauce too harsh tasting. Scaloppine Marsala is always too heavy on the Marsala, which ruins the delicate flavor of the veal. The best seafood dish is the scampi fra diavolo, the herb-laden tomato sauce a perfect foil for the fresh-tasting shrimp. Dessert choices, as it goes with most Italian restaurants, are nothing to write home to Italy about. One dessert, coppa Romana, used to be a nice piece of work, but in recent years it has diminished in stature: The scoops of ice cream don't seem as large, the once-thick piece of chocolate cake is now a thin, almost-not-there slice, and the chocolate sauce isn't as rich. What can we say about an Italian restaurant that uses the French spelling for zabaglione (and then spells the French word wrong)? Well, we can say don't order the strawberries with that custard sauce. About $70 for two, with wine.

The Pump Room

(Omni Ambassador East
Hotel),
1301 N. State St.
266-0360
AMERICAN
Open Mon.-Thurs. 7 a.m.-
11 p.m., Fri.-Sat. 7 a.m.-
1 a.m., Sun. 7 a.m.-
10:30 a.m., 11 a.m.-
2:30 p.m. & 5 p.m.-10 p.m.
All major cards.

12/20

New York's talking and gawking emporia are legion—from Sardi's, where a look at the next table *always* precedes a look at the menu, to Elaine's, where who you are determines, with cartographical precision, where and whether you'll be seated. For the most part, Chicago doesn't have time for "all this faddle," as Marianne Moore said, though here and there, as might be expected, an exception clamors for attention. Such is the case with The Pump Room, whose low-numbered booths are reserved for the filthy rich, royalty and public figures. Don't bother trying for booth Number 1: Liza Minnelli owns it, we're told. But do take a gander at the stills packed onto every square inch of the foyer: a just-married Bogie and Bacall, Ronald Colman, Her Majesty Elizabeth II and so on. The decor casts a backward glance at Chicago's speakeasy grandeur; spacious booths, comfortable chairs and spotless tableware make eating pleasant for anyone who's there to eat. And the food at The Pump Room can be fun. Stick to the house pâté (more of a full-flavored chicken-liver mousse), the stone crab or the black-bean soup to start, or order superb beefsteak tomato slices topped with sweet, red onion rings. The corned beef hash is justly famous, a throwback to hearty, uncomplicated food, a dish James Beard might have fussily approved. Simple grilled fish, roasts, ribs and the calves' liver and bacon heaped with grilled onions are reliable. Avoid anything that smacks overly of nouvelle this or that. We lean toward cheesecake and pecan pie at the end, but the hot fudge sundae has made many a nostalgic 40-year-old blissfully happy. A late-night supper menu, live music and a dance floor small enough to make contact dancing a necessity add to The Pump Room's popularity. A full bar (fourteen Cognacs and four Armagnacs in addition to wine, beer, cocktails and coolers) also helps. Two should plan on leaving about $80 lighter after dinner with wine.

Restaurant Suntory Chicago

13 E. Huron St.
664-3344
JAPANESE
Open Mon.-Fri.
11:30 a.m.-2 p.m. &
5:30 p.m.-10 p.m., Sat.
5:30 p.m.-10 p.m.
All major cards.

11/20

Suntory is a multilevel, multiroom, modern restaurant where order and understated beauty greet the eye at every turn. On the first floor is the bar/lounge area; to the rear are the formal shabu-shabu room and three private tatami rooms, each with a view of the immaculately groomed Japanese gardens; and on level two are the teppanyaki dining room and sushi bar. This tidy package offers a full range of Japanese cuisine, but the prices are as steep as the sharply pitched roof, and the chances of getting a meal that befits the price are just as precipitous. A lack of spirit pervades here, not only in the kimono-clad waitresses, but in the kitchen as well. Dishes do not expand in imagination and good taste beyond that which is absolutely necessary to get the job done. More attention is given to how a particular dish looks than how it tastes; it's more form than substance—and at $18 a throw for beef teriyaki, and $20 for sukiyaki or beef shabu-shabu, there needs to be more of both. About $40 per person, with saké or beer.

Rico's

626 S. Racine Ave.
421-7262
ITALIAN
Open Sun.-Thurs. 4 p.m.-
10 p.m., Fri.-Sat. 4 p.m.-
midnight.
Cards: AE, MC, V.

12/20

Chicago has numerous Italian restaurants, and most leave something to be desired. Rico's is an exception. Situated on the ground level of a beautifully restored four-story building on the Near West Side, Rico's decor is as straightforward as its food. Ceiling fans drop down from the high, pressed-tin ceiling. Walls are adorned with outsize color-tinted photographs that depict scenes from the early 1900s. Tables are topped with white tablecloths, which are then covered with white butcher's paper. The complete picture is one of casual elegance. If the menu pays allegiance to any particular part of Italy, it is south of Rome. Start with one of the well-crafted, richly flavored soups. Minestrone is zesty and a far cry from the thick, tasteless miscreants that have given this soup a bad name. Fettuccine carbonara is alive with flavor; the delicate, homemade pasta lightly coated with a prosciutto-studded cream sauce that is distinguished and delicious. Vermicelli alla puttanesca is an exuberant combination of marinara sauce, olives and capers. Veal dishes are generally good, though they fall off a bit when the kitchen is rushed. Seafood entrées (especially those combined with pasta) are exceptionally good, as are the daily specials. About $50 for two, with a bottle of Spaghetti Red or Linguine White.

Rinconcito Sudamericano

1954 W. Armitage Ave.
489-3126
PERUVIAN
Open Wed.-Thurs. noon-10 p.m., Fri.-Sat. 1 p.m.-10:30 p.m., Sun. 1 p.m.-9:30 p.m.
Cards: MC, V.

12/20

Low prices, an extensive menu and better-than-average cooking make this cheerfully decorated storefront worth a visit. Pottery and llama-wool hangings spruce up the walls, while a Peruvian rug attempts to do the same for the floor, which is already spruced up with nail polish–glossy red enamel. Plants here and there break up the space. Our favorite opener is anticuchos, two skewers laden with juicy chunks of beef heart, accompanied by first-rate roast potatoes; green-chile salsa, for contrast, completes this exciting and unusual dish. Papas rellenos, cigar-shaped mashed potatoes stuffed with ground beef and fried to a mahogany brown, suggest the blissfully satisfying meatloaf and mashed potatoes of our youth. Though loaded with crustaceans, the creamy shrimp soup is only fair, a victim of the limp-shrimp syndrome; the cilantro that gives character to the dish is strangely absent. Caucau, on the other hand, chewy-sweet tripe stewed with potatoes, peas and corn in a delicately piquant white sauce, needs no apologies. Aji de gallina, chicken in an almost-too-rich nut cream, might be best shared. Lobster appears by itself or in combination with other shellfish. Seafood lovers may also choose from less pricey offerings, such as garlic-creamy red snapper or a minitureen of steamed crab, shrimp and fish flavored with both wine and beer. Fixed-price dinners for two enable couples to sample a variety of dishes, including paella. Desserts are heavy on the sugar, and dark-roasted coffee, rich and full-bodied, can be muddy. No beer or wine is served, but patrons can bring their own for a $2.50 corkage fee. Amateurish service may result in long waits between courses. Dinner for two, including corkage, will run about $35.

Rio's Casa Iberia

4611 N. Kedzie Ave.
588-7800
BRAZILIAN/SPANISH
Open Tues.-Thurs. & Sun. 5 p.m.-midnight, Fri.-Sat. 5 p.m.-1 a.m.
All major cards.

11/20

No, it won't replace dining in Oviedo on fabada asturiana (blood sausage and white fava beans), or in Setubal on cod baked with potatoes and onions, or in Rio on churrasco, the ultimate, mind-boggling mixed grill. Still, it's pleasant to know that representative and serviceable examples of three neglected traditions can be obtained under one roof. The food sticks closely to the originals, though some substitutions—American for Catalonian ham, for example—are inevitable. As appetizers, octopus marinated in olive oil and wine vinegar and steamed to tenderness, or chourico assado, the mildly pungent Portuguese analogue of Spain's chorizo, might be paired with Brazil's ameijoas cataplana, cherrystones strewn with smoked ham sautéed with green pepper, tomato and onion. Soups, such as Portuguese caldo verde, are robust meal-in-a-bowl affairs; a cup is plenty for openers. Feijoada is altogether more refined than the ham-hock and plate-beef affair we've had in Rio. The muqueca de camarao, however, could pass for the shrimp-and-coco-nut-milk dish popular in Carmen Miranda country. That oddly satisfying pork-and-clam concoction called porco com ameijoas a alentejana (Portugal) and a garlicky seafood brochette with a name almost as long as the skewers—banderillas de mariscos rias bajas (Spain)—make happy appearances; daily specials round out the offerings. Those who visit after 10 p.m. are likely to enjoy a taste of flamenco, or a singer with or without a backup combo. Dinner will run $65 per couple, with wine.

Ritz-Carlton Hotel/ The Dining Room

160 E. Pearson St.
266-1000
FRENCH
Open Mon.-Sat. 6 p.m.- 11 p.m., Sun. 10:30 a.m.- 2 p.m. & 6 p.m.-10 p.m. All major cards.

Hotel dining is the Russian roulette of gastronomy. The exigencies of preparing hundreds of meals, often for several restaurants, while satisfying calls for anything from snacks to complete dinners to be served in the room, make formidable demands on the most skilled and dedicated kitchens. Some, notably The Dining Room, transcend the category, becoming fine restaurants in their own right. Those diners without caloric cares might begin with a sybaritic ensemble of duck liver, avocado and tomato presented in a lovely mosaic, or crab cakes, baked rather than pan-fried and heady with fresh tarragon. Those on a cholesterol or fat watch may opt for the starred items; an appetizer and entrée add up to fewer than 650 calories. It will be a minor hardship on the palate, with such possibilities as sliced mango and lobster, saffron-infused red snapper, veal-and-sweetbreads ravioli sauced with wild mushrooms and broiled fish teased by a sprightly lobster vinaigrette. Unfortunately, your pocket-book will lose even more weight than you do.

Original yet solidly based on classic French cooking, The Dining Room offers such elegant departures as a breast and leg of duck braised with Pinot Noir and served with a fritter made from the liver; swordfish meurette with beef marrow; or, more conventionally, beef with mustard and baked shallots or salmon on savory cabbage flavored with bacon. Paring-thin apple tart has no superiors and few peers, but for decadent abandon you should try the fruit-mousse-filled nougatine presented on raspberry purée. When no glitches occur, dining here is an aesthetic experience. Multitiered grand chandeliers scatter light against burnished dark-wood walls. Tables are generously spaced. The banquettes along the walls, slightly raised from the main floor, seat four comfortably but are routinely allotted to two. A world-class wine list at world-class prices provides the expected Latours and Grands Echézeaux, along with a few well-bred lesser luminaries, while Cognacs and vintage ports head an admirable list of postprandial libations. For dinner with wine, a couple should figure on $140 or more.

Rosebud Cafe
1500 W. Taylor St.
942-1117
ITALIAN
Open Mon.-Fri. 11 a.m.-3 p.m. & 5 p.m.-11 p.m., Sat. 5 p.m.-11:30 p.m. All major cards.

The beauty of the bar's intricate wood carvings alone is worth a trip to this popular hangout for the culinary cognoscenti. The big, open dining room is a random load of tables that, more often than not, are filled at lunch and dinner with eager eaters. There's plenty to be eager about here, including an excellent selection of appetizers: Baked clams, fried calamari and stuffed artichokes are masterpieces of good taste. Pasta dishes range from the ubiquitous and oversauced fettuccine Alfredo to a flavorfully pungent linguine with oil and garlic, with such basics as lasagne, ravioli and linguine carbonara in between. Shrimp and broccoli over linguine is exceptionally good, as is the pasta with red or white clam sauce. Many of the veal dishes are embellished too much with extras that tend to mask the quality veal that's used here. But clearly the fowl is the fairest of them all—chicken Vesuvio is an outstanding dish, the addition of peas a true inspiration; bell peppers and mushrooms bring alive the flavor of chicken cacciatore. None of the dessert choices are worth mentioning. Dinner with wine runs about $30 per person.

Sabrina Cafe Club
660 N. Orleans St.
649-5522
CALIFORNIA
Open Mon.-Fri. 11:30 a.m.-2 p.m. & 4 p.m.-2 a.m., Sat. 4 p.m.-2 a.m. All major cards.

People go to Sabrina to watch the VCR playing *Breakfast at Tiffany's*, or to perch on wobbly bar stools while confabulating earnestly across tables the size of checkerboards, or to pull wetly at a tepid Bud that's fast on its way to becoming warm. They go to table-hop, looking to score a name, a number or a network, making connections for the never-too-distant world of bucks, more bucks and megabucks. All of which must frost the bottom of Daniel Castro, a young, talented chef who deserves a better vehicle for his California-style, tapas-size offerings. An upscale pig-in-a-blanket, grilled asparagus swaddled by grainy beef tenderloin, suggests the tone: Contrast taste and texture but keep the ingredients simple and the preparation to a minimum. Thus, smoky, thin-crust pizzas come decked with sesame-sweetened leeks, charred salmon medallions enclose a nugget of crunchy shrimp, and linguine gets the twin blessings of avocado and blue crab. Our favorite dessert remains the white-chocolate strawberry cheesecake, whose caramel sauce contributes an elegant burnt-sugar note to the composition. A brief wine list is heavy on sparklers. By 10 p.m., tables in the center section have been removed and the suddenly empty space becomes—presto!—a dance floor. Banquettes, infinitely preferable to the absurdly minuscule tables, are worth waiting for. For us, the bar, which gets socked in four-deep with bright young things standing chic-to-chic, is strictly a spectator sport. Service manages to flow, if by fits and starts. Decor is eclectic: Bauhaus chairs, conical, space-cadet chandeliers, a tripartite, bilevel floor and splashes of mirror against otherwise-bare walls. Dinner for two should come to about $62, including wine.

Samavar

1040 W. Belmont Ave.
348-1440
INDIAN
*Open Mon.-Thurs. 4 p.m.-
10:30 p.m., Fri. 4 p.m.-
11 p.m., Sat. 11 a.m.-
11:30 p.m., Sun.
11:30 a.m.-10 p.m.
Cards: AE.*

11/20

Frankly, we don't quite know what to make of this over-size double storefront. The menu is seriously limited, yet the place has pretensions. Its decor shuffles toward elegance—white tablecloths, linen napkins, fresh flowers, mir-rored pillars, charcoal-gray carpeting—and then stops short with a large, vinyl-covered central square of floor, chairs stacked against a wall and a cluttered, makeshift service station. Vegetable preparations are especially good—biry-ani, for example, basmati rice studded with tomato, mush-room, peas, chickpeas, turnip, cilantro and cubes of home-made Indian cheese. Samosa, a pair of triangular fried dumplings stuffed with savory potato and peas, and bengan bhartha, tomato-rich eggplant stew, also get high marks. Shrimp masala, whole shrimp jostling chunks of cauliflower in a piquant chili-tomato sauce, lags only a little behind. Carnivores will be happy to know that tandoori (clay oven) roasted meats—boneless chicken tikka, lamb tikka (mildly spiced lamb sausage) and bone-in chicken tandoori—are all first-rate. Breads, unfortunately, are only fair, and the dhal makhani (stewed lentils) lacks the complex balance of fla-vors we've come to expect from the dish. Joujeh kabab, charbroiled saffron-marinated chicken that wasn't boneless as the menu had promised, was unevenly cooked and tasted rank and unpleasant on one of our visits. Strangely, only one chutney is served here, an excellent tangy mint sauce that goes well with most items. Dessert offerings, too, are few in number. We've been able to get only cinnamon-spiked rice pudding that was soupy though pleasant and not too sweet. Wine and beer are available, but surprisingly, not spiced Indian tea. Dinner for two, with beer, will run around $45.

Sayat Nova

157 E. Ohio St.
644-9159
ARMENIAN
*Open Mon.-Thurs.
11:30 a.m.-11 p.m., Fri.-
Sat. 11:30 a.m.-midnight,
Sun. 2:30 p.m.-9:30 p.m.
All major cards.*

12/20

Oyster-white rough-textured walls, banquettes set into cozy alcoves and fretwork brass lamps make a gesture at Middle Eastern ambience, but a TV set at one end of the bar and a service station at the other negate some of the room's potential charm. Lamb dominates the menu and is reasona-bly good, though it's sometimes past the stage of tangy freshness and sometimes even on the way to acquiring a muttony overtone. An oval platter of raw kibbe—chopped lamb and cracked wheat surmounted by fresh parsley, a small jug of oil to one side—makes an excellent shared opener. Dinner entrées come with a zesty, vegetable-flecked lentil soup, oil-and-vinegar-dressed lettuce and commercial pita bread, the last referred to misleadingly as Armenian bread. Hummus, just slightly granular with a tart undertone complementing its nutty richness, improves the pita bread immeasurably. Stuffed vine leaves (sarma) are tough, a failing the bland meat-and-rice filling does little to alleviate. The beoreg, however, are satisfyingly crisp, flaky pastries wrapped around a core of spicy meat or cheese. Kufta, finely ground lamb meatballs served with minted yogurt (mahdzoun), comes off better than the shish kebab, which needs utterly young, tender meat to be first-rate. Chicken comes either sautéed or in kebabs. The lamb chops often transcend the other lamb served, and the Middle Eastern lamb stew is worth a try, especially at lunch. Mixed drinks and wine are available, though the latter selection is severely limited. Service is generally efficient. Medium-thick, moderately sweet Armenian coffee and a chewy circlet of walnut-filled pastry called paklava make a traditional and satisfying end to a better-than-average meal. Dinner with wine runs about $50 per couple.

Scoozi!
410 W. Huron St.
943-5900
ITALIAN
Mon.-Thurs. 11:30 a.m.-
2 p.m. & 5 p.m.-10:30 p.m.,
Fri. 11:30 a.m.-2 p.m. &
5 p.m.-11:30 p.m., Sat.
5 p.m.-11:30 p.m., Sun.
5 p.m.-9 p.m.
All major cards.

For the maximum dining-as-theater plus first-rate Italian food, scuttle down to W. Huron Street where Scoozi! holds forth. Joe Decker, Avanzare's culinary magician, has transferred his talents to the West Side and has cranked the food up from good to excellent. His pastry chef, Joe Ferguson, does for profiteroles and tiramisu and fresh-berry tarts what Decker does for the serious stuff. The menu is huge. Sharing a thin pizza topped with asparagus and mushrooms or eggplant and lamb sausage seems popular, but it's a shame to bypass homemade mozzarella or grilled shrimp with charred tomato and pepper sauce or smoked pheasant with wild mushrooms or... well, you get the idea. For main dishes, one of the frequent lamb specials or braised veal shank (osso buco) are particularly appealing. Waitpersons know the food, and Kevin, the wine steward, knows his wines; their advice is never perfunctory and often is helpful. Scoozi!, however, isn't the place for quiet conversation, starry-eyed romance or anyone averse to bucking shoulder-to-shoulder crowds for an hour or more while waiting to be seated. Two people should dine with wine and considerable brio for $65.

> *We are always happy to hear about your discoveries and to receive your comments about ours. We want to give your letters the attention they deserve, so when you write to us, remember to state clearly exactly what you liked or disliked. Be concise, but convincing. Do take the time to argue your point.*

Shaw's Crab House

21 E. Hubbard St.
527-2722
SEAFOOD
Open Mon.-Thurs.
11:30 a.m.-2 p.m. &
5:30 p.m.-10 p.m., Fri.
11:30 a.m.-2 p.m. &
5:30 p.m.-11 p.m., Sun.
5 p.m.-10 p.m.
All major cards.

Until Shaw's Crab House opened some four years ago, the only decent seafood houses in the entire city were the Cape Cod Room in the Drake Hotel and Nick's Fishmarket; Chicago was not exactly in the swim of things when it came to good seafood restaurants. Shaw's has helped to alleviate the situation, and this big, busy, bustling place has that seafood-house spirit and attitude down perfectly. Hardwood floors, wood paneling, high ceilings and white tablecloths are all we need say about the decor—a good seafood house shouldn't be decorated to death. Oysters, always pristine and select, leave no bed unturned when it comes to variety. The Maryland crab cakes are the best this side of Baltimore. In season, Shaw's does soft-shell crabs and stone-crab claws better than any place in town. Other seafood-house regulars, such as lobster and shrimp, are studies in simplicity—they stand on their own freshness and are not overworked with unnecessary sauces. Daily specials trail closely behind whatever the fishing boats are bringing in from the briny deep and generally are good. On occasion, however, we've run afoul of some fish that clearly had spent too much time on the heat. The key lime pie is excellent. Dinner for two, with wine, runs about $75.

The Blue Crab Lounge across the hall from the main dining room is Chicago's answer to the Grand Central Station Oyster Bar (albeit less noisy and more sane). Oysters, clams, gumbos, chowders, shrimp and crabs are served in an oyster-bar setting. The Blue Crab Lounge is open from lunch into the late evening.

Shiroi Hana Restaurant

3242 N. Clark St.
477-1652
JAPANESE
Open Mon.-Tues. & Thurs.
4:30 p.m.-12:30 a.m., Fri.-
Sat. 4:30 p.m.-1:30 a.m.,
Sun. 4 p.m.-10 p.m.
Cards: DC, MC, V.

12/20

Alternating panels of frost-white and matte-black tiles have lost some of their gloss, and the bare-filament bubble lamps no longer cast as theatrical a glare across booths and tables and onto the sushi bar. Still, yellowtail remains curd-sweet, smoked sea eel pungent and briny, and mirugai (giant clam) startlingly meaty, a liver-like pâté, it might seem, cradled by the clam's tough mantle. The best strategy is for two to share a sushi/sashimi combination, which will generally include salmon, smoked or fresh, flying fish roe wrapped in a sheet of pressed seaweed, a butterflied shrimp, octopus, mackerel or fatty tuna and so on, along with salmon-pink shaved ginger and a dash of explosive wasabe. This can be rounded out by a selection of appetizers, such as chawan mushi, egg custard laced with bits of fish and chicken and steamed in a cup; ankino, bitter monkfish (a.k.a. lotte) roe; goma ae, sesame-dressed boiled spinach; and ika-uni-ae, strips of chewy and astringent raw squid tossed with a spoonful of pungent sea urchin roe. Halibut, sautéed or teriyaki-style, makes a particularly good entrée, but the tempuras and teriyakis are all competently prepared. It's said that a Japanese chef's reputation rests on his sukiyaki. Here, it's a shade too sweet, but the stock merits kudos; the beef, alas, can be flavorless and stringy. Much better are yosen-abe, a seafaring pot-au-feu with some stowaway chicken and lots of cabbage. Nabeyaki, a meal-in-a-bowl for $6.95, fills one up with thick, chopstick-defiant noodles, a tangle of greens and occasional shrimp or chunks of chicken. Japanese green-tea ice cream and red-bean gelatin are oddly appealing alternatives to the more traditional fresh-fruit finish. A couple should count on spending upward of $55 for a full meal with beer or saké, or about $35 for a moderate selection and saké at the sushi bar.

Sieben's River North Brewery

436 W. Ontario St.
787-7313
AMERICAN
*Open Mon.-Thurs. 11 a.m.-10 p.m., Fri.-Sat. 11 a.m.-11 p.m., Sun. noon-10 p.m.
Cards: AE, MC, V.*

9/20

This is a go-for-the-gusto, fire-up-the-*gemütlichkeit* kind of place that, on occasion—Friday nights, for example—is completely out of control, which is exactly the way a beer hall should be when things are really hopping. The eating and drinking sprawl over two levels. The lower level is pure beer hall, with original cobblestone flooring and long, wooden tables and benches where diners and drinkers go elbow to elbow in true beer-hall style. Upstairs, tables flow from either side of the large bar; smack in the center of the room are the gleaming copper and brass brew kettles. Real beer—Münchner, Pilsener, Dortmunder, Porter, Bock—comes out of those tanks at one time or another, and it's fresh and good. So is the food—sometimes. Stick with basic beer-hall grub like hamburgers, Bratwurst, sandwiches, chili and onion loaf. The kitchen doesn't do as well with "advanced cooking," so chicken is overcooked, pork chops are overseasoned, and steaks are cooked too much or too little. The Friday night fish fry is good or bad, depending on who's doing the frying. Desserts are overpriced and mundane. No reservations are taken, so be prepared on a weekend night to drink a lot of beer while you wait for a table. Dinner for two, with a stein of beer each, can range anywhere from $20 to $45.

Phil Smidt & Son

1205 N. Calumet Ave.,
Hammond, IN
(219) 659-0025
SEAFOOD
*Open Mon.-Thurs. 11:15 a.m.-9:30 p.m., Fri.-Sat. 11:15 a.m.-10:30 p.m.
All major cards.*

11/20

This place has grown mightily since its humble beginnings in 1910 as a bar and seafood grill. Today there are seven separate dining rooms that hold a total of 450 people, and on any given weekend evening there could be a wait for a table. What lures so many? Lake perch and frogs' legs—all you can eat, if you wish—are the two most popular menu attractions. Frogs' legs come either sautéed or fried, and the flesh is tender and delicate with a sweet, pleasant flavor much like that of young chicken. Lake perch comes whole in butter, boned in butter or boned sans butter. Any way you go, it's good eating—the pan-fried filets firm and full of good flavor. All is not fish or frogs' legs, however. There's decent fried chicken, shrimp, lobster tails and three cuts of beef. Entrées are preceded by bowls filled with potato salad, cottage cheese, coleslaw, beets and kidney beans. It's doubtful that you will leave feeling hungry. There's a fine selection of homemade pies, the best of which is the gooseberry when it's available. About $20 per person for dinner, with wine.

Sole Mio

917 W. Armitage Ave.
477-5858
ITALIAN
Open Mon.-Thurs. & Sun.
5 p.m.-11 p.m., Fri.-Sat.
5 p.m.-midnight.
All major cards.

The decor is fresh and simple, much in keeping with the style of a true trattoria. In the front, as you enter, is the main dining room with a ten-seat bar. A hallway leads to three smaller dining rooms (one for nonsmokers). Dropping down from the high tinned ceilings are parchment-shaded lights; white walls hold photographs of the Italian countryside, and tables are covered with checkered cloths. Back in the kitchen, plenty of creative Italian cooking is going on. Polenta al tegame is an innovative appetizer, the polenta pan-fried and paired with grappa-marinated prunes, an inspired touch that transforms simple cornmeal into something sensational. Bresaola di cervo (salt-cured venison) is served paper thin. The meat, rosy pink in color and anointed with olive oil, has a mild, pleasant taste that defies association with venison prepared any other way. Grilled mozzarella is perfectly taste matched with spinach and a grilled tomato half. Pizzas are outstanding; we particularly like the roast garlic, grilled onion, Parmesan béchamel and pancetta number, a dazzling harmonization of tastes. Pasta .choices are inviting, too: black pasta with tender rings of squid in a fresh tomato sauce, rigatoni with veal meatballs and sautéed escarole, spinach pappardelle laced and graced with cream, prosciutto, garlic and zest of lemon. Entrées are not as interesting as the appetizers, pizzas and pastas, but daily fish specials can be exciting. Grilled sea bass in a silky pimiento sauce is a rousing dish, as are the grilled sea scallops. Desserts not to be missed are the tiramisu, which will lift you on high, and the fresh strawberries glazed with simple syrup and balsamic vinegar. If those two don't get you, the sinfully rich gelati will. About $35 a person with wine.

Song Huong

5424 N. Broadway
271-6702
VIETNAMESE
Open Mon. & Wed.-Thurs.
11 a.m.-10 p.m., Fri.-Sun.
11 a.m.-11 p.m.
Cards: MC, V, Discover.

11/20

Named after the "perfume river" that flows through the heart of Vietnam, Song Huong is a two-room storefront with grass-cloth and pseudo-red-brick walls, parquet floors, glass-topped linen-decked tables and generous scatterings of greenery that raise the decor several notches above the ordinary. The food, too, is above the ordinary. More than 100 items grace the menu, and the ones we've sampled range from acceptable to first-rate examples of what Craig Claiborne once called the subtlest and most sophisticated cuisine in Southeast Asia. Crisp, chewy egg crêpes folded around whole shrimp and bean sprouts, served with lettuce, cilantro and a piquant, sweet dunking sauce, is an interesting opener. So is Viet coleslaw—a dozen steamed shrimp on a bed of delicately pungent, lightly pickled cabbage—and rolls of pork-stuffed rice paper topped with Vietnamese pâté, a kind of mild bologna. Herb-simmered duck soup in a rich cilantro-scallion broth full of eggy wheat noodles is a winner. But nam vang, a smoky brew of liver, heart and pork in a bowl of chewy rice noodles, doesn't lag far behind. We can also recommend the sour catfish casserole, a bubbling cauldron of catfish steaks simmered with bean sprouts, tomato, celery, pineapple, cilantro and lime. But skip the venison curry—the meat is tough and indistinguishable from beef, and the peanut-sprinkled coconut cream sauce is a bit too heavy-handed. Opt instead for lime beef, strips marinated ceviche-like in lime juice, or succulent roast duck with soy and black-bean sauce. Curried frog, eel with lemon grass, stuffed crab and fried quail are other tempting possibilities. Desserts are typical: "Tripple Crown Sweetie" (sic) turned out to be a tall glass layered with sweet red beans, mung beans and coconut cream, studded with chunks of ice and served with a straw. A better bet might be steamed banana with coconut milk and tapioca. Vietnamese coffee is a cross-cultural ritual—dark French-roast café filtre is allowed to drip into sugar-laden condensed milk, stirred and poured over ice cubes in a tall glass. No wine or beer is served, but corkscrews and glasses are cheerfully provided for those who bring their own. About $32 will cover dinner for two, sans wine or beer.

Spiaggia

980 N. Michigan Ave.
280-2750
ITALIC *ITALIAN*
Open Mon.-Thurs.
11:30 a.m.-2:30 p.m. &
5:30 p.m.-9:30 p.m.,
Fri.-Sat. 11:30 a.m.-
2:30 p.m. & 5:30 p.m.-
10:30 p.m.
All major cards.

Spiaggia translates from the Italian as "beach," and the view of Oak Street Beach and the lake from this multilevel, glamorous and not-inexpensive casa di alta cucina is splendid. The food is not always as splendid as the view, however—chef Anthony Mantuano sometimes bites off more than he can chew by concocting elaborate, extremely complex dishes. Once the Parmesan has settled, though, and if you choose carefully, you will experience some of the most interesting and innovative Italian cooking in this part of the country. Pizzas, baked in a wood-burning oven, are topped with all that is trendy on pizzas (duck sausage, goat cheese, sun-dried tomatoes, pesto), and all are excellent. Pasta creations are no less status-conscious, like the butterfly-shaped farfalle, tinted with tomato, which float in a light cream sauce with asparagus and snow peas. A trio of spinach, tomato and egg pastas married to cream, walnuts, mozzarella, Romano, provolone and Gorgonzola cheeses is a flavor-busy dish that suffers from too many ingredients. And so it goes with daily pasta specials that are even more complex. We don't know how the kitchen keeps it all straight. If it swims, flies or hangs around the farm or fields, it's on the menu: oven-roasted breast of duck, grilled veal chop with fresh sage, grilled fish, lamb, calves' liver with onions and fresh sage on grilled polenta and so on. Grilled sirloin anointed with olive oil and lemon is beef at its simple best. Salads are creations and a half. For example, insalata Spiaggia is a combination of mixed greens, quail eggs, enoki mushrooms and duck cracklings glossed with olive oil and balsamic vinegar. This is Italian food that goes above and beyond the ordinary. Spiaggia should get a Best Desserts in an Italian Restaurant in Chicago award—outstanding tiramisu, a supernal whole poached pear with zabaglione and chocolate, and marvelously rich gelati to mention a few. Dinner for two, with wine, will run about $120.

Standard India Restaurant

871 N. Rush St.
943-1050
INDIAN
*Open daily 11:30 a.m.-
3 p.m. & 5 p.m.-10 p.m.
All major cards.*

12/20

We've never quite known how to take the name—standard of Indian food? standard Indian food?—but the menu offers a generous sampling of the subcontinent's diversity in a setting that's part Arabian nights and part pure carny. Octagonal mirrors in gilt frames, gold-spattered wallpaper, burgundy-red drapes, velveteen chairs and scoop-backed banquettes set the mood for excellent murgh akbari, a spicy cream-based chicken curry; a complex medley of coconut, chili and garlic that gives character to Goanese fish curry; and gosht vindaloo, a lemony-sharp lamb-and-potato curry. Vegetarians may feast on mutter paneer, ricotta or cottage cheese that is strained, shaped into balls and braised with fresh peas; dhal makhani, creamed lentils; or aloo gobi, sautéed cauliflower and potatoes. Chicken tikka and lamb shish kebab surpass the tandoori chicken, which has lacked the properly incarnadine surface, dry and chewy, that should cover a moistly tender interior. Several of the biryanis, dishes of gently fried saffron-flecked rice, have few peers in the city, and the customary Indian breads—naan, roti and poori—arrive with the oven's glow still on them. Cold rice pudding doesn't sound enticing, but garnish it with almonds and pistachios and it becomes kheer, our favorite dessert here (after the homemade mango ice cream, that is). Sweet or salted lassi, a yogurt drink, and spiced masala tea make excellent nonalcoholic alternatives to classy Indian beer. Two people will spend about $45 for dinner and drinks.

Steven B's

817 University Pl.,
Evanston
864-3280
ITALIAN/CALIFORNIA
*Open Mon.-Thurs. 11 a.m.-
3 p.m. & 5:30 p.m.-10 p.m.,
Fri.- Sat. 11 a.m.-3 p.m. &
5:30 p.m.- 11 p.m., Sun.
5 p.m.-9:30 p.m.
All major cards.*

Suburbia may offer greater chic and higher tabs, but on a cost-efficient basis, Steven B's stands by itself. Pasta (fresh, of course) has a toothy give and silken texture in all its forms—traditional spaghetti with marinara, linguine primavera redolent of tangy romano, elegant spinach fettuccine seconding poached salmon with basil cream sauce, or romano fettuccine giving a robust boost to veal piccante. Serviceable salads take a back seat to vegetable accompaniments. A seasonal medley of zucchini, new red potatoes, broccoli florets and carrot nuggets does the honors for game specials (venison or pheasant), filet mignon Vesuvio, trout stuffed with a slight and moist salmon mousse, and a variety of other Italian and nouveau-California entrées. Desserts, alas, no longer exhibit the variety that once sustained us to the unbitter end. Now the dismal cheesecake, cannoli, spumoni and one daily special make abstinence, or just cappuccino, as easy on the stomach as the conscience. Well-selected wines at reasonable prices, pleasantly efficient service and stylish piano music from an upstairs alcove help offset such drawbacks as a wall of noise and drifting smoke on weekend nights. Dinner with wine will set a couple back about $60.

La Strada

151 N. Michigan Ave.
565-2200
ITALIAN
Open Mon.-Thurs.
11:30 a.m.-2:30 p.m. &
5 p.m.-10 p.m., Fri.
11:30 a.m.-2:30 p.m. &
5 p.m.-11 p.m., Sat. 5 p.m.-
11 p.m.
All major cards.

Despite the startling salmon walls and theater-heavy drapery, despite the ornate brass espresso machine that's reminiscent of a puffed-out majordomo, despite picturesque landscapes and dewy-eyed signorinas in gilt frames, La Strada takes its food and wine seriously. A microcosm of Chicago's well-heeled middle and upper classes, padded out by business people and conventioneers, crowds the plush banquettes and linen-napped tables almost every day. Signore Alberto Brondi, the maître d', leads patrons through the intricacies of Italian wines, weighing the merits of a Brunello di Montalcino against a San Giovese di Romagna or one of Antinori's highly acclaimed Tignanellos. Most of the dishes hew to the standards: pastas with wild mushrooms or shellfish, either split as appetizers or as secondi piatti; any number of veal preparations, from piccata to saltimbocca Romano; a wonderful pollo scarpariello, the bone-in chicken chunks musky with garlic and rosemary. Some, however, offer a modicum of novelty: involtine di melanzana, a layering of eggplant, mozzarella and egg; bresaola, air-dried, aromatic beef; a daily fish, perhaps sea bass surrounded by mussels, then boned and served with its wine-intensified natural juices. Desserts are iffy. Almond cheesecake has risen above its siblings, but the strawberries with balsamic vinegar usually steal the show. A couple will have to shell out about $80 to do things right.

StreetSide Restaurant and Bar

(1 First National Plaza),
Clark St. & Monroe St.
346-4700
AMERICAN
Open Mon.-Thurs. 11 a.m.-
3 p.m. & 5 p.m.-10 p.m.,
Fri. 11 a.m.-3 p.m. &
5 p.m.-11 p.m., Sat. 5 p.m.-
11 p.m.
All major cards.

A bronze-and-glass wine cupboard greets you at the entrance. Inside, opulence vies with high-tech glitz: Rich brown mahogany trim and somber carpeting are offset by turquoise and purple neon lines snaking around the walls. Floor-to-ceiling windows allow you to gaze at the plaza fountain or watch the passing parade on Clark and Monroe streets. Better yet, pay attention to the fine dishes from the seasonally changing menu. Creamy-smooth crab bisque laced with sherry is a delicious starter; you can also try that same bisque in the three-soup sampler, which may include a wonderful cream of broccoli and a chunky gazpacho. The sampler plate of appetizers is another option for grazing types. We love the zucchini pancakes topped with American caviars and crème fraîche, and we adore the spicy meat-and-cheese-stuffed won tons and peppery, piquant seafood sausage. Broiled rack of lamb, eight pink-in-the-center chops on a bed of homemade lemon-rosemary fettuccine, is first-rate, as is Louisiana catfish, which is seasoned with Cajun spices, pan-fried, topped with strips of Smithfield ham and served in a pool of silky black-pepper cream. Make sure to accompany your meal with a side order of excellent, garlicky-buttery string beans. Desserts, alas, don't measure up: Overly sweet white-chocolate cheesecake runs second to banana-rice pudding, which is full of flavor but too soupy. Except for a few sparklers, the wine list sticks to reasonably priced and well-selected American vintages. With wine, dinner for two will be $70 or so.

Michael Stuart's
140 S. Wells St.
558-4700
FRENCH
Open Mon.-Fri.
11:30 a.m.-10 p.m., Sat.
6 p.m.-10 p.m.
All major cards.

12/20

Chef Dominique Fortin, formerly of Ciel Bleu, rules the roost here, and every day he produces a new menu, which usually favors fish and poultry and pork over beef. Fortin leans more toward classic than nouvelle cuisine, as seen in such dishes as grilled pork with couscous, sturgeon with caviar butter and free-range chicken with a vegetable medley, all done simply and generally dressed with natural juices instead of complex reduction sauces. Unfortunately, not everything measures up to the menu descriptions, often because of overcooking; pork, for example, has a seared crust, and a composed salad holds tough sautéed calves' liver (besides, bitter curly endive isn't a good match with liver). Entrées come with a house salad, which bears a hefty $1.50 surcharge for blue cheese dressing. And when there's no hint of blue cheese *in* the salad, the surcharge moves from insult into injury. The once-splendid desserts are now perfunctory. The chic interior—circular brass fixtures against a green ceiling, shades of rose and gray framed by dark-wood moldings—contrasts pleasantly with the dingy South Loop streets and El tracks just outside. A selective list of fairly priced wines, mainly from France and California, and professional service complement the handsome setting. Two will spend about $100 for dinner with wine.

Su Casa
49 E. Ontario St.
943-4041
MEXICAN
Open Mon.-Fri. 11:30 a.m.-
12:30 a.m., Sat. 5 p.m.-
12:30 a.m.
All major cards.

12/20

Su Casa is about as Mexican-looking as it gets (at least in Chicago), with white brick walls, Mexican tile-topped tables, massive dark-wood ranchero chairs, carved wood statues and Mexican artifacts in abundance. You've seen it all before. The tables' proximity to one another adds to the convivial atmosphere, which grows a few decibels louder when the strolling guitarist makes his appearance. This is a Mexican restaurant that people either love or hate. We happen to love it—not to death, for there are some shortcomings, especially when the kitchen is set on the fast spin cycle. But for consistently good Mexican food, it's a safe choice. The guacamole is fresh, nicely textured and well seasoned. Whole red snapper is a swimmer to catch when it's running on the daily-specials list. Chalupa compuesta is a multitextural affair that piles pieces of tender white chicken, cheese, shredded lettuce, avocado and sour cream atop a crisp tostada. The chili is some of the best around, thick with shredded beef and a rich, flavorful sauce that's spicy, spicy hot. Mexican basics, such as steak ranchero, shrimp touched with garlic, chile rellenos and chimichangas, fill out the menu. The best dessert in the house is the sopapilla— the crisp version (buñuelo) not the puffed-up one—which is topped with honey and cinnamon. About $20 a person, with a good Mexican beer.

Sulo

3510 W. Irving Park Rd.
463-9875
PHILIPPINE
Open Sun.-Tues. & Thurs.
11:30 a.m.-8 p.m., Fri.-Sat.
11:30 a.m.-9 p.m.
All major cards.

11/20

There are a number of Chinese dishes on the menu of this spanking-clean, homey little storefront, but we recommend that you stick to the Filipino fare, an odd pastiche of Spanish and indigenous island food. Lumpiang sariwa might serve as a good beginning: an oversized, egg-rich pancake folded around crunchy string beans, shredded carrots and water chestnuts. Request patis, fermented fish juice similar to Vietnamese nuoc man; or bagoong, fermented shrimp paste, condiments that add a briny, faintly decadent, flavor to the food. Though good by itself, kare kare—chewy, gelatinous oxtails simmered in a robust peanut sauce with green beans and eggplant—benefits from an added touch of bagoong. Chicken and pork adobo, a tangy, garlic-scented stew of meat, tomatoes, potatoes and red pepper, is eminently appealing. Pickled pork and pork ear, the latter cartilaginously crunchy, may be something of an acquired taste for most people, though we find ourselves drawn to it on occasion. Desserts run to ice cream, flan or canned lychees. A combination of these, plus whatever is sweet and sticky in the kitchen, including beans, is called halo-halo—layers of everything served in a tall glass with crushed ice, to be stirred prior to ingestion. Kids love it. No wine or beer is served, but you may bring your own. About $25 should cover a dinner for two.

Superior Street Cafe

311 W. Superior St.
787-4160
AMERICAN
Open Mon.-Fri. 7 a.m.-
10:30 a.m. & 11:30 a.m.-
3:30 p.m., Tues.-Thurs.
5:30 p.m.-9 p.m., Fri.-Sat.
5:30 p.m.-10:30 p.m.
Cards: AE, MC, V.

12/20

This place is loaded with '80s chic—slate blue soldered onto earthtones, the dull ocher of exposed brick, blond bentwood chairs, unfinished wooden pillars leading up to track lighting and bare wood beams. The woven rug in blue, off-white and brown and the massive pottery platters hint at the Southwest. Add the bar, a chopped-off oblong, plus huge circular mirrors that reflect the crazy quilt of the ensemble back into the room, and the result is a trendy but enjoyable environment for a snack or a meal.

Fish gets the nod, though the menu lists a veal chop, Cornish hen, chicken and rib steak. Grilled sea scallops start the meal off on a high note, seared, smoky chunks that become sweet and creamy as one chews. On one visit, the puff pastries as delicate as a spring breeze enfolded ordinary cultivated mushrooms, and not the wild variety promised by the menu (a substitution the waiter should have mentioned). Grilled roasted veal salad should be shared or eaten as a light entrée, the abundant veal tender and well complemented by a tartly pungent dressing. A good house salad precedes and is included in the price of the regular entrées, which come with vegetables and either excellent roasted potatoes or cakes of white and wild rice. Grilled calamari steak once made a magnificent special, but the halibut wasn't far behind. The ubiquitous rib-eye steak, grilled chicken and veal chop keep salmon and whitefish company, as do three pasta dishes and a quintet of sandwiches. Desserts—chocolate-mousse pie and pumpkin cheesecake—deserve better presentations than they receive, an intentionally plain service that, we were told, is intended to keep the restaurant from appearing too fancified. There's a small but well-chosen wine list. A takeout section offers sandwiches, homemade breads, cake and ice cream in and out of shakes, malts and sundaes. About $65 for dinner for two, with wine.

Tap & Growler

901 W. Jackson Blvd.
829-4141
AMERICAN
Open Mon.-Thurs. 11 a.m.-
10 p.m., Fri. 11 a.m.-
11 p.m., Sat. 3 p.m.-
11 p.m.
Cards: AE, MC, V.

10/20

The Tap & Growler is a recent entry in the great suds race going on throughout the city. Brew pubs, they're called, and a brew pub should have a good-size bar, which this one does. It also has an open kitchen and five brew tanks tucked behind a wall of glass. The 100-seat dining room has both booths and red-topped bistro tables with bentwood chairs. Period lighting fixtures adorn the high, wood-beam ceilings. The floors are marble; the walls are ceramic tile. And in the fashion of taverns where good drink is dispensed, good food is dispensed, too. Actually, some is good, and some is so-so. Appetizers lean heavily toward seafood and dip mightily into the batter and fritter families. Beer-batter shrimp is just fine, the shrimp clean-tasting and crunchy under a light, pleasant-tasting batter. Cheese fritters the size of golf balls are filled with a mix of cheddar, mozzarella and blue cheese and served with a terrific roasted tomato sauce on the side. Soups are excellent, with a different choice each day of the week; the kale soup is the best of the lot. Fish dishes run fair to good, as do such other entrées as meatloaf and grilled flank steak, but the best bets are in the B & B category: burgers and Bratwursts. Desserts to die for are the Dutch apple pie and the carrot cake. Beers to cry for are Lairdog and Eagen's Irish Ale. About $18 per person, with a stein or two of beer.

Tehran Restaurant

6619 N. Clark St.
338-0677
PERSIAN
Open Mon.-Thurs. noon-
11 p.m., Fri.-Sat. noon-
midnight, Sun. noon-
midnight.
No cards.

11/20

One man's exotic ethnic cuisine is another man's home cooking; that the cooking may leave the home to camp out in an uptown storefront makes little difference. Families bring their children (in our experience, generally well behaved), single men stop in for a meal after work, couples or pairs of couples come here on the way to a movie. Hand-painted leather hangings and hammered metalware alternate on plastery white walls with colorful lithographs of the *Rubaiyat.* The plastic table coverings always bear live flowers, a reminder of the Persian saying, "If a man have two loaves of bread, let him sell one and buy a flower." The food here is good, copious and cheap. Add soup, salad or a serving of cheese and vegetables, rice pudding and tea or coffee to an entrée, and the tab will be under $7. A brace of grilled quail justifies the top-price splurge; the birds are moist and mildly pungent under their grill marks. Khoresht ghemeh happily weds beef with yellow split peas and eggplant, and the ubiquitous Middle Eastern vine leaves, dolma in this incarnation, make a tender swaddling for rice, chopped beef and more yellow split peas. Cheloukabab, a pairing of a charbroiled filet mignon with a ground lamb-and-beef combination, should satisfy inveterate carnivores. Persian tea and robust Turkish coffee end the proceedings on a traditional note. Patrons bring their own wine or beer, so a meal for two fritters away a mere $15, plus the cost of the booze.

Three Happiness Restaurant

209 W. Cermak Rd.
842-1964
CHINESE
Open daily 9 a.m.-2 a.m.
All major cards.

2130 E. Wentworth Ave.
791-1228
Open Mon.-Thurs.
10 a.m.-midnight, Fri.-
Sat. 10 a.m.-1 a.m.,
Sun. 10 a.m.-10 p.m.
All major cards.

"Of the making of dim sum," it is wisely said, "there is no end." Thank goodness. We have tried it in Vancouver, B.C., and Sydney, Australia, and a few dozen cities in between, and we're as crazy for these delicacies now as when we first tried them in New York several decades back. Three Happiness has two locations (down from three), both of which offer approximately the same variety and quality of dim sum from the traditional rolling carts. We favor the Wentworth address because its greater size means more elbow room and quicker seating. Several caveats apply: Arrive after 10 a.m. on weekends and the wait will run from twenty minutes up; corner tables tend to be ignored despite frantically waved hands; and depending on the waitress, explanations of the more arcane goodies may veer from clear and accurate to muddled.

Dim sum, often and inappropriately called tea pastries, are snacks originally offered to visitors in much the same way Westerners trot out coffee and cake for a guest. They may be ordered from a menu in restaurants but are more fun selected from carts, which make a circuit of the dining room, returning to the kitchen to be replenished. At Three Happiness, we're particularly fond of torpedo-shape dumplings stuffed with sweet pork and taro and fried to a crisp;

cartilaginously challenging braised duck feet; har gow, shrimp steamed in translucent wheat starch wrappers; puffy bao buns filled with barbecued pork; shu mai, like miniature dough baskets filled with savory minced pork and steamed; and slabs of sticky-sweet turnip dumplings, best when dipped in an incandescent chili paste. As an alternative to choosing strictly from the cart, there's a brief menu of larger dishes. Mixed seafood with broad rice noodles will keep the table happy in the lulls between carts, as long as no one objects to octopus and braised sea cucumber along with shrimp. Desserts would be a letdown if we didn't stuff ourselves beyond such frivolity. For those who require them, an assortment of custards, coconut puddings and tricolored gelatins circulates along with the real food. A feast with beer will cause two people to deplete their savings by $20 to $25.

Thunderbird Bar and Grill
1960 N. Racine St.
525-1380
SOUTHWESTERN
Open daily 11 a.m.-2 a.m.
Cards: AE, MC, V.

11/20

From its looks and its location one might not guess that the Thunderbird would host designer leather as often as blue jeans, or that draft Watneys and swordfish ceviche would give Dos Equis and guacamole a good run for the money. There's a crowded, TV-blasting bar that segues to a hall-like room whose neon beer signs plaster sheets of hectic red, dirty white and cool blue on raucous green and salmon-pink walls; and it's located in a grimy stretch of factory sites in the throes of gentrification. Still, so it goes, as Vonnegut noted, in this typical Chicago hybrid, where Tex-Mex meets floor-pounding rock 'n' roll seven days and nights of the week. Most of the food's good, though the Southwestern accent tends to slip: Muffalatta or croissant sandwiches creep in alongside buttery-unctuous queso fundito and floury tortillas. Green chile gives the chicken stock oomph in the tortilla soup, and toasted tortilla shreds contribute a sweet crunchiness. In fajitas, smoky chicken and firm, briny shrimp rise above the only adequate beef. "The Thunderbird" is a pair of surprisingly satisfying grilled-chicken filets topped by Monterey jack, cheddar, green onions and tomato. Sides of zucchini and yellow squash, as well as rice and beans, accompany all main courses. Sprightly red and green salsas and tangy guacamole make good preludes to a meal and keep beer or margaritas company after 10:30 p.m., when mirrored panels rise at one end of the room and a megadecibel disco comes into being like a jackhammer. Dinner with beer or wine will set a couple back about $45.

Tijuana Yacht Club

516 N. Clark St.
321-1160
MEXICAN/SOUTHWESTERN
Open Mon.-Fri. 5 p.m.-
11 p.m., Sat. 5 p.m.-
midnight, Sun. 5 p.m.-
10 p.m. (longer hours in
the Surf Room).
Cards: AE, MC, V.

12/20

Think about the wildest, craziest restaurant you've ever been to. Now add 100 pounds of wacky, 100 quarts of outrageous and 100 gallons of margarita-driven fun. Stir up the whole mess, add a ton of people, and you get Tijuana Yacht Club. The outside of the building was purposefully deconstructed to make it look like an abandoned boarding house. The corrugated-metal canopy over the sidewalk is straight from the Pee-Wee Herman school of anxiety-driven architecture. Inside, the decor only gets worse. Old hubcaps hang over the bar, the floor is concrete and on one wall a shark chases a water skier (you have to see it). All this declassé stuff was created on purpose (including the strolling musicians who can't sing a lick) to create... well, something. Novelty, we imagine. The craziest thing about this place is that the food, which is priced lower than a desert-sliding snake, is actually very good. Before there was Mexican food, though, there was the margarita, and at TYC they come by the mug, half liter or full liter (including the "margarita lite"). With the margarita comes about a half bushel of tortilla chips.

Some of the best dishes are the exceptionally good fajitas—chicken or beef—which weigh in at a full pound; the clean, crisp Gulf shrimp sautéed in lime butter; the guacamole salad, which is a meal in itself; and the Caesar, another meal-size salad. Entrées come with excellent borracho beans, pico de gallo (like salsa), guacamole and flour tortillas. Desserts are typical of this style of restaurant—terrible. Instead, have a strawberry margarita for dessert, then float next door to the Surf Bar, where the dancing (the deejay is perched in the back of a rusty pickup truck) and the footloose spirit are even more frenetic. The surf is always up at TYC. Dinner for two, with margaritas or Mexican beers, will run about $42.

Le Titi de Paris

1015 W. Dundee Rd.,
Arlington Heights
506-0222
FRENCH
Open Tues.-Fri. 11:30 a.m.-
2:30 p.m. & 5 p.m.-
10 p.m., Sat. 5:30 p.m.-
10:30 p.m.
All major cards.

Simple, assured elegance (worlds apart from those insistent stepsisters, kitsch and glitz) isn't common once one ventures beyond the Loop or its northeasterly Lake Shore Drive extensions. Le Titi de Paris's reincarnation in Arlington Heights, then, has cheered a goodly contingent of suburbanites and city dwellers alike. Salmon mousseline, lobster bisque, roast pigeon and thyme-scented lamb fare well in a decor whose subdued gray and mauve is brightened by a crystal-drop chandelier and mirrored walls and whose seating soothes the body. The restaurant's move from Palatine seems to have made Pierre Pollin's kitchen more consistent, or consistently good, the occasional overcooking happily a thing of the past. Such combinations as pearlescent striped bass beside dark-pink salmon, napped by Nantua and saffron sauces, or basil-accented Maine lobster paired with gulf shrimp, characterize the "Poissons" side of the menu. Under "Viandes," one finds cassis-stroked duck breast, faintly pink at the center, complemented by a confit of the leg; thyme and mustard-ginger sauce lending their fragrance to rack of lamb; and sweetbreads given a savory dose of Sauternes. Starters range from garlicky snails with bell peppers and a terrine of sweetbreads and wild mushrooms to sevruga, osetra or beluga caviar from Petrossian. An assiette assortie offers a sampling of homemade sorbets, chocolate truffles and pastries for dessert, but seasonally determined fruit soufflés, served for two, make a more festive conclusion. Many wines, predominantly French, may be ordered by the glass or half bottle. Service manages to be concerned and efficient without sliding into fussiness. Dinner for two, with a modest wine, will be about $100.

Topo Gigio

1437 N. Wells St.
266-9355
ITALIAN
*Open Mon.-Sat. 5 p.m.-
11 p.m.
Cards: MC, V.*

Those of us old enough will certainly remember Topo Gigio, the likable little Italian mouse that was a regular on *The Ed Sullivan Show*. (Topo Gigio translates from the Italian as "gray mouse.") The really big show at Topo Gigio is the food, but in a simple sort of way the ambience plays a nice supporting role: hardwood floors, butcher paper over the tablecloths, shelves around the room filled with Italian food-à-brac, and a table count that doesn't exceed sixteen, which creates an air of coziness that makes this little gray mouse all the more likable. More than likable is the food—this is real Italian cooking cooked by real Italians. Start with the bruschetta, a thick slice of grilled Italian bread rubbed with garlic, drizzled with oil, topped with fresh tomato and flecked with strips of fresh basil—it's simply delicious. No less exciting is the cozze alla marinara: Served in a large skillet, the steamed-open mussels, plump in their shells, ride atop a thick, zesty marinara sauce. Pasta dishes are magnificently crafted. Rigatoni al filo di fumo combines rigatoni pasta with a spicy tomato sauce, pancetta, pecorino cheese, fresh basil and fresh mozzarella. Another tongue tantalizer, fusilli ai quattro formaggi, brings together blue cheese, Swiss cheese, Parmesan and mascarpone with heavy cream and lays it lovingly on fusilli pasta. Roasted chicken with fresh rosemary, grilled chicken breasts, veal with eggplant and fresh fish specials are always eminently worthy entrées. Desserts, unfortunately, pale in comparison; better to finish your meal with fresh fruit and espresso. Expect to put forth about $50 for dinner for two, with wine.

> *Remember to phone ahead to reserve your table or your room and please, if you cannot honor your reservation, be courteous and let the restaurant or the hotel know.*

106

Toulouse

51 W. Division St.
944-2606
FRENCH
Open Mon.-Thurs.
5:30 p.m.-10:30 p.m., Fri.-
Sat. 5:30 p.m.- 11:30 p.m.
All major cards.

Still one of the city's top romantic spots, Toulouse is a great place for cozying up in dimly lit banquettes along the walls or opposite the piano bar. And the food makes cozying fun—a romantic dinner, after all, should be worth eating. And if music is the food of love, the ragtime, jazz and golden oldies emanating from the piano are stiff competition for Toulouse's fare. The small menu is augmented by daily specials, and the ingredients are always utterly fresh. Chef Richard Stewart's preparations tend toward the simple and the classic. Delicate crab cakes with creamy mustard sauce, lightly steamed asparagus and an assortment of pâtés are typical, and excellent, openers. Moist and meaty roast squab in its natural juices on a bed of cabbage is flawless; and grilled Norwegian salmon, seconded by creamy eggplant flan and garnished with artichokes, olives and peppers, is the best we've had in some time. We can also vouch for the veal, particularly the sautéed steak with wild-mushroom ravioli in a pool of chive-scented cream sauce. A daily low-sodium/low-cholesterol special—perhaps grilled swordfish made zesty with lemon sauce—is available for those on special diets. The flaky apple tart, rich, smooth crème brûlée and dark, intense chocolate feuilleté are all memorable. The small but choice wine list includes several reasonably priced selections. Coffee is first-rate. A romantic dinner for two, with wine, will set a couple back about $85.

La Tour

(Park Hyatt Hotel),
800 N. Michigan Ave.
280-2230
FRENCH
Open Mon.-Fri. 6:30 a.m.-
10:30 a.m. & 6 p.m.-
10:30 p.m., Sat. 7 a.m.-
10:30 a.m. & 6 p.m.-
10:30 p.m., Sun. 7 a.m.-
10:30 a.m., 11:a.m.-
2:30 p.m. & 6 p.m.-
10:30 p.m.
All major cards.

One of the handsomest hotel dining rooms in the city, La Tour looks out onto Water Tower Square through two-story-high street-level windows. It's especially romantic in winter, when thousands of shimmering lights form a festive backdrop to the bustling world outside. For the ultimate in sybaritic indulgence, begin your meal in the lobby, at the caviar bar, where dollops of beluga, sevruga and osetra on miniblinis can be washed down with lemon- or pepper-spiked vodka—properly iced, of course. Then enter the elegantly appointed room. Chef Jeff Jackson's menu changes seasonally, but his approach remains the same: an imaginative, often-daring juxtaposition of textures and flavors. Sometimes he succeeds splendidly: Witness the memorable salad of rabbit and sweetbreads bathed in a white-truffle-flecked Champagne sauce. Sometimes the results are more intriguing and provocative than truly satisfying, as with the sea urchins bedded on homemade noodles and crowned with beluga caviar. Chicken and foie gras nestled in a brioche, accompanied by a millefeuille of potatoes and morels, was a winner on one occasion, but roast breast of mallard rouennaise suffered from too lengthy a stint on the fire. Desserts can sometimes fall short, but when hot apple charlotte appears on the cart, go for it. Four-course prix-fixe dinners ($47 without wine and $75 with) are available.

Generally excellent service is marred by the occasional incongruous lapse. But the check never lapses: Dinner with wine will set two of you back a sobering $160.

Trattoria Bellavia

3811 N. Harlem Ave.
286-5568
ITALIAN
Open Mon.-Thurs.
4:30 p.m.-11 p.m., Fri.-Sat.
4:30 p.m.-midnight.
Cards: AE, MC, V.

Trattoria Bellavia, a neat and tidy restaurant with about eighteen cloth-covered tables, knows what it is. That it calls itself a trattoria as opposed to the more lofty-sounding ristorante says something about the honesty of the food and the friendliness of the family that cooks and serves it. Start with panzarotti. A member of the calzone family (it's fried instead of baked), this cheese-and-tomato-stuffed creation is most gratifying. As openers, calamari fritti (fried squid) and mussels marinara are no less appealing. The menu is a textbook study when it comes to pasta choices: Cheese-filled ravioli covered with a light and flavorful tomato sauce are delicate and delectable. Small rolled dumplings called cavatelli are chewy little jewels glossed with a captivating red sauce. Linguine with red or white sauce is a standout. Seafood specials are creative and well crafted. And when osso buco is on the daily-specials list, don't miss it—the veal shanks are meaty, tender and suffused with flavor from the light sauce in which they are swathed. Veal is prepared eight ways, and those we've sampled have always been excellent, as well as reasonably priced. Desserts, as it goes with a lot of Italian restaurants, are limited, but the cannoli is one of the best around. The wine list is basic and brief and all Italian, but who's complaining when the price for a Brugo Gattinara is only $16? About $45 for two, with wine.

Trattoria Gianni

1711 N. Halsted St.
266-1976
ITALIAN
Open Mon.-Sat. 4 p.m.-
11 p.m., Sun. 4 p.m.-
10 p.m.
No cards.

12/20

Still a relative newcomer, Trattoria Gianni came upon the Chicago restaurant scene quietly but in a matter of several weeks exploded like a thousand pounds of firecrackers. It was neat and new and going through some of its growing pains when we first dined here (service crunched down to a slow and low level on an evening when the place was on full spin cycle), this white-tablecloth trattoria redeemed itself mightily on our second visit by serving some of the best real Italian cooking we've had in Chicago. But then we returned a third time and found the cooking considerably less accomplished. Clearly the growing pains haven't stopped—consistency isn't (yet) Trattoria Gianni's strong suit. The Italian owners worked at Trattoria Pizzeria Roma when it first opened, before it got carried away with its success and began slinging food at its customers in a surly, disinterested way.

Calamari fritti can be wonderful eating, the squid rings tender under their light coating. Nutty, mildly sharp, delicate and creamy are the sensations that tread across the taste buds after one bite of the rigatoni with four cheeses—and, as it is said in Rome, the pasta is cooked "just until the bone is out of it." The menu, which changes frequently, is distressingly brief (only four entrées at last count), but when the petti di pollo Francesca or the grilled chicken shows up, we're content. The only veal dish we have encountered was saltimbocca sorrentina, an excellent (and basic) combination of veal topped with a thin slice of prosciutto and mozzarella cheese. The desserts aren't worth the calories, except for the fresh fruit splashed with Sambuca. The woeful wine list needs work and more work. With luck on your side, you could have a terrific meal here, but we can't guarantee it. Dinner for two, with wine, costs about $75.

Trattoria Pizzeria Roma
1557 N. Wells St.
664-7907
ITALIAN
*Open Mon.-Fri. noon-
11 p.m., Sat. 5 p.m.-
11 p.m., Sun. 4 p.m.-
10 p.m. No cards.*

8/20

Why this small, fourteen-table restaurant is so popular is beyond our comprehension. The tables are so close together they should call this place The Elbow Room (only). The coziness would be tolerable by itself. But when you factor in the sometimes-amusing, less-than-cordial, mostly Italian waiters in T-shirts (who make macho while slinging dishes as if they were in a bocci-ball tournament), the sum of the parts just doesn't add up to anything pleasant. If you order, say, three plates—an appetizer, pasta and main course—don't count on much breathing time between courses; eat fast, because there's no turning back. The menu changes frequently, but the chef has an infatuation with certain pastas like rigatoni and spaghetti, which show up under different sauces quite often—not the worst situation if they were good dishes, but they're not. The fried calamari is usually tough; and on our last visit, the suppli al telefono—a golf-ball-size sphere of rice—was small and dry, a pale comparison to the authentic Italian version; the pizzas aren't too bad, provided they aren't burned on the bottom. The menu seldom lists more than four entrées, three of which are usually chicken. The only good dessert was the cannoli, but now that's gone. Cakes, which come in the back door, are not, as the waiter would lead you to believe, "pretty good." This place does serve a great cup of espresso, though. No wine or liquor is served, but you can bring your own wine. About $20 per person for dinner.

Charlie Trotter's
816 W. Armitage Ave.
248-6228
AMERICAN
*Open Mon.-Thurs.
5:30 p.m.-9:30 p.m., Fri.-
Sun. 5:30 p.m.-10 p.m.
All major cards.*

Rumor may, like Cyrano's nose, anticipate a restaurant's arrival and, even after the event, preclude an objective evaluation. Press agents deluge the media with manufactured reputations, type-hype begets apocrypha, and before either public or critic has sampled the reputed wunderkind's food, hosanna overwhelms judgment. Something of the sort happened here, which is a pity—for Charlie Trotter's can, on occasion, rise to its reputation. The successes are typified by a trio of salmon preparations (smoked in-house, mild gravlax and tartare accented by olive); filets of sea bass on a bed of roasted garlic noodles, the whole napped by cashew-ginger butter; and cabbage-wrapped slices of squab breast steamed gently and arranged in a double row flanked by saffron risotto and savory tomato-pepper stew. To these we might add a splendid marquise laden with candied fruit and a tarte tatin enhanced by caramelized pecans and a wisp of ginger. Unfortunately, cheek-and-jowl with these fine efforts have been such failures as an acidic ratatouille in aspic; dry and tasteless frogs' legs; cultivated mushrooms (the menu having promised wild); watery lobster and granular sweetbreads (in a bold salad of arugula, radicchio, mâche and curly endive); and saccharine chocolate mousse. The tarte tatin, good as it was by itself, suffered from an incongruous addition of banana ice cream. Stark wine bins rise ceilingward behind the front room bar and lounge. A less-mannered upstairs dining room looks down on a bar dotted with a group of settee and side chairs; downstairs, dusky, textured silk-lined walls are lit by art deco sconces. The effect is pretty but not warm, just as the service is smooth and knowledgeable without being gracious. A serious wine list weighted toward American bottlings includes 24 champagnes and assorted bubblies, and ten or more wines are always available by the glass. Two people will pay upward of $105 for dinner with wine.

Tucci Benucch

900 N. Michigan Ave.
266-2500
ITALIC
*Open Mon.-Thurs. 11 a.m.-
10 p.m., Fri.-Sat. 11 a.m.-
11 p.m., Sun. noon-9 p.m.
All major cards.*

Tucci Benucch is an Italian restaurant designed to look like an Italian country home that one might find, say, in the hills of Tuscany—at least that's what the designer and Richard Melman, Chicago's famous restaurant impresario, would like you to believe. (If you do believe it, we have a few original Michelangelo paintings to sell for ten bucks a piece...) The restaurant has separations and such to evoke the effect of a multiroom casa di campagna, the chalet ceiling has baskets and stuff hanging from its rafters, the floors are wood, the tables and chairs don't match, the waiters are peasant-garbed... it may be phony, but it's a nice "house" that shows well. The food shows well, too. Pizza is the extra-thin, cracker-style-crust version, with plenty of good taste and flavor combinations: Eggplant, fresh tomato, Italian olives, sun-dried tomatoes, alone or in combination, are quite good. Tuscan bean soup, when available, is a knock-out bowl of zippy zuppa, but the house salad tends to get sogged down in its own dressing. Pasta dishes are formula but fine: fusilli novecento comes with a mighty good and meaty veal shank, the whole affair covered with a light, lively red sauce, and manicotti Melrose is just plain wonderful. Entrée choices are limited; try the roasted chicken with roasted potatoes, which is pleasantly imbued with herbs, oil and a gentle belt of garlic, or skip the entrée list altogether and go for the soup, pizza and pasta. Desserts won't cause you to lose your head and squander precious calories. Dinner for two, with wine, costs about $40.

Uncle Tannous
2626 N. Halsted St.
929-1333
LEBANESE
Open Mon. 5 p.m.-11 p.m.,
Tues.-Thurs. 12:30 p.m.-
11 p.m., Fri.-Sat.
12:30 p.m.-11:30 p.m.,
Sun. 12:30 p.m.-10 p.m.
All major cards.

11/20

A whiff of movietime Middle East—alcoves threaded among white stucco walls, a few fretted brass lamps—provides the setting for better-than-average Lebanese food. To sample a variety, order maza, a colorful parade of saucers laden with the likes of white turnip dyed with beet juice; aromatic black olives; fava beans in a minisea of seasoned oil; hummus and baba ghanouj, smoky dips of chickpea purée and baked eggplant, respectively; dough pockets filled with spiced meats; and the cracked-wheat salad called tabouli. Sea bass and red snapper come hot and glistening from the mesquite grill, accompanied by a small, mint-intense salad. A mixed grill of skewer-broiled minced beef, grilled marinated chicken, and lamb shish kebab makes for a filling meat gorge. Baklava, less cloyingly sweet than is usually the case, or rose-water-scented rice pudding appropriately suit the cardamom-laced coffee prepared to order in the traditional copper pot. Service has been known to flag at times, and communication may be less than clear. A couple will spend about $52 for dinner with a modest bottle of wine.

Le Vichyssois
220 W. Rte. 120,
Lakemoor
(815) 385-8221
FRENCH
Open Wed.-Thurs.
5:30 p.m.-9 p.m., Fri.-Sat.
5:30 p.m.-10 p.m., Sun.
4:30 p.m.-9 p.m.
All major cards.

Bernard Cretier's charming, comfortable auberge about 50 miles from Chicago deserves more respect. Chef Cretier gets his share of publicity and his share of patrons, but few of them really appreciate Cretier's classic approach to French cuisine. The regular menu lists only eleven entrées, but they are dashing examples of all that is holy in the litany of classic French dishes. Such appetizers as duck pâté marinated in brandy and sherry and quail pâté with juniper berries could easily be models after which all pâtés should be fashioned. The vichyssoise (potato-and-leek soup) is silky rich and flavor-accented to perfection, as is the lobster and clam bisque. Fish dishes are simple, straightforward and never overcomplicated. We have found ourselves longing, on more than one occasion, for the memorable bay scallops in puff pastry. Veal loin steak with morel sauce is another simple but scintillating dish. Daily specials to order when available are salmon baked in puff pastry and quail stuffed with goose liver. Dessert selections change frequently and get the same polish and careful preparation as other dishes. Dinner for two, with wine, runs about $75.

Some establishments change their closing times without warning. It is always wise to call ahead.

The Waterfront

16 W. Maple St.
943-7494
SEAFOOD
Open Mon.-Thurs.
11:30 a.m.-midnight,
Fri.-Sat. 11:30 a.m.-
1 a.m., Sun. 11:30 a.m.-
11 p.m.
All major cards.

12/20

You won't mistake the type of restaurant you're in. From stem to stern, it's nautical and nice. Just past a small bar is a separate dining area with booths and tables. A lovely light-oak staircase leads to the second-floor dining room festooned with nautical paraphernalia. The clam chowder boasts a savory, natural-flavored broth, thick with good vegetables and chunks of clams. Steamed lobster carries an extremely fair price tag and comes with steamer clams and corn on the cob. (We prefer our lobster broiled, but that doesn't change our high opinion of the lobster served here.) Sautéed bay scallops are tender little nuggets that have not been subjected to the heat too long. Jumbo Gulf shrimp, sautéed in the shell with a touch of garlic butter and wine, is finger-eating good. Served on Sunday only, the clambake is a feast that starts with a bucket of steamers, sails merrily through chicken and corn on the cob and ends up docked alongside a one-pound Maine lobster. A few steak and chicken dishes are available for nonseafaring types. The only dessert worth mentioning is the chocoholic chocolate cake, a rich, moist, fudgy-tasting affair. The after-theater supper includes a nice and light assortment of seafood dishes. Not many wines to choose from, but all are available by the glass. From $20 to $40 per person, with wine.

The Winnetka Grill

64 Green Bay Rd.,
Winnetka
441-6444
AMERICAN
Open Sun. 5 p.m.-9 p.m.,
Tues.-Fri. 5:30 p.m.-
9 p.m., Sat. 5 p.m.-10 p.m.
All major cards.

The name is misleading—this is an elegant suburban restaurant, not a chophouse, the kind of place where suburbanites gather to plan the next charity ball. On one wall a mural depicts a pale blue sky dotted with clouds; on the other, windows look out onto a parking lot; and in between, floor-to-ceiling drapes form pillars that break up the space. A tiny entrance hall makes waiting for a table tedious. For $19.95 (ten percent less if you order before 6 p.m.) you can choose from a special four-course menu that features a half-dozen appetizers and entrées; a more extensive à la carte selection is also available. Smoky, tangy black-bean soup is one of our favorite starters, as are six sparkling bluepoints topped with dilled, horseradish-spiked sour cream and crowned with a dollop of golden caviar. Other tempting openers include grilled quail beside a small salad of radicchio, watercress and Gorgonzola in a raspberry vinaigrette; and salmon tartare, augmented by fresh dill and capers and served with toast points. Entrées are the likes of grilled jumbo sea scallops sauced with buttery wine heightened by sun-dried tomatoes and bacon; sautéed black sea bass with fresh thyme hollandaise; and loin of New Zealand venison heady with roast garlic, accompanied by shoe-string fried sweet potatoes. Such desserts as flourless chocolate cake and chocolate crêpes have been flawed, but pumpkin cake, raspberry mousse and white-chocolate ice cream have made light and elegant concluding statements at other times. A well-selected list of moderate, mainly American wines is available. Dinner à la carte for two, with wine, will average around $95.

Wrigley Building Restaurant

410 N. Michigan Ave.
944-7600
CONTINENTAL
Open Mon.-Fri. 11:30 a.m-2:30 p.m.

Not long ago this restaurant, which has been around since 1936, underwent a face-lift and added new management and a new menu. But just before we went to press, it closed for dinner, staying open only for lunch, when corporate types take over the spacious booths lining the east and west walls of the main dining room. The future seem shaky here, so we'll withhold a ranking and a review for now, and hope that glory days come once again for this venerable place.

Yoshi's Café

3257 N. Halsted St.
248-6160
FRENCH
Open Tues.-Thurs.
5:30 p.m.-10 p.m., Fri.-Sat.
5:30 p.m.-10:30 p.m., Sun.
5 p.m.-9 p.m.
Cards: AE, MC, V.

To some, the setting and the ambience of this 50-seat restaurant are charming and sophisticated. Others view it as homespun and plain. We say it falls somewhere in between, which is just fine with us. As is often the case in small restaurants, the tables are rather close together, so matters of marriage, divorce or mergers would best be handled elsewhere. On the other hand, those tables are graced with soft napery and fresh flowers, and the tableware is perfectly elegant. The waiters, though seemingly carrying the weight of the culinary world on their shoulders, know their stuff, explaining (sometimes in excruciating detail) exactly how a particular dish is put together. But then owner/chef Yoshi Katsumura is an exacting chef who is meticulous about attention to detail. Starters might include such bravura creations as lobster ravioli with a Champagne-caviar sauce or pan-fried goat cheese with radicchio and pine nuts. Dishes get a dash of color here, a garnish of unusual interest there, always with good taste and visual appeal in mind. The standards for entrées are no less exacting. Breast of chicken, sweetbreads and shiitake mushrooms in a phyllo purse with a red-pepper coulis is a dish that sparkles with originality and excellent flavor. Paupiette of veal stuffed with prosciutto and Fontina cheese is one exciting taste sensation after another. Daily seafood specials always exemplify to an even greater degree Katsumura's talent. And that's the way it goes right to the meal's end, when an ever-changing kaleidoscope of homemade desserts—devastatingly good all—is presented for the choosing. About $50 per person for dinner with wine.

Yugo Inn

2824 N. Ashland Ave.
348-6444
YUGOSLAVIAN
Open Wed.-Sun. 5 p.m.-midnight.
No cards.

12/20

The decor is unabashedly folksy: leather-covered slivovitz bottles painted with Balkan motifs hang on red-brick walls, the low ceiling is timbered, floors are wooden, and waitresses wear peasant skirts and blouses. The main dining area is a cozy room up a short flight of stairs from a street-level bar. In warm weather, tables spill out onto the street, providing additional dining space. The food is simple, hearty and good. Kajmak, cream cheese blended with feta, goat cheese and butter, virtually precedes you to the table, as does a beef-and-chicken-liver pâté and thick slices of home-made bread. Chicken soup, laden with vegetables and a dollop of sour cream, makes a satisfying starter. So do about two dozen flour-dusted, lightly fried smelts. Ciganski tanjir, sizable portions of three Serbian specialties—cevapcici, grilled veal and beef sausages; raznjici, pork or chicken shish ke-babs; and pljeskavica, a patty of savory ground round—makes sampling easy. Even better are the brains fried to a golden brown in butter, served with buttered rice and sea-sonal vegetables. The popular moussaka has at times been plagued by stringy eggplant and tough custard. Tripe, on the other hand, redolent of garlic and sherry, has always been first- class. For dessert, the gooey, rum-flavored choco-late cake wins out over somewhat tough palacinke, preserve-filled crêpes. Some acceptable Yugoslavian wines are avail-able at modest prices. Dinner with wine will set a couple back about $42.

Yvette

1206 N. State St.
280-1700
FRENCH
Café: open Sun.-Thurs.
11 a.m.-1 a.m., Fri.-Sat.
11 a.m.-2 a.m.; dining
room: open Mon.-Thurs.
5:30 p.m.-11 p.m., Fri.-Sat.
5:30 p.m.-midnight, Sun.
5:30 p.m.-10 p.m.
All major cards.

Those not blasted back through the glass doors by duo pianists Tony Zito and Bob Solone (Tuesday to Saturday) or Miguel de la Cerna and Tony Neihardt (Sunday and Monday), or hopelessly enmeshed in talky-talky by brilliant yupsters downing wine coolers in the front room, are in for a treat. The food, though not quite on a par with the city's finest, is hot on their heels. Consider a plate of charcuterie, for example, that one night may display a thin but unctuous slab of goose-liver pâté nestled in a spray of pale-green curly endive inside a blush of radicchio. Nearby, a scoop of fi-brous venison rillettes rubs shoulders with a chunk of pep-pery venison sausage. Ballotine of salmon infused with anise is a mosaic masterpiece, and warm sweetbreads, nutty and sweet, mingle amicably with woodsy morels. Deftly arranged salads of quail, squab and pheasant show up regularly. A double handful of classic entrées—roast chicken lightly perfumed with rosemary and chèvre, and veal kidneys with a bracing mustard sauce—constitute the base, in addition to six to eight daily specials. One such, red snapper, often dowdy outside of Greek and Mexican restaurants, is sparked by a sauce rich in crushed peppercorns. A pesto sauce en-hanced by Dijon mustard anoints the mussels, clams and squid in a shellfish stew. Desserts run to the likes of a crème brûlée of infinite finesse and a lemon tart like a splash of fresh fruit.

A café menu reigns in front: trout and homemade pasta, salade niçoise and brochettes of shrimp, lamb and beef basted with a vigorous chile-pepper vinaigrette. If you care more about food than show, book a table in the back room. Formal place settings on linen invite diners there to be serious, despite the mural that lightly spoofs brasserie art—alongside several contemplative Scotch terriers, a fashionably dressed fin-de-siècle woman seated at a café bar stares away from the diner, cool, distant and quite self-contained. A couple should be prepared to lay out $75 for food and a modest wine.

Zaven's

260 E. Chestnut St.
787-8260
CONTINENTAL
Open Mon.-Thurs.
11:30 a.m.-2:30 p.m. &
5:30 p.m.-10:30 p.m., Fri.
11:30 a.m.-2:30 p.m. &
5:30 p.m.-11 p.m., Sat.
5:30 p.m.-11 p.m., Sun.
5:30 p.m.-10 p.m.
All major cards.

11/20

Zaven's is one of the few old-world Continental restaurants left in the city. Like a well-cared-for doyenne, the dining rooms reflect an ageless beauty, a kind of grace that doesn't exist in restaurants built today. The walls are paneled with rich, dark wood and hung with oil paintings. The tables are covered with crisp linens atop which are tiny table lamps and fresh flowers. The service staff is tuxedoed, and the lights are properly low. The mostly Continental fare intertwines nicely with a number of Middle Eastern dishes, the first of which—hummus—arrives shortly after you are seated. Served with toasted pita points, which are used as a spoon, this hummus is hard to stop eating. Roast rack of lamb (for one or two) is redolent with rosemary and cooked to the pink of perfection, the lamb succulent and satisfying. Daily fish specials are not always handled carefully, and some of the vegetable accompaniments have a tired time-warp appearance. And when was the last time you saw châteaubriand for two on a menu? Many of the Middle Eastern specialties, such as kufta kebab, raw kibbeh and tabouli salad are quite authentic. The wine list ranges far and wide (including some Bordeaux in the $500 price range). About $80 for two, with wine.

Zofia's

6873 N. Milwaukee Ave.,
Niles
647-7949
POLISH
Open Mon.-Thurs. & Sun.
11 a.m.-9:30 p.m., Fri.-Sat.
11 a.m.- 10:30 p.m.
All major cards.

11/20

On Wednesdays and weekends the half roast duck, rich, juicy and falling off the bone, sharing a platter with chewy noodle-like dumplings and the vegetable of the day, draws a good-size crowd. Other days, it's the meaty veal stew sauced with red peppers that lures them in—or the Polish assortment of pirogi—one each of Sauerkraut, ground meat and cheese—flanked by kielbasa (Polish sausage), cabbage, mashed potatoes and an apple-stuffed blintz. Pork shank with Sauerkraut also has its following, among which we count ourselves. For only $1.50 more than the à la carte price, you get soup and salad, coffee or tea and dessert, a full meal for $6.05 to $11.95 (the higher figure for filet mignon). Czarnina soup, made from duck's blood, sweet and thick with noodles and plums, is available every day, but we recommend the daily special, which can range from delicate cream of spinach to robust tomato bisque loaded with vegetables to a tangy, smooth sour-milk borscht. Salads tend toward iceberg lettuce with bottled dressing. And desserts—kolaczki (cheesecake) is preferable to Jell-O or ice cream—are pleasant enough. Portions are as huge as the food is hearty, and service is efficient. A large room, always lively with clatter and chatter, constitutes the main dining area. A smaller room, abutting on the left as you enter, provides a lounge and watering hole for the overflow crowd. Wines are exceedingly limited. Dinner for two, with the house wine, runs about $32.

QUICK BITES

QUICK BITES

We have little to say by way of introduction to Chicago's quick bites. The reviews below say it all and make perfectly clear that Chicago is the real-food capital of the United States, perhaps even of the world. Barbecued ribs, hot dogs, Italian beef sandwiches, deep-dish pizza, stuffed pizza... Chicago is to the devotee of these most worthy art forms what Paris is to the foie-gras-crazy gourmet. And you can eat your way through a couple of dozen of these great Chicago places for the price of one four-toque meal in Paris.

But enough talk—we came here to eat!

BARBECUE

Carson's
The Place for Ribs
612 N. Wells St.
280-9200

8617 Niles Center Rd.,
Skokie - 675-6800

5970 N. Ridge - 271-4000

400 E. Roosevelt Rd.,
Lombard - 627-4300

5050 N. Harlem Ave.,
Harwood Heights
867-4200
Open Mon.-Thurs. 11 a.m.-
midnight, Fri. 11 a.m.-
1 a.m., Sat. noon-1 a.m.,
Sun. noon-11 p.m.
All major cards.

After politics and politicians, the next meatiest subject in Chicago is barbecued ribs. There is no dearth of good rib places in Chicago, but few are more popular or more well known than Carson's. The interior of its flagship location on Wells Street will win no decorating awards—heavy furniture, plasticized booths, dark colors—but the ribs at Carson's get accolade after accolade from the city's food writers and professional eaters. Consistency is the key: The consistently good, meaty baby-back ribs are a class act. The sweet-tasting ribs are cooked in the zesty sauce, not just brushed on. The barbecue sauce, which locks onto those slabs, gives the ribs a look of molten steel and a taste that is slightly fiery but most pleasing. Crunchy coleslaw and incomparable au gratin potatoes are the perfect accompaniments to the ribs. If baby-back ribs aren't your thing, there are spareribs, rib tips, chicken-and-rib combos and just about everything else a good rib house should have. About $30 for a Carson's meal for two, with a drink.

Edith's Bar-B-Q
1863 N. Clybourn Ave.
327-5160
Open Mon.-Thurs. 11 a.m.-
10:30 p.m., Fri. 11 a.m.-
1 a.m., Sat. 3:30 p.m.-
midnight.
No cards.

In the middle of this neat-as-a-pin, compact barbecue house stands a big, glass-enclosed, homemade-looking barbecue pit. This contraption lets you know immediately that you've come to the right place for ribs—sweet, smoky-tasting, meaty, succulent ribs that will put you in barbecue heaven. The secret is the sauce, and there's no way anybody at Edith's will part with the recipe: Carolina-style barbecue sauce is all they'll tell you, and that's all you really need to know. Grab a seat at the small counter or, if you're lucky, at one of the tables or booths and have at it with gusto. It doesn't get much better than this. About $11 for a slab of ribs and a soft drink.

The Fireplace Inn
1448 N. Wells St.
943-7427
Open Mon.-Thurs.
4:30 p.m.-midnight, Fri.-
Sat. 4:30 p.m.-1:30 a.m.,
Sun. 3 p.m.-midnight.
All major cards.

Restaurants come and go in this section of the city known as Old Town, but The Fireplace Inn burns on with a vengeance. The après-ski ambience comes complete with a blazing fireplace in the winter months. Despite the decor, you won't find a lot of downhill-skier types eating here, but you will find a lot of downright fanatic rib lovers sucking on bones for all they're worth. The zingy sauce makes the ribs—it's the color of ketchup and just as thick, but the analogy ends there, since it's one of the best barbecue sauces in town. Ribs as good as these deserve their accompaniments—coarsely chopped, crunchy-good coleslaw and excellent french fries, for a rib house. Ribs can be teamed with chicken, steak, shrimp or crab legs. If you prefer, barbecued Texas beef ribs are available in either full-slab or half-slab portions. About $16 for a full slab of baby-back ribs and a beer. It delivers, too.

Glass Dome Hickory Pit
2801 S. Halsted St.
842-7600
Open Mon.-Fri. 11 a.m.-
10 p.m., Sat. 4 p.m.-10 p.m.,
Sun. 2 p.m.-10 p.m.
All major cards.

Big, big rib place. The Glass Dome Hickory Pit, which is more than 40 years old, is at its busiest and loudest and craziest after a White Sox game, when fans from nearby Comiskey Park hold seige and lustily attack ribs or whatever else they crave after a day at the ballpark. The Glass Dome is another one of those "secret-sauce" places, but they're serious about it here. And it really is something—tantalizing and slightly spicy/sweet, a stick-to-the-ribs sensational beauty. Chicken, combos, shrimp and a few other rib-house requisites are also on the menu. We're not enamored of the fries or the coleslaw as much here as at other places, but the quality of the ribs makes up for that shortcoming. About $15 for a full slab of ribs and a beer.

The Original Leon's Bar-B-Q
2411 N. Clark St.
281-7427

1640 E. 79th St.
731-1454

1158 W. 59th St.
778-7828
Open Mon.-Thurs. 11 a.m.-
3 a.m., Fri.-Sat. 11 a.m.-
4 a.m.
Cards: AE, MC, V.

Leon's is takeout only—no delivery, no tables—but that singular approach to selling ribs doesn't deter people from queuing up to place orders. You can't help but develop an appetite the minute you walk through the door at Leon's. Slabs of spareribs—mahogany in color, substantial in size—roll in and out of the huge cooker/smoker that takes up most of the kitchen area, and the smell alone is enough to make you swoon. Your taste buds take a seat at the tip of your tongue in anticipation of the big event, and they are never disappointed. From one end of the slab to the other, these are meaty, juicy, saucy ribs, bathed in a hot sauce, mild sauce or mixture. Chicken wings are good, too, but we've had better hot links, which are a bit too dry for our taste. A full slab of ribs runs $9.75; a half slab, $5.75.

Randall's for Ribs

41 E. Superior St.
280-2790
Open Mon.-Thurs.
11:30 a.m.-3 p.m. &
5 p.m.-10 p.m., Fri.
11:30 a.m.-3 p.m. &
5 p.m.-11 p.m., Sat. 5 p.m.-
11 p.m., Sun. 10:30 a.m.-
10 p.m.
All major cards.

Randall's is a white-tablecloth rib house with a lot of expensive trappings. That pleases some people, but others think it's too pretty to be serious about ribs. We disagree. We won't say Randall's has the best ribs in Chicago; but it is serious— to a fault—about its ribs and the rest of the food it serves, since this is a Levy Brothers' operation, and the Levy brothers make every attempt to run fault-free restaurants. Randall's ribs are smoked slowly over applewood, which imparts a slightly different—call it sweeter—flavor. The specially made barbecue sauce has tang, but it is a bit on the tame side. At times, we have had ribs here that made our elbows move faster than a fiddler's; on other occasions, our fingers tasted better than the ribs. Cornbread is especially good. Ditto for the french fries and the fried onion strings. Texas beef ribs and veal-back ribs are tasty alternatives to the baby-backs. Seafood, chicken, steak and burgers fill out the menu. The wine list is the best around for a rib house, and there's a nice outdoor café in the summer. Limited delivery area. About $18 for a full slab of ribs and beer.

Robinson's No. 1 Ribs

655 W. Armitage Ave.
337-1399
Open Mon.-Thurs. 11 a.m.-
11 p.m., Fri. 11 a.m.-
11:30 p.m., Sat. 3 p.m.-
11:30 p.m., Sun. 3 p.m.-
11 p.m.
Cards: AE, MC, V.

North Side rib aficionados will go to the mat to defend Robinson's in any rib-off, and well they should. The ribs, succulent and sweet right down to the bone, are the result of slow smoking over hickory and laying on barbecue sauce that has just the right amount of spicy tang and depth of flavor. Robinson's maintains that the slow-smoking process removes most of the fat, so the baby-back ribs are comparitively quite low in calories. A rationalization perhaps, but we'll buy it—the ribs are, in fact, lean, meaty and delicious. Add two more winners to menu: wonderfully good celery-seed coleslaw and simply sensational french fries. It's hard to go into a rib place and not order ribs, but the barbecued chicken is so good it gives us pause. A number of the dishes on the menu get the Number-One tag, as in Number-One burger and Number-One salad. Don't believe everything you read, but when it comes to the ribs you can believe it. Limited seating, but it is cozy and pleasant. The special menu for parties and catering includes some excellent options. Limited delivery area. About $14 for a full slab of ribs and a soft drink.

We are always happy to hear about your discoveries and to receive your comments about ours. We want to give your letters the attention they deserve, so when you write to us, remember to state clearly exactly what you liked or disliked. Be concise, but convincing. Do take the time to argue your point.

Twin Anchors Restaurant and Tavern

1655 N. Sedgwick St.
266-1616
Open Mon.-Thurs. 5 p.m.-
11:30 p.m., Fri. 5 p.m.-
12:30 a.m., Sat. noon-
12:30 a.m., Sun. noon-
11 p.m.
All major cards.

An Old Town fixture for more than 50 years, this neighborhood bar/restaurant has so many loyal customers you'd think they all owned a piece of the action. Twin Anchors gets the Best Jukebox Selections in a Bar award, hands down. No one has ever laid any ribs awards on the place, but then the Twin Anchors doesn't need that kind of publicity. The regulars know, and they don't like passing the good word around, since that'll just make it more difficult for them to get a table or booth. The baby-back ribs are meaty and succulent, and the barbecue sauce is as spirited as the patrons. Burgers are good, too. About $15 for a slab of ribs and a beer.

CAFES & COFFEE SHOPS

Albert's Café & Pâtisserie

52 W. Elm St.
751-0666
Open Tues.-Thurs. 10 a.m.-
9:30 p.m., Fri. 10 a.m.-
10 p.m., Sat. 9 a.m.-
10 p.m., Sun. 10 a.m.-
8 p.m.
No cards.

This small café exudes charm. Though not quite as alluring as the atmosphere, the food does have some memorable moments. The smoked Norwegian salmon plate with sourcream dill sauce is one such moment, and the salade niçoise is as authentic as you'll find this side of Nice. But chicken in puff pastry is mangled mush, and the Monte Cristo sandwich is not worth the price. Daily specials fare much better than printed menu items. There's a great selection of made-on-the-premises cakes, tortes and other sweet treats and lots of liquid assets—beer, wine, coffee (the cappuccino is one of the best around), sparkling apple cider, Cognacs and so on. Dinner for two, with wine, will run just $26.

Café on Grand

300 W. Grand Ave.
321-1140
Open Mon.-Thurs. 8 a.m.-
8 p.m., Fri. 8 a.m.-9 p.m.,
Sat. 11 a.m.-9 p.m.
Cards: AE, MC, V.

The smell of freshly baked goods tantalizes the nose buds the minute you walk in the door of this homey and comfortable tablecloth café. Croissants, brioches, muffins (the cinnamon raisin and mandarin orange are our favorites) and desserts are all something from the oven—something special. At lunchtime, we suggest the well-crafted salads, well-made sandwiches, excellent homemade soups and such light bites as the baked Brie wrapped in phyllo and the whipped pâté mousse. Café on Grand now serves dinner, and the menu has been expanded to include fish, grilled meats and fowl, so there's even more to enjoy. About $10 a person for lunch, with wine or beer.

Café Selmarie

2327 W. Giddings St.
989-5595
Open Tues.-Sat. 9 a.m.-
9 p.m., Sun. 9 a.m.-4 p.m.
No cards.

This combination bakery/pastry shop/café is a busy place at lunchtime and on Saturday afternoons. Fresh flowers and white tablecloths make for a charming and pleasant noontime sojourn. The menu features light Continental fare: ham, turkey, Brie and tuna-salad croissant sandwiches, fresh-vegetable quiche, soups and all sorts of seasonal dishes.

Tortes, cheesecakes and fruit tarts come by the slice or whole, to be taken out; the most popular are the Selmarie Torte and the German-style cheesecakes. Everything is made fresh. Fine espresso and cappuccino, too. About $6 per person.

Cafe Spiaggia

980 N. Michigan Ave.
(1 Magnificent Mile
Building, 2nd Fl.)
280-2764
Open Mon.-Thurs.
11:30 a.m.-10 p.m., Fri.-
Sat. 11:30 a.m.-11 p.m.,
Sun. noon-9 p.m.
All major cards.

What a wonderful little touch of Italy on Michigan Avenue! Cool marble, café tables, booths and a great view (if you're fortunate enough to get a window seat). Scenery aside, this café serves a range of Italian dishes that are truly *meraviglioso*. The salads are a breath of spring any time of year: radicchio, arugula, endive, tomatoes, mozzarella and fresh basil are glossed with a fragrant olive oil and balsamic vinegar dressing. Even the small salad of radicchio and escarole is a triumph. Pizzas baked in a wood-burning oven are just like you'd find in northern Italy—the pizza ai quattro formaggi is a classic of good taste. The antipasti selection includes an insalata di mare, a glorious, light mix of calamari, bay scallops and shrimp anointed with extra-virgin olive oil. We haven't tried all the pasta dishes, but the three of the seven offered that we have tried are exceptionally good—the spaghettini al cartoccio especially so. Entrées are limited, but the choices are well thought out. For dessert, don't miss the tiramisu. Expect to pay about $26 for two, with wine.

Cambridge House

167 E. Ohio St.
828-0600
Open daily 6 a.m.-1 a.m.
No cards.

This place is the coffee-shop's coffee shop. In this day of seafood grills and sushi bars, trattorias and tapas, spa cuisine and fast-food machines, it's getting hard to find an authentic coffee shop. Cambridge House is true to form and hard to beat. What we particularly like about the place (in addition to the food) is the friendly greeting from owners John Maniatis and John Galanos. If they're not around, which is rare, you can count on an equally friendly reception from Nick or John, the co-hosts. That may sound like a lot of floor talent for a coffee shop, but this place, just off Michigan Avenue, is busy, busy, busy from early morning to late evening. Visitors to Chicago who know of it gladly walk blocks to eat here. We haven't had a breakfast here yet that we didn't thoroughly enjoy: pancakes, fluffy omelets, french toast, steak and eggs, excellent coffee... And you won't find a better (or nicer) serving staff. The chicken-breast sandwich is a particularly good lunch choice. At dinner, try the roast-beef or fried-chicken dinners; the oven-browned potatoes are outstanding. An orange juice, omelet and coffee will run about $6 a head.

Hard Rock Cafe

63 W. Ontario St.
943-2252
*Open daily 11 a.m.-
midnight.
Cards: AE, MC, V.*

Damn the noise, full speed ahead. Damn the food, I came here to get a Hard Rock T-shirt. That's pretty much the way it goes with the rocking horde that descends on this hard-rock pop-culture palace day in and day out. Inside the noisy, sprawling, multilevel, neo-Georgian café (loose use of the word café) are enough rock mementos to set to rolling the eyes of even the most jaded music fan: Elton John's glasses and diamond-studded platform shoes, David Bowie's saxophone, Eric Clapton's guitar and hundreds of other pieces of rock ornamentalia adorn the walls and ceiling. Yes, Virginia, there is food, and some of it isn't all bad. The burger is a beauty—one-third pound of hand-patted chopped steak. Though the burgers don't always arrive as ordered, they are juicy and flavorful. If you have a powerful hunger, go for the half-pounder; it will wrestle you to the ground. Ribs aren't great, but they're decent enough, as is the barbecued chicken. Chili has just enough fire to cause a mild sweat. The apple pie is awesome, almost too good, and the chocolate devil's-food cake borders on idolatry. About $12 for a hamburger, beer and dessert.

Lou Mitchell's

563 W. Jackson Blvd.
939-3111
*Open Mon.-Fri. 5:30 a.m.-
4 p.m., Sat. 5:30 a.m.-
2:30 p.m.
No cards.*

Lou Mitchell's is the kind of place to which you'd take your out-of-town mother or favorite aunt or uncle. They'd approve of your good taste and the fact that you are eating well. The fourteen kinds of omelets—from California broccoli and old-English cheddar to garden-fresh zucchini and tomato—are a house specialty. We would wait in line (in fact, we often have) for the exceptionally good french toast (which we set afloat in pure maple syrup) or the Belgian waffle. The pastries—Danish, donuts, pecan rolls, muffins—are all made in the kitchen, and they're all seriously fresh and seriously good. Juices are freshly squeezed, and the rich coffee (made with specially filtered water) is flawless. It's a busy place, but the logging-camp conviviality is good fun, and Uncle Lou—always smiling, always up—is always at the door handing out small boxes of Milk Duds to the ladies waiting in line. Breakfast runs about $6 per person.

Oak Tree

25 E. Oak St.
751-1988
*Open daily 24 hours.
No cards.*

Our kingdom for a waitress who doesn't call you "Hon"! No danger of losing the castle at this place. The waitresses are all graduates of the "What'll ya have today, hon?" School of Inane Banter, but they hit the tables at a running start, so we forgive and forget. This is one of the few coffee shops in the city where you can get a lox-and-smoked-fish combo or a jumbo smoked-fish platter for breakfast. All the requisite breakfast stuff is in place: breakfast sandwiches, griddle cakes, waffles, omelets, lox and bagels. The doyennes of the Gold Coast and the denizens of Rush Street find amusement mingling with one another at the Oak Tree, and they just can't seem to get enough of one another. Breakfast for two will cost about $12.

Piccolo Mondo Cafe

2460 N. Clark St.
528-8389
Open daily 11 a.m.-11 p.m.
Cards: AE, MC, V.

The newest North Side entry in the café scene, Piccolo Mondo is the Italian café of our dreams. Bright and light with lots of glass and light oak, it's the perfect spot to get an Italian-food fix at prices that won't ruin your appetite. The tight, tidy menu covers the basics—an antipasto plate, calamari fritti, salads, pastas and sandwiches, along with innovative daily specials. The melanzana alla romana is particularly good: Slices of fried eggplant are stuffed with ricotta cheese and topped with a fresh tomato sauce. The Romanuccis, the owners, supply fresh pasta creations to many Chicago-area restaurants from their commissary on N. Harlem Avenue, so you can count on some excellent pastas at Piccolo Mondo. (There's one in Hyde Park, too.) Tortellini alla carbonara is so fragrant, so delicious, so beautifully crafted that it deserves an award. Accolades, too, to the octopus salad, a masterpiece of good taste, and to the homemade tiramisu. Excellent cappuccino and espresso top off the meal, and wines accompany it. It's a nice place for eating in (limited number of tables) or for takeout. About $13 a person for pasta, dessert and cappuccino.

Ann Sather's

929 W. Belmont Ave.
348-2378
Open Mon.-Thurs. 7 a.m.-11 p.m., Fri.-Sat. 7 a.m.-midnight, Sun. 7 a.m.-11 p.m.
Cards: MC, V.

As the plaque on the outside wall says, when this restaurant opened in 1945, the Lakeview area around Belmont Avenue was largely Scandinavian. Ann Sather's is the only remnant of that ethnic neighborhood, and it's a worthy symbol of days past, especially since its refurbishment a couple of years ago. Its newly expanded dining area is done in a soft beige that offsets the dark woodwork. Touches of slate blue, stained-glass windows and Scandinavian folk art remain, as do many of the original menu items. Sather's is still one of the most popular weekend breakfast spots around. In addition to good eggs and omelets, there are feather-light Swedish pancakes with a tart-sweet lingonberry sauce, french toast served with peach compote, waffles and the homemade baked goods Sather's is known for: melt-in-your-mouth cinnamon rolls, biscuits, muffins, Swedish limpa and various pastries and breads of the day. Breakfast meats are a class act, particularly the excellent, thickly sliced bacon. Swedish standards with American touches make up the lunch and dinner menu. Though heavy, the Swedish sampler—duck breast glazed with lingonberries, meatballs, dumplings, potato-and-veal sausage, Sauerkraut and brown beans—is a good introduction to Swedish fare. There's another location at 5207 N. Clark Street, 271-6677. Breakfast for two runs $10 to $20, sandwiches and salads, $3 to $5, and dinner entrées, $6 to $9.

Tempo Restaurant

1 E. Chestnut St.
943-4373
Open daily 24 hours.
No cards.

The menu at Tempo is everything you'd expect from a coffee shop—and more. Open 24 hours a day, every day, Tempo is the place to be when everything else is closed, but feel free to visit for breakfast, lunch or dinner whenever the spirit moves you. Rich Chicagoans didn't get rich by squandering their money , but Tom Thrifty III and Fiona Frugal are not about to eat food that isn't good. So they choose Tempo—prices notwithstanding. And when the calendar finally creaks around to May, the tables go onto the sidewalk in front, which allows for some of the best see-and-beseen action in the city. The heaviest action is at breakfast, when the regulars tuck into the excellent omelets. Picture this: Your waitress takes your order, and before your first cup of coffee has kicked in, she returns bearing a skillet brimming with a fluffy omelet packed with feta cheese, onions and tomato (the Greek); or asparagus and cheddar; or fresh mushrooms and Swiss cheese; or just about anything else you can think of. With it she delivers thick Greek toast, homemade marmalade and American fries. Not a bad way to start the day—whether you're rich or not so rich. Breakfast for two is about $10.

Walker Bros. Original Pancake House

153 Green Bay Rd.,
Wilmette
251-6000

1615 Waukegan Rd.,
Glenview
724-0220
Open Mon.-Thurs. 7 a.m.-10:30 p.m., Fri.-Sat.
7 a.m.-midnight, Sun.
7 a.m.-10:30 p.m.
No cards.

We challenge you to find any ingredient at Walker Bros. that hasn't entered the kitchen in its raw, fresh, unadulterated state. Cooking everything from scratch accounts for the quality of the menu offerings and, consequently, for the crowds on the weekends. The meats—ham, bacon, Canadian bacon, sausage—are custom-cured in St. Louis and sent north weekly. Orange and grapefruit juices are freshly squeezed. Is it any wonder that Robert Redford used to stop in here when he was nearby making *Ordinary People?* Omelets are stuffed with vegetables that practically still have dewdrops clinging to them. And those omelets, blended and baked rather than cooked on the stove, are among the fluffiest we've seen anywhere. But it's the sweet items that keep us and most other regulars coming back. The apple pancake is a wonder, the Dutch baby is downright devastating, and the fresh blueberry pancakes evoke memories of childhood summers. Breakfast for two is about $15.

Unless otherwise noted, the prices given for restaurants are for a complete dinner for two, including an appetizer, main course and dessert. The prices also include tax, fifteen-percent tip and one of the least expensive bottles of wine on the wine list. Please don't hold it against us if you end up spending a bit more!

DELICATESSENS

Bagel Nosh
1135 N. State St.
266-6369
*Open Mon. 7 a.m.-
midnight, Tues.-Thurs.
7 a.m.-1 a.m., Fri.-Sat.
24 hours, Sun. 7 a.m.-
midnight.
No cards.*

The State Street/Rush Street neighborhood teems with restaurants, bars and nightspots, and it's to Bagel Nosh that the crowds go for rejuvenation and noshing on the morning after. If you've squandered most of your cash the night before, you'll appreciate the 7 a.m.-to-noon special breakfast, which includes a first-rate omelet, freshly baked bagel, hash browns and coffee. A good alternative is the hand-cut lox draped over a fresh bagel smothered in cream cheese with all the requisite trimmings. At lunchtime, sandwiches are the thing to order—corned beef, roast beef, turkey and fish are all laudable—though there are two hot specials every day. As strange as it may sound for a deli, Bagel Nosh makes a vegetarian chili, which we've never had the nerve to try. Soups are interesting, but they can fall short on flavor when, we suppose, the alternate soup maker is on duty. Breakfast for two is $5 to $15; sandwiches for two, about $10.

Belden Corned Beef Center
2315 N. Clark St.
935-2752
*Open daily 24 hours.
No cards.*

A fixture in lively Lincoln Park, Belden is a home away from home for neighborhood residents who like a deli atmosphere—a place in which you can sit down, eat and linger. Obviously, the signature sandwich is the corned beef, and it's a model of the genre (available extra-lean for a slight surcharge). But Belden's also has all the other deli-sandwich basics—pastrami, roast beef, turkey, tongue... A lot of Chicago delis could do a better job with desserts, and Belden is no exception, but we think the homemade cheese-cake (plain, strawberry or chocolate) has enough creamy richness to keep any sweet tooth happy. A sandwich, dessert and soft drink will run about $8.

Finkl's World Famous Deli
760 N. Ogden Ave.
666-6666
*Open Mon.-Fri. 5 a.m.-
7 p.m., Sat. 6 a.m.-2 p.m.,
Sun. 10 a.m.-2 p.m.
No cards.*

Finkl's has one foot in the Old World and one foot in the new. When the place is really perking, the folks behind the counter sometimes forget which foot is which, and whose order is whose, but they get it straight sooner or later. Soups are like those your grandmother used to make (chicken noodle, matzo ball, kreplach), assuming you were blessed with a Jewish grandmother. Stay away from the tuna- or chicken-salad sandwiches (too skimpy) and go with the basics—corned beef, brisket, pastrami. Potato pancakes are good, not great. A few dishes make us wonder. Salad made with goat cheese (new world) in a Jewish deli? How about prosciutto and melon? You can take comfort, however, in knowing that the breakfast fare is more traditional, low in price (four eggs, five strips of bacon and three slices of toast for $2.95) and top-quality. Finkl's also gets high marks for its spiffy decor, all the objets d'argh notwithstanding. Free parking in the back. Soup, sandwich and a New York Seltzer run a mere $5.

D. B. Kaplan's Delicatessen

845 N. Michigan Ave.
(Water Tower Place, 7th Fl.)
280-2700
Open Mon.-Thurs. 10 a.m.-11 p.m., Fri.-Sat. 10 a.m.-midnight, Sun. 10 a.m.-11 p.m.
No cards.

The menu is three feet long from top to bottom (luckily it folds up) and is printed on both sides. Another Levy Brothers' production, D. B. Kaplan's is not bashful about taking deli to dizzying heights. Sandwiches (numbers 1 through 148) all carry cutely phrased bold-copy lead-ins: Number 21—"What's the Good Bird?"—layers breast of turkey, chopped liver, cheddar, lettuce, tomato and mayo on Rosen's Jewish challah bread. Numbers 110 through 148 are the deli sandwiches (four- and eight-ounce sizes) you dream about, from roast beef to peanut butter and jelly. Soup? Of course. Homemade chicken with noodles, matzo balls or kreplach are all vintage stock. Potato pancakes are excellent, as are the many-flavored blintzes. Gefilte fish, kishke, stuffed cabbage, chicken in the pot—it's all here, and it's all good. To accompany your meal are beer, wine, booze creations (Kahlúa Bankhead mixes Kahlúa and coffee-Cognac ice cream), fountain drinks, cheesecake and cakes and on and on—it takes a lot of food to fill a three-foot menu. Free delivery to area offices. Soup, sandwiches and soft drinks for two will run about $15.

Manny's Coffee Shop and Deli

1139 S. Jefferson St.
939-2855
Open Mon.-Sat. 5 a.m.-4:45 p.m.
No cards.

Manny's is the quintessential deli: noisy, big and loaded with people of all flavors. This place is heavenly bliss for the fur-coat, no-coat and poly-coat sets alike. Grab a plastic tray (shake off the water from the dishwasher), get in line and head down the food-service line. From steam table to soft drinks, it's loaded with more seduction than a romance novel. The chicken soup with matzo ball or kreplach is one of the best in town. Corned beef, chopped liver, tongue, brisket and pastrami merely scrape the sandwich selection. Daily specials (posted on the board just inside the entrance) will take you to deli nirvana and back. Oxtail stew, gefilte fish, beef stew, liver and onions, meatloaf... the selection is amazing, but the best part is that it all tastes great. Manny's makes one of the best potato pancakes around, too. About $6 for soup and a sandwich.

Milty's Super Deli

65 E. Wacker Dr.
641-1477
Open Mon.-Fri. 6:30 a.m.-6 p.m., Sat. 8:30 a.m.-3 p.m.
No cards.

Milty's has a spartan, bright, fast-food atmosphere, but that's okay—what draws the Michigan Avenue crowd is the fresh, well-prepared food. At the top of the list for most customers are the hot dogs, hamburgers, freshly cut fries and sausages—but it's a long list. We favor the standard deli sandwiches (kosher-style corned beef; tangy, tasty pastrami; roast beef), but the Nova Scotia lox omelet has made our day on more than one occasion. Turkeys are cooked on the premises; tuna and chicken salads are made here, too. The soup of the day is always interesting, but the chicken noodle—rich, golden and loaded with noodles—continues to win and warm our hearts. Breakfast selections hold up their end of the day (the bologna omelet is particularly good). Breakfast specials are $2 to $3, and sandwiches are $2 to $4.

Moe's Deli Pub
611 N. Rush St.
828-0110
Open Mon.-Fri. 6:30 a.m.-10 p.m., Sat. 7:30 a.m.-5 p.m.
Cards: AE, V.

In sampling the deli delights concocted by Moe and staff, the lean, well-seasoned corned beef is probably the best place to start. But if you intend to wend your way through the entire menu, plan to eat here a couple of times a week for the rest of your life. The offerings cross a number of ethnic borders, from standard Jewish deli fare to Italian dishes and even a taste or two of Mexican food. You may have to tiptoe your way through some of the ethnic tulips, but we have plucked more good stuff than not from this place. We recommend highly the corned beef and other basic meats, such as roast beef and salami, but it would be a major felony to pass up the combo sandwiches, which you order by number. We're especially devoted to the corned beef, pastrami and Swiss cheese with Russian dressing (the Number One). Another punishable offense is to ignore the homemade soups, particularly the extravaganza called Moe's Bowl, in which a bowl of chicken soup is filled with kreplach, noodles and matzo ball. And if you're on the run, ready-made sandwiches, including a dynamite Italian sub, are on the counter ready to go. Soup, sandwich and a beer are about $8.

Morry's Old-Fashioned Deli
345 S. Dearborn St.
922-2932
Open Mon.-Fri. 7 a.m.-7 p.m., Sat. 8 a.m.-5 p.m.
No cards.

Morry's is one of a somewhat rare breed in Chicago. It's a real family-run Jewish deli with all the trappings in place: kosher dills on every table, Dr. Brown's cream soda and New York Seltzer on the counter, the owners' friendly cajoling to try the soup. It also has that cluttered look one expects from a deli. Opt for a messy but not-too-fatty pastrami with Swiss cheese and hot mustard on rye, or the corned beef. Homemade soups are satisfying; a rich, flavorful chicken broth is the liquid setting for a huge, light and luscious matzo ball. Breakfast is worth a visit if only for the french toast made from challah. Come lunchtime, the place is chaotic, but tables turn over quickly and most of the regulars order takeout. Soup, sandwiches and soft drinks for two cost about $12.

Mrs. Levy's Delicatessen
233 S. Wacker Dr.
(Sears Tower)
993-0530
Open Mon.-Fri. 6:30 a.m.-7 p.m., Sat. 10 a.m.-7 p.m., Sun. 10:30 a.m.-5 p.m.
No cards.

The Levy Brothers, Larry and Mark, own a lot of eateries in town, so they have a considerable influence on what Chicagoans eat. And when they brought their mother into the act, as they did in naming this deli after her, they knew they had to get it right—or else. They got it right. At noon, it seems that every living soul in Sears Tower is dumped from the elevators into Mrs. Levy's. Crowd control is handled amazingly well, and one way or another everyone gets fed without too much fuss. This is real deli food—no fooling around here. The soups (terrific chicken noodle), the sandwiches (marvelous tongue, corned beef, pastrami), the toppings (just about every type of bread, condiment and cheese), the imaginative triple-decker sandwiches (try the Number Seven) and, yes, even the desserts—fountain creations, cheesecakes, chocolate éclairs—are all first-rate. Soup, sandwich and milk shake for about $8.

HAMBURGERS

Come Back Inn Pub

1913 W. Lake St.,
Melrose Park
343-7490
*Open Mon.-Sat. 11 a.m.-
1 a.m., Sun. noon-
11:30 p.m.*
Cards: AE, MC, V.

If you're willing to slog through the snow from the city to the suburbs, you won't find a warmer winter haven than this rambling, dark, antique-laden, convivial pub. Cozy up to a fireside table (if you can get one) for a romantic evening (though you may find the halves of a stuffed moose implanted into the fireplace a bit disconcerting). Burgers, which range from a quarter to a full pound, are thick, juicy and always cooked as ordered. Our choice is the half-pound Kodiak burger on dark Bavarian bread. It may be artery-clogging, but it is one state-of-the-art hamburger. Ribs, sandwiches, fish and steak are also available, but the burger is the way to go here. Huge selection of imported beers. About $15 for burgers and beer for two.

Ed Debevic's Short Orders Deluxe

640 N. Wells St.
664-1707
*Open Mon.-Fri. 6 a.m.-
11 p.m., Sat. 11 a.m.-
midnight, Sun. 11 a.m.-
11 p.m.*
No cards.

The fictitious Ed has done a darn good job creating a tongue-in-cheek replica of a '50s diner. The blasting, blasted rock 'n' roll music may drive you bonkers. The gum-chewing, sassy food-slingers may be a bit too contrived. The wait for a table may be unbearable. The burgers may be too greasy. The amusing signs may be too cute. In fact, the whole place may be just too, too darling. But everybody—ages 6 to 60—loves Ed's; it's a happening that borders on cult worship. And if it happens that you eat here, which you will, you'll probably enjoy it. The hamburger may be greasy, but it's good. As evidence that the beef is freshly ground, there is a life-size plastic steer in the meat room. We prefer the chiliburger, because believe or not we think Ed's chili is the best around. Ditto for the greasy french fries. The meatloaf isn't terrific, and Ed really falls off his counter stool when it comes to desserts, which are terrible. But Ed's serves an authentic diner breakfast—the scrambled eggs with onions, ham and peppers are terrific, and the banana pancakes and fried-egg sandwich are good, too. Two of you can get out of here, any time, for $16 or less.

Goldyburgers

7316 Circle Ave.,
Forest Park
366-0750
Open Mon.-Fri. 5 p.m.-
11 p.m., Sat.-Sun. noon-
11 p.m. (bar open until
2 a.m. Mon.-Thurs. &
Sun., until 3 a.m.
Fri.-Sat.).
No cards.

There are times in every epicure's life when haute cuisine, nouvelle cuisine, unsure cuisine—anything that even hints of the gourmet—simply won't do. At these times a really good American burger is the only acceptable thing to eat. Goldyburgers, whose motto is "Never Had a Bad One," offers a lot of choices in the ground-beef category, any one of which can be satisfying, but the Royalbleuburger (sic) is simply sensational. It's a half pound of ground sirloin that's broiled to perfection, draped with a veneer of blue cheese and slabbed with strips of bacon. And the bun fits the burger, and the burger gives fits to our taste buds. If you're even slightly crazy, you might want to give The Big Daddy a go—it weighs in at three-quarters of a pound. Homemade soup, several variations on the shrimp theme, a Friday fish fry and a bunch of french-fried veggies are as ambitious as the menu gets, but considering that this is just a neighborhood bar, that's ambitious enough for us. And the price—$8 for two—is right.

Hackney's on Harms

1241 Harms Rd.,
Glenview
724-5577
Open Mon.-Thurs. 11 a.m.-
11 p.m., Fri.-Sat. 11 a.m.-
midnight, Sun. 11 a.m-
10 p.m.
All major cards.

Though several other sandwiches are tried-and-true tasty possibilities, it would be a mistake to forego the half-pound Hackneyburger, a marvel of juicy, quality beef topped with mellow cheddar and laid between home-baked dark rye. This beauty is escorted by fine fries, which are sweet tasting and perfectly al dente every time. But to gild the lily, order Hackney's original french-fried onion rings, a crispy, crunchy loaf of onions that will leave you breathless. On Thursdays, pass on the burgers and have the corned beef and cabbage. This quaint little spot is nearly 50 years old and still going strong. Majestic silver poplars make the summer patio especially appealing; inside is a cozy bar with friendly bartenders who you'll get to know, since there's usually a wait for a table. Two can eat and drink for less than $10.

Hamburger Hamlet

44 E. Walton St.
649-6601
Open Mon.-Thurs. 11 a.m.-
11 p.m., Fri.-Sat. 11 a.m.-
midnight, Sun. 11 a.m.-
11 p.m.
All major cards.

More baloney than beef, Hamburger Hamlet seems to have forgotten that customers come first. We have no idea why the young and nubile still hang out here—it's certainly not for the hamburgers, which, though once great, certainly aren't so now. The service has sunk to Captain Nemo depths—but then, how would you like to be on the butt end of customers' beefs night after night? About $7 for a burger and a beer.

Moody's Pub

5910 N. Broadway
275-2696
Open daily 11:30 a.m.-
2 a.m.
No cards.

Dark-wood walls, wood tables and booths, a big bar, a jukebox, ashtrays on the tables, which are big enough to hold a bale of tobacco... Moody's evokes memories of pubs you used to crawl your way through in college days. The only update is the big-screen TV, which you can barely see when the place is really perking and the smoky haze is up. Most of the haze comes from the burger grill in the far-right corner of the one big room. The menu lists a steak sandwich and a couple of kinds of steaks and chicken. But burgers are the thing here: half-pound burgers made with quality beef; big, juicy burgers in big buns cooked exactly as ordered more often than not; burgers in a wicker basket, topped with cheese or bacon or mushrooms and buried under a mound of crispy, hand-cut Idaho fries (would that they were hotter more often). In the summer months the action moves to the outdoor beer garden on the south side of the building, which on any given weekend evening is on full spin cycle. Beer by the glass or pitcher, wine (vin de table) and specialty cocktails (Singapore sling, peach passion, planters punch and so on) keep the bonhomie at a high level. About $6 for a burger and a stein of beer.

Redamak's

2263 N. Lincoln Ave.
787-9866
*Open Mon.-Thurs.
11:30 a.m.-midnight,
Fri.-Sat. 11:30 a.m.-
1:30 a.m., Sun. noon-
11 p.m.
Cards: AE.*

Sleekly modern in an art deco style, yet comfortable and casual, Redamak's serves a perfectly good one-third-pound hamburger on light or dark rye or a sesame-seed bun. Have it topped with grilled onions, chili, olives, bacon or mushrooms— in addition, of course, to cheese. On the side you may want to try the crunchy onion rings, though the fries are good, too. The beef is ground daily, and burgers can also be ordered as doubles. Other commendable offerings include Martha's Madness, a deep-fried boneless chicken breast with Swiss cheese and Dijon mustard on grilled rye. Redamak's recently added malts, shakes and sundaes to its menu, and they've been eliciting raves from the regulars. Burgers, onion rings and beer for two will run about $20.

HOT DOGS

Byron's Hot Dogs

850 W. North Ave.
266-3355

1017 W. Irving Park Rd.
281-7474

1701 W. Lawrence Ave.
271-0900
*Open Mon.-Thurs.
10:30 a.m.-midnight, Fri.-
Sat 10:30 a.m.-1 a.m., Sun.
10:30 a.m.-midnight.
No cards.*

Byron's is undeniably the most upscale hot dog stand around. A multicolored rotating spiked sphere that looks like a satellite built by Pee-Wee Herman crowns the place. Inside it's all spit and polish with touches of art deco, booths and stylized food art—this is one good-looking hot dog stand. The menu ranges far and wide through all that Chicago's hot dog stands are famous for: Vienna hot dogs (the skinless variety), Polish sausages, hamburgers, grilled chicken sandwiches, french fries, eat al. The hot dog comes with all (if you choose) the important bun-stuffing stuff: mustard, relish, onions, tomatoes, pepper, pickle and celery salt—and it's simply great. The Polish is a big one that sticks out a half inch on either side of the steamed bun, and it has a nice snap to it. French fries are terrific. If you don't think you should, but you're made of weak stuff, finish things off with cheesecake or a Ben & Jerry's Brownie Bar. About $3 for a hot dog, fries and soft drink.

Demon Dogs

944 W. Fullerton Ave.
281-2001
Open Mon.-Fri. 6 a.m.-
10 p.m., Sat.-Sun.
10 a.m.-8 p.m.
No cards.

There's nothing demonic about the hot dogs here—except that they keep you coming back, ordering more than your cholesterol count would like you to. This relative newcomer to the Chicago wiener arena has become a contender by serving up classic dogs, always steaming hot, always with the requisite crunch. Tucked under the El tracks near DePaul University, the place really jumps at lunchtime, in the early evening and sporadically throughout the afternoon, but nothing fazes the cheerful, efficient counter help. Students on break between classes, patrons of the library branch across the street and neighborhood regulars are privy to the fastest service around. However, if you want to dawdle over your dog, there's a free jukebox loaded with the tunes of the band Chicago, once managed by owner Peter Schivarelli, plus photos, gold-album plaques and other rock memorabilia to peruse. French fries are good; try the cheese fries if you need some added bulk. Polish sausage is a popular alternative to the hot dog. Hot dog, fries and a soda are about $2.

Gold Coast Dogs

418 N. State St.
527-1222
Open Mon.-Fri. 7 a.m.-
midnight, Sat. 8 a.m.-
8 p.m., Sun. 11 a.m.-8 p.m.
No cards.

804 N. Rush St.
951-5141
Open Mon.-Thurs. 10 a.m.-
midnight, Fri.-Sat. 10 a.m.-
2 a.m., Sun. 10 a.m.-
midnight.
No cards.

2100 N. Clark St.
327-8887
Open Mon.-Thurs. 7 a.m.-
midnight, Fri.-Sat. 8 a.m.-
2 a.m., Sun. 10:30 a.m.-
midnight.
No cards.

Kudos, kudos and more kudos for One Magnificent Dog, as Gold Coast calls its pure-beef Vienna boiled red hot. And magnificent it is, in the pure Chicago tradition. All the extras you'd expect are here, and then some: You can have your onions grilled or raw; and if you're from out of town, note the celery salt— it's a must topping for frankophiles from the city of the big shoulders. If the natural casing of the boiled version has a bit too much snap to it, opt for the char-broiled red hot instead; it's just as tasty. Fast food this may be, but it's fast food raised to new heights; everything is super fresh, and Gold Coast even makes one of the best burgers in town, too. A hot dog, fries and soft drink will set you back only about $3.

Golda's

711 W. Roosevelt Rd.,
Maywood
344-7797
Open Mon.-Sat. 11 a.m.-
10 p.m., Sun. 11 a.m.-
9 p.m.
No cards.

Fresh and kosher are Golda's bywords—from the pure-beef kosher hot dogs and award-winning, freshly peeled and cut french fries to the homemade, secret-recipe chili and old-fashioned milk shakes and malts. Plenty of satisfaction, lots of choices. The red hots come in three sizes; the largest is too big for a bun, so it's served on Italian bread. And how many places these days still serve phosphates (vanilla, chocolate and strawberry)? If you pass up the malteds, try another Chicago tradition—the Dove Bar—for dessert. A hot dog with fries goes for $2 to $3.50, depending on the size.

Pig Outs
3591 N. Milwaukee Ave.
282-1200
Open Mon.-Fri. 6:30 a.m.-
9 p.m., Sat.-Sun. 11 a.m.-
9 p.m. (closed Sun. from
Dec.-Feb.).
No cards.

If you think W. C. Fields had the right idea about kids, Pig Outs won't be your kind of place—it swarms with teens from nearby Schurz High School. But age is no obstacle when it comes to enjoying juicy Vienna beef hot dogs, and this place serves them up fast and friendly to frank fans of all ages. In fact, though high school students get "special" prices, the same deal is extended to everyone—just expect a lot of teasing and a request for your ID. Seriously, Pig Outs really cares about its young customers: It serves a bargain-price egg sandwich to provide a more traditional, healthful breakfast option to the droves of ravenous students who pour through the doors the minute they open. There's a good chicken-filet sandwich and tangy fresh lemonade, too. A hot dog with fries and a sixteen-ounce soft drink will cost less than $2.

Tasty Dog
701 W. Lake St., Oak Park
383-9860
Open Mon.-Fri. 10 a.m.-
9:30 p.m., Sat. 10 a.m.-9
p.m., Sun. 11 a.m.-7 p.m.;
summer: open daily 10 a.m.-
10 p.m.
No cards.

The first-rate hot dogs are, of course, the meat of the issue at this spick-and-span stand, but if your taste runs toward garden-in-a-bun red hots, Tasty Dog is your Eden. A nimble-fingered line of servers piles on mustard, relish, onion, lettuce, cucumber, pickle, tomato and hot pepper with abandon; it's a lot like getting a free salad with your dog. The sit-down hot dog stand has plenty of indoor tables and counter seats, and on summer's dog days, wilted commuters hop off the El and take refuge in the picnic area. Kids can get a hot dog or hamburger for less than $1. About $3 for a hot dog, fries and soft drink.

Wolfy's Hot Dogs
2734 W. Peterson Ave.
743-0207
Open Mon.-Thurs. 10 a.m.-
10 p.m., Fri.-Sat. 10 a.m.-
10:30 p.m., Sun.
10:30 a.m.-10 p.m.
No cards.

This unassuming, cheerful hot dog stand is becoming a Chicago institution. Award-winning red hots come in a traditional steamed poppyseed bun with a choice of crunchy condiments—we suggest trying one slathered with cheese or chili. Wolfy's caters especially to hearty, after-school appetites: Every sandwich on the menu is available as a double. But if you eat like the proverbial bird, forego the double and leave room for the crispy fries. You'll spend just over $2 for a hot dog and fries.

ITALIAN BEEF

Al's Bar-B-Q
1079 W. Taylor St.
733-8896, 226-4017
Open Mon.-Sat. 9 a.m.-
1 a.m.
No cards.

If you want to capture the essence of things Chicago-style, look no further than Al's. Known as Little Al's to the neighborhood cognoscenti, this beef stand is a bastion of Chicago's Little Italy—the Taylor Street area—where roasted-on-the-premises beef, sliced superthin and heaped onto soft Gonnella bread, has been the Italian-beef sandwich of choice for half a decade. No amenities here (it's sort of like a two-car garage, with only stand-up counters to hunch over while you eat), but the Taylor Street show will keep you entertained while sandwich juices ooze between your fingers. Test the great french fries, with just the right amount of greasy softness; Italian sausages sizzling on the grill are awfully tempting, too. In the summer, Mario's Italian Ice just across the street is a mandatory stop if Al's hot peppers blaze your tongue a little too much. Silk dresses and vested suits mingle cordially with hard hats, and Al's gets its share of celebrities as well. About $4 for an Italian beef sandwich, fries and soft drink.

Buona Beef

6745 W. Roosevelt Rd.,
Berwyn
749-BEEF
*Open daily 10:30 a.m.-
10:30 p.m.*
No cards.

Buona means "good," and the Buonavolanto family who runs this megamagnificent beef stand is onto something mighty good. Actually, this is more than just an Italian-beef stand: There's an Italian deli, a dining area, a catering kitchen, an ice cream shop and outdoor seating in the summer. Buona Beef is all Italian and every inch Chicago. The spicy beef unique to the city is prepared on the premises according to an old family recipe and comes with your choice of hot peppers or thick strips of roasted sweet peppers. The lean, tender beef is perfectly matched with a wonderfully soft and delicious bun, and the resulting sandwich goes beyond buona. Italian lemonade, served al fresco in the summer, is a tongue-tingling thriller of a cooler. If you have even a drop of Italian blood in your veins, you'll head to Buona on Fridays for a lush and lovely, generous and mellow pepper-and-egg sandwich. If you're starving, try the beef-and-a-half sandwich. About $4 for an Italian beef sandwich, fries and a soft drink.

Johnnie's Beef

7500 W. North Ave.,
Elmwood Park
452-6000
*Open Mon.-Sat. 11 a.m.-
midnight, Sun. noon-mid-
night.*
No cards.

Lots of Italian-beef stands lurk in the suburbs, and they all have something good to offer, but Johnnie's is, well, special. Maybe it's Big John—an *abbondanza* sort of a guy—who presides over the premises, or maybe it's the low-impact atmosphere. Whatever the reason, this is a busy, busy beef stand. Johnnie's is a home away from home for those who suffer lunch, dinner and late-night hunger attacks. Just follow the scent of spicy beef and sausage wafting from the free-standing stand. The sausage is as good as the beef; have the best of both worlds and order the beef-and-sausage combo. Whatever your choice, don't miss the homemade Italian ice—lemons are squeezed daily for this tasty glacier in a cup. If it's Friday, it must be pepper-and-egg sandwich day, and Johnnie's loads the peppers and eggs into a bun with the best of them. You can eat at the outside tables in the summer; the rest of the year you'll have to find your own seating. An Italian-beef sandwich and fries will run about $3.

Mr. Beef on Orleans

666 N. Orleans St.
337-8500
Open Mon.-Fri. 7 a.m.-
5 p.m., Sat. 10 a.m.-2 p.m.
No cards.

This Italian beef stand has enough regular customers to fill Wrigley Field. They come by truck, by car, on foot... whatever way possible to get their Italian beef fix. And since the outdoor eating area has been enclosed, the hordes of daily customers have a bit more elbow room, so the feeling at any given time is more like a skirmish than a major assault. The Italian-beef sandwich at Mr. Beef is one of the best in the city. There's a spicy, tantalizing sweetness to the beef that is incomparable. It's loaded with a heavy hand into a soft-inside, crispy-outside Gonnella roll, the peppers (sweet or hot) are piled on top, you can have it "wet" or "dry"... it's a fine piece of work, this beauty-and-the-beef sandwich. The Italian sausage, made by a little sausage maker in the suburbs, has a marvelous texture and flavor (good hit of fennel) that holds up beautifully under the grilling. Less than $4 for an Italian-beef sandwich, fries and soft drink.

PIZZA

Bacino's of Lincoln Park

2204 N. Lincoln Ave.
472-7400
Open Mon.-Thurs. 11 a.m.-
10:30 p.m., Fri.-Sat.
11 a.m.-12:30 a.m., Sun.
noon-10 p.m.
Cards: AE, MC, V.

You can stuff yourself silly at Bacino's. The featured attraction at this Near North Side hangout for the glitterati is stuffed pizza: The spinach supreme (spinach and four types of cheeses), Bacino's special (sausage, mushrooms, green peppers, onions), vegetarian and broccoli pizzas rise high and wide and are deliciously handsome. Those who think pizza is swell but are concerned with staying svelte can take comfort in Bacino's thin-crust version—it's not as exciting, but it's not as filling either. We know it's hard to go to a pizzeria and not order pizza, but we'll let you in on a secret: Bacino's serves one of the best meatball sandwiches in town. You'll also enjoy a broad selection of imported and domestic beers and a decent selection of Italian and California wines that are fairly priced. Another location at 75 E. Wacker Drive, 263-0070. Delivery is available. A pizza dinner for two, with wine, costs about $20.

California Pizza Kitchen

See "Restaurants."

> *DON'T FORGET: Gault Millau introduces you to the Best of New York, the Best of Washington D.C., the Best of Los Angeles, the Best of San Francisco, the Best of New England, the Best of France, the Best of Paris, the Best of Italy, the Best of London.*

Connie's Pizza

2373 S. Archer Ave.
326-3443
Open Mon.-Thurs. 11 a.m.-
midnight, Fri.-Sat. 11 a.m.-
1 a.m., Sun. 11 a.m.-
midnight.
Cards: AE, MC, V.

Connie's is a tour de force in the great Chicago pizza race, in more ways than one. On any given day, some 35 Connie's trucks are out delivering pizza—from the city location alone. Connie's is also a full-menu restaurant (appetizers, soups, salads, sandwiches, pasta, chicken). And, of course, pizza can be enjoyed at its restaurant on S. Archer Avenue, which looks like an old warehouse that has been rehabbed to its former glory. In fact, it was built from scratch, and it's quite impressive. The pizza is impressive, too—most of the time. The delivered version isn't as good as that served in the restaurant; it tends to slide in on the greasy side too often. Pizzas come in a variety of styles: middleweight (a little thicker crust), deep-dish, stuffed and, on request, thin crust. If you're negotiating a big business deal and can't break for lunch, Connie's will deliver 100 pizzas with less than two hours' notice. Less than $15 for two, with beer.

Edwardo's Natural Pizza Restaurant

1212 N. Dearborn St.
337-4490
Open Mon.-Thurs. 11 a.m.-
midnight, Fri.-Sat.
11 a.m.-1:30 a.m., Sun.
noon-11:30 p.m.
Cards: AE, MC, V.

Edwardo's has several locations spread around the Chicagoland area, but we like the sleek, modern location on N. Dearborn Street best. The pizza isn't any better at this particular location—in fact, Edwardo's rapid expansion has resulted in corporate-formula pizza, which means that pizzas are made by the book and the book isn't always right. But the help is a little more savvy and the customers are, too. Nobody could question the quality of Edwardo's pizzas, because only the freshest ingredients are used in constructing the stuffed pizzas, which are the strength of the menu. The stuffed spinach is delicious, as is the soufflé pizza, a mix of fresh spinach, broccoli and chopped walnuts. There is also a pesto pizza, and for the health-conscious, a whole-wheat crust is available in both the stuffed and thin-crust versions. Some excellent salads and several pasta dishes (the pasta needs work) are included on the menu, along with a good selection of bottled beer and wine. About $20 for stuffed pizza and beer for two.

Geppetto's

113 N. Oak Park Ave.,
Oak Park
386-9200
Open daily 11 a.m.-
11 p.m.
All major cards.

Geppetto's makes excellent pizza, whether it be thin crust, deep-dish or stuffed. If those seem basic and mundane, look at the next column on the menu, where you'll find Geppetto's signature pizzas, which are quite out of the ordinary. The deli pizza has Grey Poupon mustard and enough cold cuts to heat up an igloo. The sombrero pizza is, as you have already guessed, covered with ingredients you'd find in a taco. The West Side gets barbecue sauce, chicken and mozzarella cheese... pizza schizophrenia! But wait! Don't order yet! If you still can't make up your mind, there are 35 topping choices, ranging from alfalfa sprouts to crabmeat to pastrami, right on through to turkey and zucchini. The rest of the menu has its own personality, too, and regulars are crazy for the complex sandwiches, Italian specialties and seafood dishes. After you've stumbled through all those choices and are still undecided, you can always fall back on a quiche or two. And you can wash it all down with imported and domestic beer, California Coolers or one of the other requisite beverages. Takeout and delivery also, along with another location at 6457 N. Sheridan Road, 274-8300. A pizza dinner for two, with beer, will cost about $16.

Gino's East Pizzeria
160 E. Superior St.
943-1124
*Open Mon.-Thurs. 11 a.m.-
11 p.m., Fri.-Sat. 11 a.m.-
midnight, Sun. 2 p.m.-
10 p.m.*
All major cards.

The aroma of the deep-dish pizza will make your taste buds scream and your stomach roar during the inevitable weekend wait for a table. But steel yourself—both will be duly rewarded once your server slides onto your plate a slab of yellow-crusted wonder from a deep, black pizza pan. The atmosphere is loud and lively, and the graffiti etched into the tables by patrons past makes for some interesting reading. In recent years, pizza aficionados—especially those in the city—have not loved Gino's pizza as much as they used to. But visitors from other cities who have never experienced authentic deep-dish pizza are truly enamored of these pies. Pasta dishes, though, are scandalously oversauced, ravioli is overcooked, and if you order a hamburger, you deserve what you get. Gino's got a lot of national press several years ago, which was when it got too comfortable and went to sleep on its press clippings. Another location at 1321 W. Golf Road in Rolling Meadows, 364-6644. About $20 for pizza and beer for two.

Giordano's Restaurant
747 N. Rush St.
951-0747
*Open Mon.-Thurs. 11 a.m.-
midnight, Fri.-Sat. 11 a.m.-
1 a.m., Sun. noon-midnight.
Cards: AE, CB, DC,
Discover.*

There is as much controversy in this city over who originated stuffed pizza as there is about the latest political brouhaha. We have our own opinion about the birth of stuffed pizza, but the story is too long to recount here. Suffice it to say, then, that Giordano's got rolling about fifteen years ago, and for a long time the only pizza it made (and some say brought to perfection) was stuffed. Today it also serves thin-crust pizza, but it isn't half as interesting as the stuffed version, which is stuffed with plenty of choice ingredients, from vegetables and sausage to shrimp and beyond. It's well-made pizza, and the overall taste has its moments, but the sauce isn't consistent from one location to another. It's spicy here, not so spicy there; harsh-tasting here, mellow and sweet there. But it never misses on the crust—it's consistently good. As it goes these days, pizzerias have to offer something for everybody, so Giordano's has the basic (and basically uninteresting) salads, token pastas (most of them in the linguine family), sandwiches, soups and the Italian desserts that dot Chicago's Italian restaurant landscape: spumoni and tortoni. Delivery and takeout are available. About twenty other locations are scattered throughout

Chicagoland. A stuffed pizza dinner for two, with beer, runs about $20.

Home Run Inn, Inc.
4254 W. 31st St.
247-9696
Open Mon.-Thurs.
11 a.m.-12:30 a.m., Fri.-
Sat. 11 a.m.-1:30 a.m.
(no seating after midnight),
Sun. noon-midnight.
No cards.

You can tell a Chicagoan, but you can't tell him much—about pizza, that is. The city is a sharply divided camp when it comes to favorite pizza places, pizza styles, who was the first to do this or that to a pizza... it's all as messy and loose as a Pee-Wee Herman movie. But there is substantial agreement around these parts when it comes to who has the best thin-crust (actually it's more of a medium-thick-crust) pizza: the Home Run Inn. It's all in the consistency. The pizza here is as good today as it was 40 years ago when owner Nick Perrino started the whole thing. The size of the place has expanded fivefold since then, and on any given evening it seems as if the customer base has expanded tenfold. It's a well-oiled machine, though, so pizzas (it makes about 7,000 a week, some destined for the freezer section of local supermarkets, some for takeout) come without too much wait. When you do wait, however, the people-watching is as interesting as the pizza is excellent. Why is the pizza so good? Home Run bones pork butts to make its own sausage, blends three different kinds of mozzarella cheese and makes a lush, tasty sauce and a properly chewy crust. What more can you ask of a pizza? About $20 for an extra-large cheese-and-sausage pizza and a couple of beers.

Leona's
3215 N. Sheffield Ave.
327-8861
Open Mon.-Thurs. 11 a.m.-
1 a.m., Fri.-Sat. 11 a.m.-
2:30 a.m., Sun 11 a.m.-
2:30 a.m.
All major cards.

This frenetic pizzeria and Italian restaurant has grown like topsy since 1950 to accommodate its ever-increasing legion of fans, so eating here is not exactly a tranquil experience (actually it's like a college mess hall run amuck). Fortunately, for those who can't stand the din or the wait, Leona's has one of the largest and most reliable delivery teams in Chicago. We say "fortunately" because Leona's has the greatest variety of pizzas in the city and makes them all with élan. We think the thin crust is the best of the lot, but there are also respectable versions of the pan, double-deck, stuffed, whole-wheat crust and white (with a Parmesan cream sauce instead of tomato sauce) pizzas. With no fewer than 27 toppings to choose from— including such bizarre possibilities as cauliflower, turkey breast and whipped eggs—you really get pizza your way here. Leona's is not timid about adding and deleting menu items, but some permanent entries, like the excellent lasagne and the toothsome ravioli trio (meat, cheese and spinach) are definitely worth a try. Meal-size salads will feed an entire college dormitory, as will many of the other dishes here. Dinner for two, with drinks, runs about $16. Two offshoots are Leona's Daughters, 6953 N. Sheridan Road, 764-5757, and Leona's Neighborhood Restaurant, 1936 W. Augusta Boulevard, 292-4300.

Lou Malnati's Pizzeria

439 N. Wells St.
828-9800
*Open Mon.-Thurs. 11 a.m.-
11 p.m., Fri.-Sat. 11 a.m.-
1 a.m., Sun. 3 p.m.-
10 p.m.
All major cards.*

Lou Malnati started his pizza operation in the suburbs, and with this latest location in the trendy River North area, sons Marc and Rick are continuing the family tradition. Burnished wood, comfortable booths, high tables with stools and tile floors give this century-old building a traditional but upscale look enlivened with sports memorabilia, including framed shirts of some of Chicago's biggest sports stars. It's a fine atmosphere in which to sidle up to one of the best deep-dish pizzas in the town where deep-dish pizza began. Try the buttercrust pizza, unique to Malnati's, or the chicken parmigiana sandwich. Six other locations are scattered throughout the suburbs. About $15 for cheese-and-sausage pizza and beer for two.

O'Fame

750 W. Webster Ave.
929-5111
*Open Mon.-Sat. 4 p.m.-
midnight, Sun. 2 p.m.-
midnight.
Cards: MC, V.*

From the spotless white decor to the open kitchen, O'Fame boasts a pristine atmosphere, and just as much attention is given to the great, fresher-than-fresh pizza ingredients. If you like your pizza crust thin and crisp and your vegetables unfailingly crunchy, you'll find this pizza irresistible. Simple toppings like sausage are excellent and never boring, but it's the vegetable toppings that stand out—thinly shaved mushrooms, wisps of onion and slivers of green pepper are piled on generously; slicing them thin ensures that they're cooked but retain their individual textures. There's also pan and stuffed pizza, pasta with fresh-tasting sauces, an imaginative antipasto plate for two and a fantastic Italian sub sandwich. Pizza and beer for two will run about $15.

Pizzeria Uno

29 E. Ohio St.
321-1000
*Open Mon. 4 p.m.-11 p.m.,
Tues.-Thurs. 11:30 a.m.-
11 p.m., Fri.-Sat. 11:30
a.m.-midnight, Sun.
1 p.m.-8 p.m.
All major cards.*

This is where it all began, in June 1943, when Pizzeria Uno opened and the business of serving pizza—not just in Chicago, but around the world—took a giant leap forward. Stories abound about would-be competitors who dug into the trash can behind Uno's to try to discover the ingredients that go into Uno's deep-dish pizza. The hunt was for good reason: Uno's had customers lined up outside, waiting for a taste of the sensational "new pie." And a lot of people wanted more than just a piece to eat—they wanted some of that booming business. Uno's is as busy today as it was then, and just about every celebrity—from rock star to movie star to Brenda Starr (well, maybe her creator)—who visits Chicago has been to Uno or to her sister, Due, just a block away. This is a magnificently constructed pizza, from the crust to the toppings. The dough is made daily, the cheese is the best available, the sausage and other toppings are choice and fresh, and the sauce is natural and perfectly seasoned. Deep-dish pizza doesn't get much better than this, and in this setting, which is pure Chicago pizzeria from the checkered tablecloths to the snappy wait staff, pizza never tasted so good. About $16 for a pizza-and-beer dinner for two.

NIGHTLIFE

ON THE TOWN IN CHICAGO

From Lincoln Park's funky blues bars to River North's stylish nighteries and Rush and Division streets' plethora of singles bars, Chicago is home to as broad and sophisticated a nightlife scene as in any of the world's great cities. While visitors often make a beeline for Rush and Division streets, this city of diverse neighborhoods has much more to offer than touristy fern bars. Chicago is, of course, the "Home of the Blues," but it's also home to thriving jazz and reggae scenes. And, needless to say, the Second City also knows a thing or two about comedy.

Keep in mind that all bars within the Chicago city limits are open one hour later on Saturdays. That means bars that close at 2 a.m. Sunday to Friday are open until 3 a.m., and late-hour license holders that normally close at 4 a.m. stay open until 5 a.m.

For up-to-the-minute nightlife and live-music listings, check the *Chicago Tribune* and *Chicago Sun-Times*'s Friday entertainment sections, the free weekly *Chicago Reader*, *Chicago* magazine's "Events" listings and the *Illinois Entertainer*.

BARS

Acorn on Oak
116 E. Oak St.
944-6835
Open daily 11:30 a.m.-2 a.m.
Cards: AE.

Pianoman Buddy Charles—he of the seemingly limitless repertoire—has long been a fixture here, but even non–music lovers will enjoy a visit to the Acorn. Frequented primarily by those over 35, the dark and chummy pub is populated by everyone from society matrons to lonely guys out on the town. Seated at the small bar, you might hear snatches of conversation that sound like dialogue from a soap opera, but one thing they'll never be is dull. The burgers are among the city's best.

John Barleycorn Memorial Pub
658 W. Belden St.
348-8899
Open daily 11 a.m.-2 a.m.
Cards: MC, V.

Some bars show sporting events or music videos on their large-screen TVs. No such proletarian drivel here: This venerable Lincoln Park pub instead projects slides of paintings and sculptures by the masters. Busts of Mozart and Beethoven share space with stuffed birds, moose heads and more than twenty painstakingly assembled wooden-ship models. You don't have to be an art lover or highbrow to fit in here, where the atmosphere is casual and conversation is the main event. Excellent burgers and appetizers are served, as well as a selection of more than 30 beers.

The Berghoff Cafe
17 W. Adams St.
427-3170
Open Mon.-Thurs. 11 a.m.-9 p.m., Fri.-Sat. 11 a.m.-9 p.m.
No cards.

Other than the fact that women are now allowed in the bar, not much has changed at the Berghoff in the last 50 years, and for that we're thankful—this classic Chicago saloon has a lot of tradition and history. Opened by Herman Berghoff, who came to Chicago in 1893, Berghoff's long, stand-up oak bar (with a convenient brass rail to hang onto should you feel faint) remains as popular as its restaurant. Dressed nattily, the bartenders pour some 1,600 steins of beer daily, much of it brewed specially for the Berghoff and bearing its name; the house fourteen-year-old bourbon is specially distilled in Kentucky. And the Berghoff's clientele runs the gamut, though you can expect to see plenty of white-collar office workers bellying up to the bar after 5 p.m.

Billy Goat Tavern
430 N. Michigan Ave.
(lower level)
222-1525
Open daily 7 a.m.-2 a.m.
No cards.

This is one of Chicago's most famous and colorful bars. Semihidden on the lower level of Michigan Avenue, the Billy Goat has been a favorite of journalists and staff from the neighboring *Sun-Times* and *Tribune* buildings for generations. A funky, no-frills kind of place, the Billy Goat is a living museum of Chicago journalism. Blowups of columns and bylines of famous writers from days past fill the place, as do yellowing clips and hundreds of photos of famous Chicagoans. The food is quick and cheap; this place is said to have been the inspiration for John Belushi's famous *"Cheezebugah, Cheezebugah!"* bit from *Saturday Night Live.* If you thrive on loud talk, greasy food and cheap drinks, this is your nirvana.

Brehon Pub
731 N. Wells St.
642-1071
Open Mon.-Sat. 11 a.m.-2 a.m., Sun. noon-8 p.m.
No cards.

If the trendy razzle-dazzle of River North begins to grate on your nerves, this somewhat dingy Irish bar should provide some welcome relief. Whether you come in a group or solo, you'll find Brehon to be one of the city's friendlier pubs, a place where you can still find Beer Nuts and beef jerky behind the old oak bar. You can get a pint of Guinness on tap, which goes perfectly with the Irish flags, pictures of Chicago's Irish politicians and the "Erin Go Bragh" banner above the door. From two-fisted blue-collar workers to three-piece-suiters, everyone feels at home here.

Harry Caray's
33 W. Kinzie St.
465-9269
Open Mon.-Fri. 11 a.m.-1 a.m., Sat. 11:30 a.m.-1 a.m., Sun. noon-midnight.
Cards: AE, MC, V.

Longtime baseball broadcaster Harry Caray is one of the most beloved Chicagoans, and his multiroom restaurant/bar is equally beloved. Caray has collected loads of baseball memorabilia—uniforms, autographed photos, red-white-and-blue World Series banners—during his 40 years behind the microphone, and he's put it to good decorative use in his long bar. This is a beer-drinking kind of joint, frequented by a young and well-dressed crowd, guzzling Budweiser and munching gratis homemade potato chips. And—as an added bonus—from April to October, the avuncular Caray is often in attendance, kissing young women and pressing the flesh.

City Lights
223 W. Ontario St.
280-7660
Open nightly 9 p.m.-4 a.m.
Cover $5.
All major cards.

Nostalgic for the disco '70s? Then head for City Lights, the watering hole attached to Ditka's that's crawling with people decorated with lots of gold chains, jewelry and out-of-season tans. Between bouts of looking to meet Mr. or Ms. Right, they admire the autographed photos of sports and show-biz personalities on the walls and keep an eye out for celebrities in-the-flesh. High-tech lighting grids over-look the central dance floor, where music ranging from Madonna to Roy Orbison keeps things busy. Jeans, tennis shoes and sweatshirts are verboten, and men without sport coats might find the tuxedo-clad wait staff a bit snooty while pouring $4 bottles of domestic beer.

Coq D'Or
(The Drake),
140 E. Walton Pl.
787-2200
Open Mon.-Fri.
11:30 a.m.-2 a.m., Sat.
11:30 a.m.-2 a.m., Sun.
11:30 a.m.-midnight.
All major cards.

A link to the Chicago of yesteryear, the Coq D'Or in The Drake hotel retains the charm it displayed during its open-ing days in the late 1920s. The room is beautifully paneled in dark wood with appointments reminiscent of an early 1800s tavern. A pianist tinkles away in the background, though the melodies never interfere with the conversation. Food is available at the bar— try the excellent chili or clam chowder. Though it's not the fashionable place it once was, the Coq D'Or remains a room rich in Chicago tradition.

Cricket's
(The Tremont),
100 E. Chestnut St.
280-2100
Open daily 11 a.m.-1 a.m.
All major cards.

The city's rich Gold Coast socialites and other persons of renown meet at Cricket's in The Tremont hotel to gossip and name-drop shamelessly ("I was with Eva Gardner once and she said to me: ..."). The atmosphere is understated and clubby; many of the bar's patrons are on a first-name basis with the bartender. Although a pianist plays standards off in a corner, this intimate room is primarily a place for convers-ing over an expensive glass of Cognac or Champagne. If you can't match all the caricatures of the regulars on the walls with names, you're probably not one of them.

Earl's Pub
2470 N. Lincoln Ave.
929-0660
Open nightly 6 p.m.-2 a.m.
No cards.

For nearly 25 years, Earl Pionke's Earl of Old Town was the focal point for Chicago's folk-music community. It was the launching pad for both Steve Goodman and John Prine and, under Earl's gruff but benevolent tutelage, nurtured two generations of the city's singer-songwriters. At his new location, Earl—looking like ZZ Top's father with his long, pointed gray beard—pours drinks and flips burgers while presenting local acoustic-music acts from Tuesday to Sun-day (happily free of cover charge). The place is funky but comfortable, with plain brick walls, scarred tabletops and bar stools whose upholstery has seen better days. A large-screen TV shows sporting events most of the time, while a mixture of old bohos wearing tweed sport coats and more fashionably attired yupsters wash down Earl's chili and burgers with a few cold ones. If Lincoln Park's trendiness becomes overwhelming, this is a good alternative.

Fourth Edition
(Chicago Marriott),
540 N. Michigan Ave.
836-0100
Open nightly 5 p.m.-
12:30 a.m.
All major cards.

Unlike the noisy, retro-disco atmosphere of the Marriott's other lounge, the Upper Avenue Room, the Fourth Edition is a civilized spot for a cocktail and some music. The room resembles an English library, appointed with bookshelves, richly upholstered chairs and couches and stained glass on the ceiling. In the middle of the intimate room is a piano, which is put to good use by musicians performing standards and show tunes Tuesday through Saturday beginning at 9 p.m. Yes, this is a hotel bar, filled with the requisite tourists and business travelers, but it's one of the nicer ones in the city.

Gaslight Corner
2858 N. Halsted St.
348-2288
Open daily 10 a.m.-2 a.m.
No cards.

This corner tavern is many things to many people. For locals, it's a neighborhood place to grab a beer and a burger or sandwich; for performers and audiences from the neighboring Steppenwolf Theater Company, it's a preshow and postshow hangout; and for armchair jocks, it's a sports bar showing football, baseball, basketball and hockey games on one of the better big-screen projection TVs in town. Okay, we'll admit that the bar service can be slow, and the bartenders sometimes border on being surly, but the mix of people makes for one of the more interesting bar crowds on the North Side.

The Green Door Tavern
678 N. Orleans St.
664-5496
Open daily 11 a.m.-
midnight.
Cards: AE.

Long before the fern bars on Division Street in the suburbs started raiding antiques shops for bits of faded Americana, this historic restaurant/tavern was filled to the rafters with timeworn relics. From ancient brass cash registers to vintage Ex Lax and *Ladies Home Journal* ads, The Green Door presents a visual feast without coming off like a tourist trap. While the wood-frame building dates back to 1872—one year after the Great Chicago Fire—the building changed from a grocery store to a tavern/restaurant in 1921 and retains many of the original fixtures. The lunch-and-dinner menu lists everything a good tavern should—chili, burgers, ribs—and you can almost always find room to belly up to the bar. You're in for a treat if you're a jazz fan, as music by Charlie Parker, Miles Davis and Billie Holiday continually wafts from the speakers.

The Green House
(The Ritz-Carlton),
2160 E. Pearson St.
266-1000
Open daily 11:30 a.m.-
1 a.m.
All major cards.

You'll forget, if only for a peaceful moment, that you're in the heart of the city when you settle into this relaxing open area just off the twelfth-floor lobby of The Ritz-Carlton hotel. Strategically placed plants, trees and flowers provide a lush backdrop for cocktail sipping, while a large fountain splashes in the background. Comfortable wicker chairs and couches abound, and you can munch on appetizers (shrimp, cheese plates and the like). The staff is extremely friendly—they'll be happy to leave you alone with your thoughts if you'd rather daydream than drink.

Hard Rock Cafe
63 W. Ontario St.
943-2252
Open daily 11 a.m.-1 a.m.
Cards: AE, MC, V.

While there's nothing uniquely "Chicago" about this local branch of the Hard Rock, it's a fun place to have a few brews, eat hamburgers and chili and marvel at the plethora of rock 'n' roll artifacts. Loud, nonstop music blasting from the sound system makes screaming the preferred form of conversation. But there's always plenty to look at, from David Bowie's saxophone to Roy Orbison and Sting's guitars. The crowd is young and frisky, and even though there's seating for 250 people on two levels, on weekends plan on waiting in line to get in.

Harry's Cafe
1035 N. Rush St.
266-0167
Open Sun.-Thurs.
11:30 a.m.-midnight, Fri.-
Sat. 11:30 a.m.-2 a.m.
All major cards.

Even before the term "yuppie" was invented, Harry's was a well-established favorite among upscale baby boomers out to do some power partying. Year-round tans and the sweet smiles of success abound, with much exchanging of business cards. The decor in this restaurant/bar is your standard brass 'n' glass, with hanging plants and stained glass. In warm-weather months the ground-level area looking out on Rush Street is a prime spot for people watching.

Hunt Club
1983 N. Clybourn Ave.
549-3020
Open Mon.-Sat.
11:30 a.m.-2 a.m., Sun.
11:30 a.m.-midnight.
All major cards.

In a previous incarnation as Molly McGuire's, this was a great place to knock back a beer after work, beloved by both blue-collar workers and pioneering De Paul–area professionals. Now—to quote a friend of ours—this bar/restaurant has been colonized by the "yuppie elite." The food is decent, live blues, reggae and rock bands are featured regularly, and there's a beautiful outdoor patio area. But if you have a low tolerance for pretense, don't say we didn't warn you.

The Lodge
21 W. Division St.
642-4406
Open daily 2 p.m.-4 a.m.
All major cards.

Although this open-till-four joint is as much a singles bar as anyplace on Division Street, somehow The Lodge doesn't seem quite as predatory as the others. But it's still a crowded and rowdy place, and you'll feel like a human sardine as the occasional elbow hits you in the ribs. The jukebox plays lots of '60s rock, the table-bowling game is a nice icebreaker, and if you're wearing jeans, you won't feel out of place.

Maxtavern
2856 N. Racine St.
348-5055
Open daily 12:30 p.m.-
2 a.m.
No cards.

Globe-trotters will feel right at home—almost two dozen globes of varying sizes are either suspended from the high ceiling or displayed near the bar at this hangout for the young, artsy, North Side set, distinguished by their black clothes, berets and tortured-young-artist demeanors. A couple of hundred record albums are behind the bar, and the bartender will be happy to consider your musical request as he pours you one of several excellent regional beers. Oh yes, if you'd like to document your visit, there's a photo booth as well.

Butch McGuire's

20 W. Division St.
337-9080
Open daily 10 a.m.-4 a.m.
Cards: MC, V.

If you insist on "doing" Division Street, you might as well start out with the progenitor of Chicago's singles bars, Butch McGuire's. Since 1961, a visit to Butch's has been a rite of passage for both Chicagoans and tourists. The place is full of antiques and Irish knickknacks, and the extravagant decorations put up for Christmas and St. Patrick's Day are worth a visit alone. It's nearly always packed with singles (or wedding-ring- in-the-pocket singles), and if you're a woman, you can expect to get hit on about every 30 seconds. Still, it's all part of the game, and zealous bouncers will be happy to step in if "get lost" isn't part of your new admirer's vocabulary. Though now almost interchangeable with such neighboring bars as Mother's and She-Nannigans, Butch's remains one of the city's best-known bars.

Nick's

1973 N. Halsted St.
664-7383
*Open Mon.-Fri. 3 p.m.-
2 a.m., Sat.-Sun. 1 p.m.-
2 a.m.*
Cards: AE.

When it opened more than ten years ago, Nick's was an outpost of fun in an area best described as seedy. Now boutiques with cutesy names, designer ice cream stores and trendy nighteries glut the intersection of Halsted and Armitage, yet Nick's remains reassuringly the same. The bizarre accoutrements (a huge painting sporting a few bullet holes behind the bar, a tiger-striped surfboard, a bathroom shower mounted on the wall) make it clear that this is a great place to cut loose—and your feet will just have to move when they hear the classic Motown and soul music from one of the city's best jukeboxes. The atmosphere is casual, and the clientele predominantly young professionals from the immediate area.

O'Rourke's

319 W. North Ave.
944-1030
Open daily 3:30 p.m.-2 a.m.
No cards.

One quick look inside this dim, rather scruffy Old Town institution and you'll know this is no slick singles bar. O'Rourke's is a favorite among writers, artists, playwrights and poets of all ages, but that doesn't mean that just plain Joes aren't welcome to hoist a pint of Guinness and join in the repartee, too. Large portraits of Irish literary figures— Oscar Wilde, James Joyce, Brendan Behan and Sean O'Casey—fill one wall, with quotes from their works scribbled in chalk above each picture. Mainly a place for the lively art of conversation, O'Rourke's also has a stupendous jukebox stocked with selections ranging from Nat King Cole to Otis Redding to John Coltrane.

Kitty O'Shea's

(Chicago Hilton & Towers),
720 S. Michigan Ave.
922-4400
*Open Mon.-Sat. 11 a.m.-
1 a.m., Sun. 1 p.m.-
midnight.
All major cards.*

One might expect phoniness from a hotel bar, but they don't come any more Irish than this multiroom, street-level pub across the street from Grant Park. From pints of Guinness and Harp to shots of Jameson poured by an Irish bartender from suspended, upside-down bottles, Kitty O'Shea's provides traditional Irish imbibing fare. While sitting at the long mahogany bar and quaffing a few (or perhaps tasting the lamb stew or potato-leek soup), you'll notice that the walls are full of paraphernalia paying tribute to the old sod. Of special interest are the photos and traditional walking sticks in "Shillelagh Corner," where homage is paid to prominent Chicagoans of Irish ancestry. This is as authentic an ethnic pub as you'll find in any big-city hotel.

O'Sullivan's Public House

495 N. Milwaukee Ave.
733-2927
*Open daily 11:30 a.m.-
4 a.m.
No cards.*

Located at the intersection of Grand Avenue, Halsted Street and Milwaukee Avenue, O'Sullivan's is yet another example of the classic Chicago Irish workingman's bar. Serious darts players are among the regulars in this dark, woodsy bar filled with Irish curios. By day, O'Sullivan's is a popular lunchtime spot for both blue-collar workers and three-piece-suiters, and it's noted for its lamb stew. Live rock and blues music is featured Wednesday through Saturday with a $2 cover charge.

Out Takes

16 W. Ontario St.
951-7979
*Open daily 4 p.m.-2 a.m.
Cover $3 Fri. after 8 p.m.
& Sat. after 9 p.m.
Cards: AE, DC.*

Until the next *dernier-cri* opens, the trendy set is firmly encamped in Out Takes. From the CD jukebox stocked with Talking Heads and Echo & the Bunnymen to the 900-gallon fish-tank bar, Out Takes is an audio-visual extravaganza bound to impress even the most jaded barfly. There are several rooms to explore, along with an outdoor café, where you can sample such appetizers as duck pâté while drinking Champagne priced from $35 (Mumm's Brut) to $125 (Roederer-Cristal '82). Amid the bizarre body-parts sculptures and artsy black-and-white photographs in the "gallery," even the tragically hip will admit that one thing Out Takes is *not* is boring.

Pump Room

(The Ambassador East),
1301 N. State St.
266-0360
*Open daily 7 a.m.-1 a.m.
All major cards.*

The name evokes images of celebrities of old holding court in booth number one. And even if the Pump Room has been eclipsed by newer, trendier nightspots, it remains a Chicago must. The hundreds of photos of famous Pump Room visitors crammed onto every inch of available wall space make for amusing gazing while sipping a cocktail or listening to the musicians in the corner playing jazz, standards and cheek-to-cheek dance music. While some yupscalers come here after work for a cocktail or two and to sample the gratis spread of hors d'oeuvres, most of the clientele is over 40. This is also one of the few places in the city that still requires men to wear jackets.

The Ranch

56 W. Randolph St.
263-8207
Open daily 7 a.m.-2 a.m.
No cover charge.
All major cards.

Blues and jazz clubs abound, but Chicago has never been a mecca for country music. Nonetheless, we've found this little bit of Dixie in the heart of the Loop, a haven for those longing to hear popular country music. For more than 25 years the rock-solid Sundowners have played classic country standards (Wednesday through Saturday at 8:30 p.m.) for no cover charge—surely one of the city's best entertainment values. Set below street level, The Ranch is like a western museum, filled as it is with cowboy memorabilia and an impressive collection of antique pistols and guns. This is a popular lunchtime spot noted for its chili, and the clientele is among the most heterogeneous of any bar in the city.

Riccardo's

437 N. Rush St.
787-2874
Open daily 11:30 a.m.-
11 p.m.
All major cards.

Like the Billy Goat, this handsome restaurant/bar is a hangout for hard-boiled journalists, along with slickly dressed advertising people. Camped around the palette-shaped bar (original owner Rick Riccardo was a painter), the mixed-media patrons toss down double scotches and vodka on the rocks while boisterously discussing politics, business and whatever else comes to mind. Huge surrealistic paintings by Riccardo hang behind the bar, and photos of notable Riccardo's regulars grace the walls. If the cigar and cigarette smoke gets too intense, you can escape to the streetside café during warm-weather months.

Sieben's River North Brewery

436 W. Ontario St.
787-7313
Open Mon.-Thurs.
11 a.m.-midnight, Fri.-
Sat. 11 a.m.-2 p.m.,
Sun. noon- 10 p.m.
Cards: AE, MC, V.

Sieben's is a beer-lover's paradise, a boisterous working brewery offering food, live jazz and a great atmosphere. Located on the western fringe of River North, Sieben's brews excellent lager, ale and stout, as evidenced by the huge copper kettles in the middle of this sprawling two-tier room. Wooden picnic tables and benches give a beer-hall atmosphere to the downstairs beer garden, while separate tables and a copper-topped bar make for a slightly quieter setting upstairs in the bier stube. There's lots of exposed brick, wooden beams and pipes, with turn-of-the-century photos and posters recalling the halcyon days when Chicago boasted dozens of breweries. The drinkers, who come in all varieties, are held together by a common love of suds.

Sweetwater

1028 N. Rush St.
787-5552
Open Sun.-Thurs. 4 p.m.-
10:30 p.m., Fri.-Sat.
4 p.m.- midnight.
All major cards.

The bar in this sophisticated restaurant attracts a well-heeled, dressed-for-success, over-35 crowd anxious to meet their own kind. Tastefully furnished throughout, with twin chandeliers and a vaulted skylight high over the bar, Sweetwater is a sports bar for those whose sport of choice is people watching. To make the game even more fun, Sweetwater's glass walls allow the pedestrians on Rush Street to ogle you while you ogle them.

Tap Root Pub
636 W. Willow St.
642-5235
Open daily 11 a.m.-
1:30 a.m.
All major cards.

If you want to experience a historic Chicago tavern, you won't find one more authentic and colorful than the Tap Root Pub. The original Tap Root on Larrabee Street was demolished in 1972, though the building it has occupied since then has been a bar for more than 100 years. Legend has it that Al Capone used to store bootleg whisky in the warehouse behind the beer garden, and that infamous local politician Paddy Bauler once shot a cop here for insulting him. From the elaborately designed tin ceiling to the pot-bellied stove, antique carpentry tools and old bottles, there's a strong sense of tradition. Dressed in his trademark suspenders, longtime owner Harley Budd (how's that for a barkeep's name!) is always happy to share the bar's lore with his customers, who include neighborhood young professionals, old-timers and the occasional cop on the beat. The attached Four Seasons Restaurant is known for its seafood, with a fish fry every Friday night and a clambake on Sundays. Oh yes, the Tap Root also has one of the city's biggest beer gardens.

Ultimate Sports Bar & Grill
354 W. Armitage Ave.
477-4630
Open Sun.-Thurs.
11:30 a.m.-2 a.m., Fri.-
Sat. 11:30 a.m.-4 a.m.
All major cards.

This was one of the city's first yuppie sports bars and it remains one of the most boisterous—a fact that has had residents of bucolic Lincoln Park up in arms from time to time. Although they've since become sports-bar clichés, the Ultimate has continuous sporting events on multiple TVs, a basketball free-throw shooting cage and walls full of Chicago sports memorabilia. Burgers and beer-friendly appetizers are available, and the dining area is situated inside a boxing ring. The club attracts a young, hard-drinking crowd who can easily cross the border into obnoxiousness the later the hour gets.

Zebra Lounge
1220 N. State St.
642-5140
Open daily noon-2 a.m.
No cards.

Located just a half block north of Division Street, the Zebra Lounge is an oasis of sanity amid the singles-bar hustle. This tiny piano bar semihidden in the Canterbury Court building is aptly named, for the zebra motif is incorporated throughout the room, including the walls, booths and artwork. A homey and friendly bar, the Zebra Lounge is also a great place to check out some of the neighborhood Gold Coast eccentrics, while listening to standards and show tunes from the piano player. Though the preponderance of black-and-white stripes may have you seeing double if you've had one too many, the Zebra is a wonderful place to escape to.

Some establishments change their closing times without warning. It is always wise to call ahead.

BLUES

Blue Chicago
937 N. State St.
642-6261
*Open Mon.-Sat. 8 p.m.-
2 a.m. Shows nightly 9 p.m.
Cover $3-$6.
Cards: MC, V.*

If you're staying in or around the Loop, this is the city's most accessible blues club. Tourists, business travelers and conventioneers sometimes outnumber locals, but we don't care—this joyously raw music is the real thing. Such stalwarts of the local blues scene as Magic Slim and Valerie Wellington frequently hold the stage in this good-sized room, which features a long bar, small dance floor and portraits of (mostly) departed blues greats along the walls.

B.L.U.E.S.
2519 N. Halsted St.
528-1012
*Open nightly 8 p.m.-2 a.m.
Shows 9 p.m.
Cover $3-$5.
No cards.*

At first glance, the city's best blues bar hardly looks worthy of such an honor. It's a cramped room with an equally small stage that doesn't always accommodate all the members of larger groups. Seating is on a first-come, first-serve basis, and if you *do* find a place to sit, you might be squeezed in closer to your immediate neighbors than you like. But when the music starts—provided by the city's top blues men and women—you'll immediately forget these shortcomings as this cozy, smoky club turns into an instant party. Crowds are a mix of area yuppies, blues purists and out-of-towners.

B.L.U.E.S. Etcetera
1124 W. Belmont Ave.
525-8989
*Open nightly 8 p.m.-2 a.m.
Shows Sun.-Thurs. 9 p.m.,
Fri.- Sat. 9:30 p.m.
Cover $3-$6.
Cards: AE, MC, V.*

While lacking that "wang-dang doodle" ambience of its sister club on Halsted Street, B.L.U.E.S. Etcetera is larger and more generous with creature comforts. You can readily find a seat on most nights, you won't have to wait long to use the rest room and, if the spirit moves you, you can even shake your money-maker on the dance floor right in front of the stage. The club also tends to be more catholic in its booking policies, bringing in out-of-town blues, R & B and even Cajun-Zydeco groups. The crowds tend to be composed of primarily young professionals from the immediate area.

Kingston Mines
2548 N. Halsted St.
477-4646
*Open nightly 8:30 p.m.-
4 a.m. Shows nightly
9:30 p.m. Cover $4-$7.
No cards.*

This funky North Side institution is a haven for night owls who refuse to quit when the 2 a.m. clubs close. Blues bands play continuously in two different rooms, which are always jam-packed by midnight. Be prepared to have the occasional beer spilled on your Gucci loafers—this rough-hewn club attracts a hard-drinking crowd. Such top blues artists as Otis Rush and Junior Wells are featured in the main room, while a solid house band alternates in the second room. This is also a regular haunt for visiting pop stars and other celebrities. If your idea of heaven is greeting the sunrise with a few fading blues notes, plan to spend some wee hours at Kingston Mines.

Lilly's

2513 N. Lincoln Ave.
525-2422
Open nightly 4 p.m.-2 a.m.
Shows Wed.-Sat. 9:30 p.m.
Cover $2-$5.
No cards.

This charming Lincoln Avenue standby attracts a more genteel crowd than such nearby clubs as B.L.U.E.S. and Kingston Mines. Piano-based blues is the specialty here, and most people come to listen rather than talk. The club's friendly namesake tends bar and serves an impressive selection of domestic and imported beers. An added bonus are the large picture windows on one side of the room, which let you check out the always-interesting foot traffic on Lincoln Avenue.

New Checkerboard Lounge

423 E. 43rd St.
624-3240
Open daily 11 a.m.-2 a.m.
Shows Mon. & Wed.-Sat.;
showtimes vary.
Cover $3-$5.
No cards.

The New Checkerboard is located in one of the most dangerous parts of the city, but the club remains popular, especially for out-of-towners who think they'll be hearing a different brand of blues than that found at the North Side's clubs. In reality, the North Side clubs usually host the bigger names, but this landmark is not without its charms. Once inside you'll find a friendly crowd that is a 50-50 mix of neighborhood residents and visitors. The place is functional at best—linoleum floors, rickety chairs and tables, a barely adequate sound system—yet the New Checkerboard is to be commended for keeping the blues-mecca heritage of 43rd Street alive and well.

Wise Fools Pub

2270 N. Lincoln Ave.
929-1510
Open Mon.-Sat. 4 p.m.-
2 a.m.; Sun. hours vary.
Shows Mon. 8:30 p.m.,
Tues.-Sat. 9:30 p.m., Sun.
4:30 p.m. Cover $3-$6.
No cards.

Take one look at the classic photos and drawings of blues greats in this club's outer bar and you'll have no doubt as to the kind of music played here. This is a cozy, classic-looking Chicago bar, with some of the friendliest patrons, bartenders and waitresses in town. Wise Fools is pretty rustic looking, which perfectly suits the rough-'n'-tumble style of Chicago blues. The music room seats only about 100 people, so be ready to cool your heels in the outer bar for a while, especially on weekends.

CABARET

Boombala

2950 N. Lincoln Ave.
871-2686
Open nightly 6 p.m.-2 a.m.
Shows Tues.-Thurs. 8 p.m.
& 9:45 p.m., Fri.-Sat.
9 p.m. & 10:45 p.m.
Cover $4-$8.
Cards: MC, V.

With its overstuffed couches, fresh flowers, snow-white appointments and cozy ambience, this 50-seat club resembles a comfortable living room more than it does a nightclub. Boombala's intimate setting complements the entertainment, which leans toward sophisticated jazz, pop and musical comedy and appeals to an over-30 crowd. A limited menu of chic food is available, and reservations are highly recommended.

George's

230 W. Kinzie St.
644-2290
*Open daily 11:30 a.m.-
2 a.m. Showtimes &
cover vary.
All major cards.*

An elegant nightclub and northern Italian restaurant, George's can be faulted only for its excessive ambient noise— the sound of people conversing and eating their linguine can sometimes compete with the music. Still, waiters and maître d's have become adept at politely hushing the worst offenders. George's used to be almost exclusively a venue for top mainstream jazz names, but in recent years new-age music and stand-up comedy have become integral parts of the entertainment schedule. There is a two-drink minimum.

Moulin Rouge

200 N. Columbus Dr.
565-7440
*Shows Tues.-Thurs. & Sun.
9:30 p.m., Fri.-Sat. 9 p.m.
& 11 p.m. Cover $22-$25.
All major cards.*

As you might expect from the sky-high cover charge, this is the city's premier supper club. An elegantly handsome room done up in scarlet and black, the 400-seat Moulin Rouge presents a mix of old-guard showbiz names (Carol Channing, Tony Bennett) along with relatively hipper acts (James Brown, B. B. King). The house orchestra features some of the city's top jazz players, playing for dancers before and after the main act. There's no official dress code, but you'd be best advised to leave your Levis at home.

Roxy

1505 W. Fullerton Ave.
472-8100
*Open Mon.-Sat. 11 a.m.-
2 a.m., Sun. 5 p.m.-2 a.m.
Showtimes & cover vary.
Cards: MC, V.*

This unassuming night spot presents everything from comedy to jazz and occasional rock 'n' roll. The outer bar is filled with silver-screen memorabilia (hence the club's name), and serves sandwiches and appetizers with such foolish names as "Hedda Gobbler" and "Chili Chaplin." The entertainment room is intimate, which is a nice way of saying you should arrive early to guarantee yourself a seat. In this friendly place, almost everyone seems to be on a first-name basis with the owner, so we'll give you an insider's tip—her name is Betty. There's a two-drink minimum on weekends.

Ruggles Cabaret Bar

1633 N. Halsted St.
988-9000
*Open nightly 7 p.m.-2 a.m.
Shows Wed.-Sun.; times vary.
Cover $3-$18.
All major cards.*

Housed in the labyrinthine Royal-George Theatre Centre, Ruggles has dabbled in musical revues, although pop and jazz acts are more the norm. Filling the large, T-shape room with seating on several levels is a predominantly over-30 audience that is a mix of after-show theater patrons and sophisticates with a penchant for jazz and show tunes. Reeboks and jeans are seen as frequently as somber suits, and there's a two-drink minimum.

Unless otherwise noted, the prices given for restaurants are for a complete dinner for two, including an appetizer, main course and dessert. The prices also include tax, fifteen-percent tip and one of the least expensive bottles of wine on the wine list. Please don't hold it against us if you end up spending a bit more!

COMEDY

Catch a Rising Star
(Hyatt-Regency Chicago),
151 E. Wacker Dr.
565-4242
*Open nightly 7:30 p.m.-
2 a.m. Shows Sun.-Tues. &
Thurs. 8:30 p.m., Wed.
5:30 p.m. & 8:30 p.m.,
Fri.-Sat. 8:30 p.m. &
10:30 p.m. Cover $5-$10
with two-drink minimum.
All major cards.*

This snazzy new stepsister of the famed New York comedy factory is located in the elegant Hyatt-Regency Chicago— not exactly the setting you'd expect for a comedy club. The comfortable, 220-seat room has a stage that one wag has described as looking like "Ward Cleaver's den," with its easy chair, bookshelves and bric-à-brac. The comedic talent ranges from nationally known yucksters to unknowns, and there's plenty of talent to be found, but the club has yet to develop its own distinctive comedic atmosphere.

Funny Firm
318 W. Grand Ave.
321-9500
*Open Mon.-Wed. & Fri.-
Sun. 7 p.m.-end of show,
Thurs. 6:30 p.m.-end of
show. Shows Sun.-Wed.
8:30 p.m., Thurs. 7:30 p.m.
& 9:45 p.m., Fri.-Sat.
8 p.m. & 10:30 p.m.
Cover $8-$10; no cover
Mon. with two-drink
minimum.
All major cards.*

One of two recent comedic additions to the River North nightclub scene, the Funny Firm is a large (300 capacity), multilevel club that trades intimacy for glitzy, high-tech flash. While we much prefer the homeyness of Zanies, if you want to see the same comedians in person that you see on late-night TV, this is a good bet. There's no cover for the Friday midnight "blue" show, which might not be appropriate entertainment fare for your Aunt Clara.

Second City
1616 N. Wells St.
337-3992
*Showtimes vary.
Cover $7.50-$9.50.
No cards.*

Don't expect to see stand-up comedy at the legendary spawning ground for talent ranging from John Belushi and Bill Murray to Joan Rivers and David Steinberg. The house specialty is ensemble humor: skits, vignettes and blackouts that often have their origin in the famed after-show improvs. One of Chicago's chief artistic contributions to the world, the weekend shows at Second City's 290-seat main stage are often sold out weeks in advance, so reservations are a must. And don't worry about interruptions from the occasional boorish conventioneer, as the cast has great expertise in dealing with hecklers.

Zanies
1548 N. Wells St.
337-4027
*Open one hour before shows.
Shows Tues.-Thurs. & Sun.
8:30 p.m., Fri.-Sat. 7 p.m.,
9 p.m. & 11:15 p.m.
Cover $8.50 with two-
drink minimum.
Cards: MC, V.*

Zanies was presenting top stand-up comics long before the current comedy boom hit the city (and the nation). And despite competition from newer, larger competitors like the Funny Firm and Catch A Rising Star, this 100-seat club still snares its share of *Tonight Show* and *Late Night with David Letterman* regulars. A long, narrow room furnished with tiny cocktail tables and decorated with artist Bob Fischer's "bizzart," Zanies has nurtured the careers of such home-grown comedians as Emo Phillips and Judy Tenuta, who have since gone on to national acclaim. Reservations are highly recommended.

DANCING

Clubland

3145 N. Sheffield Ave.
248-7277
*Open Wed.-Sat. 9 p.m.-
2 a.m. on nonconcert
nights; immediately after
concerts otherwise.
Cover $5.
Cards: AE, MC, V.*

Housed in the beautifully restored Vic Theatre, Clubland is a good example of the dance club as multimedia spectacular. A bank of 75 video monitors and five giant-screen TVs fill the stage with both music videos and specially prepared videos created by the club's own production team. Choreographed dancers and house musicians complement the videos, and there's plenty of dance space both onstage and on the large dance floor. The music is a mix of contemporary pop and oldies, attracting a rowdy but clean-cut postcollegiate crowd.

Exit

1653 W. Wells St.
440-0535
*Open nightly 8 p.m.-4 a.m.
Cover $3 Fri.-Sat.
No cards.*

This dark, foreboding-looking place is one of Chicago's longest-lived punk-rock clubs. Sure, you'll see lots of people wearing leather, spikes and geometrically bizarre haircuts, but don't let that stop you from checking out the action on the sunken dance floor. The music is loud and tends toward British and other European dance records. Nothing much goes on until midnight, though the later the hour the more mainstream the clientele becomes.

F/X 1100

1100 N. State St.
280-2282
*Open daily 11 a.m.-4 a.m.
Cover $5 Fri.-Sat.
All major cards.*

A sleek, relatively new addition to the Rush Street area with an equally sleek clientele adorned in the latest fashions. Some of the city's most beautiful women turn up here, which means there are lots of men clamoring to get to know them a little better. There are several rooms and levels, and the dance floor is always packed. Crowds tend to be young, single and willing to wait in line to get in on weekends. No jeans are allowed.

Jukebox Saturday Night

2251 N. Lincoln Ave.
943-0998
*Open nightly 7 p.m.-2 a.m.
Cover $5 Fri.-Sat.
Cards: AE, MC, V.*

The music of the '50s and '60s lives on at this shrine to the baby boomer, chock-a-block with classic jukeboxes, posters, signs and other pop-culture collectibles from days gone by. A deejay spins music by Dion, the Beach Boys and the Rolling Stones from the rear end of a '57 Chevy, while aging boomers hit the dance floor. Because of its proximity to several hospitals, it usually draws a profusion of nurses and other medical professionals.

Karl's Satin Doll

820 N. Orleans St.
642-1948
Open Fri.-Sat. 8:30 p.m.-
2 a.m. Cover $7.50.
All major cards.

If you long for the days of the Big Bands, or even if you're too young to have experienced them firsthand, this elegantly appointed 350-seat club is right up your alley. Tastefully decorated in peach-colored tones, Karl's is a classy and romantic spot for dancers who don't mind touching each other. The dance floor has plenty of room, and the house orchestra features some of the city's top jazz musicians. Karl's attracts a well-dressed clientele that is primarily over 40. There's a two-drink minimum.

Limelight

632 N. Dearborn St.
337-2985
Open nightly 9 p.m.-4 a.m.
Cover $5 Sun.-Thurs., $7
Fri.- Sat.
Cards: AE.

When it first opened, this huge, multiroom club was blasted for bringing a New York–style arrogance to Chicago. Still, slowly but surely it has become an important part of the city's nightlife scene, though some pretentious vestiges remain. In fact, some people come to the Limelight only for its freak-show aspect—bizarre performance artists doing their thing in glass showcases, oddly coiffed waiters wearing skirts—but if you feel like dancing to the big beat after 2 a.m., this is a good spot to try. Crowds range from black-clad, tragically hip scenemakers to straight-looking business people. Live music is occasionally presented on weeknights.

Medusa's

3257 N. Sheffield Ave.
935-3635
Open Fri.-Sat. 9 p.m.-
2 a.m. Cover $3-$5.
No cards.

Located in a former public-school building just two blocks north of Clubland, Medusa's is philosophically miles apart from its neighbor, attracting a young and defiantly arty crowd. This is a juice bar, and as such admits patrons age 17 or older, so you might feel a bit out of place if you came of age when the Fab Four ruled the dance floor. The first level is a gymnasium-size dance club with an ever-changing decor and plenty of room to move to deejay-spun Euro-pop dance music and occasional live acts. The second level displays new-wavish art and sculptures and some eerie holograms. And on top is a maze of small rooms and one bigger one featuring a wall of TV monitors. If you have trouble finding Medusa's, just look for the long line of spiky-haired, mohawked, black-leather-clad people stretching down the street.

Neo

2350 N. Clark St.
528-2622
Open Sun.-Thurs. 8 p.m.-
4 a.m., Fri.-Sat. 6 p.m.-
4 a.m. Cover $3 Fri.-Sat.
No cards.

Like Exit, this is one of the city's oldest new-wave dance clubs, but the wave isn't so new anymore. Set back from Clark Street at the end of a long alley, the club resembles a graveyard until well after midnight, when those evicted from the 2 a.m. clubs descend. Neo is a large, multilevel space with plenty of room to move to the beat-heavy new-wavish music on the black-and- white linoleum dance floor. Crowds are mixed and generally friendly, and if you come alone you shouldn't have any trouble finding a dance partner.

Riviera Night Club

4746 N. Racine Ave.
769-6300
Open Fri.-Sat. 9 p.m.-
4 a.m. Cover $5.
Cards: AE, MC, V.

The "Riv" is a painstakingly renovated classic popcorn palace that serves double duty as a concert facility and dance club. Though the neighborhood is a bit on the rough side, inside you'll find bartenders and doormen wearing tuxedos and a well-dressed and varied mix of people out on the dance floor. Computer-controlled lighting and lasers add some glitz to the mix of pop, urban and Latin dance music blasting out of the high-powered sound system. The Riviera isn't a scene-maker hangout like the Limelight, but if you just want to dance, this is a good bet.

Eddie Rockets

9 W. Division St.
787-4881
Open nightly 8 p.m.-4 a.m.
Cover $5 Fri.-Sat.
All major cards.

Of the Division Street "meet markets," Eddie Rockets is one of the least obnoxious. Perhaps we're damning with faint praise , but you have to consider the surroundings. After climbing a steep flight of stairs you'll find yourself in a two-level room with brick walls, neon fixtures and a perennially packed dance floor shaking to high-volume Top-40 dance music under a high-tech lighting system. The club draws a young, single, late-night crowd heavy on leather miniskirts and Members Only jackets.

JAZZ

Andy's

11 E. Hubbard St.
642-6805
Open Mon.-Wed.
11:30 a.m.-8 p.m., Thurs.-
Fri. 11:30 a.m.-8:30 p.m.,
Sat. 6:30 p.m. -1 a.m.
Shows Mon.-Fri. noon &
5 p.m., Sat. 9 p.m.
Cover $3-$4.
All major cards.

Andy's is an extremely popular lunchtime and after-work stop for both hard-core and borderline jazz fans. Located near lower Michigan Avenue, a block from both Riccardo's and the Billy Goat (see "Bars"), Andy's is a comfortably unostentatious club that attracts both well-dressed professionals from nearby offices and more casually dressed devotees. Some of the city's top jazz talents play mainstream jazz from a stage in a corner of the large room, with banners from past years' Chicago Jazz Festivals providing a backdrop. While the roar from the revved-up after-work crowd at either the oval bar or back tables might occasionally intrude, this is primarily a listener's room. A menu of (mostly) grilled food is available.

The Bulls

1916 N. Lincoln Park West
337-3000
Open nightly 8 p.m.-4 a.m.
Shows 9:30 p.m., 11:30 p.m.
& 1:30 a.m. Cover $3-$5.
All major cards.

This subterranean room in the heart of Lincoln Park's nightlife area needs only stalactites to complete the cave ambience. The Bulls is a longtime jazz-lovers' favorite, drawing a varied crowd from all over the city, especially after the 2-a.m. clubs close. Jazz styles from bebop to Latin are feature seven nights a week; be warned that conversation can easily drown out the music at the tables in the back of the room. Sandwiches and appetizers are available.

Gold Star Sardine Bar

680 N. Lake Shore Dr.
664-4215
Open Mon.-Fri. noon-
2 a.m., Sat. 7 p.m.-3 a.m.
Shows Mon.- Sat. 7 p.m.;
lunch shows Mon.-Fri.
4 p.m. No cover.
Cards: AE, MC, V.

This minuscule nightclub nearly hidden in the cavernous 666 N. Lake Shore Drive building has become one of the most talked-about nightclubs in the city. Why? It may be because of the surprise one-nighters by the likes of the entire Count Basie Orchestra or Bobby Short—in a club barely able to seat 50 people. Or perhaps it's the ambience: equal parts upscale (elegant appointments, wicker swivel chairs and large fine-art photographs) and "just plain Chicago" (White Castle hamburgers, known locally as "sliders," are served). No reservations are taken, and the long line to get in on weekends can be daunting. There's a one-drink minimum, and jeans and running shoes are frowned upon.

The Green Mill

4802 N. Broadway
878-5552
Open daily noon-4 a.m.
Shows nightly 9 p.m.;
late show Fri.- Sat.
1:30 p.m. Cover $2-$5.
Cards: AE.

This notorious room was a prime gangster hangout in the '20s and '30s, the place where comedian Joe E. Brown had his throat cut for making fun of the wrong guys. These days The Green Mill is an oasis of civility in rough-'n'-tumble Uptown. The recently renovated club attracts a core clientele of true jazz lovers of all stripes, especially during the postmidnight Saturday jam sessions. The Green Mill offers an unbeatable blend of old Chicago and great jazz.

Jazz Showcase

(The Blackstone), 636 S.
Michigan Ave.
427-4300
Open Tues.-Thurs. & Sun.
7 p.m.-2 a.m., Fri.-Sat.
8 p.m.-4 a.m. Shows Tues.-
Thurs., Sun. 8 p.m. &
10 p.m., Fri.-Sat. 9 p.m.,
11 p.m. & 1 a.m.
Cover varies. No cards.

For more than 40 years Jazz Showcase maven Joe Segal has been synonymous with jazz in Chicago. Over the years his Jazz Showcase has had several locations, but it looks like it's finally found a permanent home at The Blackstone hotel. This is Chicago's premier location for world-class jazz talent—from Max Roach to Dexter Gordon, this comfortable, sophisticated, classy room has seen and heard it all. Reservations are recommended, as are slick duds. There's a two-drink minimum on weekends.

Moosehead Bar & Grill

163 W. Harrison St.
922-3640
Open daily 11 a.m.-1 a.m.
Shows Mon.-Fri. 6 p.m.,
Sat. 9 p.m., Sun. 11 a.m.
Cover $4; no cover Sun.
All major cards.

Like Andy's, this is a popular after-work haunt for Loop workers. Moosehead is an Americana-lover's dream, with antiques, photos, stuffed animals and—yes—a moosehead. While the look of the place suggests a hunting lodge, the fine jazz is as city-slicker as it gets. Reasonably priced drinks and decent hamburgers, sandwiches and salads complete the picture.

Oz

2917 N. Sheffield Ave.
975-8100
Open nightly 4 p.m.-2 a.m.
Shows Thurs.-Fri. 10 p.m.
Cover $2-$4.
Cards: AE, MC, V.

Oz calls itself a "Premium Neighborhood Bar." We're not exactly sure what that means, but we do know that on weekends *seating* is at a premium. With its glass-brick bar and clean, modern look, Oz is a cozy, upscale little room that attracts a local upscale clientele. There's no stage to speak of, so prominent local jazz musicians play from one corner of the room. A beer garden is open during the summer, and the bar stocks an impressive selection of wine, brandy and Cognac.

Pops for Champagne
2934 N. Sheffield Ave.
472-1000
Open Mon.-Sat. 4 p.m.-
2 a.m., Sun. 11 a.m.-2 a.m.
Shows Thurs.-Fri. 9 p.m.,
Sun. 11 a.m. & 9 p.m.
Cover varies; no cover Sun.
All major cards.

Located across the street from Oz, this even-more-upscale jazz club pours a wide variety of Champagnes by the glass while talented musicians play. We contend that jazz is better suited to scotch on the rocks or bourbon and water, but those who like bebop and bubbly will undoubtedly like Pops.

ROCK

Batteries Not Included
2201 N. Clybourn Ave.
348-9529
Open daily 4:30 p.m.-
2 a.m. Shows Wed.-Sun.
10 p.m. Cover $2-$6.
No cards.

Only in Chicago will you find a cutting-edge rock club owned by a Haitian immigrant located on the edge of one of the city's most desirable neighborhoods. This tiny place attracts a young, artsy, adventurous crowd that likes its music loud and fast. The music room is really too small for such bombastic fare, but if you want to see some of the city's more interesting rock acts, start here.

Biddy Mulligan's
7644 N. Sheridan Rd.
761-6532
Open Tues.-Sat. 8 p.m.-
2 a.m. Shows Tues.-Wed.
9:30 p.m., Fri.-Sat. 10 p.m.
Cover $2-$10.
No cards.

Though not easy to get to because of its location on the city's extreme North Side, Biddy Mulligan's is worth the long cab ride if you're partial to unpretentious rock 'n' roll. There's nothing fancy in this roomy club with a postcollegiate atmosphere, where overturned barrels function as tables, yet top national, regional and local musicians make Biddy's one of the city's best clubs. Such blues artists as Albert King and Albert Collins, as well as such long-in-the-tooth rock acts as Humble Pie and Bachman-Turner Overdrive are liberally sprinkled into the music mix, as are occasional reggae and jazz acts.

Cabaret Metro
3730 N. Clark St.
549-3604
Concert room open on
concert nights 6:30 p.m.-
4 a.m.; Smart Bar open
nightly 9:30 p.m.-4 a.m.
Showtimes & cover vary.
No cards.

This is the city's top rock venue, whether it's presenting the latest English funny-haircut band or the best new local acts. The live music room is actually a mini concert hall, complete with balcony and large dance floor. After concerts on weekends, the room turns into a video dance club. Downstairs is a club within a club, the Smart Bar, where deejays play cutting-edge dance music until the wee hours in a sweaty room reminiscent of mom and dad's rec-room basement. Crowds here tend to be young and artsy, dressed in whatever is au courant this week.

Cubby Bear
1059 W. Addison St.
327-1662
Open daily during baseball season 10 a.m.-2 a.m.; open nightly during off-season 8 p.m.-2 a.m. Showtimes & cover vary. No cards.

Located across the street from Wrigley Field, the Cubby Bear is a pregame and postgame haunt by day and a music club by night. This is a rambling place that features a large outer bar filled with baseball memorabilia and a semienclosed music room whose brick wall mirrors the one in the ballpark's outfield. Music ranges from local thrashers to Texas R & B, with crowds as varied as the acts. Every few years or so the Cubby Bear decides to drop live music, so you might want to call ahead.

Gaspars
1359 W. Belmont Ave.
871-6680
Open Mon.-Sat. 4 p.m.- 2 a.m. Showtimes & cover vary. No cards.

Once upon a time this bar was attached to a Schlitz brewery, and that oldtime ambience remains in the club's comfortable outer room. Live music is featured in the back room, a rather cozy space whose decor can best be described as early German beer hall. Local acts are the main focus—very modern "new music" bands incongruously performing in a room designed for oompah music. The clientele is varied and refreshingly unpretentious.

Orphans
2462 N. Lincoln Ave.
929-2677
Open daily 3 p.m.-2 a.m. Shows nightly 9:30 p.m. Cover $2- $6. No cards.

"Eclectic" is the password at this venerable North Side music club, where you'll find everything from Latin jazz to pure pop. This is a great place in which to check out Chicago talent in a relaxed atmosphere that fosters listening. Orphans has a casual, corner-bar atmosphere, and you'll encounter some of the city's friendliest waiters and bartenders. Weekday acts presented in the spacious music room tend to be a bit more adventurous than weekend attractions.

Park West
322 W. Armitage Ave.
929-5959
Open 1 hour before early show (usually 7:30 p.m. or 8 p.m.). Cover varies. Cards: AE, MC, V.

Essentially a concert venue, Park West often books local acts during the middle of the week. This beautiful 750-seat hall is one of the country's top showcase rooms and has hosted everyone from Hall and Oates to Third World and Suzanne Vega. The sound and lighting systems are state of the art, and there isn't a bad seat in the house. Unfortunately, drinks are expensive and rest-room lines often long. The audience varies as much as the music, with some as dressed up as others are dressed down. The club turns into a video dance club on Saturdays after concerts.

Wild Hare
3530 N. Clark St.
327-0800
Open nightly 8 p.m.-2 a.m. Shows nightly 10:30 p.m. Cover $2-$6. No cards.

While Chicago may be best known for its blues music, the city boasts a thriving reggae scene as well, thanks to a large Jamaican community. Jamaican posters and flags cover the walls at this club, where Red Stripe beer and a large selection of rums nicely complement the music. Dancing is encouraged, though space on the dance floor is minimal. Crowds are a mix of local Rastas and North Side yuppies.

HOTELS

MIDWESTERN HOSPITALITY

As large as Chicago has grown, as far as its fabulous skyline has spread along the western shores of Lake Michigan, and as far west and north as the city's considerable gentrification has reached, when it comes to greeting its visitors, Chicago's open arms extend only a short breadth: about a three-mile stretch that runs through the Magnificent Mile south toward the Loop and to the affluent Gold Coast and River North neighborhoods.

In Chicago, Midwestern hospitality is as important a standard as luxurious accommodations. As the city grows into a flourishing haven for conventioneers and business travelers, local hostelries must extend themselves to the weary, the overworked and the aggravated, as well as to the tourist.

If there has been a shift in hotel popularity over the last several years, it has been northward, away from the large, opulent landmarks on S. Michigan Avenue and State Street, where nocturnal safety has become a concern. While the city's financial district and a good deal of its commerce remain centered in the Loop, it is no longer Chicago's entertainment capital. The Windy City's modern spirit has moved closer to N. Michigan Avenue and its environs. Hotels in this area offer both convenience and some contemporary touches that have not yet caught on farther downtown.

Often left empty on weekends (when business travelers disappear), even the finest hotels slash rates nearly in half in order to attract guests, as well as offer packages including such things as theater tickets, dinners and sight-seeing tours.

Our reviews of Chicago's noteworthy hotels are divided into four price ranges based on single occupancy: Top of the Line ($160 and up), Deluxe ($110 to $159), Moderate ($80 to $109) and Inexpensive ($50 to $79). Please note that the four distinctions are based not on our evaluation of these establishments but only on how much they cost.

Our opinion of the comfort level and appeal of each hotel is expressed in a ranking system, as follow—we remind you that these distinctions are based only on the price:

   Exceptional comfort

   Very good comfort

Average comfort

 Modest comfort

Symbols in red denote a degree of charm; no ranking at all means we cannot recommend the establishment. Keep the price range in mind when noting the ranking; one "hotel" is not good for an expensive hostelry, but it's just fine for a budget place.

TOP OF THE LINE

The Ambassador East
1301 N. State St.
787-7200

This Gold Coast gem sparkles with the romantic elegance of Chicago's past. The horse-drawn carriages en route from Michigan Avenue that frequently pass by add to the traditional old-world charm of this Omni Classic hotel. Shining green-and-white marble floors and an attentive bell staff welcome guests into a lobby resplendent with fresh flowers. Destined for Byfield's entertainment cabaret or the Pump Room, one of Chicago's premier eateries, some of the world's most celebrated personalities have passed under The Ambassador East's white canvas awnings—including Alfred Hitchcock and the entire cast and crew of *North by Northwest*. A recent $5-million renovation has left the 275 rooms and suites immaculately appointed, plush and cheerful. Amenities, however, are surprisingly few. A stay in a suite or Omni Club room will get you robes, a hair dryer and a scale; suites also feature large wet bars. Valet parking is $16, with no in-and-out privileges.
Singles: $175; doubles: $185; suites: $235-$700. Weekend packages available.

Chicago Marriott
540 N. Michigan Ave.
836-0100

Its size, its location on the Magnificent Mile and its Marriott parentage attract an often-frenzied convention and business clientele, who appreciate the hotel's warmth and comfort. A plushly furnished atrium bar/lounge rises one step up from the marble-floor lobby, which is encircled by myriad hotel shops. Rooms are standard hotel fare, though quite comfortable; accommodations are more luxurious on the Marquis floor, which is available for higher rates or to members of Marriott's Marquis Club. Use of a full health-club facility, including an indoor swimming pool and outdoor tennis courts, is complimentary for guests. Expect long lines when checking in. Valet parking is $17.
Singles: $168-$188; doubles: $188-$208; suites: $1,000. Weekend packages available.

The Fairmont
200 N. Columbus Dr.
565-8000

One of Chicago's newest hotels, The Fairmont is our favorite for its indulgent amenities, inviting decor and ebullient staff. The lobby, luxuriously executed in marble and velvet, is one of the most comfortable in the city—as are the rooms. Few Chicago hotels offer such a wealth of personal touches: two-line speakerphones with call-waiting and modem capabilities; standing butlers; tie racks; upright shoeshines; separate dressing areas accented with brightly lit vanities; TVs and phones in both the bedrooms and the generously sized marble bathrooms; his-and-hers terry robes (with distinctive pink and blue bordering); hair dryers; and generously stocked minibars. A good night's sleep is assured in beds covered with thick, tufted down quilts, 100-per-cent-cotton sheets and oversized down pillows. Each of the 700 rooms is decorated with cheerful pastels and marble-topped cherrywood furnishings. Lakeside rooms offer magnificent views of Navy Pier, while south-facing rooms overlook splendid vistas of Lake Michigan, Grant Park, the Art Institute and Buckingham Fountain. Serious French cuisine is available at Entre Nous, Italian food at the upbeat Primavera and Chicago-style sandwiches at the stately Metropole; live entertainment is staged at the Moulin Rouge. Valet parking is $13.50.

Singles: $160-$230; doubles: $185-$255; suites: $500-$650. Weekend packages available.

Hotel 21 East
21 E. Bellevue Pl.
266-2100

Since it opened its sleek glass doors in the summer of 1988, the 21 East on the Gold Coast has played gracious host to a decidedly international crowd that demands first-rate luxury. Not only does each of the 247 rooms have a VCR built into the TV set, but each room is also equipped with a compact disc player, three two-line speaker phones, mini and wet bars, a deep-soaking tub and Sebastian hair-care products. Six duplex suites have window shades that open and close with the touch of a bedside button. Common areas include the striking black-marble lobby; the richly decorated four-story atrium lounge, over which the clear glass elevator rises; Cafe 21, a promising new restaurant; Bar 21, with a 25-foot-long copper-topped bar and a panoramic view of Rush Street's party scene; and a fabulous mahogany board room that makes the perfect business impression. But nothing reveals the chic atmosphere of the 21 East as much as the two shiny black BMW 735i's parked in the cul-de-sac entry, ready to whisk business travelers to meetings and vacationers to the theater. Valet parking is $17 a day.

Singles: $160-$215; doubles: $175-$235; suites: $235-$425. Weekend packages available.

Hyatt-Regency Chicago
151 E. Wacker Dr.
565-1234

If Lawrence Welk decided to build a spaceship, it would resemble the Hyatt-Regency Chicago's lobby. The multi-level space-center-like atrium, constructed of marble and steel, oozes futuristic schmaltz, from the droning of the white, mini grand piano in the open-air Midway Lounge suspended above a bed of orchids and azaleas to the long strings of teardrop lights crying from the ceiling on the other side of this massive room. With 2,030 rooms, it's easy to get lost in all the corridors that lead guests around like blind mice. The accommodations are minimal in comfort—beds are uncomfortable, sound sometimes travels through walls, and the decor is drab. Still, conventioneers rave about the place, insisting that service transcends that found at some other higher-end hotels, like The Palmer House. Amenities include minibars in the West Tower (management fears that student groups staying in the East Tower may get out of hand), makeup mirrors, cable TV (with speakers in the bathroom) and hair dryers. The Hyatt has several restaurants: Scampi's, Stetson, Mrs. O'Leary's and the Skyway, none of which are frequented by locals. Valet parking is $14.

Singles: $175; doubles: $200; suites: $325-$2,000. Weekend packages available.

The Mayfair Regent
181 E. Lake Shore Dr.
787-8500

An exquisite hotel parked on the shores of Lake Michigan, The Mayfair Regent exudes an intimate, elegant charm often lost in the city's older and larger hostelries. The lobby is regally appointed with Louis XVI furnishings, chandeliers and fresh flowers. Rooms—there are 209—are spacious, comfortable and bathed in warm pastels. Request a lake view; The Mayfair Regent is blessed with some of the loveliest views in the city. Rooms are also chock-full of personal amenities, including robes, scales and telephones in the bathrooms, which boast marble vanities. Other indulgences include a walk-in dressing area in almost every room and an umbrella for a rainy day. Hand-painted Chinese murals decorate the lobby bar, which is one of the few in the city that actually uses its fireplace. The Mayfair Regent is home to two of the most popular and expensive eateries in town: The Palm, known for its juicy steaks and casual ambience, and the Ciel Bleu on the eighteenth floor, with its fancy French fare and panoramic vista of the lake. Valet parking is $12.

Singles: $185-$205; doubles: $205-$225; suites: $275-$850. Weekend packages available.

The Park Hyatt
800 N. Michigan Ave.
280-2222

In Chicago, The Park Hyatt is best known for its elegant restaurant, La Tour, a power-breakfast mecca for the city's intrepid politicians and press. A small, extremely expensive hotel located on Water Tower Square overlooking Michigan Avenue, The Park Hyatt is rich in understated, modern elegance. A two-story travertine lobby is cheered by a generous wall of light that falls softly on plush, velvet couches. Rooms are comfortably sized and regally decorated in peach or forest green, with marble-topped rosewood furnishings. Bathrooms are well stocked with phones, TVs and hair dryers. Valet parking is $16.50.

Singles: $210-$285; doubles: $235-$310; suites: $575-$2,500. Weekend packages available.

The Ritz-Carlton
160 E. Pearson St.
266-1000

Aside from the water-spitting brass heron in the center of the Greenhouse Lobby Bar, The Ritz-Carlton is a bastion of indulgent good taste. The twelfth-floor lobby is among the cushiest in the city, with floral-pattern furnishings that pass the "sit-till-you-sink" test with flying colors. Called the Greenhouse for good reason, the lobby is splendidly lit by a rounded glass wall that meets the roof, much like a greenhouse. A light lunch is served here, as well as in The Café. Opulent dinner fare is offered in The Dining Room, which also serves what many consider Chicago's most delicious (and generous) Sunday brunch. The Bar, designed with an art deco motif, presents jazz or blues on most nights. A member of the auspicious Four Seasons chain, The Ritz-Carlton stresses service, which is why so many high-brow celebrities stay here. All rooms offer king-size beds, as well as two-line speakerphones, hair dryers, makeup mirrors and a 24-hour valet laundry service. Glass French doors separate bedrooms from plush, well-lit parlors in the "petite suites." Regular rooms are spacious and furnished with comfortable love seats and chairs. Valet parking is $18.

Singles: $185-$270; doubles: $205-$270; suites: $600-$2,000. Weekend packages available.

Swiss Grand Hotel
323 E. Wacker Dr.
565-0565

The exterior of the Miracle Mile's Swiss Grand Hotel is chilly indeed: Rows of black glass alternate with rows of mirrored glass, all the way up to the 43rd floor. And the geometric glass awning is as wholly uninviting as is the gray-granite entrance to the lobby. Yet the interior of this 645-room art-techno palace has as much warmth as a sultry Southern summer. The multilingual staff couldn't be friendlier or more accommodating. A huge fishbowl of Swiss chocolates awaits sugar-starved guests at the registration desk. And the rooms, appointed in cheerful pastels and cherrywood furnishings, are both elegant and comfortable; many have superb views of Lake Michigan or the Chicago River (request a corner king room, which has views of both). Although the Swiss Grand Hotel opened for business just as we went to press, it wasn't yet complete, so we can't tell you about the 36 suites on the highest floors, the five duplex suites or the presidential suite, which has a wood-burning fireplace. Also unfinished was the fitness center, which by the time you read these lines will boast an indoor pool, exercise equipment, a sauna, a whirlpool and massage services. But if these facilities feature the same attention to dignified detail as others in the Swissôtel chain, which is run by Swissair and Nestlé, you are assured a most pleasurable stay. Valet parking is $14 a day.

Singles: $175-$220; doubles: $195-$240; suites: $450-$2,500.

The Westin
909 N. Michigan Ave.
943-7200

If elegance or regional flavor is important to you, avoid The Westin, a haven for conventioneers who have downtown business. Situated north of the John Hancock Building and a block away from Water Tower Place, this concrete monstrosity is ideal for the corporate traveler who likes to shop as well as conduct business. Accommodations offer the comfort one would expect of a large chain hotel, although we've heard some complaints from annual conventioneers about a perennial problem with overheated rooms. A pleasant pink-tone lounge/bar supplies some of the comfort that is missing in the stark, marble-wall lobby. Dining choices vary from the casual Chelsea Restaurant to the more austere Fine Dining Room. Our favorite is the wood-paneled Lion Bar & Grill, which serves up jazz Tuesday through Saturday evenings. Health-club facilities with designated weight rooms for men and women, as well as saunas and steams, are available for a nominal fee. Valet parking is $18.50 a day.

Singles: $175-$240; doubles: $215-$280; suites: $425-$2,500. Weekend packages available.

The Whitehall
105 E. Delaware St.
944-6300

Owned by John Bennett Coleman, the stalwart force behind the resurrected elegance of the Tremont Hotel across the way, The Whitehall is a similar European-style, service-oriented hotel for discriminating business and leisure travelers. Aged pine treated in England covers the lobby walls, which adds to the dignified charm of this relatively small, 222-room hostelry. Although the rooms are starkly furnished, they are tastefully appointed. Some have bay windows built in the days when The Whitehall had an unobstructed view of Lake Michigan. The Whitehall Club, once a members-only room for fine dining, is now open to hotel guests. Valet parking is $16.50, without in-and-out privileges.

Singles: $165-$205; doubles: $185-$225; suites: $375-$950. Weekend packages available.

DELUXE

The Ambassador West
1300 N. State St.
787-7900

Although many Chicago hostelries purport to have the ambience and elegance of a small European hotel, The Ambassador West is one of the few that actually achieves that goal. The stately oak-paneled lobby, aswirl with baroque music, has true English character. So do certain artifacts here, such as the Thomas Vernon long case clock (circa 1740) and a seventeenth-century portrait of Lady Faversham. The Royal Court Café, set off the lobby, offers a free Continental breakfast to all guests. Some patrons complain that the 217 rooms, most of which are spacious and tastefully decorated, are a bit run-down, a problem that should be cured when renovations are completed in April 1989. Amenities include wet bars, stocked minibars, cable TV and complimentary shoe-shine and newspapers. Guests can charge meals to their rooms, as well as order 24-hour room service from The Pump Room, located across the street in The Ambassador East. Valet parking is $14.

Singles: $135-$150; doubles: $150-$165; suites: $180-$700. Weekend packages available.

The Barclay Hotel
166 E. Superior St.
787-6000

This black-glass tower housing 120 suites is just a block east of the Magnificent Mile. Although the concept of an all-suite luxury hotel is enticing, the owners might have spruced up the rooms to match the heady prices. But we must admit that the suites—six per floor—are quite spacious and boast living and sleeping rooms with functionally sized efficiency kitchens tucked neatly in a corner. From the small, handsome oak-paneled lobby, pad down the spiral staircase into the dimly lit Bookmark Lounge, where built-in bookshelves contain a slew of tattered volumes; closer inspection reveals their likely origin: a used-college-textbook sale. This pseudo-homeyness is not reflected in the Bookmark's wait staff; when we asked for a cup of coffee, we were gruffly informed that there was none and if we wished to remain at one of the many empty tables, we'd have to order a drink. The Barclay Club on the seventh floor serves expensive French cuisine to hotel guests and club members only (a doorbell outside the eatery ensures that the riffraff is kept out). Valet parking is $13 a day, without in-and-out privileges.

Singles: $155-$195; doubles: $175-$215; parlors: $285-$460. Weekend packages available.

Chicago Hilton & Towers

720 S. Michigan Ave.
922-4400

If you like hotels built in a grand scheme, this one just east of the South Loop will suit you. Built in 1927 as the Stevens Hotel, it was once touted as the largest hostelry in the world. Several renovations later—the most recent completed in 1985 at a cost of $150 million—the Chicago Hilton & Towers has reduced its number of rooms to a mere 1,620. As a result, rooms are large, comfortable and well appointed with cherrywood furnishings; many sport two full bathrooms. And each of the many restaurants is a visual treat that should at least be seen—if you can find your way around the many chandelier-dripping hallways. While some have compared the lobby ceiling in The Palmer House with that of the Sistine Chapel, the mural looming above the Hilton's atrium entrance is a closer call. Other attractions of note: The Lakeside Green and the Normandy Lounge, both overlooking Grant Park, are perfect spots for high tea or cocktails. Also, the complimentary health club is the finest to be found in a Chicago hotel (not counting the Charlie Club, which is actually a fitness center with guest rooms, and the Marriott, which has its own tennis courts). A running track surrounds exercycles and weight equipment, a large skylit pool is set off to one side, and aerobics classes are held twice daily (for $4 a class). Valet parking is $14.

Singles: $115-$190; doubles: $140-$215; suites: $380-$6,000. Weekend packages available.

The Drake

140 E. Walton Pl.
787-2200

The Drake has played host to the prime ministers of Australia and Tunisia, to the queens of Thailand and the Netherlands and to First Lady Nancy Reagan. But the friendly attitude of the immense staff (the staff-to-guest ratio is approximately one to one) extends just as warmly to ordinary travelers. Like The Palmer House several blocks south, The Drake bills itself as the "Grand Dame" of Chicago's hostelries. It earns the appellation because of its opulent but not off-putting interior design, its four award-winning dining facilities and its obliging personal services. Amenities include in-house movies, 24-hour room service, a multilingual concierge, same-day valet and complimentary newspapers. Also, The Drake maintains manned elevators complete with velvet benches for the weary. The Vista Executive floor houses a self-contained executive complex with a full range of personal services. Although each of the 535 rooms is uniquely designed, our only complaint is that some of the regular rooms are too small and drably furnished. Listed in the National Register of Historic Places, The Drake recently completed a $21-million renovation that restored the building to the luxurious style of its original 1920 incarnation. Since it sits at the northern tip of the Magnificent Mile, The Drake has many rooms with choice views of Lake Michigan and Oak Street Beach—so request a lakeside view. Some must-dos at The Drake include taking high tea in the Palm Court Lobby, sampling the bookbinder's soup in the Cape Cod Room and touring the elegant function rooms. These include the Italian-style Gold Coast Room, resplendent with 24-carat-gold filigreed columns and 25 crystal chandeliers, and the incredibly romantic Georgian-style Grand Ballroom. Valet parking is $17.50.

Singles: $155-$195; doubles: $180-$220; suites: $350-$1,200. Weekend packages available.

The Executive House
71 E. Wacker Dr.
346-7100

The 415 rooms in this recently renovated addition to the Ramada chain are spacious, comfortable and warmly decorated in rich greens and blues, with large, handsomely appointed bathrooms. Pitched diagonally on the Chicago River (between the North Loop and the Magnificent Mile), The Executive House offers more extensive river vistas than any other downtown hotel. River-view rooms with king-size beds are slightly more expensive than rooms with city views, which are best on the twentieth and higher floors. Although the penthouse suites have breathtaking views, they are decorated in an overcrowded hotel-lobby fashion, with three large wood-and-glass card tables and big, velvet pit couches. The staff is courteous and enthusiastic, and the expected amenities are available. Valet parking is $15 a day.

Singles: $120-$170; doubles: $135-$185; suites: $175-$275; penthouse: $400-$800. Weekend packages available.

The Knickerbocker
163 E. Walton Pl.
751-8100

Request a room on the fourteenth floor of this 60-year-old hotel for a firsthand glimpse of Prohibition-era Chicago. Secret doors leading to a central stairwell are carved into papered walls, making for quick escapes into the twenties, when these rooms were used as speakeasies. Chicago's first lighted dance floor still glows beneath removable carpeting in the Georgian-styled Grand Ballroom. With renovation recently completed, the darkly stained oak-paneled lobby bar, flanked by tall cathedral windows, still seems just the spot for fedora-wearing mobsters. The accommodations suit this hostelry's intimate, romantic charm, with comfortable sitting areas in each room. Decor and amenities vary from room to room; those with canopy beds are the most charming, while the rooms with two bathrooms can create peace for the traveling couple. Continental food is available in the Prince of Wales restaurant and lighter fare in the café overlooking Walton Street. Valet parking is $17.50.

Singles: $150-$185; doubles: $172-$207; suites: $225-$1,100. Weekend packages available.

The Morton
500 S. Dearborn St.
663-3200

The Morton, now part of the Omni chain, is one of the few Chicago hotels that faithfully represents the unique flavor of its neighborhood. Once a printing shop in historic Printer's Row, one section of The Morton is listed in the National Register of Historic Places. A primarily red-brick facade invites you into the teak-paneled lobby, which is sparsely appointed with modern, streamlined furnishings that were custom designed for the hotel. A dropped tray ceiling, however, lends some homeyness to the room. A mahogany-lined elevator lifts you to one of The Morton's seven floors, which are done in grays and greens and feel futuristic. Spaciousness abounds in the 160 rooms, which boast thirteen-foot, loft-like ceilings. Tight, cushioned furnishings complement this stark style, and blocks of warehouse windows shed plenty of light on the original local artworks in each room. Larger-than-life travertine-marbled bathrooms house a host of personal amenities, including an upright scale, hair dryer, TV, phone and Pierre Cardin bathrobe. Other amenities include a minibar, cable TV and video player. The 21st-century-looking Presidential Suite, with its view of the Midwest Stock Exchange and Sears Tower, is not to be missed. The Prairie Restaurant, whose design pays tribute to Chicago's favorite architectural son, Frank Lloyd Wright, serves Midwestern cuisine at moderate prices. Valet parking is $12.50.

Singles: $120-$140; doubles: $135-$155; suites: $350-$1,200. Weekend packages available.

The Nikko
320 N. Dearborn St.
744-1900

East meets Midwest at The Nikko, the city's only hotel located on the banks of the Chicago River. Be sure to request a River King room, which affords a view of both the river and some of the city's newest architecture, via floor-to-ceiling bay windows. Accommodations are comfortable, if a bit stark in their concise Eastern design. Extra-large bathrooms are outfitted in Italian marble; room amenities include minibars, three phones, terry robes and 24-hour dining. A cardiovascular-oriented health club with three trainers is available for $10 per visit. The Hana Lounge, a sunken lobby bar encircled by an outdoor Japanese garden, is a delightful spot for a light lunch or a spot of saké. Some other distinctly Japanese touches include hand-woven inset rugs; carved ash elevators (they talk, too); rich mahogany trim throughout the hotel; and the Benkay Restaurant, with its Japanese-style dining room, sushi bar and six private tatami rooms for parties of two to twelve. Valet parking is $17.

Singles: $155-$195; doubles: $175-$215; suites: $250-$2,500. Weekend packages available.

The Palmer House
17 E. Monroe St.
726-7500

Rising like a jeweled phoenix from the State Street pavement since 1873, The Palmer House originally opened on September 26, 1871, just thirteen days before the great Chicago fire reduced it to ashes. Chicago real estate baron Potter Palmer, never one to admit defeat, immediately built a new hotel at three times the size of the original and ten times the cost. It included such state-of-the-art technology as fireproofing, elevators, electricity and telephones in each room, all firsts for Chicago's hotel industry. The resting place of some of history's most colorful figures—Mark Twain, Sarah Bernhardt, Oscar Wilde, Rudyard Kipling, Charles Dickens and President Ulysses S. Grant—The Palmer House grew with its fame and underwent another complete renovation in the twenties (without a single business day lost). A recent $85-million restoration under the guidance of the Hilton chain, in which The Palmer House has been a link since 1945, once again restored this centrally located downtown hotel to its inimitable opulence. Each of the 21 French canvasses gracing the lobby's two-story ceiling has been cleaned, and the plush sitting areas have been refurbished. Rooms are large and exquisitely appointed. We've heard some guests complain, however, of sluggish room service and spotty maid service. The Palmer House is home to some popular, touristy restaurants: Trader Vic's, the French Quarter, Palmer's Steak and Seafood House and the Boca Raton Café. The Towers on the 22nd and 23rd floors offers "Hotel within a Hotel" services; a concierge and a new health club are available to all guests. No valet parking.

Singles: $110-$165; doubles: $135-$190; suites: $260-$1,500. Weekend packages available.

The Tremont
100 E. Chestnut St.
751-1900

In 1975, when John Bennett Coleman was searching for a name for the fifteen-story residential building (circa 1923) he was renovating as a hotel, he stumbled upon the saga of The Tremont. The legendary grand hotel was thrice razed during fires in 1839, 1849 and in the more famed conflagration of 1871 (it was in the old Tremont in 1858 that Abraham Lincoln debated Stephen Douglas). The Tremont was also thrice rebuilt, until it at last met with the fatal slap of the demolition ball in 1931. The newer Tremont upholds its namesake's tradition of Midwestern hospitality coupled with European charm. A small hotel, The Tremont has 129 rooms warmly furnished in burnt oranges and browns; junior suites feature two bathrooms. The Tremont is home to Cricket's, one of the city's more popular eateries, where trucks, hats, planes and other knickknacks hang from the ceiling, livening up the hotel's otherwise stately ambience. Valet parking is $17.50.

Singles: $150-$190; doubles: $170-$210; suites: $350-$850. Weekend packages available.

MODERATE

The Allerton
701 N. Michigan Ave.
440-1500

Although still elegant, this older hotel located just off the center of the Magnificent Mile has become slightly faded and run-down. Nonetheless, it offers one of the city's better French restaurants, L'Escargot, and has its own entrance to Gucci. Although the deep-pink-and-gray granite art deco lobby is charming and inviting, it is a bit worn, despite recent renovations. The same holds true for the 450 rooms, which even on higher floors are subject to the not-so-sweet sounds of construction below. We prefer the decor in the larger regular rooms to that in the suites. Valet parking is available next door at the Sheraton Plaza for $14.50.

Singles: $89-$103; doubles: $99-$113; suites: $120-$265. Weekend packages available.

Best Western Inn of Chicago
162 E. Ohio St.
787-3100

Guests on a budget don't seem to mind getting what they're paying for at the Inn of Chicago, but we think you can do much better for the money. Rooms are cramped and appointed in the same dreadful color scheme as the orange-marble lobby; bathrooms are among the smallest we've seen; and double-pane windows don't muffle street noises. A half block east of the Magnificent Mile, this hotel is a tolerable place to stay only if you don't intend to spend a lot of time in your room. Valet parking is $10, without in-and-out privileges.

Singles: $92-$102; doubles: $108-$128; suites: $205-$375. Weekend packages available.

The Blackstone
636 S. Michigan Ave.
427-4300

Like so many S. Michigan Avenue hotels whose elegant lobbies greeted the great politicians and socialites of another time, The Blackstone heralds itself as the "Home of the Presidents." The hotel's relatively small size—300 rooms—permits it to retain much of the stately feeling it had when it was built in 1910. Consistent with the older downtown hotels (except the extravagantly renovated Chicago Hilton & Towers), room amenities are few—a phone, TV and bathroom scale are the most noteworthy. Still, the recently renovated rooms are spacious and handsome, and lakeside rooms offer breathtaking views of Lake Michigan, Grant Park and Buckingham Fountain. The Blackstone's other attractions include an elegant lobby offset by a lovely marble stairway, the Mayfair Theatre and Joe Segal's Jazz Showcase, which spotlights popular national and international jazz greats. Valet parking is $11, without in-and-out privileges.

Singles: $79-$89; doubles: $89-$99; suites: $119-$350. Weekend packages available.

Charlie Fitness Club & Hotel
122 S. Michigan Ave.
726-0510

Jane Fonda would love it here! Included in the price of your room is membership in a 24-hour health club, complete with an indoor running track, indoor swimming pool, aerobic and dance studios, basketball court, 90 weight machines, computerized rowing machines, 40 computerized exercise bikes and 10,000 pounds of free weights. Nominal fees are charged for use of racquetball/handball/ squash courts, private spa rooms and tanning beds. After all that exercise, you'll appreciate the rooms, which are large and comfortable, if a little institutional looking. If you have the money, splurge on a lakefront view. An L.A.–style four-story atrium lounge with a winding staircase affords not only a dramatic view of the lake but also a floor-to-ceiling peek into the workout rooms and aerobic studios. Another great lake view can be had from the Café Med dining room. No valet parking.

Singles & doubles: $70-$90; lakefront doubles: $120; suites: $150.

The Claridge
1244 N. Dearborn St.
787-4980

Set apart from the downtown frenzy, The Claridge is a quiet, European-style hotel with easy access to the Windy City's business and attractions. Nestled in the heart of the wealthy Gold Coast residential district, The Claridge is rich with an inviting elegance that extends to its rooms. They are tastefully appointed with silk wallpaper and art deco headboards over firm beds. Other furnishings are a bit stiff, which is of little consequence when you consider that the rates are about ten percent below others of its caliber. J. P.'s Eating Place, one of Chicago's favorite seafood canteens, can be found in back of the distinctly European lobby bar, which is more cramped than cozy. Valet parking is $14, with no in-and-out privileges.

Singles: $75-$125; doubles: $125-$140; suites: $250. Weekend packages available.

Days Inn Lake Shore Drive
644 N. Lake Shore Dr.
943-9200

The Days Inn may not offer the glamour or indulgent amenities of other downtown hotels, but it does have a terrific view of Lake Michigan lapping the shores of Olive Park—and for a much better price than you'll find elsewhere. This hotel is at its best in the warmer months, since there is no free transportation to the Magnificent Mile just four blocks away—a wearisome trek during Chicago's excruciating winters. The 580 rooms, decorated in classic Americana, are comfortable and well kept, except for some tables and chairs you'll find a little worse for wear; unfortunately, since it is located directly behind Lake Shore Drive, street noise may be a problem. The revolving rooftop Pin-

nacle Restaurant makes up for its banal food with its splendid vista of the entire city. An outdoor pool is available for
guests in the summer. Park-it-yourself for $7, with in-and-
out privileges.

Singles: $89-$119; doubles: $99-$129. Weekend rates
available.

Holiday Inn-City Centre
300 E. Ohio St.
787-6100

We counted lines of about 50 people waiting to check in
on the three occasions we visited this centrally located hotel,
which is just a few blocks east of the Magnificent Mile.
Name tags distinguish veteran guests from new arrivals; as
you would expect, the Holiday Inn-City Centre is a popular
convention spot. There are 500 rooms, and guests seem to
be quite pleased with them once checked in. One of this
hotel's prime features is its connection to a private health
club, which is free to all guests (nominal fees are charged for
court time, aerobic classes and massages); an outdoor pool
and sun deck on the eighth floor are exclusively for hotel
guests. Park-it-yourself for $6 a day, with in-and-out privi-
leges.

Singles: $99-$146; doubles: $115-162; suites: $300-$650.
Weekend packages available.

Holiday Inn-Mart Plaza
350 N. Orleans St.
836-5000

If you can find this Holiday Inn, which is sequestered
fifteen floors above the Apparel Mart, you might be in for a
pleasant surprise—that is, after you swim through the fish-
bowl-like atrium lobby and settle into your room. Done in
dark blues and light browns, most of the 525 rooms have
spectacular views of the city and the Chicago River. South-
facing rooms afford a glimpse of Wolf Point, the Kennedy
clan–owned property upon which the Apparel Mart and the
Holiday Inn are built, and also the home of Chicago's first
white settlers (in the early 1800s). Avoid the cabana rooms
off to the side of the skylit pool—they tend to be smaller
than others and much noisier. Since the hotel's eight floors
are perched high above street level, city noise is never a
problem. One word of warning: This is primarily a convention hotel, so be prepared for big crowds. Park-it-yourself
for $8.50, with in-and-out privileges.

Singles: $94-$112; doubles: $109-$128; suites: $290-$350.
Weekend rates available.

Hyde Park Hilton
4900 S. Lake Shore Dr.
288-5800

Since the Hyde Park Hilton is the only acceptable hotel
near the University of Chicago and the city's South Side,
guests with local business have no choice but to stay in one
of 314 rooms, which are in obvious need of the scheduled
renovations. Although spacious, these rooms are worn and
drably decorated. And we've heard complaints of poor service in both the hotel and the adjoining restaurant, The
Chartwell, as well as dissatisfaction with leaky bathroom

fixtures and incessant humming from the main cooling system. To make your stay more pleasant, request a lakeside room. Courtesy vans will take you to various points of interest and business throughout the city. Room discounts are provided for guests with U. of C. business.

Singles: $79-$109; doubles: $89-$119; suites: $125-$180. Weekend packages available.

The Lenox House

616 N. Rush St.
337-1000

Just a few blocks west of the Magnificent Mile, The Lenox House has 330 adequately furnished efficiency suites that are just right for those who want some of the conveniences of home during their Chicago stay. Although recently renovated, the place still looks a bit run-down and unkempt (when we visited, piles of laundry were stashed quite visibly next to the elevator). If you don't care to cook in your room, the hotel is attached to Houston's Restaurant, a lunch and dinner spot popular with businesspeople and nearby residents. No valet parking.

Singles: $95-$150; doubles: $105-$160. Weekend rates available.

McCormick Center Hotel

23rd St. & Lake Shore Dr.
791-1900

Smack in the center of McCormick Center, the world's largest convention space, the McCormick Center Hotel could pass for just another selling floor—except that it is carpeted and has a few obligatory partitions. Although free shuttle buses will take you downtown, the location is too remote for travelers who want to discover Chicago. And, of course, it's packed to the rafters with conventioneers. Built in 1973, the place still smacks of that decade's most dismal decor—each door to the 650 rooms is adorned with a multicolored Peter Max–like design. The rooms, however, have been renovated and are cheerfully appointed and comfortable—except for chairs and couches, which for some inexplicable reason have hardwood armrests, another misguided design touch from the '70s. Most rooms have great views of the lake, and a skylit pool and workout room are free to all guests. Valet parking is $9.

Singles: $99-$145; doubles: $119-$165; suites: $180-$950. Weekend packages available.

The Midland Hotel

172 W. Adams St.
332-1200

In the heart of the financial district, The Midland Hotel is a friendly, neighborhood place with some pleasant accommodations for a fairly pleasant price. Ask for a room on a renovated floor, because the unrestored corridors in this 1920s hotel are dimly lit and a bit dingy. Rooms are comfortably decorated in typical hotel fashion. Its three restaurants include the Ticker Tape Bar & Grill, the Over-The-Counter Café and the more formal Exchange Restaurant, which has some lovely seats overlooking the travertine-

covered lobby. Above looms a ceiling-length gilded Florentine relief. Our one complaint: The lobby has no seating
area. Special amenities include a limousine that will take you
throughout the city. No valet parking.

Singles: $95-$105; doubles: $115-$120; suites: $125-$450.
Weekend packages available.

The Richmont
162 E. Ontario St.
787-3580

If only the rooms in this lovely, whitewashed building
weren't so cramped, The Richmont would be one of our
favorites of the city's small hotels. The cheery, French-style
lobby is inviting, the Rue de St. Clair Bistro and Outdoor
Café are charming, and the staff is congenial. Unfortunately, the rooms are unbearably small. Still, if you want a
friendly taste of Chicago, this is a lovely neighborhood
hotel, albeit with not too much room to savor it. Valet
parking is $14, with no in-and-out privileges.

Singles: $90-$120; doubles: $102-$132; suites: $145.
Weekend packages available.

The Raphael
201 E. Delaware St.
943-5000

We love this fetching, moderately priced hotel, located just
a block east of the Magnificent Mile, for enveloping its
guests in the intimacy and warmth of a small country inn
amid the frenzy of a big city. Walk through the beveled-
glass front door of the Gothic red-brick building and bask in
the sunlight streaming through a triptych of cathedral windows in the two-story lobby. Although The Raphael doesn't
offer concierge services, the gracious front-desk staff will do
its best to take care of you. The 172 rooms are quaint, with
true European character: stucco walls topped with beamed
ceilings, comfortable king-size beds and, in most rooms,
sitting areas. Valet parking is $17, without in-and-out
privileges.

Singles: $95-$120; doubles: $115-$140; suites: $120-$155.
Weekend packages available.

Sheraton Plaza
160 E. Huron St.
787-2900

This 234-unit converted condominium complex was a
pleasant surprise. Although the lobby resembles that of an
office building, the well-kept rooms are cheerfully decorated in pink tones with attractive stained-oak furnishings,
and bathrooms are reasonably large and modern. Amenities
include 24-hour room service from Tiffs Too, the hotel
restaurant, as well as pay TV, minibars and makeup mirrors
in the bathrooms. Because nearly half of the units are suites,
the front desk is generous with upgrades. And the location
is perfect, just half a block east of the Magnificent Mile.
Valet parking is $14.50.

Singles: $105-$165; doubles: $120-$185; suites: $195-
$405. Weekend packages available.

INEXPENSIVE

The Bismarck
171 W. Randolph St.
236-0123

The Bismarck has gone the way of many a once-regal downtown hostelry. At first sight, its lobby is magically inviting—teeming with the spirit of old Chicago. But a closer look reveals tattered woodwork, peeling wallpaper, faded carpeting and outdated, worn furnishings. Sadly, the decor in the 504 rooms is downright tacky, the bathrooms are small, and the beds are a bit soft. Even the renovated rooms, in orange and brown hues, cry for modern styling. The Bismarck receives two poor-achievement awards: one for the slowest and noisiest elevators in town (we waited for twelve minutes on the twelfth floor), and the other for the least-knowledgeable hotel staff around (we had to define the words "concierge" and "amenities" to one bellman and to another the concept of valet parking, which, by the way, is $10.25 for the first day and $8.25 for the second and third). Two saving graces: Room service delivers pizza, and prices are slightly lower than at other downtown establishments.

Singles: $70-$85; doubles: $80-$95; suites: $135-$145. Weekend packages available.

The Congress Hotel
520 S. Michigan Ave.
427-3800

Once known as "The Home of the Presidents" (FDR rehearsed his 1932 acceptance speech in a Congress suite), this well-known hotel, which opened in 1892 for the 400th anniversary of the discovery of America, has seen brighter days. Although the lobby's intricately tiled mosaic ceiling and gilded Florentine clock are worth a look, we would not recommend a stay here. Despite the hotel's reputation of days past and the recent renovations to restore the 825 rooms, we found the furnishings drab, outdated and tattered, the walls stark and the amenities too few to mention. The fact that this was the Chicago den of many presidents, including Grover Cleveland, Teddy Roosevelt, Woodrow Wilson, Herbert Hoover and Richard Nixon, along with such notables as Buffalo Bill Cody, Thomas Edison, Jean Harlow, the Rockefellers and the Rothschilds, underscores the notion that the Congress is alive with ghosts of eras past. If reincarnated, they would be too spooked to stay here today. No valet parking.

Singles: $70-$80; doubles: $80-$100; suites: $150-$425. Weekend packages available.

The Essex Inn
800 S. Michigan Ave.
939-2800

If money is an issue and you don't need to walk through an elegant lobby on your way to bed, The Essex Inn offers affordable, tastefully decorated rooms, some with magnificent views of Lake Michigan and Grant Park. Don't fret about the Inn's southern address (although we would not recommend an evening stroll in the area); an hourly shuttle bus will deliver you to and from Water Tower Place. Our only complaints are that bathrooms are excruciatingly small, and the lobby Muzak doesn't mix well with the rock 'n' roll pumped in from the hotel deli. Tip: In the suites' parlor areas the Spectravision movies are free; you pay for them in the bedrooms. Outdoor pool on premises. Parking is 90 cents per visit.

Singles: $68-$82; doubles: $78-$92; suites: $150-$350. Discounts for AAA members. Weekend packages available.

The Talbot
20 E. Delaware St.
943-0161

The Talbot's all-suite facilities are the best we've seen in town. Efficiency kitchens are roomy, modern and well stocked, and the well-kept suites are well decorated in warm tones. Although you won't find any restaurants in this 153-unit hotel, it is close enough to myriad Michigan Avenue restaurants. Also, Continental breakfast is served daily, and there is a generous Sunday brunch in one of the larger meeting rooms. Discount rates are available for extended stays. No valet parking.

Singles: $65-$150; doubles: $75-$300. Weekend packages available.

AIRPORT

O'Hare Hilton
O'Hare International
Airport
686-8000

Since it's located just an escalator ride from O'Hare's four major terminals, it may as well look like a fifth one, complete with departure information highlighted on monitors off to the side of the curved front desk. The decor is horrific—lime-green carpeting in the corridors, silver-lined paper on the walls and funky orange covers on the beds—but if you're stuck in town on a layover or have to catch an early plane, there are worse places to sleep. Maybe. Park it yourself for $12 a day, without in-and-out privileges.

Singles: $110-$130; doubles: $130-$150; suites: $220. Special weekend rates available.

AIRPORT

SHOPS

MIDWESTERN MERCHANDISING

Where you shop in Chicago depends not so much who you are or how much money you have, but on what you know. Rare is the out-of-towner who hasn't heard of Water Tower Place's seven glorious atrium-style levels lined with merchandise for the budget-conscious and the fat-of-wallet alike. No sooner does one touch down at O'Hare than one schedules a trip to the $200-million marble mecca of merchandise, with its more than 100 shops, accounting for nearly half the stores on the Magnificent Mile. And far be it for us to tell that out-of-towner *not* to visit Water Tower Place, for it is home to so many worthy wares. It's also the site of two of the most venerable retail institutions known to plastic: Lord & Taylor and Marshall Field, Chicago's oldest and most popular department stores.

And with the recent grand opening of the first Midwestern branch of Bloomingdale's, at 900 N. Michigan Avenue, and the adjoining eight-level Avenue Atrium, the beautiful new home of restaurants, movie theaters and 85 upscale shops, sophisticated downtown shoppers are in retail heaven. Some of the internationally known boutiques in Avenue Atrium (which had just opened at press time) include Henri Bendel, Fogal, Mondi, Neuchatel Chocolates, Aquascutum, Christofle, Maxima and The Coach Store.

But to savor a taste of true Chicago shopping, venture beyond those megamalls. After all, Water Tower is just another branch, albeit a particularly nice one, in the chain-store tree that has spread to nearly every city in America. Even the Magnificent Mile, which is to Chicago what Fifth Avenue is to New York, offers the same opulence—Cartier, Tiffany, I. Magnin—found in Beverly Hills, San Francisco, Palm Beach, Dallas and elsewhere. It's on Chicago's side streets, or at least off the beaten path a bit, that the city's character can be bought, wrapped and taken home to your closet, kitchen or living room.

The hunt begins near downtown, at the northern tip of the Magnificent Mile on Oak Street, Chicago's answer to Rodeo Drive, where labels are as important as quality and high price tags reign. Jump south a block to Chestnut Street, and you'll find more high-end boutiques professing the same top-labels-for-top-dollar philosophy. But our favorite Chicago shopping areas take a little more effort to reach. The further north you travel, the quirkier—and more exciting—it gets.

River North, the city's loft and gallery haven, is also home to some of the city's trendier shops and boutiques. The area is bounded by W. Chicago Avenue, Kinzie Street, N. Clark Street and the Chicago River. At N. Halsted Street, beginning a stone's throw south of W. Armitage Avenue, the real fun begins; good prospects are found as well along N. Lincoln Avenue, N. Clark Street and N. Broadway, which begins at W. Diversey Parkway. And things get wonderfully imaginative north of Diversey along Halsted, Clark and Broadway, where you'll find a most eclectic assortment of shops that sell antiques, vintage clothing and books, along with some daring avant-garde clothing. And scattered hither and thither on some out-of-the-way streets are shops worthy for their great bargains and/or unusual wares. We've unearthed the best of each lot, from the well-known chains to the one-of-a-kind gems, in the pages that follow.

ANTIQUES

ART DECO & ART NOUVEAU

Fly-by-Night Gallery
714 N. Wells St.
664-8136
Open Mon.-Fri. 10 a.m.-6 p.m., Sat. 10 a.m.-5 p.m.

A truly glorious antiques boutique, Fly-by-Night stocks exquisite art nouveau and art deco objets d'art—furnishings, statuary, jewelry—all displayed with painstaking care and elegance. Browsing through Fly-by-Night is not unlike browsing through a small museum. A detailed history of its origin accompanies each perfectly restored piece.

Steve Starr Studios
2654 N. Clark St.
525-6530
Open Mon.-Thurs. 2 p.m.-6 p.m., Fri. 2 p.m.-5 p.m., Sat. noon-5 p.m., Sun. 1 p.m.-5 p.m.

Starr carries some of the finest art deco treasures to be found in the city: etched glassware and mirrors, cut-glass and crystal perfume bottles, silver cigarette cases, chrome cocktail shakers and glorious rhinestone jewelry. Don't get too attached to one of the hundreds of deco frames with photographs gracing his walls—they're not for sale. Time your visit for after 2 p.m., when Starr himself mans the store. He's quite a character—a little ornery, very excited about his wares and quick to tell you how much you're saving by shopping in his store, which is stretching the truth just a little.

State Street Collection
609 N. State St.
951-1828
Open Tues.-Sat. 11 a.m.-6 p.m.

This collection is strongest in art deco kitchen collectibles—stoves, spice racks and manual appliances from that era are its specialty.

BOOKS, MAPS & PRINTS

Hamill & Barker
1719 Howard St.
475-1724
*Open Mon.-Fri. 9 a.m.-
4:30 p.m., Sat. 10 a.m.-
4 p.m.*

Established in 1928, Hamill & Barker, Chicago's oldest antiquarian bookseller, carries the city's widest stock of incunabula—books printed before 1501. Its forte is texts printed prior to 1900; and it carries a thorough selection of old theological volumes and the earliest books of the Greeks and Latins—Plato, Socrates and Aristotle—which start at about $1,000. It also has one of the best collections of early Chicago history to be found. Most volumes are in meticulous condition.

Kenneth Nebenzahl
333 N. Michigan Ave.
641-2711
*Open Mon.-Fri. 9 a.m.-
5 p.m.*

Located on the 28th floor, Nebenzahl is Chicago's leading dealer in antique maps from the late fifteenth century to 1850. The book collection spans the same period, but it also carries more recent texts on Chicago history. The selection is broadest in Americana, early medicine and travel, many of which contain explorers' accounts from the days of Columbus, as well as books on early-American and Western settlement and a fine array of antique atlases.

Old Print Store
1407 N. Wells St.
266-8631
*Open Tues.-Fri. 10 a.m.-
6 p.m., Sat. noon-6 p.m.*

Owner James S. Nowik is a member of the American Historical Print Collectors Society, and his expertise shows as he guides you through his overstuffed treasure trove of rarefied prints, maps and books. His inventory, which spans the last three centuries, includes natural-history plates, botanicals, limited-edition European prints and eighteenth-century English architectural plates. Nowik is especially proud of his collection of original Currier & Ives prints, which he sells for $200 to $1,200. He also has a limited selection of Audubon prints and etchings from the '20s and '30s.

FURNISHINGS

Aged Experience
2034 N. Halsted St.
975-9790
*Open Mon.-Sat. noon-
6 p.m., Sun. noon-5 p.m.*

Although this rustic-looking shop specializes in early-twentieth-century American pine and oak furniture, the real finds are the hand-stitched quilts (about $225) and some miniature hanging cabinets. A tempting copper ink-and-blotter set typifies the smaller, well-priced treasures found here.

Antique Palace
3020 N. Lincoln Ave.
477-6700
*Open Mon.-Fri. 9 a.m.-
6 p.m., Sat. 11 a.m.-6 p.m.*

Enter through glass doors and be trapped by more doors made of black wrought iron. The sign asks you to ring, and it tells you that no salespeople work the floor and that all questions should be brought to the long desk in back. This huge, half-block-long shop is filled to the brim with every antique imaginable—from seemingly every period and every country. But the buzz that opens the gates bounces off the ultra-high ceilings with an echo, setting an eerie tone in this palace of the past. Furnishings are in good condition, as are the statuary, prints, silver and gold, glassware and jewelry. The collection of finer pieces is roped off and accessed through assistance from the subdued staff. You can spend an entire day milling among the long rows of desks, tables, chairs, curios and armoires, and the prices are quite reasonable, even without the designer discount.

Margaret Bauer Antiques, Ltd.
172 E. Walton St.
649-0509
Open Mon.-Fri. noon-5:30 p.m., Sat. noon-3 p.m.

This quaint antiques shop adjacent to the Drake Hotel sells a small, tasteful collection of turn-of-the century art glass, bronzes, porcelain, paintings, rugs, silver and jewelry. Prices may be a little high, but quality seems to be good, and some of the silver and jewelry are absolutely exquisite.

Brass Works
2142 N. Halsted St.
935-1800
Open Mon.-Fri. 9:30 a.m.-6 p.m., Sat. 11 a.m.-5 p.m.

Brass Works could be the end of a long search for that Victorian-style brass doorknob or keyhole plate you need for your restoration project. Other great (and expensive) finds include a neoclassic torchère brass bowl shade (circa 1925) for $425 and an emeralite adjustable banker's lamp with the original shade (circa 1917) for $575. Brass beds and bathroom fixtures are also Brass Works specialties.

Caledonian
209 W. Illinois St.
923-0098
Open Mon.-Fri. 9 a.m.-5 p.m., Sat. 11 a.m.-4 p.m.; hours vary in summer.

Caledonian feels like a stately English sitting room, which is no surprise considering it's one of Chicago's most elite importers of fine—and terribly expensive—British furnishings from the late eighteenth and early nineteenth centuries. Most tables, chairs, breakfronts and armoires from the Chippendale and George III periods are made from mahogany and have been fastidiously restored. The pieces are for the most part magnificent, some of the loveliest and most elegant we've seen: for example, the flame mahogany George III breakfront with glass shelves and interior lighting that sells for $38,000.

Cathay Gallery
620 N. Michigan Ave.
951-1048
Open Mon.-Sat. 10 a.m.-5 p.m.

Specializing in Oriental art from the Neolithic period through the early 1900s, Cathay's fifth-floor Michigan Avenue suite sells quality Chinese antiques in mint condition. Pieces come in all forms—ceramics, jade, paintings, bronze, ivory, cloisonné and clothing. Ceramic bowls from the Han-Tang Sung Dynasty (200 B.C. to the thirteenth century) are perfectly preserved and range in price from a few hundred dollars to more than $25,000. Other interesting items include a rosewood and ceramic Chinese deco screen from the 1920s and an intricately embroidered imperial robe for $1,500.

Formerly Yours
3443 N. Halsted St.
248-7766
Open Mon.-Sun. noon-
6 p.m.

If it's not in near-perfect condition, proprietors Jamie Murawski and Ron Holtzman won't consider selling it in their store. Specializing in American Victorian furnishings from 1830 on, Formerly Yours is loaded with well-priced finds in top condition—from a mahogany table inlaid with rosewood, pine and ebony (circa 1910) for $285 to an American mahogany Federal-style desk with tambour front for $975. Some beautiful Chinese lacquered panels inlaid with mother of pearl, quartz, ivory and jade sell for a reasonable $355.

Malcolm Franklin
56 E. Walton St.
337-0202
Open Mon.-Fri. 9 a.m.-
5 p.m., Sat. 9 a.m.-3 p.m.;
summer hours vary.

Dan Sullivan now runs the shop his grandfather opened many years ago on Michigan Avenue, and he'll be the first to tell you that the Chicago flagship and the New York branch are recognized as among the finest antiques stores in the country. But Sullivan says this earnestly, even with a touch of humility, and we couldn't disagree with him. Malcolm Franklin sells the finest English furnishings, from William & Mary through the Regency periods, with a smattering of Victoriana. Last we checked, Malcolm Franklin carried one of the few complete sets of eight Queen Anne chairs to be found. Walnut with a paper-scroll top rail, the circa-1710 set was selling for $65,000. Other treasures have included a George I carved and gilt gesso console table with a marble top (circa 1725) and an elaborately carved Charles II mirror made about 1670.

Gallery Vienna
750 N. Orleans St.
951-0300
Open Mon.-Fri. 10 a.m.-
5 p.m., Sat. 11 a.m.-5 p.m.

Exquisitely restored and refinished Austrian furnishings from the Jugendstil period between 1900 and 1930—Gallery Vienna sells complete dining sets from this era, as well as other sturdy and well-preserved pieces. It also carries expertly detailed miniatures by Italian designer Ettore Sobrero. (See also listing under "Galleries" in Arts.)

International Antiques
2907 N. Clark St.
528-4602
Open Mon.-Sat. 11 a.m.-
7 p.m., Sun. noon-6 p.m.

It's difficult to find your way around Chicago's largest importer of Scottish antiques: Narrow aisles are stacked with Scottish artifacts, some of which are in markedly poor condition. Prices are high, as evidenced by the severe markdowns made to move merchandise. For example, an Edwardian leaded-glass cabinet in fair condition was knocked from $2,750 to $1,900. If you look hard enough, however, there are some good finds, such as a Scottish baronial breakfast cabinet and secretary selling for $2,275.

O'Hara's Connoisseur Gallery
707 N. Wells St.
751-1286
Open Mon.-Sat. 10 a.m.-
6 p.m.

Five rooms are so stacked with antiques from every part of the world and every period that it's difficult to sort the quality pieces from those unworthy of a second look. But Richard O'Hara will be glad to guide you through his treasures. He's particularly proud of a $175,000 Tiffany-glass window he bought in Wilkes Barre, Pennsylvania, along with his collection of authentic Tiffany lamps, even though this part of his immense shop is poorly lit and a bit dusty. O'Hara targets the upper bracket of the antiques market, who come here for such lavish pieces as a Biedermeier child's canopy bed inlaid with oak, walnut and tulip wood, sixteenth-century gilded salon tables and eighteenth-century French tapestries. If you feel a bit lost, don't be too shy to ask O'Hara—he loves the attention.

Parenteau Studios
230 W. Huron St.
337-8015
Open Mon.-Fri. 8:30 a.m.-4:30 p.m., Sat. 10 a.m.-4 p.m.

Parenteau Studios is divided into two sections: one for Paul Parenteau's furniture designs, the other for one of the loveliest antiques galleries in the city; it's spacious and easy to get around. Parenteau specializes in European antiques, mainly French pieces from the eighteenth and nineteenth centuries. Most of the pieces have been exquisitely restored and are displayed in realistic settings. Some furnishings even have their original fabrics—a little worse for wear, but beautiful just the same, such as the Louis XVI lacquered settee upholstered in pale blue and white silk damask. Oddly enough, Parenteau also carries Oriental stone statuary from the second to tenth century A.D. A definite must-look.

Victoria Peters
449 N. Wells St.
644-5855
Open Mon.-Fri. noon-4 p.m., Sat. 11 a.m.-5 p.m.

That Gucci and Burberry's use pieces from Victoria Peters for their seasonal displays is a sure sign of her refined and classic taste. Peters specializes in smaller furnishings: end tables, stools, small desks. All pieces are bought in London, though not all were made there. For instance, a large mahogany armoire inlaid with ivory shows a distinct Indian influence, and a luscious collection of blue and white ceramics hails from the Orient. Her pieces are perfectly restored, tastefully chosen and highly priced.

Portals Limited
230 W. Huron St.
642-1066
Open Mon.-Fri. 10 a.m.-4:45 p.m., Sat. 10 a.m.-4 p.m.

After leaving Parenteau Studios, hop on the manned wrought-iron elevator to the seventh floor and venture into Portals, which specializes in English aesthetic furnishings as well as contemporary naïf art. This bright, airy gallery is conducive to browsing, and the pieces are breathtakingly beautiful, magnificently restored and absolutely one of a kind. The artwork is vibrant and fairly priced. But the most appealing aspect of Portals is its owner, Nancy McIlvane, a genuinely warm woman who shares her enthusiasm with everyone who walks through her doors, whether or not they are knowledgeable about her passion.

George Rettig Antiques
715 N. Franklin St.
642-9180
Open Tues.-Fri. 10:30 a.m.-5:30 p.m.

George Rettig is another one of Chicago's highly respected antiques dealers who specializes in decorative English and French furniture from the eighteenth and nineteenth centuries, as well as fine replicas. Spiral staircases connect two floors of lovely, well-restored pieces. But one of the best features of this River North antiques shop is

Rettig himself, an affable man who will take time to talk even when he's rushing out the door at closing time. He spent twenty years working with the city's biggest dealers before opening his own shop six years ago, and his knowledge is boundless. If he doesn't have exactly what you're looking for, he'll tell you where you can get it.

Jay Roberts Antiques Warehouse
149 W. Kinzie St.
222-0167
Open Mon.-Sat. 10 a.m.-5 p.m.

"Things you drooled over in Europe but didn't know how to bring back." That's how Jay Roberts describes his 50,000 square feet of inventory of nineteenth-century European appointments. It is all moderately priced, in mint condition and a step ahead of what other local antiques dealers carry. Roberts makes several trips abroad annually and ships everything himself, thus eliminating the middleman and bringing better prices to his customers. The first floor is filled with museum-quality tables, curios, bookcases, brass beds and commodes. Walls are lined with fine collections of functional antique wall and grandfather clocks. The second floor houses fireplace mantles shipped whole from Europe and often redesigned as headboards. A kaleidoscope of stained-glass windows, as well as a glittering array of crystal and glass chandeliers, hangs from the ceiling.

The Time Well
2780 N. Lincoln Ave.
549-2113
Open Sat.-Mon. noon-5 p.m., Wed.-Fri. 3 p.m.-8 p.m.

This large consignment shop sells used and antique furnishings in very good condition from the eighteenth century to more recent times. The staff is exceptionally good at helping you find the right piece, which is fortunate, since the inventory is dauntingly vast. But the selection is choice; only tasteful pieces in fine condition are displayed, and if a piece doesn't sell within 30 days, it's returned to the owner.

Turtle Creek Antiques
850 W. Armitage Ave.
327-2630
Open Mon.-Fri. 11 a.m.-6 p.m., Sat. 10 a.m.-6 p.m., Sun. 11 a.m.-5 p.m.

Proprietor Mary Popma personally oversees the restoration of the turn-of-the-century wicker furniture she sells, often reupholstering them herself to ensure the best quality. But exquisitely preserved hand-stitched quilts and European embroidered-and-laced linens from the late nineteenth century through the 1930s are the shop's forte. The antique jewelry from the arts and crafts period through art deco and into the '50s is also noteworthy.

GLASS & LIGHTING

Aunt Edie's Glass
3339 N. Halsted St.
528-1617
Open Wed.-Sun. noon-7 p.m.

The city's largest dealer of Depression-era glassware, Aunt Edie's is chock-full of reasonably priced, authentic tinted glass from that period. Although it doesn't repair china, it does have an efficient locator service that can help find replacement pieces.

Stanley Galleries
Antique Lighting
2118 N. Clark St.
281-1614
Open Mon.-Sat. noon-
7 p.m., Sun. noon-6 p.m.

Crystal drips from the ceilings in this quaint Lincoln Park antiques shop. It's aglow with the light of hundreds of chandeliers, wall sconces and floor, desk and table lamps that date from 1840 to 1935. Although lighting specialists, Stanley Galleries has an exquisite American collection of art glass by Tiffany and Steuben, as well as objets d'art. Everything is magnificently preserved, particularly some of the older furniture, which dates back to the late 1800s and is mostly European and fairly high priced.

Tiffany
Stained Glass
216 W. Ohio St.
642-0680
Open Mon.-Fri. 9 a.m.-
5 p.m., Sat. 10 a.m.-3 p.m.

No, it's not the real thing. But these detailed reproductions could fool all but the best-trained eye. Tiffany Stained Glass reproduces the lamps that elsewhere sell *starting* at $50,000; here they sell for a fraction of that price. Skilled artisans on the premises hand-cut a vibrant assortment of glass, making painstaking efforts to reproduce exact patinas.

MARKETS

Chicago
Antique Mall
3343 N. Clark St.
929-0200
Open Mon.-Thurs. & Sat.
11 a.m.-6 p.m., Fri.
11 a.m.-7 p.m., Sun. noon-
5 p.m.

A mere upstart when we first visited, the Chicago Antique Mall was readying its ground floor to accommodate another 21 independent dealers, which will bring the total to 50. Specializing in Americana from the Victorian era through the twentieth century, the unusually airy and cheerful mall is full of many great finds. Prices range from $1.50 into the thousands for fine furniture, vintage jewelry and clothes, crystal, glassware and art deco pieces. Of note is the old book and map collection, with some maps dating as far back as 1500.

BEAUTY

BEAUTY PRODUCTS

Caswell-Massey
835 N. Michigan Ave.
(Water Tower Place)
664-1752
Open Mon. & Thurs.
10 a.m.-7 p.m., Tues.-Wed.
& Fri.-Sat. 10 a.m.-6 p.m.,
Sun. noon-7 p.m.

So proud is it of its distinction as America's oldest chemist and perfumer, Caswell-Massey of Chicago made founding date 1752 its phone number. Finely treated oak shelving built into every nook and cranny of this old-world apothecary maintains the traditional charm that has kept this place in business years beyond its bicentennial birthday. Come here for some old-fashioned pampering, whether you need a menthol dome to cure that headache or a luscious Caswell-Massey shaving cream—the kind you apply with a brush. In addition to a wide and aromatic supply of cachets, hand-milled soaps, fragrances, face powders, natural sponges, oils and creams—made with such ingredients as seaweed, almonds, rainwater and tomatoes—this parfumerie also carries some European products not easily found in this neck of the woods: like Roget Galet lip balm, the most effective lip balm known to man.

Crabtree & Evelyn

835 N. Michigan Ave.
(Water Tower Place)
787-0188
Open Mon. & Thurs.
10 a.m.-7 p.m., Tues.- Wed.
& Fri.-Sat. 10 a.m.-6 p.m.,
Sun. 11 a.m.-5 p.m.

Truly a garden of aromatic delights, Crabtree & Evelyn offers a respite from the Water Tower melee, as well as from the harsh reality of city life. When combing through the lavender cachets, buttermilk lotions and cinnamon soaps, it's hard not to fantasize about sinking ever so slowly into the luxuries this British parfumerie has to offer. If only we could pamper ourselves as delicately and indulgently as Crabtree & Evelyn carefully coddles its products: from the triple-milled soaps in every imaginable shape, color and fragrance to the ultra-moisturizing jojoba hair products. Children are not forgotten here; they'll be charmed by soap figurines from *Alice in Wonderland* and *The Tales of Beatrix Potter*, which are tucked into lovely painted tins. A range of comestibles is also available, from cooking oils and spices to cookies and jams.

FACE & BODY

Elizabeth Arden

717 N. Michigan Ave.
266-5750
Open Mon.-Wed. & Fri.-
Sat. 9 a.m.-6 p.m., Thurs.
9 a.m.-8 p.m.

These three floors comprise the lap of luxury. Arden's beauty products are sold on the first floor, the second floor belongs to Tiffany & Co., and the third provides pampering of the highest order in salons bathed in pink and offset with white wicker. Elizabeth Arden's Maine Chance Day, named for her Maine retreat, consists of five hours of completely forgetting the world outside this Michigan Avenue spa. A visit to the steam cabinet, a massage, hair styling, manicure, pedicure, facial, daytime makeup and a light lunch can be yours for $200. A "miracle morning," which does not include the steam and lunch but does give you an eyebrow arch, lasts an hour and costs $150. Other packages and à la carte services are available for the asking. An airy lingerie salon sporting Christian Dior's finest adjoins the beauty area, and the first-floor salon displays some lovely clothes by Donna Karan, Louis Ferout, Valentino and Adele Simpson.

Che Sguardo

716 N. Wells St.
440-1616
Open Mon.-Wed. & Fri.
8:30 a.m.-5:30 p.m.,
Thurs. 8:30 a.m.- 8 p.m.,
Sat. 11:30 a.m.-5 p.m.

Certainly Chicago's most state-of-the-art cosmetic studio—the bright, spacious atmosphere is accented by exposed brick walls, angled mirrors and natural-oak floors—Che Sguardo also creates some of the trendiest, most upscale and elegant face fashions around. Owned by the city's most renowned makeup artist, Kathy Schmalen, Che Sguardo serves the city's professionals in the performing arts, modeling and photography, as well as women seeking the latest in fresh facial looks. Several European cosmetic lines are available, including Diego dalla Palma. The two-and-a-half-hour makeup and skin-care consultation runs $100, and a facial costs $50. Manicures, pedicures and tanning beds are also available.

Georgette Klinger
835 N. Michigan Ave.
(Water Tower Place)
787-4300
Open Mon. & Thurs.
9:30 a.m.-6 p.m., Tues.-
Wed. & Fri.-Sat.
9:30 a.m.-4 p.m.

The ultimate pampering place for both men and women, Georgette Klinger will take you for a day and bathe you in creamy luxury. Services range from a simple manicure for $13 to a deluxe, full day of beauty that includes a facial, body massage, manicure, pedicure, scalp treatment, shampoo and blow-dry, makeup lesson and lunch—all for $235. A full day for men, which includes all of the above except, of course, the makeup lesson, costs $185.

Ilona of Hungary
45 E. Oak St.
337-7161
Open Mon., Wed. & Fri.
10 a.m.-6:30 p.m., Tues. &
Thurs. 10 a.m.-8 p.m.,
Sat. 9 a.m.-5:30 p.m.

The skin-care specialists here are European-trained, and each brings to Ilona's at least fifteen years' experience. Neither machines nor any unnatural ingredients are used in the extensive line of skin-care products. Still, prices are competitive with larger skin-care outfits, and the service is just as lavish. A one-hour facial is $50. Other services include herbal waxings, cellulite treatments, full body massages and bull-blood treatments (don't worry, it's pseudo bull blood: a blend of Hungarian wine and cream used to rejuvenate older skin).

Marilyn Miglin
112 E. Oak St.
943-1120
Open Mon.-Fri. 10 a.m.-
5:30 p.m., Sat. 10 a.m.-
5 p.m.

Sit down at one of Marilyn Miglin's well-lit makeup stations and learn how to look the very best by using the very least. Makeup artists here are skilled in subtlety and never rely on heavy colors to bring out your beauty. Two-hour skin-care and makeup consultations run between $35 and $50, and all products used are available for purchase. An exceptionally kind staff makes a visit here all the more enjoyable.

HAIR SALONS

Brady C'est Bon
835 N. Michigan Ave.
(Water Tower Place)
664-3600
Open Mon.-Wed. & Fri.-
Sat. 8:30 a.m.-4:30 p.m.,
Thurs. 8:30 a.m.-6:30 p.m.

In the finest Chicago boutiques, Brady C'est Bon is the name most often heard when people are seeking hair-salon referrals. Few customers leave this busy salon dissatisfied. The price is high, but most get what they pay for. Other services include manicures, pedicures, hair treatments, facials and massages.

Paul Glick

701 N. Michigan Ave.
751-2300
Open Tues. 8 a.m.-8 p.m.,
Wed. & Fri.-Sat. 8 a.m.-
5 p.m., Thurs. 8 a.m.-
6:30 p.m.

A Glick haircut is a status symbol in Chicago. And when it's done right, there is no better. While some of Chicago's grandest dames swear by these coifs—as do many celebrities breezing in and out of the city—the results aren't always in step with the salon's fine reputation. Although Glick himself has turned in his scissors, for $75 he will spend an hour evaluating the psychological implications of your hair. We found this consultation ridiculous, but some women swear by Glick's word. Cuts range from $35 to $75, depending on the stylist; perms are $70 and up. Body wraps, manicures, pedicures and coloring are also available.

Charles Ifergon

106 E. Oak St.
642-4484
Open Tues.-Wed. & Fri.-
Sat. 9 a.m.-5 p.m., Thurs.
9 a.m.-7 p.m.

Like Paul Glick, Ifergon is an elite salon that has trouble with consistency. Some of its stylists are the most skilled in town, but we hesitate to make any individual recommendations; even though stylists covet their chairs at Ifergon, turnover does exist. We can say that we don't consider Ifergon himself to be worth the money. He charges $10 more than other stylists and schedules appointments every fifteen minutes; in our experience, he's spent those fifteen minutes quickly ruffling through his clients' hair, wooing them with his thick French accent and barely making a difference. We've also had some harrowing experiences with permanents—solutions left on too long, styling assistants too inattentive to notice. Still, if you get the right stylist, and a good assistant for coloring or perms, Ifergon can make you as beautiful as Mother Nature will allow.

Jean-Pierre Coiffures

70 E. Walton St.
944-4311
Open Tues.-Sat. 9 a.m.-
5 p.m.

This large Gold Coast salon has a reputation for customer satisfaction. Stylists listen to their clients and will concoct new hair designs only when asked. There's also a nice jewelry selection. Other services include electrolysis, waxing and makeup consultation.

Leigh Jones

12 E. Walton St.
944-3366
Open Mon.-Sat. 9 a.m.-
6 p.m.

Leigh Jones, who once worked with Jean-Pierre, opened this understated, yet elegant, salon with the same service-oriented attitude of his former employer. Hair styles here are certainly vogue, but stylists are not ashamed to be conservative if that's what customers want. The full-service salon also offers facials, manicures, pedicures and sculptured nail treatments.

Maxine Ltd.

64 E. Walton St.
751-1511
Open Mon.-Wed. & Fri.-
Sun. 9 a.m.-5 p.m.,
Thurs. 9 a.m.-7 p.m.

This high-tech hair palace has many Sassoon recruits who value customer satisfaction over trendiness. Space-age cubicles painted in black, chrome yellow and purple service Chicago's elite, who always leave pleased. It's one of the few salons that makes Sunday appointments.

Vidal Sassoon
835 N. Michigan Ave.
(Water Tower Place)
751-2216
Open Mon.-Thurs. 9 a.m.-
5 p.m., Fri.-Sat. 8:30 a.m.-
5:30 p.m., Sun. 10 a.m.-
5 p.m.

Although many clients come back for more, others avoid this high-tech salon for its slave-like adherence to current, not necessarily attractive, hair trends. If you need a new look, Sassoon may be the place to find it, since its stylists are well trained, if not a little scissor-happy. Sassoon takes clients on Sunday. Manicures and pedicures are available.

BOOKS & STATIONERY

BOOKS

All American Adventures
2936 N. Clark St.
281-9673

6130 W. Belmont St.
286-2676
Open Mon.-Wed. & Sun.
noon-7 p.m., Thurs.-
Fri.noon-8 p.m., Sat.
noon- 6 p.m.

Stocking all-new main line and small-press comics, All American will keep you current on the latest adventures of the most popular adventure heroes, including the X-Men, Batman, Superman, Wonder Woman and the Teenage Mutant Ninja Turtles. All American also sells a wide array of fantasy role-playing games, as well as back issues and collectors' comics. A No. 1 Spiderman recently sold for $560.

Aspidistra Bookshop
2630 N. Clark St.
549-3129
Open Mon.-Sat. noon-
8:30 p.m., Sun. 1 p.m.-
7 p.m.

Aspidistra carries a superb selection of used books of twentieth-century literature; all the major names are represented in volumes that are in excellent condition. Most titles are stocked according to subject, so it's easy to find your way around this huge used-book palace. Some used-book aficionados complain that prices are a little high, and we have to agree, but its superlative selection, including a large collection of volumes on the Civil War and Vietnam, makes Aspidistra worthwhile.

Barbara's Bookstore
1434 N. Wells St.
642-5044

2707 N. Broadway
477-0411
Open Mon.-Sat. 10:15 a.m.-
9:45 p.m., Sun. 11 a.m.-
8 p.m.

Barbara's Bookstore is a perfect place to lose yourself for a couple of hours on a rainy afternoon. It does a big business in paperbacks, which line the walls from floor to ceiling. It also carries an extensive, updated selection of hardcover best-sellers, though its strong suit seems to be in smaller presses, obscure and little-known periodicals, and books on the performing arts. The children's section is superb, with a delightful sitting area to peruse the volumes.

Bookseller's Row
2445 N. Lincoln Ave.
348-1170
Open daily 11 a.m.-
10:30 p.m.

A most civilized used-book store, Bookseller's Row prides itself on the condition of its used, rare and out-of-print volumes, which are always clean and untattered. It carries some 40,000 titles on every topic imaginable, and sections are clearly marked according to subject. A roped-off section of finer used books contains full sets of Limited Edition

Club volumes from the '20s and '30s, including the complete plays of Shakespeare.

Stuart Brent
670 N. Michigan Ave.
337-6357
Open Mon.-Fri. 9 a.m.-
8 p.m., Sat. 9 a.m.-6 p.m.,
Sun. noon-5 p.m.

A favorite of Noel Coward, Ernest Hemingway, Nelson Algren and Ben Hecht when they came to town, Stuart Brent is a classic old-world bookstore for serious readers. Don't be surprised if a gray-haired man with a big smile tries to sell you his favorite book. It's probably Brent himself, a man who cherishes his customers and enjoys getting personally involved in their reading habits. Downstairs is a fine children's section, with shelves of classics intelligently interpreted for the young, as well as some sophisticated current releases.

Crown Books
24 N. Wabash Ave.
782-7667
Open Mon.-Fri. 9 a.m.-
7 p.m., Sat. 9:30 a.m.-
6 p.m., Sun. noon-5 p.m.

A reasonably good discount general bookstore; the range of titles is spotty, but books on computers, travel and cooking (plus, of course, best-sellers) are well represented. A wide-ranging selection of magazines is another plus of this major bookstore chain. Call for other locations.

B. Dalton Bookseller
645 N. Michigan Ave.
944-3702
Open Mon.-Sat. 10 a.m.-
6:30 p.m., Sun. 11 a.m.-
5 p.m.

This branch of the ubiquitous national chain is a good, moderately sized bookstore stocking about 25,000 titles. The selection is broad but not deep, and best-sellers are discounted. Other locations are scattered around town and in the suburbs, including 129 N. Wabash Avenue (236-7615) and 175 W. Jackson Street (922-5219).

Europa Bookstore
3229 N. Clark St.
929-1836
Open Mon.-Thurs. 10 a.m.-
10 p.m., Fri.-Sat. 10 a.m.-
11 p.m., Sun. noon-11 p.m.

Europa is Chicago's best source for foreign-language books from every country in Europe. It has a terrific selection of books in French, German, Spanish and Italian, as well as volumes translated from these and other languages into English. Sections are marked by country, and there are particularly thorough selections of foreign literature, how-to books, flash cards, tapes, dictionaries and other language-learning tools. Europa also sells flags from all over Europe, as well as cigarettes, newspapers and magazines.

N. Fagin Books
1039 W. Grand Ave.
829-5252
Open Mon.-Fri. 10 a.m.-
5 p.m., Sat. 10 a.m.-3 p.m.

Chicagoans with a lifelong passion for the natural sciences—anything from dinosaurs to primitive art—have a second home in N. Fagin Books. The store is an internationally known resource for specialty books and journals on anthropology, archaeology, zoology and botany. N. Fagin has served the academic and library communities since 1980 with new and used obscure titles, 75 percent of which are on anthropological or archaeological subjects. Owner Nancy Fagin provides a free search service, takes mail and phone orders and sells a small selection of folk art and native American prints.

Guild Books
2456 N. Lincoln Ave.
525-3667
*Open Mon.-Sat. 11 a.m.-
10:30 p.m., Sun. noon-
10:30 p.m.*

If you're just dying to read the most recent issue of *Paris Match,* or need an inspirational shot of social consciousness, come to Guild Books. Magazines from just about every European country line the walls in the back room, along with many small-press publications you might not find elsewhere. Mainstream books displayed strategically in the window lure the less heady Lincoln Park crowd into this gem of a bookstore, which is best known for its historical, sociological and political publications.

I Love a Mystery Bookstore
55 E. Washington St.,
Ste. 616
236-1338
*Open Mon.-Fri. 10 a.m.-
5 p.m., Sat. 10 a.m.-3 p.m.*

One of the oldest mystery bookstores in the country, I Love a Mystery houses some 10,000 titles, mostly paperback but with a selective smattering of hardcovers. Owner John Morginson claims to have read most of them and loves to make recommendations. He carries books that are hard to find in the U.S., including a large selection of British paperbacks published long before the American hardcover editions hit the presses.

Kroch's & Brentano's
29 S. Wabash Ave.
332-7500
*Open Mon. & Thurs.
9 a.m.-7 p.m., Tues.-Wed.
& Fri.-Sat. 9 a.m.-6 p.m.*

The biggest of Chicago's chain bookstores, and one with many branches, Kroch's stocks an impressive range of titles on just about every topic. The Wabash store is the best stocked; look here first when you need a book in a hurry. The accommodating staff will be happy to do title and author searches and will gladly special-order books as quickly as possible. In addition to expansive collections of the obvious—best-sellers, self-help, children's, cooking, travel—Kroch's also finds room for the obscure, often carrying editions that have been long out of print. For bargains, check out Kroch's & Brentano's Bargain Book Center at 62 E. Randolph Street (263-2681). Call 332-7500 for other locations.

Oak Street Bookshop
54 E. Oak St.
642-3070
*Open Mon.-Sat. 10 a.m.-
6 p.m., Sun. 11 a.m.-5 p.m.*

Not the biggest bookstore in town, and certainly not the most complete, but certainly worth a look. This cozy shop earned some regional fame for its role in the '70s movie *Harry and Tonto,* but the fame, unfortunately, didn't seem to bring in much business. Still, owner Carol Stoll carries some interesting volumes, from books on Renaissance art to how to have a better sex life. A separate room in back houses a superlative collection of books on theater and film.

Occult Bookshop
3230 N. Clark St.
281-0599
*Open Mon.-Sat. 11 a.m.-
7 p.m., Sun. noon-5 p.m.*

If the further reaches of spirituality are beckoning, the Occult Bookstore is for you. It's the city's oldest and most respected bookstore specializing in mysticism, witchcraft, magic, astrology, yoga and Oriental philosophy. In the market for a psychic? The Occult Bookstore has one in residence who charts horoscopes and reads tarot cards; it's best to make an appointment. Having a seance? Greet the spirits in style with lovely candles, crystals and incense.

Powell's

2850 N. Lincoln Ave.
248-1444
Open daily noon-9 p.m.

Powell's may sell used books, but it looks like a well-stocked, well-kept, new-book shop. Its three giant rooms are packed with about 100,000 titles on just about every subject imaginable: Oriental philosophies, theology, mythology, folklore, histories of numerous countries, the Renaissance, railroads, aviation... Prices are considerably less than at some other used-book emporiums. Call for information on special events, such as the poetry readings on the first Thursday of the month and the children's story-telling hours on the first Saturday of the month.

Prairie Avenue Bookshop

711 S. Dearborn St.
922-8311
Open Mon.-Fri. 9:30 a.m.-5:30 p.m., Sat. 10 a.m.-4 p.m.

The historic Printer's Row neighborhood, once the home of Chicago's booming publishing trade and now the site of the city's most creative residential and commercial restoration, is an appropriate spot for the shop that purports to have the country's largest selection of architecture books. A printed-and-bound feast for architectural professionals and students, the Prairie Avenue Bookshop keeps its customers abreast of the newest titles via its monthly newsletter. It also distributes a guide to building a professional library for architectural ingenues.

Rand McNally Map Store

23 E. Madison St.
332-4628
Open Mon.-Fri. 9:30 a.m.-6 p.m., Sat. 10 a.m.-4 p.m.

Going on a trip? Rand McNally will provide street maps for just about any destination, along with atlases, travel guides, wall maps, globes and an array of Rand McNally business products, including zip-code finders, and sales and marketing atlases.

Rizzoli

835 N. Michigan Ave.
(Water Tower Place)
642-3500
Open daily 10 a.m.-10 p.m.

Oak-beamed ceilings and built-in bookshelves give Rizzoli an Oxfordesque reading-room air. You'll feel like an intellectual just being here, what with Emily Dickinson's love poems poised elegantly on the octagonal wooden sales desk and a heady collection of Penguin classics lining an entire wall off to the side. Selling Jane Austen to Jackie Collins, Rizzoli is the book- lovers' bookstore, a wonderful place to browse to the strains of classical music. International newspapers are available, as are most every foreign and domestic magazine. On the back wall you'll find one of the most comprehensive travel sections around.

Sandmeyer's Bookstore

714 S. Dearborn St.
922-2104
Open Tues.-Fri. 11 a.m.-6:30 p.m., Sat. 11 a.m-5 p.m., Sun. noon-5 p.m.

Designed very much like a magazine section of a library, Sandmeyer's permits easy browsing. Wooden floor, exposed-brick walls and piping are indicative of the design trend in Printer's Row, where the shop is located. Although selection is small, it's quite accessible—all the books lay in full view on black, metal racks.

The Savvy Traveler

50 E. Washington St.
(2nd Fl.)
263-2100
*Open Mon.-Sat. 10 a.m.-
6 p.m.*

Being savvy travelers ourselves (or so we like to think), we love this unusual store for its exceptional breadth and intelligence. Sandye Wexler devotes about two-thirds of her floor space to a great collection of guidebooks, both mainstream and obscure, that'll take you to just about any destination on the planet, along with travel-oriented novels, photo essays, first-person accounts and even cookbooks. The rest of the roomy, friendly shop is filled with all sorts of nifty travel accessories, from globes and maps to luggage and clever money belts.

The Stars Our Destination

2942 N. Clark St.
871-2722
*Open Mon.-Sat. 10 a.m.-
8 p.m., Sun. noon-6 p.m.*

Trekkies and Whovians unite! Carrying only science fiction, The Stars Our Destination represents owner Alice Bentley's lifelong obsession with the outer limits. The best known sci-fi authors are represented: Isaac Asimov, Robert Heinlein, William Gibson, Orson Scott Card. Bentley claims she carries the largest selection of Philip K. Dick books in the city, and perhaps the country, and has dedicated the entire back wall to Star Trek and Dr. Who volumes.

Unabridged Bookstore

3251 N. Broadway
883-9119
*Open Mon.-Fri. 11 a.m.-
9 p.m., Sat. 10 a.m.-7 p.m.,
Sun. 11 a.m.-6 p.m.*

This is the sort of place that locals love to hang out at and read the latest issue of *People* or even the first few chapters of Gabriel García Márquez's most recent novel. The staff is disarmingly friendly and willing to help find titles. Strong sections in cinema, travel, softcover science fiction and gay literature.

Waldenbooks

616 W. Diversey Pkwy.
549-3292
*Open Mon.-Fri. 9 a.m.-
9 p.m., Sat. 10 a.m.-7 p.m.,
Sun. 10 a.m.-6 p.m.*

A national chain known to practically every mall shopper in the country, Waldenbooks is a reasonably large general interest bookstore with an especially well-rounded selection of business titles. Best-sellers are discounted 25 percent, and the staff will special-order any current title that's not in stock. Aside from books, you'll find a good range of greeting cards and games. The several other locations around town include branches in the Sears Tower (876-0308) and at 127 W. Madison Street (236-8446).

Women & Children First

1967 N. Halsted St.
440-8824
*Open Mon.-Tues. 11 a.m.-
7 p.m., Wed.-Fri. 11 a.m.-
9 p.m., Sat. 10 a.m.-7 p.m.,
Sun. noon-6 p.m.*

The city's finest selection of books for, by and about women. Although all the fiction is written by women, many of the nonfiction titles—self-help, addiction recovery, psychology and the like, as they relate to women—are written by men. It also carries comprehensive selections of child-care and birthing books. A healthy supply of journals, anthologies and small-press publications dealing with women's issues are displayed by the front desk. Children and teens are well-represented as well, and co-owner Linda Bubon holds a storybook hour for children between the ages of two and five every Wednesday at 10:30 a.m.

STATIONERY

Arcadia
36 S. Wabash Ave.
641-8300
Open Mon. & Thurs.
9:45 a.m.-7:45 p.m.,
Tues.-Wed. & Fri.- Sat.
9:45 a.m.-5:45 p.m.,
Sun. 11 a.m.-5 p.m.

If only we had more friends to send these remarkably appropriate and funny greeting cards to! Rows and rows of chuckles are found in one of the best humorous-card selections in the city. Of course, Arcadia doesn't ignore the serious side of life, also catering to those more sweet and sensitive than us. It even carries those teeth-rotting epithets of love by Susan Polis Shultz. T-shirts, stationery, kites, candy and funky school supplies round out the selection; there's also an interesting selection of adult beach toys. Call the above number for other locations.

He Who Eats Mud
3247 N. Broadway
525-0616
Open Mon.-Fri. 11 a.m.-
7 p.m., Sat. 11 a.m.-6 p.m.,
Sun. noon-6 p.m.

An odd name for an odd store. But what a delightful one it is. The greeting cards here will have you bellyaching in the aisles. For more serious correspondence, head for the back room, which is home to more demure invitations and greeting cards, including some particularly lovely imported boxed ones by Caspari. An entire display is devoted to Crabtree & Evelyn products and another to Fitz & Floyd porcelain dinnerware.

Horder's
184 N. Wabash Ave.
648-7272
Open Mon.-Fri. 8:15 a.m.-
5 p.m.

Horder's is one of Chicago's oldest stationery and office-supply stores; it's also the most complete and certainly the most ubiquitous. "Order from Horder's" is the slogan, and we suggest you do. If it doesn't carry a particular accessory for your office, desk, computer or classroom, an employee will get it for you as quickly as possible for as little as possible. Call for other locations.

Paper Source
730 N. Franklin St.
664-5440
Open Mon.-Fri. 10 a.m.-
6 p.m., Sat. 10 a.m.-5 p.m.

A kaleidoscope of fine-art papers made from cotton and tissues, some Oriental and quite delicate. Although the papers are most commonly used for artwork, shelving or in panels as wallpaper, the creatively minded can invent their own stationery designs from these beautifully textured papers. They are marbled, dripped and splattered in an endless array of colors.

The Water Mark
109 E. Oak St.
337-5353
Open Mon.-Sat. 10 a.m.-
6 p.m.

The Water Mark's staff will be happy to take you through volumes of invitation samples from Cranes and other fine paper houses until you find the perfect summons to your affair. The prices aren't excessive for the quality, though some staff members can't hide a greedy glint in their eyes when pointing out the exquisite invites Chuck and Di sent to close friends for their wedding. In addition to prepackaged cards and invitations, you can order personal stationery and business cards. If you really want to go all out, The Water Mark will create flamboyant invitations complete with ribbons and satin boxes for $125 a pop.

CHILDREN

BOOKS

The Children's Bookstore
2465 N. Lincoln Ave.
248-2665
Open Mon.-Wed. 10 a.m.-6 p.m., Thurs.-Sat. 10 a.m.-10 p.m., Sun. noon-6 p.m.

Chicago's largest children's bookstore received a national events-programming award for bringing in late Mayor Harold Washington and preparing kids to interview Illinois Senator Paul Simon during the 1988 presidential campaign. Other activities include storytelling hours (Mondays and Fridays at 10:30 a.m.) and writing workshops. The Children's Bookstore carries most categories found in adult bookstores—sports, humor, biography, science, poetry and reference. It specializes in nonfiction, which is usually lacking in other children's book departments.

CLOTHES

All Our Children
2217 N. Halsted St.
327-1868
Open Mon.-Wed. & Fri. 10 a.m.-6 p.m., Thurs. 10 a.m.-7 p.m., Sat. 10 a.m.-5 p.m., Sun. noon-5 p.m.

A small, friendly boutique for kids newborn to size 12. Clothes are fashionable and reasonably priced, as are accessories. The christening dresses are in particularly good taste, though they're much more expensive than everything else. More prolific brands include OshKosh, Hoo Hodders and Maggie Mackall.

And Baby Makes Three
1435 N. Wells St.
280-BABY or 642-KIDS
Open Mon.-Fri. 10 a.m.-7 p.m., Sat. 10 a.m.-6 p.m., Sun. noon-5 p.m.

And Baby Makes Three is three floors of the highest quality, most adorable clothes for infants, toddlers and kids. Dresses by Mouse Feathers come with matching hats; those by Sarah Kent are positively demure. Antique christening gowns are as enchanting as they are delicate. Jumpers and overalls come in every style, color and fabric. Among our favorite togs here are the Kermit The Frog rubber rain boots and rain jackets appliquéd with clouds. We could go on and on, but we'd rather you go and see for yourself.

Banana Moon
554 W. Diversey Pkwy.
525-8080
Open Mon.-Fri. 11 a.m.-6 p.m., Sat. 10 a.m.-5 p.m., Sun. noon-4 p.m.

Banana Moon carries some of the most endearing dresses for little girls that we've ever seen. Many of them are made by Maggie Mackall and have a Laura Ashley flair; other brands include OshKosh, Sweet Potatoes and Mufflings. The selection is thorough and the staff extremely helpful with clothes and accessories, which include teething spoons and cups, ID bracelets, ribbons, bows and socks.

Benetton 012
121 E. Oak St.
944-0432
*Open Mon. & Thurs.
10 a.m.-7 p.m. Tues.-Wed.
& Fri.-Sat. 10 a.m.-6 p.m.,
Sun. noon-5 p.m.; summer:
open Mon.-Fri. 10 a.m.-
7 p.m.*

Be sure to know your child's bodily dimensions when shopping here, because Italy's Benetton sizes its children's clothing differently than American stores. It doesn't carry a lot for newborns, but the selection for toddlers and kids is wide and colorful. Call the above number for other locations.

Born Beautiful
3206 N. Broadway
549-6770
*Open Mon.-Wed. & Fri.
9:30 a.m.-6 p.m., Thurs.
9:30 a.m.-8 p.m., Sat.
10 a.m.-6 p.m., Sun.
noon-5 p.m.*

Born Beautiful has a large selection of kids' clothes at a slight discount. Diversity is key here; the assortment ranges from conservative to funky. We particularly enjoyed the jackets with fringes, ribbons and rhinestones. Born Beautiful also carries plenty of children's accessories and some warm winterwear.

Gap Kids
2108 N. Halsted St.
281-0354
*Open Mon.-Fri. 10 a.m.-
8 p.m., Sat. 10 a.m.-6 p.m.,
Sun. noon-5 p.m.*

Adorable kids' fashions just like mom and dad wear. Of course, some of the kids' stuff is a lot cuter, both due to the tiny sizes and the design, which tends to be a bit more brightly colored than the Gap's adult clothing. Kids will be as comfortable in these clothes as parents will be with the prices.

LolliPop
2828 N. Clark St.
248-7311
*Open Mon.-Fri.
10:30 a.m.-9 p.m., Sat.
10:30 a.m.-6 p.m., Sun.
noon-5 p.m.*

Although the shop is a little cramped, teeming as it is with terrorizing toddlers bopping back and forth on hobby horses, the trendy designer kidwear makes it worth a visit. The London Fog flannel jackets, winter coats and rain gear are positively adorable, as are the Guess denims and leather jackets. Prices aren't too frightening.

My Own Two Feet
2148 N. Halsted St.
935-3338
*Open Tues.-Wed. & Fri.
10 a.m.-6 p.m., Thurs.
11 a.m.-7 p.m., Sat.
10 a.m.-5 p.m., Sun.
noon-
5 p.m.*

Shoe fetishes get an early start at this shop. From flannel-lined Converse All-Stars to shiny Capezio Mary Janes, these shoes will have you yearning for your lost youth. In the meantime, your kids can play grown-up in their very own pair of down-sized, adult-style shoes, like the boys' Cole-Haan loafers and white bucks ranging from $65 to $78. A play area in the corner helps out with toddlers-in-tow. Although the salespeople are great with kids, talking in those squeaky high voices that only children can relate to, they unfortunately tend not to lower the octave when speaking with adults.

Over the Rainbow
835 N. Michigan Ave.
(Water Tower Place)
943-2050
*Open Mon. & Thurs.
10 a.m.-7 p.m., Tues.-Wed.
& Fri.-Sat. 10 a.m.-6 p.m.,
Sun. noon-5 p.m.*

Eclectic fashions for babies and kids at a range of prices. An OshKosh jumper sells for a mere $19, but an Irene Clayaux knit dress is a splurge at $90. One favorite item here is the House of Hatan musical pillow for $15.

The Second Child
954 W. Armitage Ave.
883-0880
Open Mon.-Sat. 10 a.m.-
6 p.m., Sun. noon-5 p.m.

This upscale children's resale boutique is a great find for mothers with little attic room to store their child's every jumper and bib. It's an even better find for those unwilling to spend a fortune on garments that will get only short-term use. Everything is sold on commission, and togs with tears or stains are not accepted. The trendy Lincoln Park location helps The Second Child attract some high-quality clothing, which it sells for a fraction of the new cost. It may take some searching to find what you need, but the prices make the hunt worthwhile.

FURNITURE

Bellini
2001 N. Halsted St.
943-6696
Open Mon.-Sat. 10 a.m.-
5:30 p.m., Sun. noon-5 p.m.

For the infant already convinced of his right to have the best, Bellini sells upscale, Italian-crafted designer baby furniture, bedding and accessories. As can be expected, prices are high. The Fabio, an art deco–styled crib done in cherry-stained beech, is $689; the Judy, another Bellini design, is $769. Some very plush accessories are also sold.

CLOTHES

ACCESSORIES

Accents Studio
611 N. State St.
664-1311
Open Mon.-Sat. 11 a.m.-
7 p.m.

Accents sells artsy kitsch from local and New York–based jewelry and accessory designers. Some of it borders on tacky, but some of the way-out styles are wonderfully endearing, like the rhinestone-studded sunglasses topped with a matching set of dinosaurs for $60. It also carries some wild belts and a small but ultra-trendy selection of shoes.

Accessory Lady
835 N. Michigan Ave.
(Water Tower Place)
280-1662
Open Mon. & Thurs.
10 a.m.-7 p.m., Tues.-
Wed. & Fri.-Sat 10 a.m.-
6 p.m., Sun. noon-5 p.m.

This nationwide chain of accessory stores offers a gamut of put-togethers to complete office and casual outfits. The jewelry isn't real and therefore isn't expensive, though in some cases it's utterly undesirable anyway. Still, there are some nice handbags in the rear of the store and a limited selection of tops and hats that will cheer up otherwise-drab ensembles.

Fire & Ice
2551 N. Clark St.
327-3732
Mon.-Sat. 11 a.m.-6 p.m.,
Sun. noon-5 p.m.

Fire & Ice carries a fabulous collection of highly stylized costume jewelry. But that's not all—the leather belts and handbags are also innovative and often one-of-a-kind. But we're still trying to figure out what to do with the suede handkerchiefs.

Glorious Hats
66 E. Walton Pl.
787-8899
*Open Mon.-Fri. 10 a.m.-
5:30 p.m., Sat. 10 a.m.-
5 p.m.*

Glorious Hats employs three milliners who custom design hats, caps, bows and head pieces. Some of the hats in stock are brought in fully decorated with the loveliest of ribbons, bows and netting from Paris and Canada, but the imaginative women here will create exactly what you want from any material for an extremely reasonable price.

Hats in the Belfry
835 N. Michigan Ave.
(Water Tower Place)
266-9723
*Open Mon. & Thurs.
10 a.m.-7 p.m., Tues.-
Wed. & Fri.-Sat. 10 a.m.-
6 p.m., Sun. noon-5 p.m.;
summer: open Mon.-Wed.
10 a.m.-7 p.m., Thurs.-Sat.
10 a.m.-9 p.m., Sun. noon-
5 p.m.*

There are far too many hats to count in this Water Tower alcove, but none surpass the quality or imagination seen in those in Marshall Field's hat department. It does, however, carry some attractive fun hats, especially models in straw, felt and canvas twill for men and women, at refreshingly low prices. When entering, be sure to look up—the ceiling is bordered with endless novelty hats, from conductors' caps to Indian headdresses.

Panache
2252 N. Clark St.
477-5437
*Open Mon.-Fri. 10 a.m.-
7 p.m., Sat. 10 a.m.-6 p.m.,
Sun. noon-5 p.m.*

You'd be hard-pressed not to find what you want at Panache, one of Chicago's best-stocked accessory and handbag boutiques. Panache sells not only a wide and dynamic selection of belts but also a never-ending supply of handbags and costume jewelry. The attitude is a little haughty, as are the prices, but the selection makes these minor aggravations tolerable.

That's Our Bag
734 N. Michigan Ave.
984-3517
*Open Mon. & Thurs.
9 a.m.-7 p.m., Tues.-Wed.
& Fri. 9 a.m.-6 p.m., Sat.
10 a.m.-6 p.m., Sun.
noon-5 p.m.*

That's Our Bag carries such a vast inventory of ladies' handbags, suitcases, briefcases and accessories, it's no wonder prices are far cheaper than anywhere else on the Magnificent Mile. Not everything is top quality, but there are some great buys, particularly Bosca leather goods and Liz Claiborne purses.

Theodora
50 E. Oak St.
266-2285
*Open Mon.-Sat. 11 a.m.-
5 p.m.*

You can't help but have fun in Theodora's, an Oak Street boutique teeming with whimsical baubles, trinkets and knickknacks. Theodora's innovative lines include vintage and reproduction jewelry, as well as lacy scarves, beaded wall coverings and antique purses. It even sells beaded baby sandals. Prices are high, as is expected on this ritzy block, though some are positively outrageous, especially for the antique watches. But don't let that keep you away from this eclectic boutique, which also has an enticing selection of vintage cotton dresses and lingerie.

> *Some establishments change their closing times without warning. It is always wise to call ahead.*

This Little Piggy

835 N. Michigan Ave.
(Water Tower Place)
943-7449
Open Mon. & Thurs.
10 a.m.-7 p.m., Tues.-Wed.
& Fri.-Sat. 10 a.m.-6 p.m.,
Sun. noon-5 p.m.

The ultimate sock store, This Little Piggy will keep all your little piggies laughing. It's full of great designs for those with a sense of humor. Bright-green-and-pink watermelon socks complete with seeds come in all sizes. Other designs of note include athletic socks with bandannas that tie at the ankle and bobby socks laced with ribbons and charms. There's also a good selection of women's pantyhose.

CASUAL (MEN & WOMEN)

Aca Joe

622 N. Michigan Ave.
337-0280
Open Mon.-Thurs. 9 a.m.-
9 p.m., Fri. 9 a.m.-mid-
night, Sat. 9 a.m.-10 p.m.,
Sun. 10 a.m.-6 p.m.

Since it began assimilating the latest fashion trends, like tie-dyed sweatshirts, Girbaud baggy slacks and European-designed shirts, Aca Joe has lost some of its campy, south-of-the-border appeal. That may come as a relief to those frustrated by the omnipresent Aca Joe logo emblazoned in black on virtually every garment sold here. Still, the clothes are big, boxy, comfortable and affordable.

Banana Republic

835 N. Michigan Ave.
(Water Tower Place)
642-7667
Open Mon.-Fri. 10 a.m.-
8 p.m., Sat. 10 a.m.-7 p.m.,
Sun. 11 a.m.-6 p.m.

As ubiquitous as Banana Republic has become, you never walk out feeling like you're going to look like every other Joe about to embark on a safari—urban or otherwise. Two huge plaster elephant tusks arcing at the entrance immediately sweep you away from Water Tower's mall mania into this jungle-crazed environment, complete with bongo music. You can't beat the comfort these great prices afford, and as casual as Banana Republic purports itself to be, some of these duds can be dressed up for the office or a light night on the town. Take, for instance, the women's cotton high-necked cardigan sweater or the ultra-trendy cotton sarong skirt. Some terrific men's fashions include an Italian waiter's jacket that will pass most successfully as a summer blazer and the cotton canvas Kenya convertibles that unzip at the leg to become walking shorts. In addition to the cotton shorts, tops, dresses and jackets, our favorite for women is the slimly cut women's expedition flight suit.

Benetton

608 N. Michigan Ave.
944-2904
Open Mon. & Thurs.
10 a.m.-7 p.m., Tues.-Wed.
& Fri.-Sat. 10 a.m.-6 p.m.,
Sun. noon-5 p.m.

Benetton's colorful wools and cottons have made its casual sportswear a most popular commodity in Chicago—and just about everywhere else on the planet. Whether you prefer the button-down look or the convenience of a pullover, Benetton usually carries both. Slacks for men and women are boxy and quite comfortable, though some tighter-fitting styles can be found. Benetton displays all its wares on racks centered in the middle of the store; a friendly staff member will retrieve your choice from one of the many built-in shelves on which clothes lie neatly folded. Prices have shot up over the years, however, making this playful Italian line less affordable than it once was. Call the above number for other locations.

The Gap

835 N. Michigan Ave.
(Water Tower Place)
787-7992
*Open Mon.-Sat. 10 a.m.-
8 p.m., Sun. 11 a.m.-6 p.m.*

What we love about The Gap is that you can buy a sweater in four different colors for the price you'd pay for one in some of Chicago's ritzier boutiques. Gap-brand clothes—pants for men and women, sweaters, pullovers, shirts, skirt and dresses—are unpretentious clones of more expensive brands. But their quality gives them a character of their own. Recently, The Gap has ventured into printed fabrics—using paisley and floral designs—to upscale the merchandise. But the prices, as always, are eminently affordable. Call the above number for the many other Gap locations.

The Limited

835 N. Michigan Ave.
(Water Tower Place)
266-0700
*Open Mon.-Sat. 10 a.m.-
7 p.m., Sun. noon-6 p.m.*

Let's face it, no matter how many zillions of women are sporting the same Outback Red khakis and jeans or Forenza cotton pullovers, you won't be able to resist such well-priced, trendy and comfortable clothing. And with the ever-changing display of accessories, including belts, scarves and costume jewelry, there's plenty of opportunity to make a stylish statement of your own. Although The Limited's growing popularity has given way to slightly higher prices over the years, its sales are unbeatable, and its heavily stocked inventory makes them worth waiting for. If you're an Ann Taylor kinda gal with a restrictive budget, The Limited carries many of the same styles in suits and separates for sometimes half the price—including some attractive wool coats by Cassidy, but again, wait for a sale. Call the above number for other locations.

Soho

835 N. Michigan Ave.
(Water Tower Place)
642-0991
*Open Mon. & Thurs.
10 a.m.-7 p.m., Tues.-Wed.
& Fri.-Sat. 10 a.m.-6 p.m.,
Sun. noon-5 p.m.*

These are casual, sporty fashions with a trendy twist for men and women. Big, floppy T-shirts and overgrown sweaters by Gotcha are big sellers here, as are the retail-priced line of Girbaud slacks for men.

LEATHERWEAR

Bally of Switzerland

919 N. Michigan Ave.
787-8110
*Open Mon.-Fri. 10 a.m.-
7 p.m., Sat. 10 a.m.-6 p.m.,
Sun. noon-5 p.m.*

Although primarily a fine shoe store for men, Bally recently branched out to apparel and now carries some well-crafted leather jackets and leather-and-wool combination sweaters for men. It offers the same for women, as well as similar outstanding quality in finely constructed, if not a bit conservative, shoes. Briefcases and other leather accessories are available, but all the merchandise is extremely high priced.

Bottega Veneta

107 E. Oak St.
664-3220
*Open Mon.-Sat. 10 a.m.-
6 p.m.*

You'll find a wonderfully warm atmosphere in which to choose a $350 woven leather bag that melts like butter between your fingers or other finely made leather goods. The purses, wallets, briefcases, belts and some luggage are equally expensive (except for a leather-bordered canvas beach bag that sells for $65). Some conservative women's shoes go for between $150 and $200. The staff is refreshingly unpretentious.

Robert Elliot

43 E. Oak St.
787-0767
Open Mon.-Sat. 10 a.m.-6 p.m.

Robert Elliot boasts impressive leather work for an equally impressive price. All skirts, slacks, shirts and jackets are made from lambskin, which is among the softest leathers around. Some garments are adorned with interesting yet tasteful appliqué work, like polka dots and flowers. Jackets sell for $575, tank tops for $195. The staff is friendly and helpful but a bit pushy, particularly when it comes to odd-colored leathers in which we wouldn't be caught dead.

Gucci

900 N. Michigan Ave.
(The Avenue Atrium)
664-5504
Open Mon.-Sat. 10 a.m.-8 p.m., Sun. noon-6 p.m.

Don't walk into this branch of Italy's most famous leather snootery with your nose in the air—this Gucci defies its sister stores' holier-than-thou demeanórs with some good Midwestern hospitality. Of course, prices for the G-laden lines of leather goods, clothes and accessories are not as kind as the staff, but who comes here looking for bargains anyway?

North Beach Leather

835 N. Michigan Ave.
(Water Tower Place)
280-9292
Open Mon.-Wed. & Fri.-Sat. 10 a.m.-6 p.m., Thurs. 10 a.m.-7 p.m., Sun. noon-5 p.m.

We're always suspicious of stores boasting franchises in, among other dubious spots, Las Vegas. Our intuition proved accurate at North Beach, a collection of fine leather cut in the most vulgar fashions imaginable. The turquoise merry-widow bustiers and peach-colored tight-as-tangerine-skin dresses accented with shoelaces from bust to waist prove our point. But passing the true test of tacky is the large leopard-print jacket, snap-bra top and skirt with mother-of-pearl snaps. Madonna must get her leatherwear here.

Tannery West

835 N. Michigan Ave.
(Water Tower Place)
943-0908
Open Mon. & Thurs. 10 a.m.-7 p.m., Tues.-Wed. & Fri.-Sat. 10 a.m.-6 p.m., Sun. noon-5 p.m.

The leatherwear at Tannery West is pretty simple and therefore timeless. Straight skirts run from $110 to $150, shirts about $175 and jackets usually about $575. More contemporary items are available, such as bustiers for $150 or men's gym shorts for $110. We've had problems with Tannery West's skirts, however: After some wear, the lining tends to drop below the hem.

MENSWEAR

Baskin

835 N. Michigan Ave.
(Water Tower Place)
943-3000
Open Mon.-Fri. 10 a.m.-8 p.m., Sat. 10 a.m.-6 p.m., Sun. noon-5 p.m.

We just don't get it. Why, in such an open-minded metropolis as Chicago, are there so many stylish and upwardly trendy stores available for women and so few for men? Don't expect an answer from Baskin, where ennui persists like a second-grade history lesson. Ultra-conservative suits by Austin Reed and Hickey Freeman start at about $300.

Baskin's pride is that most of its merchandise is made in the U.S. and constructed of cotton, wool and polyester blends. Prices are reasonable, as is the quality, but the styles of the suits and separates and the never-ending range of silk rep ties is sure to put you to sleep.

Eddie Bauer
123 N. Wabash Ave.
263-6005
Open Mon. & Thurs.
10 a.m.-7 p.m., Tues.-Wed.
& Fri. 10 a.m.- 6 p.m.,
Sat. 10 a.m.-5:30 p.m.,
Sun. noon-5 p.m.

Once primarily a camping outfitter, Eddie Bauer has expanded to a full line of reasonably priced preppy wear for men, women and children. It still carries a full array of camping supplies, but that department pales beside the influx of clothing, which is well made, slightly conservative and very casual. We like the cotton sweaters best, which are almost always on sale.

Bigsby & Kruthers
1750 N. Clark St.
440-1750
Open Mon. & Thurs.
10 a.m.-9 p.m., Tues.-Wed.
10 a.m.-8 p.m., Fri.-Sat.
10 a.m.-6 p.m., Sun. noon-
5 p.m.

What Ann Taylor is to women, Bigsby & Kruthers is to men, only more so. This men's-only department store is on the cutting edge—fashions by New Man, Mondo and Armani earn Bigsby's fine reputation for vogue style and design. Prices are high, but it should cost to look this good. Bigsby & Kruthers has an especially fine selection of ties, Italian suits and tuxedos, and the casualwear is superb. Avventura, the fabulous men's shoe store, has rented out space here to help complete the picture. Other locations in Water Tower Place and at 10 S. LaSalle.

Brittany Ltd.
999 N. Michigan Ave.
642-6550
Open Mon. & Thurs.
10 a.m.-7 p.m., Tues.-Wed.
& Fri. 10 a.m.- 6 p.m.,
Sat. 10 a.m.-5:30 p.m.,
Sun. noon-5 p.m.

Rumor has it that when it comes to fashion, the Midwest is about ten years behind either coast, and Brittany does its best to uphold Chicago's classically conservative reputation. Southwick's suits, Brittany's house-brand line, are constructed with exacting detail and are worth the price for those hesitant to venture into more trendy modes. Brittany also carries costly lines from Ralph Lauren, Izod, Alan Paine and Braemar, as well as other purveyors of fine, orthodox fashion for men and women.

Brooks Brothers
74 E. Madison St.
263-0100
Open Mon.-Sat. 9 a.m.-
6 p.m.

What can we say about Brooks Brothers' sleek, Ivy League prep appeal that you don't already know? Brooks has always been a hallmark of quality, a status symbol among the conservative, but rarely a statement of style. There's nothing *unstylish* about the straight lines of well-crafted Brooks suits made from the finest English wool—they just haven't changed with the times and therefore have become classic in their own timeless sort of way. Traditional oxford shirts, ties, footwear and casualwear are also staples here, as are a comparably restrained line of women's clothing. Brooksgate for boys and slimmer men offer similar styles at lesser prices.

Burberry's
633 N. Michigan Ave.
787-2500
Open Mon.-Wed. & Fri.-
Sat. 9:30 a.m.-6 p.m.,
Thurs. 9:30 a.m.-7 p.m.

As staid a fashion statement as it may be, Burberry's signature plaid never goes out of style. And either through osmosis or a keen marketing strategy, it has spread with unrelenting verve from the collars of the classic trench to the scarves, hats, umbrellas, bathrobes—and even desk accessories for those who need constant reassurance of their social condition. Of course, not everything here is plaid, and Burberry's sustains a strong line of conservative and costly clothes for men and women, including some luxurious silks.

Capper & Capper
1 N. Wabash Ave.
236-3800
Open Mon.-Sat. 9 a.m.-
5:30 p.m.

We didn't think clothes could get more conservative than Brooks Brothers' or Burberry's, but we were wrong. Capper & Capper, a small, Midwestern chain of repressed fashion for men and women, offers solid styles and extraordinary personal service for slightly less than Brooks Brothers'. It has a nice selection of sweaters, as well as finely made suits and a small line of sturdy, well-made shoes.

Dunhill
835 N. Michigan Ave.
(Water Tower Place)
467-4455
Open Mon. & Thurs.
10 a.m.-7 p.m., Tues.-Wed.
& Fri.-Sat. 10 a.m.-6 p.m.,
Sun. noon-5 p.m.

Dunhill will fit you, send your measurements to Italy and, in six weeks, deliver an elegant, English-style suit made from the finest imported wool, silk, linen or cashmere—appropriate for the most dignified boardroom. Custom-made suits start at $1,200. Ready-to-wear suits, also made by Zegna of Italy, range from $840 to $1,150. Dunhill offers the most debonair of casualwear as well—cotton and wool slacks, ascots and sea-island polo shirts. Don't bypass the distinguished line of accessories, including the timeless fourteen-karat-gold-plated Dunhill Rologas lighter for $295. A humidor in back carries Dunhill's fine line of cigars, along with several other brands.

In Chicago
63 E. Oak St.
787-9557
Open Mon.-Tues. & Thurs.
10:30 a.m.-7 p.m., Wed. &
Fri. 10:30 a.m.-8 p.m.,
Sat. 10 a.m.-6 p.m.

This is another of the few shops that brings men's fashion up to date. The cheerful staff will be happy to put your look together if you're having trouble doing it alone. But if you'd rather do it yourself, the plentiful racks of New Man and Girbaud jeans should give you a good start. Swanky suits by Marzotto, Lubiam, Bill Robertson and Talia range from $400 to $600. And for those who think Mickey Mouse is still chic, cotton sweaters bearing his likeness are $125.

Intrinsic
440 N. Wells St.
644-6212
Open Mon.-Fri. 11 a.m.-
7 p.m., Sat. 10 a.m.-6 p.m.

Originally a men's boutique, Intrinsic should have stayed just that. Exquisite upscale fashions are designed by the most exclusive and expensive Italian designers, including Umberto Ginocchetti, Roberto Cavalli, Piero Panchetti and Valentino. In contrast to merchandise found in the newer women's department, which boasts some loud and tasteless clothing, the menswear here is superbly styled. Intrinsic carries an exciting and imaginative line of unisex jewelry by Navaro, Windy Gal, Nina Ricci and Diva.

Jeraz
51 E. Oak St.
266-7300
Open Mon.-Fri. 10:30 a.m.-
7:30 p.m., Sat. 10:30 a.m.-
6 p.m., Sun. noon-5 p.m.

Exclusive, expensive and somewhat exotic, Jeraz is for men who invest in image, care deeply about style and have plenty of money. Suits by Maurizo Baldassari and Kaisserman are constructed with exacting attention to form and cost $800 to $1,500. Knit shirts range from about $200 to $500; and Italian ties start at $50.

Polo
960 N. Michigan Ave.
280-1655
Open Mon. & Thurs.
10 a.m.-7 p.m., Tues.-Wed.
& Fri.-Sat. 10 a.m.-6 p.m.,
Sun. noon-5 p.m.

In some circles, conservative means stodgy, outmoded and downright boring. Not in this one. Ralph Lauren has redefined conservative fashion with more than a touch of class. Few men, on or off the cricket field, won't look deadly in Lauren's cream-colored wool-gabardine pleated slacks. Even fewer won't look smashing in the fastidiously tailored khaki linen suits. There are some outmoded traps to fall into, however, but we trust the discriminating shopper will bypass the outdated and head for the demure—for there is no man so handsome as he who dresses beautifully yet seemingly without effort.

Russo
2209 N. Halsted St.
348-8558
Open Tues.-Sat. 11 a.m.-
p.m., Sun. noon-5 p.m.

High-fashion funk reigns here in a most pricey way. Men's Luciano Soprano unlined trench coats sell for $600. There's some other priceless stuff, particularly for men, including some wonderful Jean-Paul Gaultier ties. The women's section is not as classy, but it's worth a look. Our favorite: a pair of $36 socks resembling turn-of-the-century lace-up boots.

Saeed
750 N. Franklin St.
337-6572
Open Mon.-Fri. 11 a.m.-
7 p.m., Sat. 11 a.m.-6 p.m.

This small River North shop caters to men with contemporary tastes. All the European clothing is bought from young, talented designers soon to make a name in this country. A small selection of bigger names like Maurizio Baldassari is available, but we suggest the more distinctive works by such unknowns as Mario Bernini. Our favorite is an unconstructed black tuxedo jacket for $275.

Seno Formal Wear
111 E. Oak St.
280-0800
Open Mon. & Thurs. 10
a.m.-8 p.m., Tues.-Wed. &
Fri. 10 a.m.- 6 p.m., Sat.
10 a.m.-5 p.m., Sun. noon-
5 p.m.

Eminently reasonably priced tuxedos by Pierre Cardin, Lord West, Christian Dior and Robert Stock—all averaging $425—are sold here, and rentals are competitively priced between $47 and $75. The biggest plus: personal service attentive to every detail, something you don't always find at bigger formalwear chains. Seno has another branch on Randolph Street (see Tuxedos under "Where to Find").

Sirreal
2204 N. Clark St.
929-8538
Open Mon.-Fri. noon-
8:30 p.m., Sat. 10:30 a.m.-
6 p.m., Sun. noon-5 p.m.

Sirreal is among Chicago's trendiest boutiques for men, and fairly expensive as well: Boss sweaters go for $125, and Italian-made suits sell for an average of $500. When we last checked in, Sirreal, always on the cutting edge of men's fashion, was selling sexy Go Silk separates: butter-smooth pants and silk bomber jackets. It also carries one of our favorite collections of silk ties, always in the most daring and dynamic styles and colors, along with a wide selection of dress and casual slacks, some of which, surprisingly, sell for less than $100.

Stuart
102 E. Oak St.
266-9881
*Open Mon.-Fri. 11 a.m.-
6:30 p.m., Sat. 10 a.m.-
5 p.m., Sun. noon-5 p.m.*

All the big Italian designers are represented here, including Missoni and Umberto Ginocchetti. Prices are sky high, but so is the quality of these handsomely designed men's suits and separates. Friendly personal service is another plus.

Traffick
3313 N. Broadway
549-1502
*Open Mon.-Fri. noon-
7 p.m., Sat. 11 a.m.-6 p.m.,
Sun. noon-5 p.m.*

We like this store because it is one of the few that has a great variety of men's underwear, from Bike skimpies to silk boxers. Of course, that's not all. This casual Broadway boutique also sells a nice selection of trendy cotton shirts and wool slacks, as well as a tasteful array of printed T-shirts.

Robert Vance
835 N. Michigan Ave.
(Water Tower Place)
440-0993
*Open Mon. & Thurs.
10 a.m.-7 p.m., Tues.-Wed.
& Fri.-Sat. 10 a.m.-6 p.m.,
Sun. noon-5 p.m.*

The conservative-yet-sporty togs for men here include an attractive supply of Ralph Lauren sweaters and slacks, which offset the utter ennui of what looks like a mile-long display of Robert Talbott ties. Prices are fairly high, but worthy of the quality. The women's shop across the way is such a yawner that we decided not to include it.

SHOES

Avventura
835 N. Michigan Ave.
(Water Tower Place)
337-3700
*Open Mon. & Thurs.
10 a.m.-7 p.m., Tues.-Wed.
& Fri.-Sat. 10 a.m.-6 p.m.,
Sun. noon-5 p.m.*

What a relief to find a men's shoe store with a selection reaching beyond brown leather and tassels. Styles here are exciting and daring. So what if you wouldn't be caught dead in a pair of paisley deck shoes—at least Avventura gives you a chance to make that decision. Most shoes are Italian made, mostly by Avventura, some by Zodiac and the highest priced by Lorenzo Banfi (Ostrich loafers in many colors run about $600). Most other leather styles cost about $185. Avventura is also located in Bigsby & Kruthers (440-1750).

Brass Boot
55 E. Oak St.
266-2731
*Open Mon.-Fri. 10 a.m.-
6 p.m.*

The instant assault of aromatic leather when you walk into the Brass Boot speaks of the quality to be found here. Private label and Cole-Haan are the most prolific brands of men's shoes, though there are some good-looking Zodiac models as well.

Chernin Shoes
610 W. Roosevelt Rd.
922-4545
*Open Mon.-Wed. & Fri.-
Sat. 9 a.m.-6 p.m., Thurs.
9 a.m.-8 p.m., Sun.
9:30 a.m.-5 p.m.*

If you're looking for savings on brand-name shoes—Bruno Magli, Allen Edmonds, Rockport, Timberland, Dexter, Zodiac, Nike and Reebok—Chernin is worth the trek. Most certainly Chicago's largest discount shoe outlet, the place can get pretty hectic even during off-peak hours. But the selection is as tremendous as the bargains.

Cole-Haan

645 N. Michigan Ave.
642-8995
Open Mon.& Thurs.
9:30 a.m.-8 p.m., Tues.-
Wed. & Fri.-Sat.
9:30 a.m.-6:30 p.m.,
Sun. 11 a.m.-5 p.m.

Distinguished. It's the best word to describe the Maine-based shoe company that produces these sturdy, expensive and extremely handsome shoes for the office, as well as for casual and evening engagements. Cole-Haan doesn't create the most outrageous styles for men or women, but they are classic, always attractive and easily adaptable to racier outfits. Even the Gucci imitations and some Italian-looking styles are tastefully contrived.

Fit to be Tied

1971 N. Halsted St.
280-8910
Open Mon.-Sat. 11 a.m.-
9 p.m., Sun. noon-6 p.m.

Kenneth Cole and Zodiac dominate this small, trendy shoe shop that also has a limited but extremely tasteful collection of contemporary belts. Most of the men's and women's shoes are comfortable and au courant. A small display of more formal shoes is stylish without a lot of glitz. Frequent sales make the already reasonable prices more attractive.

Hanig's

660 N. Michigan Ave.
642-5330
Open Mon.-Fri. 9 a.m.-
7 p.m., Sat. 9 a.m.-6 p.m.,
Sun. 11 a.m.-5 p.m.

Hanig's is more adept at men's shoes than women's. Johnston & Murphy leads its fine line of men's footwear, which is followed (if not surpassed) by Salvatore Ferragamo, Bruno Magli and Cole-Haan.

Joseph

679 N. Michigan Ave.
944-1111

50 E. Randolph St.
332-2772
Open Mon. & Thurs.
10 a.m.-7 p.m., Tues.-Wed.
& Fri.-Sat. 10 a.m.-
6 p.m., Sun. noon-5 p.m.

Footwear by Walter Steiger, Petra, Anne Klein, Bruno Magli and Stewart Weitzman fill this large Michigan Avenue shoe palace, where an accommodating staff helps you forget the high prices. There is also a generous supply of accessories, some handbags, a small stationery department and, in back, a modest clothing boutique.

Charles Jourdan

835 N. Michigan Ave.
(Water Tower Place)
280-8133
Open Mon. & Thurs.
10 a.m.-7 p.m., Tues.-Wed.
& Fri.-Sat. 10 a.m.-6 p.m.,
Sun. noon-5 p.m.

You've seen the same sensibly sturdy shoes with style elsewhere, but not all in one place. You won't find many surprises here, just the classic pumps that have maintained Jourdan's healthy business over the years. Other lines change regularly, but at Jourdan, the highest of heels (they average about three inches) are always in fashion. Women's styles run about $250, and the limited, traditional selection of men's footwear, about $180. A small-but-tasteful selection of accessories and bags is displayed, as well as a smaller assortment of silk blouses and neatly cut French skirts.

Lori's Designer Shoes

808 W. Armitage Ave.
281-5655
Open Mon.-Thurs. 11 a.m.-
7 p.m., Fri.-Sat. 11 a.m.-
6 p.m., Sun. noon-5 p.m.

Charles Jourdan, Anne Klein, Joan & David and Stuart Weitzman for Mr. Seymour are among the better names in this well-stocked discount-shoe source; these more expensive brands earn 40 percent off. Many of the styles aren't exactly fetching, but great bargains abound if you look long enough. There's a terrific selection of black-satin pumps (though not always in every size), and some exquisite leather bags are good buys.

9 West
115 N. Wabash Ave.
984-0151
Open Mon.-Fri. 8 a.m.-
5:45 p.m., Sat. 10 a.m.-
5:30 p.m.

9 West is one of our favorite spots for bulk seasonal buying. Simple, well-constructed pumps and flats in a rainbow of colors are reasonably priced and probably all you need to complete just about any outfit, casual or formal. You'll find these shoes elsewhere in department stores, but they're about $5 cheaper per pair at the source. The help is patient with the fussy clientele.

Pappagallo
835 N. Michigan Ave.
(Water Tower Place)
787-2547
Open Mon. & Thurs.
10 a.m.-7 p.m., Tues.-Wed.
& Fri.-Sat. noon-5 p.m.

We remember shopping here as young girls, and little has changed since then. Classic patent and leather pumps and flats are the same as ever—conservative and sturdy in a delicate way. Prices are reasonable, and there are some attractive handbags and accessories to choose from.

Posh
50 E. Oak St.
787-0775
Open Mon.-Sat. 10 a.m.-
6 p.m.

Posh carries exclusive lines from Manalo Blahnik, Roger Vivier and Nancy Knox, as well as styles from more frequently seen designers, such as Mario Valentino. Many of these shoes are quite avant-garde, and some are downright daring. Prices are predictably high.

Poseyfisher
501 N. Wells St.
644-1749
Open Mon.-Fri. 11 a.m.-
7 p.m., Sat. 10 a.m.-6 p.m.

Unquestionably our favorite shoe store, Poseyfisher has the biggest selection outside of a department store. As au courant as the River North neighborhood, Poseyfisher is a two-story warehouse-style place, with shoes perched atop stacks of cardboard boxes containing various sizes. But don't let the casual atmosphere fool you—there are some distinctly classy styles here, and at a 20- to 40-percent discount to boot. Whether you need a pair for the beach or some smashing originals for a holiday party, you'll find the right shoes at Poseyfisher. Some recognizable brands include Giorgio Pacini, Anne Klein, Liz Claiborne, Perry Ellis, Yves Saint Laurent and some funky makes by Lisa Tucci.

S'Agaro
1712 N. Wells St.
944-6732

58 E. Chestnut St.
440-0401
Open Mon.-Fri. 10 a.m.-
6:30 p.m., Sat. 10 a.m.-
6 p.m., Sun. noon-5 p.m.

Finely crafted European shoes (mostly Italian and Spanish) for the office or for eveningwear. All styles are contemporary, some with a classic twist; they're similar in design and quality to those made by Joan & David—but for about one-third the price.

The Season's Best
645 N. Michigan Ave.
943-6161
Open Mon. & Thurs.-Fri.
9 a.m.-7 p.m., Tues.-Wed.
9 a.m.-6 p.m., Sun. noon-
5 p.m.

This place is a shoe jungle. Footwear in every conceivable shape, size and color hangs from every available space, whether on the floor, in shelves or from the walls and ceiling. Styles are mostly casual, though there are some suitable choices for the office and for eveningwear. Although basically a shoe store, The Season's Best also houses an ample selection of handbags and accessories and a few racks of trendy clothes in the back. Most of the prices are reasonable.

Slithers

2549 N. Clark St.
871-2994
*Open daily 11 a.m.-
7:30 p.m.*

"Slithers" is a strange but appropriate name for a shop with shoes and accessories made from all things that slither: eels, snakes, lizards. But a few other animals are also represented—Slithers sells some attractive items made from peacock feathers. Perhaps "Slithers and Strutters" would be a more appropriate name.

Smyth Bros.

33 E. Oak St.
664-9508

835 N. Michigan Ave.
(Water Tower Place)
642-7798
*Open Mon., Wed. & Sat.
10 a.m.-6 p.m., Thurs.-Fri.
10 a.m.- 6:30 p.m., Sun.
noon-5 p.m.*

This generous selection of all the biggest (and priciest) names in women's shoes includes Yves Saint Laurent, Charles Jourdan, Joan & David and Unisa. Don't expect to find any discounts, although Smyth Bros. is sure to have the size and style you want when you want it.

The Walking Source

847 W. Armitage Ave.
929-5568
*Open Tues.-Fri. 11 a.m.-
8 p.m., Sat. 9 a.m.-6 p.m.,
Sun. noon-6 p.m.*

The staff here goes for the hard sell, insisting you're bound for hammertoe hell if you don't invest in your feet while you're still young. Explore the large selection of sensible, fastidiously soled walking shoes by Clarks, Rockport, Timberland and H. H. Brown. Prices are high, but that goes without saying in this trendy neighborhood.

VINTAGE CLOTHING

Flashy Trash

3524 N. Halsted St.
327-6900
*Open Mon.-Sat. noon-
7 p.m., Sun. noon-6 p.m.*

The most popular vintage shop in the city, Flashy Trash plays up its image by offering plenty of old and looks-like-old clothing and accessories for men and women. The clothes, from the Victorian era through the 1970s, are on the costly side, but the quality justifies the prices—even the hand-beaded shawl from the twenties for $1,200. The jewelry cases are quite tempting, including consistent offerings from Eisenberg, the most prestigious costume jeweler in the twenties. There's also a colorful array of art deco watches.

Gloria

2730 N. Lincoln Ave.
327-9665
*Open Wed.-Fri. 9 a.m.-
5 p.m., Sat. 11 a.m.-
6 p.m.; summer: open
Wed.-Fri. 4 p.m.-10 p.m.,
Sat. 11 a.m.-6 p.m.,
Mon.-Tues. by appt. only.*

Gloria herself admits she carries junk. But what fabulous junk it is—from Carmen Miranda–like ceramic statues to TVs and radios from the '40s and '50s. Gloria sells anything that's interesting, fairly old and in fairly good condition. The deco jewelry collection is not the best we've seen, but some treasures will surface if you look hard enough. Well-kept women's clothes from the '40s and '50s are fairly priced. The best thing we've scored here was a beautiful '50s men's tuxedo, in perfect condition, for a mere $125.

Just Vintage
2935 N. Clark St.
549-7787
Open Mon-Fri. noon-
7 p.m., Sat. 11 a.m.-
6 p.m., Sun. 1 p.m.-5 p.m.

Like Frannies next door (which we didn't consider worth a review), Just Vintage is one of Chicago's lesser-quality resale shops. But some of the fashions (mostly from the '50s) are lovely and worth a look, while some are in disrepair, and others are downright tacky.

Legacy Vintage
953 W. Armitage Ave.
935-0374
Open Mon.-Sat. noon-
6:30 p.m.

Legacy Vintage is clearly among the best vintage stores in Chicago. The selection of clothes from the '20s through the '60s is endless and superbly preserved. No other store carries such a strong assembly of chiffon and satin dresses, and certainly not at these prices. Perfectly restored satin wedding dresses sell for about $95, and shirts and dresses in prime condition can go for as little as $5. Some nice menswear as well.

Lost Eras
1511 W. Howard St.
764-7400
Open Mon.-Sat. 10 a.m.-
6 p.m.

Lost Eras is a little out of the way, but well worth the trip. This is certainly the most complete vintage shop in the city, offering antique furniture from 1850 through 1960 and vintage clothing from 1890 through 1950. The accessories, jewelry and menswear are impressively preserved and reasonably priced.

Mirror Mirror
2961 N. Lincoln Ave.
929-8899
Open Tues.-Wed. & Sun.
noon-5 p.m., Thurs.-Fri.
& Sat. noon-8 p.m.

This is absolutely *the* place to go for vintage wedding gear. Elaborately beaded satin dresses in excellent condition from the '30s, '40s and '50s run between $55 and $700. Vintage cocktail and prom dresses are also available, as are some casualwear from earlier times.

Silver Moon
3337 N. Halsted St.
883-0222
Open Mon. & Wed. 1 p.m.-
6 p.m.. Tues.-Thurs. &
Fri. noon-7 p.m., Sat.-Sun.
noon-6 p.m.

Don't let the aura of a walk-in closet fool you—Silver Moon is a treasure chest of glorious vintage clothing, and you don't have to look too hard to find the good stuff. Proprietor Tari Costan takes pride in her buying; she ogles the $500 23-inch-waist Christian Dior strapless black satin gown as much as her customers do. Knowledgeable and protective of her merchandise, Costan won't let you try it on if she thinks it won't fit. Authentic hand-beaded flapper dresses in good condition sell for between $300 and $500. Definitely the place to look if you want to be the hit of the party.

Studio V
672 N. Dearborn St.
440-1937
Open Mon.-Sat. noon-
6 p.m., Sun. hours vary.

Authentic and reproduction art deco jewelry, clothing and accessories for men and women. Studio V's strong point is most certainly jewelry, in Bakelite and rhinestone and deco in design. An entire case is devoted to vintage cuff links. Another strong point is kitsch from the '20s through the '60s, including authentic black dial phones, windup clocks, decorator glasses and Barbie record albums.

WOMENSWEAR

Alcott & Andrews
430 N. Michigan Ave.
923-0112
Open Mon.-Fri. 10 a.m.-
8 p.m., Sat. 10 a.m.-6 p.m.,
Sun. noon-5 p.m.

This trilevel women's department store done in a Georgian ballroom motif complete with spindle balustrades outfits sophisticated executives with classic taste. Not unlike Ann Taylor but larger and more conservative, Alcott & Andrews softens the severe edges of today's careerwear with its own line of clothing in luxurious silk, lace, cotton, cashmere and wool. Fashions are serious but not without feminine appeal. Casualwear is understated and elegant, as are the many accessories designed to complement these outfits. Alcott & Andrews's clothes can be a bit expensive, though not outrageously so, which suits the attitude of the women who shop here.

Alexon
835 N. Michigan Ave.
(Water Tower Place)
944-3872
Open Mon. & Thurs.
10 a.m.-7 p.m., Tues.-Wed.
& Fri.-Sat. 10 a.m.-
6 p.m., Sun. noon-5 p.m.

If the salespeople at this British-based boutique held their noses at any higher an angle, they would have trouble breathing. Proud of their casual and career clothes for the woman executive on the move, the folks at Alexon never fail to remind you of the store's European success. And indeed, some of the fashions are quite nice, such as the black-and-white hound's-tooth three-quarter-length jacket and the uncrushable seersucker pantsuit with an unstructured jacket. But the Ocean Liner outfits leave as much to be desired as the attitude.

An-li Creations
15 E. Chestnut St.
280-0018
Open Mon.-Fri. 10 a.m.-
6 p.m., Sat. 10 a.m.-5 p.m.

What a delightful sight: walking into this exclusive Chestnut Street knit shop to find An-li herself ironing a panel from a yet-to-be-finished angora sweater. Most of An-li's knits are made by her own hand, and her labor is reflected in the prices. Her braided, ribbed sweaters made of 70-percent wool and 30-percent rayon go for $275, and a lovely blue-and-white knit sailor shirt and skirt costs $550. An-li also custom-designs sweaters for men and women, and she sells some creative jewelry made from semiprecious stones.

Giorgio Armani
113 E. Oak St.
427-6264
Open Mon.-Sat. 9:30 a.m.-
6 p.m.

Giorgio Armani's new Oak Street branch makes even the most well heeled feel a bit frumpy next to the racks of exquisite silks and gabardines that have earned the Italian designer his holy reputation. The $1,500 double-breasted gabardine tuxedos with silk lapels are fabulous even on the hanger, as are the finely lined men's suits. Upstairs, silk-lined rayon suits and silk dinner jackets for women that fall with amazing grace from the shoulder to the hip sell for $2,000. Even the $545 silk bibbed blouse merits its ghastly price tag. Black silk evening gowns for $1,500 and up seem reasonable given how skillfully they glide down your body's bumpiest curves.

Art Effect

651 W. Armitage Ave.
664-0997
*Open Mon.-Thurs. 11 a.m.-
7 p.m., Fri. 11 a.m.-6 p.m.,
Sat. 10 a.m.-5:30 p.m.,
Sun. noon-5 p.m.*

These expensive, trendy casual clothes are perfect for the woman who wants to hide her figure. Surely that's not the intention of this oh-so-fashionable boutique featuring handmade women's clothing from local and national designers—but the styles do tend to be on the boxy side. There's some wonderful knitwear, a unique assortment of hand-painted items and some fine, hand-crafted silver jewelry.

Artwear

2273 N. Lincoln Ave.
248-2554
*Open Mon., Wed. & Sat.
10 a.m.-6 p.m., Thurs.-Fri.
10 a.m.-8 p.m.*

We call this "participation shopping," a sport that involves more than just opening and closing your wallet. At Artwear, you create your own designs on T-shirts, sweats and jeans by painting them on the premises. Or choose some colors, hook your shirt onto the swirling paint machine and voilà!— a colorful splattering of the rainbow is yours for only about $15. This is a great place to take kids who think shop is a four-letter word.

Avenues I

2476 N. Lincoln Ave.
472-2766
*Open Tues.-Sat. noon-
8 p.m., Sun. noon-5 p.m.*

Unlike Blake (see below), Avenues I is a high-priced trendsetter that's worth the expense; the staff is as delightful as the merchandise. You won't find many separates for less than $100, but you'll find a lot that'll make you feel good, including an exceptionally large selection of the In Wear line. And there are some great hats to top off the casual fashions.

Blake

2448 N. Lincoln Ave.
477-3364
*Open Mon.-Fri. 10:30 a.m.-
7 p.m., Sat. 10:30 a.m.-
6:30 p.m., Sun. noon-6 p.m.*

Talk about attitude! The first time we visited this ultra-snooty boutique, a customer and self-admitted clotheshorse babbled about her little-girl fantasies of having the perfectly stocked closet, which so enthralled the salesgirl that she ignored us when we asked the price of a garment. The clothing here is hip and profoundly expensive. Silk running shorts, for example, sell for about $100. Most of the clothing hails from New York, and some pieces are from Europe and Japan—we think they're all overpriced. But we must admit that the casual and elegant separates, suits and dresses are fashionable and made from the most au courant fabrics.

Caroll

835 N. Michigan Ave.
(Water Tower Place)
642-8974
*Open Mon.-Fri. 10 a.m.-
7 p.m., Sat. 11 a.m.-6 p.m.,
Sun noon- 5 p.m.*

We like this French boutique's fresh, airy attitude. Fashions are primarily simple and on the classic side, though the wild-side miniskirts, bandeau tops and way-above-the-knee flowered shirtdresses prevent us from calling the shop conservative. Floral skirts, belts and ballet slippers are quite delicate, and some of the unconstructed linens are quite campy. A generous supply of Anne Klein can usually be found at prices that will shock—about $200 for a simple cotton sweater.

Cashmere-Cashmere

104 E. Oak St.
337-6558
Open Mon.-Fri. 10:30 a.m.-
6 p.m.

What a dream to be able to roll around naked in this shop—absolutely everything, for both men and women, is made from the finest Italian cashmere. Fat wallets can trim down considerably here: A long, black cashmere coat is $1,200, and sweaters go for $750. If you really want to indulge yourself, pick out a pair of $85 socks or the $150 black string bikini (no swimming or tanning oil allowed).

Cashmere il primo

835 N. Michigan Ave.
(Water Tower Place)
988-4004
Open Mon. & Thurs.
10 a.m.-7 p.m., Tues.-Wed.
& Fri.-Sat. 10 a.m.-6 p.m.,
Sun. noon-5 p.m.

The selection here is far more conservative than at Cashmere-Cashmere, though prices are just a bit lower. On the three occasions that we visited this boutique, the staff seemed more interested in making personal phone calls than in making a sale.

Chanel

940 N. Michigan Ave.
787-5500
Open Mon.-Sat. 10 a.m.-
6 p.m.

Always up to date without abandoning the treasured classicism that has made Chanel the most elite of women's clothiers, this elegant boutique is a paradigm of traditional and modern design. When hemlines lifted, so did Chanel's, but always with the sleek, straight lines that keep these clothes so enduring (and endearing). And, of course, it carries the classic collarless Chanel suit in fuzzy raw silk; along with exquisite finished silks, generally accented with the gold Chanel button; and some of the most expensive T-shirts imaginable (about $625).

Chia

2202 N. Halsted St.
248-9595
Open Mon. by appt. only,
Tues.- Fri. 11 a.m.-7 p.m.,
Sat. 10 a.m.-6 p.m., Sun.
noon-5 p.m.

Emphasis here is on the exclusive: exclusive clothes for exclusive women made by exclusive designers exclusively for Chia. This attitude is reflected in the price tags. Although there are some nice things, most aren't nearly as extraordinary as their prices, and the quality isn't as high as the snooty demeanor would imply.

Contessa Bottega

106 E. Oak St.
944-0981
Open Mon.-Sat. 10 a.m.-
6 p.m.

The Contessa prefers Parisian-made clothes, so this duplex boutique carries a chic line of Paris's finest—from career-wear to casualwear. Albert Poljan's sleek rayon and silk designs (including suits) are found here, as are Karlein Kerwin's viscose knits, which are unparalleled in fashion finesse and comfort.

Dégagé

2246 N. Clark St.
935-7737
Open Mon.-Fri. 10 a.m.-
6:45 p.m., Sat. 10 a.m.-
5:45 p.m., Sun. noon-
5 p.m.

One of Lincoln Park's flagship boutiques, Dégagé has always been ahead of its time with lively casual clothes and original ideas. Although the store is expensive, well-maintained and serviced by friendly and extremely helpful salespeople, a number of the garments were soiled, as if they had been tried on and discarded on the floor a few too many times. Point out any stains, however, and you'll get a discount for the cleaning bill.

Divine Knits
61 E. Oak St.
943-6207
Open Mon.-Sat. 10 a.m.-
6 p.m., Sun. noon-5 p.m.

All this place sells are cotton-knit separates—lovely, comfortable, solidly styled, very expensive cotton-knit separates. One of cotton's greatest advantages is that it can be worn all year long, which makes sales especially attractive in any season.

T. Edwards
835 N. Michigan Ave.
(Water Tower Place)
337-1822
Open Mon.-Fri. 10 a.m.-
7 p.m., Sat. 10 a.m.-6 p.m.,
Sun. noon-5 p.m.

We've never walked out of here empty-handed. Although much of the merchandise is on a par with that found at any Limited (at slightly higher prices), there are always surprises if you thrive on the challenge of the hunt, particularly when it comes to slacks. Most everything here is casual, for day or evening. Edwards also carries eccentric, eye-catching accessories, like the must-have calculator with large rhinestone buttons.

Erinisle
2246 N. Clark St.
975-6616
Open Tues.-Wed. & Sat.
11 a.m.-6 p.m., Thurs.-Fri.
11 a.m.-7 p.m., Sun. noon-
5 p.m.

There are lots of four-leaf clovers and emerald greens in this boutique featuring the fashions and crafts of Ireland. The biggest draw seems to be the authentic wool fishermen's sweaters—just the thing to do battle with Chicago's winter.

Fiber Works
2457 N. Lincoln Ave.
327-0444
Open Mon. 11 a.m.-6 p.m.,
Tues. & Thurs. 11 a.m.-
9 p.m., Wed. & Fri.-Sat.
11 a.m.-8 p.m.

If you'd rather make it yourself, Fiber Works may be the place to start. Walls here are lined with reasonably priced skeins of colorful and high-quality yarns that include silks, cottons and a number of wool derivatives. A small selection of ready-to-wear made from natural fibers fill the front of the shop. Several wooden looms in back are used for weaving classes. Also, Fiber Works offers instruction in hand and machine knitting. Call for times.

Flamingo Road
2121 N. Clybourn Ave.
472-0900
Open Mon.-Thurs. noon-
9 p.m., Fri. 10 a.m.-6 p.m.,
Sat. 10 a.m.-5 p.m., Sun.
noon-5 p.m.

It's a little out of the way, but may be worth it for Californians who need a taste of home. All bathing suits, pants, skirts, bandeau tops and dresses are from the West Coast and appear in a blinding array of bright colors, including acid pinks, greens, oranges and yellows. Swimsuits are particularly good buys, usually between $32 and $42.

Handle with Care
1706 N. Wells St.
751-2929
Open Mon.-Fri. 10 a.m.-
6:30 p.m., Sat. 10 a.m.-
6 p.m., Sun. noon-5 p.m.

Handle with Care does just that with its customers. It's hard not to feel ultra-feminine from the moment you walk in, what with the heady scent from the lavender and rose sachets. An attentive staff is on its toes, happy to check the storeroom for your size of that perfect skirt. These bright, cheerful (even in winter) dresses, skirts, slacks and suits, many of which are designed exclusively for the store, are moderately expensive but high in quality. Some other nifty finds include hats adorned with antique silk flowers and jewelry, white-cotton underthings and trendy jewelry made by local artists.

Hemisphere

835 N. Michigan Ave.
(Water Tower Place)
649-1302
Open Mon.-Thurs. 10 a.m.-
7 p.m., Fri.-Sat. 10 a.m.-
6 p.m., Sun. noon-5 p.m.

There are so many Casual Corner–type stores in Water Tower that it's a welcome relief to find a store that has some fashion integrity. Prices at Hemisphere are pretty high, but the natural fibers—silks, wools, linens—shine with quality. These fine shirts, sweaters, skirts and dresses are perfect for the woman who knows the difference between classic and conservative.

Honeybee

19 E. Chestnut St.
649-0013

2314 N. Clark St.
525-0059
Open Mon.-Wed. & Fri.
10 a.m.-7 p.m., Thurs.
10 a.m.-8 p.m., Sat.
10 a.m.-6 p.m., Sun.
noon-4 p.m.

Originally a mail-order catalog, Honeybee has spread its pollen to two Chicago locations. And the results are sweet. At our last visit we stumbled across one of the most attractive sweater sales we could remember. And you can't consider crew-neck cottons by Calvin Klein and Liz Claiborne for $30 mere sloppy seconds. The other clothes—dresses, slacks, shirts—provide respite for the overtaxed wallet. Some fabulous belts and scarves at equally attractive prices will top off any smashing Honeybee outfit.

Janis

200 W. Superior St.
280-5357
Open Mon.-Sat. 10 a.m.-
6 p.m.

"Feel like a work of art, wear something Janis" is the motto of this River North boutique. But if you want to feel like a work of art, we suggest a visit to the Art Institute. The fashion logic here is most questionable. Let's be serious: a flower- and butterfly-appliquéd suede suit for $3,700? It's not the sort of thing you'd don for a nature walk, but we can't imagine any other appropriate place to wear the thing. And what about the horrendously gaudy rhinestone-studded peacock necklace for $575? Janis's clothing makes little sense.

Jean Charles

30 E. Oak St.
787-3535
Open Mon.-Sat. 10 a.m.-
6:30 p.m., Sun. noon-
5 p.m.

Jean Charles is a collection of high fashion from a range of American and international designers. The avant-garde is the specialty: Dresses with conservative frontal appeal are puffed and tucked in back; daringly low necklines enliven orthodox black suits; and jackets that are restrained in front are slit to the shoulder blades in back. As you might expect, prices are exceptionally high, and it's hard to tell if the staff is a little pushy or just trying hard to make customers feel comfortable in these super-sophisticated togs. An elegant boutique in front sells pricey footwear.

Keli's

750 N. Franklin St.
664-5440
Open Mon.-Sat.
10:30 a.m.-6 p.m.

The small-but-discriminating selection showcases such contemporary designers as Reza and Betsey Johnson. Some imaginative yet tasteful designs include a three-piece snakeskin suit with bustier and miniskirt ($900) by Joseph Alexander.

Stanley Korshak

940 N. Michigan Ave.
280-0520
Open Mon.-Fri. 10 a.m.-
6 p.m., Sat. 10 a.m.-
5:30 p.m.

An elite boutique for Chicago's grande dames, Korshak's is not without contemporary appeal. Ungaro, Krizia, Valentino and Ferragamo are among its regular designers, but the selection doesn't stop there. Korshak's is a relaxing place to shop for the finest of clothes, thanks to the friendly salespeople, who never push a sale.

Lanina

3405 N. Broadway
327-2145
Open Mon.-Sat. 11 a.m.-
7 p.m., Sun. noon-5 p.m.

Recently known as the Elle Boutique, this strictly Parisian shop made headlines when publishing magnate Rupert Murdoch threatened to sue the owner for using the same name as his high-fashion magazine. Lawsuits aside, the French fashions by Claude Bert and Maxi Librati are sleek, well fitting, quite costly and slightly ahead of Chicago's fashion sense.

Guy Laroche

835 N. Michigan Ave.
(Water Tower Place)
337-0606
Open Mon. & Thurs.
10 a.m.-7 p.m., Tues.-Wed.
& Fri.-Sat. 10 a.m.-6 p.m.,
Sun. noon-5 p.m.

Perusing Guy Laroche's catalog is like reading the "ladies'" menu in a haute French restaurant—prices are never mentioned. Therefore women (presumably the guests of men) are spared the trauma of knowing the cost of the meal. But at Guy Laroche women have to use their own plastic at purchase time, and the resulting damage is considerable for these classic, beautifully cut French fashions. Simple cotton tops sell for $125, a steal compared to the lovely, ever-so-simple suits, which can run in the thousands. You can leave here feeling very pretty, but you'll pay dearly for it.

Liberty of London

835 N. Michigan Ave.
(Water Tower Place)
280-1134
Open Mon. & Thurs.
10 a.m.-7 p.m., Tues.-Wed.
& Fri.-Sat. 10 a.m.-6 p.m.,
Sun. noon-5 p.m.

Prick your finger in Liberty of London and your blood is sure to run blue. The floral and paisley fabrics of these dresses and skirts are as lovely as an English tea garden. If you want to make your own, the fabric is available by the yard.

Luv Boutique

2100 N. Clark St.
929-2330
Open Mon.-Fri. 11 a.m.-
7 p.m., Sat. 10 a.m.-6 p.m.,
Sun. noon-5 p.m.

In this shop, one of the least-expensive, highest-quality boutiques around, you won't find too many surprises, but you will take home some affordable separates in fine silks and wools. The clothing is essentially casual, with a terrific selection of slacks and jeans. The staff fashion coordinator helps out with tough decisions.

One Plus One

815 W. Armitage Ave.
975-8559
Open Tues.-Fri. 11 a.m.-
6 p.m., Sat. 11 a.m.-
5:30 p.m., Sun. noon-5 p.m.

Thirty mix-and-match cotton/polyester-knit styles are here in a rainbow of colors for no more than $50 apiece. You can create a unique look here—layered or wrapped, clingy or loose. And the attractive accessories sell for less than $50.

Parachute

22 W. Maple St.
943-9292
*Open Mon.-Fri. 11 a.m.-
7 p.m., Sat. 11 a.m.-
6 p.m., Sun. noon-5 p.m.*

Parachute's cement walls are so gray, its ceiling so high and its atmosphere so cavernous that you almost expect mildew to seep through the cracks in this cave-like, ultra-trendy unisex clothing shop. A stylish mainstay for Chicago's models and high-fashion types, Parachute has a chilling ambience that detracts from its superbly contrived but frighteningly costly merchandise. Its designs are a step ahead of those at Chicago's other au courant boutiques, perhaps because of their European flavor.

Pauline's

6 S. Michigan Ave.
726-4242
*Open Mon.-Sat. 10 a.m.-
5 p.m.*

Imagine the perfect dress: It falls softly around every curve, drapes delicately below your collarbone and flows gracefully toward the floor. It sometimes seems impossible to find just the right dress; that's when you should visit Pauline Burke. She'll tap into your imagination and create the perfect dress for you—quickly and, for originals, at a reasonable price (from $135 to $400). She'll spend as much time as needed designing her dresses, looking for materials and seeking prototypes in magazines and local stores. Her specialties are beading and draping, as well as fur design.

Polo

960 N. Michigan Ave.
280-1655
*Open Mon. & Thurs.
10 a.m.-7 p.m., Tues.-Wed.
& Fri.-Sat. 10 a.m.-6 p.m.,
Sun. noon-5 p.m.*

The second floor of this stately bleached-pine palace is dedicated to women with classic tastes. All of Ralph Lauren's forever-chic fashions are sold here, from his trademark imported-broadcloth shirts to his lovely silk twill scarves. An unending selection of his conservative but never-stodgy footwear is a display of durability—these shoes may cost you dearly, but their life spans make the prices comparatively cheap.

Port of Entry

2032 N. Halsted St.
348-4550
*Open Mon.-Wed. & Fri.-
Sat. 10 a.m.-6 p.m., Thurs.
10 a.m.-7 p.m., Sun. noon-
5 p.m.*

We love that rare creature, the honest saleslady. And at Port of Entry, a wonderful, if expensive, boutique boasting a fine, mostly locally designed selection of tastefully slinky clothes, the salesladies are a godsend when the mirror breeds only indecision. These clothes are for the fashion conscious with good figures; the emphasis is on sleek lines and close fits, in rayon and fine stretch cotton, along with lovely linens and silks.

Jackie Renwick

65 E. Oak St.
266-8269
*Open Mon.-Fri. 11 a.m.-
7 p.m., Sat. 9 a.m.-
5:30 p.m.*

One flight up from Oak Street's traffic, Jackie Renwick sells somewhat conservative fashions for the career woman who thrives on personal service. "Warm" is a word that rarely describes salespeople, but the people here deserve just that description. They're not pushy or stuffy, like so many others on this ambitious shopping block. The selection is limited but enough to keep a good many businesswomen as regular customers.

Ring-O-Livio
301 W. Superior St.
751-1850

2000 N. Halsted St.
642-4999
*Open Mon.-Fri. 10:30 a.m.-
6 p.m.*

Located in the heart of trendy River North, Ring-O-Livio has become a very "in" place to shop. The fashions are on the funky and boxy side; frankly, some look better left on the hanger. But there are some outstanding selections from Hugo Boss, Bill Chas Robinson, Axis, Krunch and Joan Vass, and the particularly good men's department has sassy overcoats, baggy slacks and ultra-hip Italian silk ties.

Rowbottoms & Willoughby Outfitters
72 W. Hubbard St.
329-0999
*Open Mon.-Fri. 10 a.m.-
6 p.m., Sat. 10 a.m.-5 p.m.*

Rowbottoms & Willoughby carries everything you'd need to go watch a damp, Sunday-afternoon polo match. But fine English tweed blazers are just the beginning. It also stocks a grand supply of wet-weather gear from Britain, Australia, New Zealand and France, including the best selection we've seen of super-water-resistant oilskin coats. Waterproof hunting and fishing boots are other big sellers, as is the line of conservative, classic and even a bit stodgy clothing and accessories for men and women.

Sonia Rykiel
106 E. Oak St.
951-0800
*Open Mon.-Sat. 9:30 a.m.-
6 p.m.*

This is another of Oak Street's hip-but-classic Parisian boutiques. Although the usually staid Rykiel is known mostly for her brightly colored knits, the back of the store displays a more feral temperament. We were charmed by the black bolero jacket thickly patched with silk flowers for $3,370, which looked great with an angled hem satin skirt for $975 and a satin camisole midriff. You may have to suffer through a long dressing-room line, but the ultra-hip staff is so friendly and entertaining you probably won't mind.

Mark Shale
919 N. Michigan Ave.
440-0720
*Open Mon.-Fri. 10 a.m.-
7 p.m., Sat. 10 a.m.-
5:30 p.m., Sun. noon-
5 p.m.*

The ambience at Mark Shale's is not so different from that of Polo's across the street, except that this miniature department store goes beyond Lauren and carries other ultra-prep labels, such as Ruff-Hewn and Gant. It sustains the classic, conservative dresser for every occasion except fancy evenings on the town. A dizzying spiral staircase winds through four levels of fine merchandise, with equal space provided for both genders. Prices are moderately high, but the quality and service are well worth the investment.

Chas A. Stevens
25 N. State St.
630-1500

835 N. Michigan Ave.
(Water Tower Place)
787-6800
*Open Mon. & Thurs.
10 a.m.-7 p.m., Tues.-Wed.
& Sat. 10 a.m.- 6 p.m.,
Fri. 10 a.m.-5 p.m.*

A large boutique for women, Chas A. Stevens has never been short on style or chic, and it carries the top brands at reasonable prices. Labels bearing the names Christian Dior, Susan Bradley and Seville are seen in the collection of suits; separates come from such makers as Claiborne, Ellis and Elan. Stevens provides personal wardrobe consultants for those without the time or the taste.

Sugar Magnolia
110 E. Oak St.
944-0885

2130 N. Halsted St.
525-9188
*Open Mon.-Sat. 10 a.m.-
6 p.m., Sun. noon-5 p.m.*

Once a Deadhead, always a Deadhead. It's a little-known secret that owner Leslie Gerston schedules her New York buying trips around the Grateful Dead's tours. But that shouldn't come as any surprise given the overpriced inventory, which includes tie-dyed gym shorts, tie-dyed cotton sleeveless sweaters and acid-green silk shirts. But not everything is Deadwear; there are some comfy cottons, a good selection of designer jeans and jackets and some adorable baby clothes. But we'll pass on the rhinestone T-shirt emblazoned with the entire lyrics of "Sugar Magnolia."

Tashiro
3309 N. Clark St.
248-1487
*Open Tues.-Sat. 11 a.m.-
7 p.m., Sun. noon-6 p.m.*

Once a primarily Japanese boutique, Tashiro has expanded to include cutting-edge local and French designers. Washable silks, viscose and light wools are used to create these stylish, airy and nicely fitting clothes for men and women. The owners haven't completely abandoned the Japanese influence: The staff pads along the wooden floors in bare feet or socks, and an elevated floor covered with rice mats separates the Western ready-to-wear from the more delicate Oriental ensembles. A fine selection of kimonos and Manpe (Japanese work pants) is folded neatly in shelves surrounding the rice mats. The staff will kindly deliver your selection should you choose to keep your shoes on.

Ann Taylor
103 E. Oak St.
943-5411

1750 N. Clark St.
337-4462
*Open Mon. & Thurs.
10 a.m.-7 p.m., Tues.-Wed.
& Fri.-Sat. 10 a.m.-
6 p.m., Sun. noon-5 p.m.*

Ann Taylor could be Everygirl's favorite clothing store. It's a history-making event when we leave without buying something. It appears, however, that quality is just a bit on the downswing. Once unparalleled for classic clothes with a contemporary twist, we've notice lately some of the fabrics are not as fine, seams not as tightly sewn and styles not as neatly cut. Once known for its fabulous sales, Ann Taylor now routinely discounts clothes that often deserve the markdown. Still, you can't help but fall in love with much of this merchandise, whether it's a perfect silk sun dress, a chic wool or linen suit or a lovely leather jacket. Accessories are perfectly matched to the clothes, though comparable pieces usually can be found elsewhere for a little less money.

That Girl Boutique
833 W. Armitage Ave.
477-3422
*Open Sun.-Mon. noon-
5 p.m., Tues.-Fri. 11 a.m.-
7 p.m., Sat. 10 a.m.-5 p.m.*

This boutique prides itself on carrying merchandise found nowhere else in Chicago. But there's good reason why you won't find this stuff elsewhere. Imagine a three-piece puckered-silk outfit with a zip-away funnel skirt for when you're in the mood for a mini. Or consider the latest in Judy Jetson fashion: a linen dress accented with a giant hoop sewn into the hem. Other "nowhere else to be found" creations include pink, sequined ball gowns and gathered-silk minidresses. The blue-collar clientele saves for months to buy these creations.

Ultimo Ltd.
114 E. Oak St.
787-0906
Open Mon.-Sat. 9:30 a.m.-
6 p.m.

Enter beneath a sheath of heavy drapery and through a small mirrored hallway furnished à la orientale and find yourself in Ultimo, the store that made Oak Street's reputation as the street for the elite. You'll immediately be asked if you need any help, and if you aren't dressed appropriately, a not-so-subtle sneer will insinuate that you don't belong. Ignore this—the fun has only just begun. Ultimo has two floors, one for ready-to-wear and one for haute couture. All the big names in European design are represented, including Krizia, Valentino, Vickie Teele and Ungaro, as well as some Japanese and American designers, such as Issey Miyake and Donna Karan. Salesclerks follow a little too closely while you peruse the rows of lovely, well-made clothing from New York, Paris and Milan. The treatment is the same for men, who *can't* walk out without buying a Valentino or Armani suit for at least $1,000.

Gianni Versace
101 E. Oak St.
337-1111
Open Mon.- Sat. 10 a.m.-
6 p.m.

The clothing from this avant-garde Italian designer is lovely, extremely well made, terribly fashionable and frightfully expensive. But the prices don't stop well-heeled models and fashion connoisseurs from flocking here for outfits to wear to the latest club opening or otherwise important social outing.

DISCOUNT

Handmoor
70 E. Randolph St.
726-5600
Open Mon.-Fri. 9:30 a.m.-
7 p.m., Sat. 10:30 a.m.-
5:30 p.m.

Handmoor is one of the choicest designer discount shops for women. Dresses, slacks, blouses and pullovers by top designers are elegantly displayed. Because the designers are top of the line, you're not going to find rock-bottom prices, but the tab is consistently about twenty percent less than at better department stores. Service is generally impeccable, except during the blow-out sales, when the staff becomes understandably harried.

Spiegel
1105 W. 35th St.
890-9690
Open Mon.-Fri. 10 a.m.-
7:30 p.m., Sat. 10 a.m.-
5 p.m., Sun. 11 a.m.-
5 p.m.

How many times have we heard Don Pardo advertise the Spiegel Catalog when he signs off for *The Price Is Right*? Well, now you can visit yourself and get 40 percent off retail on merchandise by the same top designers for men, women and children that you'll find in the downtown department stores. This outlet also has an extensive furniture and housewares department.

LINGERIE

Enchanté
835 N. Michigan Ave.
(Water Tower Place)
951-7290
*Open Mon. & Thurs.
10 a.m.-7 p.m., Tues.-
Thurs. & Fri. 10 a.m.-
7 p.m., Sun. noon-5 p.m.*

What Jane Seymour is to romance, Enchanté is to lingerie. Gowns and peignoirs of cotton lace and satin bows make for dreamy, countryside fantasies, as do most of the French-made pieces here. Satin tap pant and camisole sets can cost $160. The selection is somewhat limited and the sizes are often out of stock, but if you're in search of the perfect wedding trousseau or want to spice up your marriage in a most tasteful, romantic way, Enchanté will enchant you. And him.

Schwartz's Intimate Apparel
945 N. Rush St.
677-5828
*Open Mon. & Thurs.
9:30 a.m.-9 p.m., Tues.-
Wed. & Fri.-Sat.
9:30 a.m.-5:30 p.m.*

Fine personal service and a fabulous selection have made Schwartz's extremely popular with wealthy Gold Coast dowagers as well as with ingenues. Once specialists in bridal trousseaus, weddings still bring in big business to Schwartz's, which continues to offer a superb line of corsets and lace underthings for the bride-to-be. In addition to nightgowns by Dior and Natori, bras and panties by Olga, Bali, Subtract, Warner's, Vanity Fair and Lily of France and a small but select line of bathing suits by Gotex, Jantzen and Oscar de la Renta, Schwartz's has expanded into sportswear, offering such designer names as Adrienne Vittadini.

Underthings
804 W. Webster Ave.
472-9291
*Open Mon.-Fri. noon-
7 p.m., Sat. 11 a.m.-6 p.m.,
Sun. noon-5 p.m.*

Christian Dior, Eileen West, Calvin Klein: They're all accounted for here in lace, cotton and silk. Although the selection is limited—what's not displayed on the wire-and-clothespin racks is stored in plastic tubs behind the register—it is tasteful and surprisingly well priced. Check out the divine garters and garter belts in satin and lace, as well as the irresistibly romantic satin dressing gowns.

Victoria's Secret
835 N. Michigan Ave.
(Water Tower Place)
440-1169
*Open Mon. & Thurs.
10 a.m.-7 p.m., Tues.-Wed.
& Fri.-Sat. 10 a.m.-6 p.m.,
Sun. noon-5 p.m.*

Don't be intimidated by those impossibly svelte, freshly scrubbed girls sporting cotton and lace G-strings in Victoria's Secret's made-for-men-only catalog. Not only do they not look anything like the customers here, but we were hard-pressed to find much of the merchandise touted in the glossy catalog, neither in this branch nor the one at 2828 N. Clark Street (549-7405). The lingerie here is affordable and kind to the average woman's figure. Satin teddy and camisole sets sell for as little as $49, but the best buys are always the comfortable cotton underwear, a deal at four for $16. Silk men's boxers and briefs have been added to the inventory, as have cashmere bathrobes.

Whispers
2657 N. Clark St.
327-4422
*Open Mon. & Thurs. noon-
7 p.m., Tues.-Wed. & Fri.-
Sat. 11 a.m. to 6 p.m.*

Whispers is to Chicago what Frederick's of Hollywood is to Los Angeles—on a much smaller scale. Many a scandalous article has been written about married men buying lace nighties here for women other than their wives. Although much of the lingerie is risqué, Whispers does carry a number of tasteful items by Lily of France, Dior and Natori.

SMALL & LARGE SIZES

Lane Bryant
9 N. Wabash Ave.
621-8700
Open Mon.-Wed. & Fri.-
Sat. 9:30 a.m.-5:45 p.m.,
Thurs. 9:30 a.m.-7 p.m.

Lane Bryant is a complete store for women's sizes 12 to 28; its three floors include sportswear, suits, coats, dresses, lingerie, swimwear and accessories. Fashions are reasonably up to date and quite affordable, especially in the fifth-floor clearance department.

The Forgotten Woman
535 N. Michigan Ave.
329-0885
Open Mon.-Wed. & Fri.-
Sat. 10 a.m.-6 p.m., Thurs.
10 a.m.-7 p.m.

Designer clothes for women who are designed a bit larger than the average. These clothes are fashionable yet practical—they don't go overboard in trying to hide the larger woman's figure, but they do their best to not accentuate it, either. Of particular note are the cocktail dresses made from silks and jerseys.

Penningtons du Canada
835 N. Michigan Ave.
(Water Tower Place)
664-6164
Open Mon. & Thurs.
10 a.m.-7 p.m., Tues.-Wed.
& Fri.-Sat. 10 a.m.-6 p.m.,
Sun. noon-5 p.m.

These clothes do not flatter the larger-figured woman. Pricing is inconsistent: Some great bargains hang alongside some ridiculously expensive things. And we find the use of appliqués and metal rivets for decoration a bit tacky, if not incredibly outdated.

Petite Sophisticate
100 W. Randolph St.
782-4326
Mon.-Fri. 10:30 a.m.-9 p.m.

2828 N. Clark St.
(Century Mall)
935-3373
Open Mon.-Fri. 10:30 a.m.-
9 p.m., Sat. 10:30 a.m.-
6 p.m., Sun. noon-5 p.m.

Run by the same folks who own Sophisticated Woman for larger sizes (see below), Petite Sophisticate has an even better selection of separates, suits and dresses for the smaller woman. Silk tops are especially nice, and there's a thorough selection of sweaters (some by Ellen Tracy) and a handsome line of career suits.

Sophisticated Woman
200 W. Adams St.
621-2828
Open Mon.-Fri. 8 a.m.-
6 p.m., Sat. 11 a.m.-4 p.m.

Sophisticated Woman sells some of the most attractive separates for larger women we've seen anywhere. The silk tops are especially alluring, as are the extremely well-fitting slacks. Although many of the dresses are better left on the rack, a few shouldn't be overlooked.

Chas A. Stevens Petites
25 N. State St. - 630-1500

835 N. Michigan Ave.
(Water Tower Place)
943-6313
Open Mon. & Thurs.
10 a.m.-7 p.m., Tues.-Wed.
& Sat. 10 a.m.- 6 p.m., Fri.
10 a.m.-5 p.m.

Chas A. Stevens Petites offers all the big-name designers found in its store for regular sizes—Anne Klein II, Susan Bradley, Jones New York and Liz Claiborne, to name a few. It's one of the best smaller-size selections around and shouldn't be missed by those frustrated by limited collections elsewhere.

DEPARTMENT STORES

Bloomingdale's

900 N. Michigan Ave.
(The Avenue Atrium)
440-4460
Open Mon.-Sat. 10 a.m.-
8 p.m., Sun. noon-6 p.m.

Chicago's newest department store has taken the city by storm, as has its neighboring new shopping center, The Avenue Atrium. Bloomingdale's had just opened at press time, not giving us a chance to personally inspect it, but we can say that it promises to be as dizzyingly marvelous as its New York parent. The Avenue Atrium is home to dozens of superb American and European merchants, from Gucci to The Coach Store, Aquascutum of London to Fogal.

Bonwit Teller

875 N. Michigan Ave.
751-1800
Open Mon. & Thurs.
10 a.m.-8 p.m., Tues.-Wed.
& Fri.-Sat. 10 a.m.-7 p.m.,
Sun. noon-5 p.m.

Bonwit Teller is the smallest of Chicago's department stores, which works to its advantage—the atmosphere is intimate and the service personal and friendly. True, the selection isn't as vast as in larger stores, but you're more likely to find what you want. The merchandise is tasteful, elegant and, though riding the crest of conservatism, often quite different from that of other emporiums. Also, it is home to two of the most sophisticated men's boutiques— Hermès and Sulka.

Carson Pirie Scott & Co.

1 S. State St.
641-7000
Open Mon. & Thurs.
9:45 a.m.-7:30 p.m.,
Tues.-Wed. & Fri.- Sat.
9:45 a.m.-5:45 p.m.

Carson is housed in one of Chicago's architectural landmarks, the Schlesinger and Mayer Store building, which was designed by Louis Sullivan at the turn of the century. A few blocks south of Marshall Field, it is the other premier old-world Chicago department store, though it's certainly not as refined. You won't find specialty designer salons here, but you will find the designers' merchandise—Liz Claiborne, Cathy Hardwick, Evan Picone, Leslie Fay. The Corporate Level for the woman executive offers some finely made officewear at reasonable prices. Metropolis on the second floor is home to sporty, well-priced togs and campy footwear to match. Carson dedicates a lot of space to men, particularly sportswear, and the makeup department is among the busiest in the city, bustling even at the oddest hours.

Lord & Taylor

835 N. Michigan Ave.
(Water Tower Place)
787-7400
Open Mon.-Sat. 10 a.m.-
8 p.m., Sun. noon-7 p.m.

Always a staid purveyor of fine, somewhat conservative fashion, Lord & Taylor is Chicago's most stable and predictable department store. Men in particular like Lord & Taylor for its fabulous sales. For women, there's a complete line of designer and casual clothes, with a particularly strong selection of dresses. We can complain only about the displays on the upper floors (there are seven in all)—clothes are clumped together on racks in bargain-basement fashion, unworthy of the moderately high prices their tags demand.

I. Magnin
830 N. Michigan Ave.
751-0500
*Open Mon. & Thurs.
10 a.m.-7 p.m., Tues.-Wed.
& Fri.-Sat. 10 a.m.-6 p.m.,
Sun. noon-5 p.m.*

Displays of leather goods from Fendi, Gucci and Louis Vuitton greet you at I. Magnin's Michigan Avenue entrance, setting the store's elitist tone. I. Magnin designates its boutique-like departments the way Disneyland does its Tomorrowland, Frontierland and Jungleland. Designer salons within this large emporium include Anne Klein, Claude Montana, Donna Karan, Giorgio Armani, Valentino, Yves Saint Laurent, Laykin for fine jewelry, Carol and Irving Ware Furriers and, of course, Ms. Magnin. That there are never many shoppers milling about I. Magnin's spacious floors is a testament to the store's exclusivity. Prices are extraordinarily high, but so is the quality of personal service.

Marshall Field
111 N. State St.
781-1000

835 N. Michigan Ave.
(Water Tower Place)
781-1234
*Open Mon. & Thurs.
9:45 a.m.-7 p.m., Tues.-
Wed. & Fri.-Sat.
9:45 a.m.-5:45 p.m.*

Few Loop emporiums capture the distinct flavor of Old Chicago as tastefully as Marshall Field does. Located here since the turn of the century, Field serves commuters with the same distinguished charm it did the carriage trade when it opened in 1853 at a nearby location. Field's State Street store—450 departments resplendent with the finest clothes, antiques, furniture, crystal, furs, rare-book and stamp collections—is the flagship, a veritable paradise of shopping wonderment. It was founder Marshall Field who said, "Give the lady what she wants," an attitude that's perpetuated in the store's present-day commitment to its clients. Specialty shops include Field's Afar, a distinctive men's gift shop selling antique flasks and frames, tie clips, grooming kits, silk robes, scarves and ascots and a marvelous ship model (for $4,000); Amelia's, a private-label boutique for intimate apparel; and the 28 Shop, which houses upscale high fashion for women. Louis Vuitton and Bottega Veneta lease space here, as does a complete electronics outlet. Marshall Field's melt-away Frango Mints are shipped worldwide and made in the State Street kitchens, as are all the hand-dipped candies and baked goods sold at the fifteen branches throughout Chicago and the suburbs. Of historical note is the Tiffany-glass dome located between the sixth and seventh floors on the Washington Street side of this 73-acre edifice. Built by Louis C. Tiffany, the 6,000-square-foot glass dome was unveiled to the public in 1907. In 1897, a cast bronze clock weighing nearly eight tons was installed on the State and Washington corner; the original was replaced in 1907 and another installed on the State and Randolph corner. Field has eight restaurants, including the Walnut Room, named for for its famous walnut-paneled interior. And we almost forgot the watch-repair shop and optical store. If all this is a bit overwhelming, Field also has a personal shopping service.

Neiman-Marcus

737 N. Michigan Ave.
642-5900
Open Mon. & Thurs.
10 a.m.-8 p.m., Tues.-Wed.
& Fri.-Sat. 10 a.m.-6 p.m.,
Sun. noon-5 p.m.

If only all department stores were designed as elegantly and accessibly as Neiman-Marcus. The expanse of the first floor is entirely on view upon entering—at first, in fact, the spaciousness, further accentuated by the three atrium-style levels above, is disconcerting. But it's hard to get lost here, which cannot be said for other stores of this size. Needless to say, the prices are high, but the quality is impeccable. The second floor is home to the designer salons of Galanos, Chanel, Valentino, Sorbara furs and Ungaro. Of special note is the intimate-apparel department, which is resplendent with the delicate silks and cottons of Christian Dior, Eileen West and Jonquil. The value of shopping here lies not only in the flawless quality of the merchandise but in the accommodating attitude of the staff.

Saks Fifth Avenue

669 N. Michigan Ave.
944-6500
Open Mon. & Thurs.
10 a.m.-7 p.m., Tues.-Wed.
& Fri.-Sat. 10 a.m.-
6 p.m., Sun. noon-5 p.m.

Bring along a compass if you don't want to get lost here. The departments are designed on a circular floorplan, making it difficult to find your way around and creating a general aura of frenzied shopping. Still, Saks is unbeatable for impeccable fashions for men and women. Top-line designers include Valentino, Bill Blass, Perry Ellis, Donna Karan, Armani, Anne Klein and Calvin Klein. Revillon Fur Salon carries, as always, a most elegant line of fine and pricey furs. And the men's shop is large and up to date, yet forever in step with Saks's pristine tradition of fine, classic clothing.

FLOWERS

Fertile Delta

2760 N. Lincoln Ave.
929-5350
Open Mon.-Fri. 9 a.m.-
8 p.m., Sat.-Sun. 9 a.m.-
6 p.m.

Fertile Delta touts itself as Chicago's largest plant and garden center, and we don't doubt it for a moment. Two huge rooms are stuffed with tall trees and hanging plants. And in the spring, summer and fall, Fertile Delta carries a superb selection of outdoor plants in a vacant lot the size of the store's interior, which also houses a flower shop. The staff is warm and extremely knowledgeable, so ask away.

Flower Bucket

1162 N. LaSalle St.
943-9773
Open Mon.-Sat. 9 a.m.-
8 p.m., Sun. 10 a.m.-7 p.m.

Flower Bucket proffers one of the best deals in town for roses—$8 a dozen for cash and carry (charge it, and the price goes up to $10; having them delivered costs about $21). The Bucket's nice selection of other blossoms—gladioli, birds of paradise, carnations, pompons—sells for less. Other locations are 158 W. Washington Street (346-9773) and 1201 W. Belmont (935- 9773).

Green Inc.

1716 N. Wells St.
266-2806
Open Mon.-Sat. 9 a.m.-
7 p.m., Sun. 10 a.m.-6 p.m.

We just love strolling by and gazing in these windows in the dead of winter—Green Inc.'s tropical-plant display carries us to faraway (and much warmer) lands. But Green is much more than a florist, although it creates the arrangements for many of the city's large weddings and parties. It also has a fabulous display of plant containers made from porcelain, terra cotta and wicker, along with beautiful blue-and-white Chinese porcelain vases and antique Japanese flower baskets. Other decorative accessories include skull and antlers and Haitian and Mexican folk art.

Ronsley

363 W. Ontario St.
427-1948
Open Mon.-Sat. 9 a.m.-
5:30 p.m.

Ronsley isn't just a florist, it's a total design center. Its forte is custom arrangements of exotic flowers, and it does a remarkable job with ornaments and trinkets. Ronsley also houses a complete production center for film sets, which is also used for meetings, conventions and parties.

FOOD

BAKERIES

Bjuhr's Swedish Bakery

5348 N. Clark St.
561-8919
Open Tues.-Fri. 6 a.m.-
6 p.m., Sat. 6 a.m.-
5:30 p.m. Closed the first
three weeks of July & the
week after Christmas.

For more than a quarter of a century, Bjuhr's has served perfectly fresh European- and Swedish-style baked goods—whipped-cream cakes, coffee cakes, pastries—all made without preservatives. Although the shop recently remodeled, both the staff and the delicacies look exactly as they always have. Three best-sellers include the marzipan and strawberry torte, the limpa and the cardamom coffee cake. But we couldn't stop ourselves there: The mind-spinning aroma of anise, fennel and other spices typical of Swedish baked goods tempted us—as they surely will you—to chart new culinary paths. Some have said that the princess torte and the Andersonville coffee cake are better here than in Sweden. You can expect a long but worthwhile wait; and beware of the Christmas rush.

Cheesecakes by J. R.

2841 W. Howard St.
465-6733
Open Mon.-Fri. 8 a.m.-
8 p.m., Sat. 9 a.m.-5 p.m.

Janet Rosing grew up with a mother who was an accomplished baker. After working in several local restaurants, Rosing recognized a need for well-made baked desserts but could find nothing to rival those her mother used to make. So nine years ago she started Cheesecakes by J. R. Once a wholesaler with three cheesecake flavors, Rosing now does a big business in retail as well, and her menu has expanded to fourteen flavors, including pecan caramel, marble, chocolate chip, hazelnut, amaretto, cappuccino, lemon and raspberry. Rosing's booming restaurant business and rapidly expanding mail-order endeavor are testaments to her tasteful interpretations of America's second-favorite dessert (after ice cream), baked right here with great care and the freshest ingredients.

Dinkel's Bakery
3329 N. Lincoln Ave.
281-7300
*Open Mon.-Sat. 6 a.m.-
6 p.m.*

Dinkel's authentic old-world flavors still come through in its best-selling recipes, creations that for generations have not changed a single spoonful of sugar, a solitary pinch of salt. Danish rolls, coffee cakes and a varied selection of breads are among the mouth-watering treats. Others include a multitiered Black Forest cake, Sachertorte, stollen, Strudel and an apricot strip. Lightweights steer clear of Dinkel's Sip'n Whisky cake, a pound and a half of sweet, warm alcoholic comfort loaded with pecans and raisins.

European Pastry Shop
4701 N. Lincoln Ave.
271-7017
*Open Mon.-Sat. 9 a.m.-
10 p.m., Sun. 10 a.m.-
10 p.m.*

At the foot of the recently remodeled Lincoln Square pedestrian mall, this friendly little pastry shop is a quaint European respite from the heart of America, a prime spot for a piping pot of coffee, a butter-cream torte and a good friend. Specialties include a Black Forest cherry cake with whipped cream, napoleons, strawberry shortcake and strawberry whipped-cream cake, all made with extremely fresh fruits. The butter cookies are especially delicious as well.

Let Them Eat Cake
224 W. Adams St.
728-4040
*Open Mon.-Fri. 6:30 a.m.-
6 p.m.*

If you sneak into the kitchen at the next big party you attend, you're sure to find empty boxes that read "Let Them Eat Cake." This appropriately named full-service bake shop has garnered a fine reputation over the years for its party cakes—cakes for little get-togethers, major bashes, office parties, you name it. Its delicious cakes and pastries are baked with a grand array of fillings and frostings. And don't be surprised if, while waiting to place your order, you find yourself testing some of the cookies that lay in wait behind glass cases. House specialties include banana-walnut fudge cake, cherry cheese strudel and fresh-fruit tarts and cheesecakes. Wedding cakes and sculptured cakes are made to order. The Adams Street shop takes orders for the following locations, which unlike this one, are open on Saturdays: 60 E. Chicago Avenue, 66 E. Washington Street, 1701 W. Foster Avenue.

Lutz Continental Cafe & Pastry Shop
2458 W. Montrose Ave.
478-7785
*Open Tues.-Sun. 7 a.m.-
10 p.m.*

Lutz oozes old-world German charm. And its pink-table-clothed, well-lit café is the perfect spot to enjoy a cup of cappuccino and a pastry on a lazy Sunday morning. Or try the lovely garden café if the season is right. But if you're going to take out, give yourself some time, for the selection is endless and despairingly tempting: rich Schwarzwalder, cherry mocha, rum, hazelnut and Grand Marnier tortes; Sachertortes, Linzertortes, fruit Kuchens, napoleons, éclairs and rum balls; and truffles flavored with raspberry, orange, coffee brandy, caramel, rum and walnut nougat. Just the sight of the almond-filled coffee cakes shimmering beneath a sugar glaze is enough to send you into sugar fits. And if all this isn't enough, Lutz also serves homemade ice cream.

North Star Bakery
4545 N. Lincoln Ave.
561-9858
*Open Tues.-Sat. 8 a.m.-
3 p.m.*

North Star is an anachronism in the world of baked goods—it makes only rye bread and only in three varieties: Roggenbrot, German rye as Americans know it; Bauerbrot, round farmer bread; and Comissbrot, German army bread. But the lack of selection hasn't hindered success—Jim Meyer has been in this business for more than 50 years, since he opened up shop with his father at another location. And he knows what he's doing. Unlike commercial bread companies, North Star fires up its ovens at 2 a.m. and lets each loaf rise in a warm oven for two hours. You may have tasted these breads elsewhere in the country, for Meyer does 75 percent of his business with restaurants in other states. If you come in before noon, you can burn your hands on a piping hot loaf.

CHEESE

**Chalet Wine
& Cheese Shop**
3000 N. Clark St.
935-9400
*Open Mon.-Fri. 10 a.m.-
10 p.m., Sat. 9 a.m.-
10 p.m., Sun. noon-6 p.m.*

In addition to its superb wine collection, Chalet carries imported cheeses from all over the world, including France, Denmark, Norway, Holland, Ireland and West Germany. French-style pâtés are shipped in from New York and Canada, and a full range of gourmet products—mustards, vinegars, condiments, crackers, coffees—hail from all over the globe. Recently, Chalet has had much success with low-cholesterol and low-sodium cheeses, all the rage with health-conscious gourmets. Other locations are 444 W. Armitage Avenue (266-7155), 1525 E. 53rd Street (324-5000) and 40 E. Delaware Street (787-8555).

COFFEE

**Coffee & Tea
Exchange**
3300 N. Broadway
528-2241
*Open Mon.-Fri. 9 a.m.-
8 p.m., Sat. 9 a.m.-7 p.m.,
Sun. 11 a.m.-6 p.m.*

This is surely the finest, largest and best-priced selection of coffee around. Wooden barrels are filled to the brim with Ethiopian, Jamaican and Guatemalan beans roasted on the premises. Some tempting flavors include Linzertorte, toasted almond and piña colada. The back wall is lined with at least a hundred flavors of fresh and boxed teas, as well as a generous assortment of fresh spices. The Coffee & Tea Exchange carries every coffee or tea accessory you might need, but know what you want before you enter: The staff can be less than helpful.

Color Me Coffee

3000 N. Sheffield St.
935-7669
*Open Mon.-Thurs. 8 a.m.-
7 p.m., Fri.-Sat. 8 a.m.-
midnight, Sun. 9 a.m.-
5 p.m.*

These are probably among the freshest beans around—owners/roastmasters Greg and Rhonda Stivers roast and flavor all twenty selections on the premises. This charming Lincoln Park spot is also worth a visit to enjoy a freshly brewed cup, munch on a delicious scone or muffin at the counter and listen to the romantic rumbles of the nearby El tracks. Sixteen tea varieties are also available, along with a good selection of coffee and tea accessories.

Gloria Jean's Coffee Bean

835 N. Michigan Ave.
(Water Tower Place)
944-7767
*Open Mon. & Thurs.
10 a.m.-7 p.m., Tues.-Wed.
& Fri. 10 a.m.- 6 p.m.,
Sun. noon-5 p.m.*

It's one thing to have salespeople follow you around in an expensive boutique or jewelry shop, but in a coffee store? Prices here are ridiculous—about $9 a pound—but as the only beanery in Water Tower, Gloria Jean's gets away with it. Although selection is fairly broad, there are very few flavored coffees. Gloria Jean's does, however, carry state-of-the-art coffee-making equipment, including Rotel's espresso machine and Krups Three-in-One espresso, cappuccino and coffee maker.

Starbucks Coffee Company

2063 N. Clark St.
525-6231
*Open Mon.-Sat. 8 a.m.-
10 p.m., Sun. 10 a.m.-
10 p.m.*

This Seattle-based coffee company roasts its own "city roast," which is darker and fuller-bodied than most American coffees, and a little higher priced, since this skilled process removes more moisture. Starbucks roasts only Coffee Arabica's beans, which are 50 percent lower in caffeine than most coffees. Starbucks's pride shows in its new store here, done in faux marble with a serpentine counter. Coffees come from the Americas, Arabia, Africa and the Pacific. If you want to try a certain type, a staff member will be happy to brew a cup while you wait, or they'll make you a cappuccino, espresso or one of many specialty drinks, like steamed cider. They also sell a fine selection of teas—black, green, blended, scented and spiced. Call the above number for other locations.

CONFECTIONS

Aunt Diana's Old Fashioned Fudge and Confectionery

835 N. Michigan Ave.
(Water Tower Place)
664-1535
*Open Mon.-Fri. 10 a.m.-
8 p.m., Sat. 10 a.m.-9 p.m.,
Sun. 11 a.m.-6 p.m.*

In addition to its mouth-watering array of fudge, Aunt Diana's is best known for its caramel apple, which is dunked in the chewy stuff and then dipped into a sea of walnuts or pecans. If you come at the right time, you can watch the staff dip jumbo strawberries into a vat of chocolate. Most of the candies are made in the kitchen on the premises.

Benton Hartt Chocolates
1966 N. Halsted St.
281-6666
*Open Mon.-Thurs. noon-
11 p.m., Fri.-Sat. noon-
midnight, Sun. noon-
10 p.m.*

Mother and son Jean Saks and George Koons make all these chocolate confections by hand, from the caramels to the truffles to the chocolate-covered Oreos. But the real draw at Benton Hartt is the ice cream, some of the richest we've found anywhere. It's best when mixed with an assortment of candies, cookies or fruit.

The Fudge Pot
1532 N. Wells St.
943-1777
*Open Mon.-Thurs. & Sun.
noon-10 p.m., Fri.-Sat.
noon- midnight.*

Another worthy contestant in the Best Caramel Apple in Town competition, The Fudge Pot creates wonderfully luscious caramel confections, along with candies made from chocolate, nuts and toffee. Its late hours attract a restaurant and club crowd in the evenings, but don't let the lines scare you away—these gooey treats are worth the wait.

Godiva Chocolatier
835 N. Michigan Ave.
(Water Tower Place)
280-1133
*Open Mon. & Thurs.
10 a.m.-7 p.m., Tues.-Wed.
& Fri.-Sat. 10 a.m.-6 p.m.,
Sun. noon-5 p.m.*

These aren't the sort of chocolates that drip and goo—they're more the type to hold pointedly between index finger and thumb (pinky out) and nibble delicately, even when no one is watching. Frankly, we like our chocolates to be a little less formal and a little more flavorful than Godiva's; the tastes, like the ambience of the shop, are a bit controlled. Still, you can't go wrong sending a golden gift box to someone you want to impress. The one-pound golden gift box sells for $22; add $3 for a ribbon and silk tea rose. Chocolate-filled tins go for $15 to $25. What we most like about this store are the tables, at which weary Water Tower shoppers can unload their arms and enjoy a cup of cappuccino laden with chocolate flakes or a scoop of Godiva's gourmet ice cream.

Huwyler
535 N. Michigan Ave.
923-0028
*Open Mon.-Sat. 10 a.m.-
6 p.m.*

Huwyler's pristine little chocolates are flown in weekly from Switzerland, where they are handmade with natural ingredients and without preservatives. Each chocolate is truly a work of art—some are laced with chocolate ribbing, others inlaid with an assortment of other freshly made candies. Huwyler sells coated nuts, jellies and florentines, but its specialty is truffles, which come in such flavors as champagne, caramel, hazelnut, coconut and lemon. Of course, such frivolous luxuries have their price: about $20 a pound.

Long Grove Confectionery Co.
835 N. Michigan Ave.
(Water Tower Place)
944-7070
*Open Mon.-Sat. 10 a.m.-
8 p.m., Sun. 11 a.m.-5 p.m.*

Those who want to go to chocolate heaven when they die should make sure that Long Grove Confectionery is included in their prayers. Sure, the people behind the counter can be a bit snooty, but this chocolate transcends bad attitudes. The turtles are some of the biggest and most decadent we've ever seen (and well they should be at $11.95 a pound), but the pièce de résistance is the "ultimate" candy apple ($3.95), which is swirled in gobs of chunky milk chocolate.

ICE CREAM

Ben & Jerry's
338 W. Armitage Ave.
281-8686
Open Mon.-Thurs. & Sun.
11 a.m.-11 p.m., Fri.-Sat.
11 a.m.-1 a.m.

Since Ben & Jerry's opened not long ago, Lincoln Parkers can be spotted regularly emerging from this little, white-washed ice cream shop with Cherry Garcia and Heath Bar crunch dribbling down their chins. The ice creams are delicious, the toppings fresh, and the caloric intake scrumptiously high. If it's not too busy, you can sit down at a table to enjoy and watch others enjoy, or take home the ice cream by the pint or quart. Ben & Jerry's also sells great-looking T-shirts.

Benton Hartt

See "Confections" above.

Kid Millions
2808 N. Halsted St.
348-5865
Open Mon.-Thurs. 1 p.m.-
11 p.m., Fri. 1 p.m.-
midnight, Sat. 1 p.m.-
1 a.m., Sun. 1 p.m.-
10:30 p.m.

It's no wonder Kid Millions is Chicago's favorite ice cream store, host to lines flowing out into the street even in winter—servings are gargantuan, mounds of pure-butterfat-and-sugar heaven atop a sweet, crunchy cone. All 70 flavors are made on the premises, with about 16 featured on any one day. Some of the more esoteric flavors include cantaloupe, ginger snap and coffee Oreo. Kid Millions uses all fresh fruit in its ice creams, and it mixes in the candy by hand so that the result is more like eating candy in ice cream, rather than slurping a kind of multicolored milkshake. Waffle cones are cooked behind the counter, as is the secret-recipe bittersweet-chocolate sauce. Because ice cream is made in small, quality-controlled batches, prices are a little on the high side. But the atmosphere is fun and the ice cream delicious—we wholeheartedly recommend spending the extra few cents.

Scoops & Buns
2618 N. Clark St.
348-0220
Open daily 7 a.m.-1 a.m.

Reminiscent of an old-fashioned soda fountain, Scoops & Buns serves a tempting selection of Petersen's ice creams and apple, cinnamon, pecan and raisin buns made on the premises. It may be an odd combination, scoops and buns, but it works for this new Lincoln Park establishment. Buns are served hot from the oven with the option of a deliciously gooey sugar sauce drizzled on top.

Zephyr Ice Cream Restaurant
1777 W. Wilson Ave.
728-6070
Open Sun.-Thurs. 8 a.m.-
midnight, Fri.-Sat. 8 a.m.-
1 a.m.

This old-fashioned ice cream palace may be a little out of the way (on the North West side in the Ravenswood neighborhood), but the 42-ounce milkshakes, chocolate phosphates and egg creams are well worth the trip. Art deco reigns, with stainless steel, neon and mirrors, and the outdoor café is a particularly nice spot in which to cool down during the summer.

MARKETS

ETHNIC MARKETS

L'Appetito
30 E. Huron St.
787-9881
Open Mon.-Sat. 10 a.m.-
6:30 p.m.

L'Appetito is best known by the lunch crowd for its bulging Italian submarine sandwiches made with salami, mortadella, Provolone, lettuce, tomato, oil and seasonings deliciously wedged inside a ten-inch loaf of soft French bread. But that's not all. L'Appetito sells everything Italian, and if it's not imported, it's probably made on the premises: bread rolls filled with meat or eggplant, pasta, sweet and hot sausages, marinara sauce, mozzarella, cannoli and too many freshly made salads to mention. A mouth-watering line of cold cuts includes prosciutto, Swiss cured beef and Italian salami. L'Appetito carries everything needed for a home-cooked Italian meal, including free recipes. It also has a fine selection of French and Italian cheeses and is the only place in town that makes fresh luganeaga sausage. Call in advance to place an order.

Casa Hernandez
4409 N. Sheridan Rd.
334-3348
Open daily 8 a.m.-9 p.m.

Casa Hernandez is a large, full-service Hispanic supermarket complete with a butcher, a delicatessen and a produce department. It carries everything that goes into Spanish or Mexican cooking. But we'd suggest bringing a dictionary if you don't speak Spanish, for the staff, although friendly, has some difficulty with English.

Convito Italiano
11 E. Chestnut St.
943-2982
Open Mon.-Fri. 11 a.m.-
7 p.m., Sat. 10 a.m.-6 p.m.,
Sun. noon-5 p.m.

Convito Italiano is considered by some to be the best gourmet takeout shop in the city. Every region of Italy is represented in the homemade tomato-based sauces and the pasta, which is prepared daily in egg, spinach and tomato versions. Daily specials are flavored with the likes of garlic, pumpkin and lemon. All breads and sweets are made on the premises, the pepper-cheese bread being the most popular. The front display case is packed with hot and cold prepared foods, as well as a multitude of meat, pasta and vegetable salads. But if Convito Italiano is known for anything, it's for its staggering selection of Italian wines.

Kuhn's Delicatessen
3053 N. Lincoln Ave.
525-9019
Open Mon.-Fri. 9:30 a.m.-
7 p.m., Sat. 9:30 a.m.-
8 p.m., Sun. 9 a.m.-6 p.m.

Few shops capture the essence of Chicago's rich German heritage as convincingly as Kuhn's does, as you'll discover when you wander down the aisles stocked with imported delicacies. Food isn't the only thing that comes from Germany here—so do the salespeople. Primarily women, they'll be more than happy to take you on a tour of the most comprehensive German deli in town. The place is virtually empty during the week but packed on Saturdays. Prices are a bit high.

**Oriental Food
Market**
2801 W. Howard St.
274-2826
*Open Mon.-Sat. 10 a.m.-
6 p.m.*

The makings of virtually every type of Oriental cuisine are available here—Japanese, Filipino, Chinese, Thai. You'll find fresh vegetables, some frozen appetizers and all the cooking staples you'll need to make it yourself. The owners are generous with their culinary knowledge and will be glad to help you find what you need, including cooking utensils (which they sell and rent) and cooking classes (which they host).

GOURMET MARKETS

**The Bountiful
Board**
2560 N. Clark St.
549-1999
*Open Mon.-Fri. 11 a.m.-
8:30 p.m., Sat. 10 a.m.-
6 p.m., Sun. 2 p.m.-7 p.m.*

The Bountiful Board's country-kitchen charm just begs you to nosh on its gourmet snacks on the premises, but you can also take them home. The interesting and tasty selections include salads with smoked turkey and smoked Gouda or butterfly pasta (farfalle) and shrimp, crab-filled brioche, apple-stuffed pork loin and pesto-stuffed veal breast. For dessert, try the fresh-fruit cobbler, bread pudding with raspberry sauce or pear-almond tart. The Bountiful Board also deserves credit for its imaginative selection of packaged condiments, such as peach Melba, blueberry-cassis or apricot-amaretto preserves, and cooking oils made from avocado, peanut or walnut.

**Mitchell Cobey
Cuisine**
100 E. Walton St.
944-3411
*Open Mon.-Sat. 10 a.m.-
6 p.m.*

After Neiman-Marcus, Mitchell Cobey is the city's most distinguished gourmet shop. Established in 1977, this clean, white, epicurean palace is one of the only food stores in the city that prepares all its dishes on the premises—and with great care and imagination. Sample, for instance, salmon tartare wrapped in smoked salmon with a whipped-cream sauce, fresh turbot with red-pepper sauce or homemade Belgian truffles. Cuisine to go includes pâtés, caviars, smoked salmon and a strong selection of unusual cheeses. Catering is also available.

**LaSalle Street
Market**
745 N. LaSalle St.
943-7450
*Open Mon.-Fri. 11 a.m.-
7 p.m., Sat. 10 a.m.-6 p.m.*

A step up from Burhop Fish Market at One Fish Plaza, LaSalle Street Market carries a limited and unfortunately unimaginative selection of baked goods, flavored coffees, homemade salads and smoked meats. The store is small and the ambience a bit disconcerting—it's difficult choosing a dessert while you're being assaulted by the smell of fish a few doors down. If you're doing one-stop shopping for a fish dinner, however, LaSalle is a good bet for an accompanying salad or two. It also sells some delicious ice cream.

Neiman-Marcus Epicure Department

737 N. Michigan Ave.
642-5900
*Open Mon. & Thurs.
10 a.m.-8 p.m., Tues.-Wed.
& Fri-Sat. 10 a.m.-6 p.m.,
Sun. noon-6 p.m.*

This is truly a gourmet shop, the type you're more likely to find in New York than Chicago, which is still developing its taste for culinary sophistication. Within the multifaceted food boutique is a Petrossian shop, selling a number of superb caviars from the Caspian Sea, as well as delicate foie gras and smoked salmon. The charcuterie features gourmet foodstuffs freshly prepared by local restaurants and vendors, along with smoked meats, an extensive line of exotic cheeses, domestic and imported wines, fresh fruits, international beers and sixteen varieties of coffee. The chocolate bar sells Yoku Moku Japanese cookies, and the dessert shop is home to a tantalizing display of cakes, pastries and tarts. For gifts to send, check out Neiman-Marcus's Red River–brand food packages containing Texas-flavored novelty specialties. Prices are high, but what else would one expect from Neiman-Marcus?

Savories

1700 N. Wells St.
951-7638
*Open Mon.-Sat. 7 a.m.-
7 p.m., Sun. 10 a.m.-6 p.m.*

Without a doubt, Savories sells the most delicious, mouth-watering muffins in town. Innovative flavors include raspberry peach, zucchini bran, peach spice bran and peach lemon. Scones made with blueberry, lemon or currant should be tasted sooner or later. Just as we went to press, Savories was expanding to include homemade salads and sandwiches, which is why we have classified it as a "Gourmet Market." We suspect these new foods will be as impeccable as their baked counterparts, which include breads and tortes made in local bakeries. Savories also carries a phenomenal selection of 55 coffees and about 30 teas, as well as any accessory you may need.

Zambrana's

2346 N. Clark St.
935-0200
*Open Mon.-Fri. 10 a.m.-
8 p.m., Sat. 9 a.m.-7 p.m.,
Sun. 9 a.m.-6 p.m.*

Zambrana's, a complete food emporium, sells wines, baked goods, cheeses, smoked meats and homemade salads, and it even has a floral department. Although everything sold here is at least relatively good, particularly the fresh, zingy salsa, some gourmets have complained that Zambrana's is too eclectic to maintain consistent quality. Others say it is suffering an identity crisis. We suggest you have a taste for yourself.

MEAT, POULTRY & GAME

Big Apple

2345 N. Clark St.
880-5800
*Open Mon.-Fri. 9 a.m.-
9 p.m., Sat. 8:30 a.m.-
8 p.m.*

Those who want to bypass Gepperth's prices but retain that quality come to the Big Apple, a full-service supermarket with an excellent meat department. All beef is U.S.D.A. prime, aged 21 days and cut to order by hand. The butchers take extra care with the meat to ensure customer satisfaction. For instance, all beef liver is skinned and veined by hand before it is sold. Big Apple also prepares tasty beef and chicken kebabs marinated in Russian dressing, chicken marinated in oil and vinegar, and its own sausages.

Gepperth's Meat Market
1970 N. Halsted St.
549-3883
Open Mon.-Fri. 9:30 a.m.-6 p.m., Sat. 9 a.m.-5 p.m.

Sawdust covers the floor at Gepperth's, a small, upscale meat market with the best reputation in town. Its stock in trade is excellent corn-fed beef from the Midwest and a full line of meats (choice and prime), including provini veal from Wisconsin, pork, chicken, turkey, duck and pheasant. It makes its own extra-meaty baby-back ribs, its own sausages—Italian, Polish, Hungarian, Cajun—hot dogs and even its own smoked bacon. Gepperth's also sells a full line of specialty cheeses and meat condiments. Prices are on the high side.

Paulina Meats
3501 N. Lincoln Ave.
248-6272
Open Mon.-Fri. 9 a.m.-6 p.m., Sat. 9 a.m.-5 p.m.

Paulina Meats is a favorite of local gourmets because it stocks display cases with specialty cuts, responding to recent cooking trends. Meats are of the choicest cuts, always fresh and tender. The staff loves to talk cooking with its customers, so as a result, lines are often long.

SEAFOOD

Burhops
745 N. LaSalle St.
(One Fish Plaza)
642-8600
Open Mon.-Thurs. 11 a.m.-7 p.m., Fri. 10 a.m.-7 p.m., Sat. 10 a.m.-6 p.m.

Located in the aptly named One Fish Plaza, Burhops is one of Chicago's most popular fish markets; it's certainly the most centrally located and is rather expensive as a result. But its fish is uncompromisingly fresh, flown in daily from Alaska, Hawaii and Florida. Some of the most popular imported fish include mahi mahi, marlin, swordfish, shark, Alaskan salmon and pompano. Burhops also sells a full line of foodstuffs that go into the making of a fish dinner: wines, marinades, rice, soups, sauce ingredients and freshly baked breads. Free recipe cards accompany every purchase. Lines are long on Fridays and Saturdays. Another location is 3025 N. Clark Street (327-6570).

Chicago Fish House
1250 W. Division St.
227-7000
Open Mon.-Fri. 9 a.m.-6 p.m., Sat. 8 a.m.-4 p.m.

If you can order it at one of Chicago's fine restaurants, you'll find it at Chicago Fish House, the city's elite institutional distributor of fresh fish. Fish is flown in from all over the world: the Bering and North seas, the North and South Atlantic, the Great Lakes, the Gulf of Mexico, the Pacific, New Zealand, Ecuador, Costa Rica... The institutional business allows for a tremendous variety in this retail outlet, which tends to be less expensive than other seafood markets. Dry goods are also available: canned foods, wines, cheeses, breads, spices. Chicago Fish House also has an extensive line of seafood cookbooks. Free cooking demonstrations are held on Saturdays from noon to 2 p.m.

STAPLES

Foodworks
1002 W. Diversey Pkwy.
348-7800
Open Mon.-Fri. 8 a.m.-
8 p.m., Sat. 9 a.m.-8 p.m.

Foodworks is not the place to shop for all your household needs; it doesn't stock a full range of toiletries and cleaning supplies. But when it comes to edibles, Foodworks caters to the upscale, health-conscious gourmet. The emphasis is on natural, whether it be soda, candy, bread, condiments, meat or fruit. Meats are cut from corn-fed stock, and vegetables and fruits are organically grown. The salad bar and deli prepare some delectable and unusual combinations, and coolers are filled with fresh-squeezed natural juices. But all this earthly goodness has its price—about one-third more than you'd pay elsewhere. Another location is 935 W. Armitage Avenue (935-6800).

Treasure Island
2121 N. Clybourn Ave.
880-8880
Open Mon.-Fri. 8 a.m.-
midnight, Sat. 8 a.m.-
9 p.m., Sun. 9 a.m.-9 p.m.

Treasure Island is Chicago's most elegant supermarket, a veritable haven for the upwardly mobile professional, particularly after 5 p.m. But don't let the yuppie image scare you away, for Treasure Island does have its treasures: a wide and fine selection of cheeses, meats, domestic and imported wines, ethnic foods, baked goods, fruits and vegetables, salads and exotic delicacies. It's important, however, that you be a decisive shopper; the choices can be frighteningly overwhelming, especially if you walk in hungry. Treasure Island is surprisingly affordable, just a tad more expensive than the larger chains. And though it doesn't carry lesser-priced generic brands, frequent sales are unbeatable, and the overall selection and quality of foodstuffs surpasses that found elsewhere. Some of the branch stores offer cooking classes by the best chefs and food writers in the city, and some have video departments and extensive floral boutiques. Call the above number for details and information on other locations.

WINE

Bragno Wines
& Spirits
40 E. Walton St.
337-5000
Open Mon.-Sat. 10 a.m.-
midnight, Sun. noon-
10 p.m.

Bragno purports to have the finest wine selection in the world. We can't confirm that, but with over 4,000 bottles from all over the globe cooled in five basement wine cellars, we're not about to argue the point. In addition to better-known wines from France, Italy, Spain and California, Bragno carries vintages from Switzerland, Australia, Chile, South Africa, Hungary, Yugoslavia, Germany, Bulgaria, Rumania, Lebanon and Greece. The liqueur collection is international as well, as are the Cognacs, brandies and beers; the Champagne selection also is extensive. Bragno will deliver throughout the city. The staff is exceptionally gracious and will make good recommendations.

Chalet Wine & Cheese Shop

3000 N. Clark St.
935-9400
Open Mon.-Fri. 10 a.m.-
10 p.m., Sat. 9 a.m.-
10 p.m., Sun. noon-6 p.m.

Chalet is located in a gray brick structure very much like a castle, but the inside is pure Early American. The extensive collection of wines includes domestic vintages from California, Washington and Oregon; imported selections come from all corners of the globe. The inventory includes at least 120 Chardonnays and a complete line of ports, liqueurs and sherries; and wine futures are available. Chalet also carries about 150 brands of imported beer. Discounts are available on bulk purchases. Other locations are 444 W. Armitage Avenue (266-7155), 1525 E. 53rd Street (324-5000) and 40 E. Delaware Street (787-8555). (See also "Cheese.")

The House of Glunz

1206 N. Wells St.
642-3000
Open Mon.-Fri. 10 a.m.-
6 p.m., Sat. 10 a.m.-
5:30 p.m.

While the northern strip of N. Wells Street is developed and quite safe for shoppers on foot, the area around The House of Glunz is questionable, so you should not travel there alone. But travel there you should, for Chicago's oldest wine merchant (established in 1888) is a must for both wine connoisseurs and interested neophytes. The beautiful shop, detailed with stained-glass windows and a mural that depicts monks working in ancient vineyards, sells fine selections for equally fine prices, ranging from $10 for a 1972 Graves Rouge to $500 for an 1889 Château Capbern Gasqueton; it also has a superb Champagne collection. But there's more to The House of Glunz than mere merchandising. In back is a wine museum, in which you'll find a nineteenth-century fountain by Beneducé of Florence of a boy squeezing grapes into a wine cup, wine casks from all the great European vineyards, handmade copper wine-making utensils and antique silver accessories. And the wine-tasting room, lined with dusty bottles of fine and rare imports and overseen by a portrait of Louis Glunz, the founder of the store (which is run by his great-grandchildren), is an early-Renaissance-style marvel. Recently restored by grandson Joseph Glunz, it is furnished with intricately carved chairs (including a bridal dowry chair), illuminated shelving, hand-wrought iron light fixtures from the ancient walled city of Rothenberg, Germany, sparkling Venetian glassware, a vast beer stein collection and nineteenth-century oil paintings. Expert cooks, the friendly Glunzs will recommend wines to complement any menu. Delivery is available.

Sam's Wines & Liquors

1000 W. North Ave.
664-4394
Open Mon.-Sat. 8 a.m.-
9 p.m., Sun. noon-6 p.m.

Some places spend a lot of money to look like a warehouse; Sam's doesn't have to. Not only does Sam's sell a comprehensive selection of top-line liquors, Cognacs, brandies and liqueurs at sizable discounts, but its domestic and imported wine collection is superlative, featuring first growths of the most famous Bordeaux and Burgundies. You'll also find the Midwest's largest selection of California wines, 350 German wines, 75 Alsatian wines and about 200 Champagnes. Sam's also carries all the drinking accessories you could ever need and delivers throughout the city and the suburbs.

Zimmerman's
213 W. Grand Ave.
332-0012
Open Mon.-Sat. 8:30 a.m.-
8 p.m., Sun. noon-5 p.m.

Savvy Chicagoans never give up a search for a seemingly impossible-to-find liquor without checking at Zimmerman's. Established at this location 55 years ago, Zimmerman's is ruled by Max Zimmerman, an old-time, fedora-topped wine merchant who roams the aisles of his warehouse-size store, chatting it up with customers and making recommendations. In addition to a substantial stock of nearly every mainstream liquor imaginable, Zimmerman's carries a good many drinks you've probably never heard of: Krupnick, a Polish honey liqueur; Advoket, an egg liqueur made in Yugoslavia, Poland and the United States; Arak, a Middle Eastern liquor similar in taste to Italy's Sambuca but drier; and Wishniak, an Israeli cherry liqueur. Zimmerman's also houses 200 California wines and about 140 from France, along with bottles from Australia and Switzerland, and even kosher wines. Delivery is a flat $2.50 anywhere in the city or suburbs.

GIFTS

Accent Chicago
835 N. Michigan Ave.
(Water Tower Place)
944-1354
Open daily 9 a.m.-10 p.m.

Visitors who must humor friends and family back home with lots of stuff that spells "Chicago" will appreciate Accent Chicago, which makes the chore as pleasant as possible. T-shirts, street signs, deep-dish pizza pans, pens, paper, candy, tote bags, framed photographs—if it says Chicago, this place sells it. Other locations include shops in Sears Tower (993-0499) and, for all you last-minute shoppers, O'Hare Airport (686-1820).

Beggars Market
15 E. Chestnut St.
944-1835
Open Mon.-Wed. & Fri.
11 a.m.-7 p.m., Thurs.
11 a.m.-8 p.m., Sat. 10
a.m.-5:30 p.m., Sun.
noon-4 p.m.

This delightful store sells handmade contemporary arts and crafts. Treasures include colorful Summa knits for children (up to $200), antique quilts, handmade lace pillows and sundresses. A tantalizing case of contemporary and antique jewelry is second only to a glass sideboard full of acid-aged brass kaleidoscopes, some made with semiprecious stones and others with alternating stained-glass wheels; these range in price from $85 to $250. Some less-expensive gifts include Caswell-Massey soaps and oils and clear-glass tumblers with a relief imprint of a cow. The staff is gracious and accommodating.

Bizarre Bazaar
1517 N. Wells St.
642-0860
Open Mon.-Thurs. 11 a.m.-
7:30 p.m., Fri.-Sat.
11 a.m.-9:30 p.m., Sun.
noon-7 p.m.

This warehouse-size junkyard filled with every gonzo gift imaginable is aptly named. From top hats to silver picture frames, sunglasses to posters (some framed), lingerie to sex toys, the inventory has little discretion. Although the police have tried to confiscate cases of drug paraphernalia on several occasions, colorful water pipes, bongs and cocaine kits still attract many. The store may sound sleazy, but it's a fun spot for a visit, and don't be afraid to buy something.

La Bourse
67 E. Oak St.
787-3925
Open Mon.-Sat. 10 a.m.-
5 p.m.

Operated by the Women's Board of the Chicago Medical School, La Bourse mixes exciting treasures in with the mundane. The eclectic inventory includes antiques, silver, porcelain and crystal. Modern finds include frames made from ground stone to look like malachite.

Brookstone
835 N. Michigan Ave.
(Water Tower Place)
943-6356
Open Mon.-Thurs. 10 a.m.-
7:30 p.m., Fri. 10 a.m.-
9 p.m., Sat. 10 a.m.-
5:30 p.m., Sun. 10 a.m.-
5 p.m.

The perfect place to shop for any man in your life—anyone who appreciates fun, practical gadgets for in and out of the home. And the selection goes beyond the eminently useful to such toys as finely crafted walnut and beech chess sets for $150 and miniature Ping-Pong and pool tables for $149.95. But we especially love the can't-live-without tools, like the electric miniscrewdriver that goes where others can't or the use-anywhere dead bolt to protect you when you're away from home.

Cats 5th Avenue
815 W. Armitage Ave.
935-5332
Open Tues.-Fri. 11 a.m.-
6 p.m., Sat. 10 a.m.-
5:30 p.m., Sun. noon-
5 p.m.

Created for feline fanatics, Cats 5th Avenue sells a litter of cat-related items from the expected to the bizarre: bar sets, tableware, jewelry, books and even *Catmopolitan* magazine. Need a "Feline Reflections" stained-glass mirror? You'll find it here. Hang out by the register and hear some great cat tales, including one about a lady who lives in a one-bedroom apartment with 30 furry friends and ten litter boxes stacked one atop another.

Collector's World
835 N. Michigan Ave.
(Water Tower Place)
266-0499
Open Mon. & Thurs.
10 a.m.-7 p.m., Tues.-Wed.
& Fri.-Sat. 10 a.m.-6 p.m.,
Sun. noon-5 p.m.

Although it's a little too cute for our comfort, those into collectibles will feel right at home in this haven for things small and rosy-cheeked. You'll find figurines in every character possible, from Goebel, Royal Doulton, Precious Moments and Rockwell, which are limited editions and therefore command high prices, along with Swiss inlaid wooden music boxes with Italian movements topped with brides, grooms, animals and ballerinas. Smaller music boxes run from $27 to $38.

Cose
750 N. Franklin St.
787-0304
Open Mon.-Fri.
10:30 a.m.-6:30 p.m.,
Sat. 10:30 a.m.-6 p.m.

Small, personal gifts for the home or office include a nice selection of Alessi stainless ware and elegant diary-type books filled with handmade cotton and linen papers. Our favorite gift, however, is an upright marble nutcracker.

Eclectricity

1000 W. North Ave.
951-7333
Open Mon.-Fri. 10:30 a.m.-
7 p.m., Sat. 10 a.m.-6 p.m.,
Sun. 9 a.m.-6 p.m.

Eclectricity specializes in high-tech gifts and state-of-the-art sundries for the home, kids and office. It carries high-gloss fitness equipment along with an interesting display of futuristic clocks and miniature Ping-Pong, pool and hockey tables. But what's of the most value at Eclectricity is free—excellent gift advice. Other locations are 547 W. Diversey Parkway (929-0045) and 225 N. Michigan Avenue (856-9239).

Gamesters

835 N. Michigan Ave.
(Water Tower Place)
642-0671
Open Mon. & Thurs.
10 a.m.-7 p.m., Tues.-Wed.
& Fri.-Sat. 10 a.m.-
6 p.m., Sun. noon-5 p.m.

These are games and novelty gifts for the young at heart. Toward the back are handsome wood inlaid chess, checker and backgammon sets. Gamesters is a great place to shop for April Fool's Day gifts—an entire wall is lined with gag gifts that are sure to get a rise out of even the most unflappable.

Good Taste

653 W. Armitage Ave.
664-1455
Open Mon.-Fri. 11 a.m.-
7 p.m., Sat. 10 a.m.-
6 p.m., Sun. noon-5 p.m.

Come here for that special wedding or housewarming gift that's sure not to be returned. Owned by the same people who run Art Effect (see "Clothes"), Good Taste is just that. Exquisite patina candlesticks and brightly painted dishes and pitchers are our favorites. Everything is original and handcrafted, which justifies the high prices. Unless you are incurably thin, avoid the food counter in back—you won't be able to pass by banana-split cakes, white-chocolate-strawberry cheesecakes, peanut-butter patty cakes and tuxedo brownies (layers of brownies, cheesecake and chocolate cheesecake topped with a dark-chocolate swirl) without trying something.

Hammacher Schlemmer

618 N. Michigan Ave.
664-9292
Open Mon.-Sat. 10 a.m.-
6 p.m.

Hammacher Schlemmer is to adults what F.A.O. Schwarz is to kids—a playground of state-of-the-art toys for the young at heart and thick of wallet. What big kid can resist the solar-powered golf cart? Or the clock that tells time in 70 cities across the globe? You may think you'll have no use for such things in your mundane life, but once you come in for a browse, you'll start to imagine the possibilities.

A Joint Venture

1704 N. Wells St.
440-0505
Open Mon.-Fri. 10 a.m.-
6:30 p.m., Sat. 10 a.m.-
6 p.m., Sun. noon-5 p.m.

It's a jewelry store. It's a gift shop. It's an art gallery. It's A Joint Venture, a clever, one-of-a-kind boutique. Up front you'll find hand-painted T-shirts and knickknacks for the house. A shelf toward the back features gag gifts: plastic ants, teeth and babies, as well as a good selection of humorous cards. Next to that is a long, glass counter displaying imaginative (and expensive) jewelry made by international artisans. And in back is the art gallery, which promotes the work of fine local talent and African unknowns. If you're not sure what you're looking for, or why, A Joint Venture will help you figure it out.

Kangaroo Connection

1113 W. Webster Ave.
248-5499
Open Mon.-Wed. & Fri.
11 a.m.-6 p.m., Thurs.
11 a.m.-7 p.m., Sat. noon-
6 p.m.

If you missed *Crocodile Dundee*, one and/or two, this small Lincoln Park shop specializing in the land down under will make up for it. Shoppers are greeted with an authentic "G'day" from proprietor Kathy Shubert and a lick from Gretchen, a miniature schnauzer bearing a strange resemblance to a koala bear. From oilskin coats and akubra hats to koalas emblazoned on everything from T-shirts to sheets, this moderately priced gift shop sells authentic and not-so-authentic Australian sundries, including Vegemite, the awful-tasting brown concoction the Aussies swear by.

The Museum Shop at The Art Institute of Chicago

S. Michigan Ave. &
S. Adams St. - 443-3536
Open Mon. & Wed.-Thurs.
10:30 a.m.-4:30 p.m., Tues.
10:30 a.m.-7:30 p.m., Sat.
10 a.m.-5 p.m., Sun. &
holidays. noon-5 p.m.

Along with the fine collection of art books, prints and posters you'd expect to find at one of the world's leading museums, The Museum Shop sells a most elegant and sophisticated selection of gifts—jewelry, silver and pewter frames, ceramics, silk scarves, ties and meticulous reproductions of a number of exhibit items. Everything selected is of exquisite taste; allow plenty of time for browsing.

Nonpareil

2300 N. Clark St.
477-2933
Open Mon.-Fri. 11 a.m.-
7 p.m., Sat. 10:30 a.m.-
6 p.m., Sun. noon-5 p.m.;
summer: open Mon.-Wed.
11 a.m.-7 p.m., Thurs.
11 a.m.-8 p.m., Fri. 10:30
a.m.-6 p.m., Sun. 11 a.m.-
5:30 p.m.

It's difficult to classify Nonpareil; we're classifying it as a gift shop, though it offers much more. From washable silks to bug bottles, suede slippers to lovely new and antique jewelry, Nonpareil really does seem to have something for just about everyone. Although the clothing selection is small and ever-changing, suffice it to say that you can always find a well-made, reasonably priced skirt, shirt or dress. The boutique often carries graceful silk scarves, and the restored antique watches are always tempting.

Penguins on Ice

445 W. Diversey Pkwy.
248-7684
Open Tues.-Fri. noon-7 p.m.,
Sat. noon-6 p.m., Sun.
noon-5 p.m.

Penguin-decorated beach towels, highball glasses, posters, clothing, dishes—you name it, if it has a penguin on it, Penguin on Ice carries it. But it doesn't stop at Penguins—the animal mania spills over into a line of gifts with images of cows, pigs and ducks.

Pine Cone Christmas Shop

835 N. Michigan Ave.
(Water Tower Place)
943-6969
Open Mon. & Thurs.
10 a.m.-7 p.m., Tues.-Wed.
& Fri.-Sat. 10 a.m.-6 p.m.,
Sun. noon-5 p.m.

This is a hot spot for perennial Christmas shoppers—those who can't make it through the summer without knowing how they're going to decorate the Christmas tree. We find it pretty weird walking into this snowflake-covered store abuzz with Christmas carols in the middle of spring, but we've included it for all those type-A hyperorganizers for whom Christmas shopping knows no seasonal boundaries. Ornaments, lights, trinkets and wrapping paper are always available, regardless of the temperature outside.

HOME

CHINA & CRYSTAL

Marshall Field
111 N. State St.
781-4808
Open Mon.-Sat. 9:45 a.m.-5:45 p.m., Sun. 9:45 a.m.-7 p.m.

Marshall Field's Crystal Gallery has one of the largest crystal collections in the world, its four rooms glistening with pieces from Hoya, Riedel, Lalique, Kosta Boda, Waterford, Cheska, Wedgwood, Rogaska, Lenox, St. Louis, Christian Dior, Cartier, Baccarat and Steuben. In fact, the Crystal Gallery is the exclusive distributor of Hoya and Steuben. Although it doesn't sell complete collections, anything can be special-ordered.

Spaulding & Co.
959 N. Michigan Ave.
337-4800
Open Mon.-Fri. 10 a.m.-5:30 p.m., Sat. 10 a.m.-5 p.m.

Since 1855, Spaulding has upheld a fine Midwestern tradition for classic, even a bit conservative, quality. Except for the department stores, Spaulding has one of the largest selections of china and crystal—mostly from Europe and all quite expensive— in the city. It also carries several fine lines of sterling, flawlessly made gold jewelry and an exclusive line of stationery and watches.

Waterford/ Wedgwood
636 N. Michigan Ave.
944-1994
Open Mon.-Sat. 9:30 a.m.-5:30 p.m.

One side of this Michigan Avenue shop is devoted to Irish-made Waterford crystal, the other to Britain's Wedgwood china. Both lines are comprised of flawlessly made, classic designs that brought each U.K. maker fame long before Waterford took Wedgwood under its wing two years ago.

FABRIC

Fishman's Fabrics
1101 S. Des Plaines St.
922-7250
Open Mon.-Sat. 9 a.m.-5:30 p.m., Sun. 9:30 a.m.-5 p.m.

Fishman's out-of-the-way location is offset by its selection—the largest in the city. Three floors hold a mind-boggling array of designer fabrics in every conceivable material, as well as some funky fake furs. Reasonable prices.

Fraerman
314 W. Adams St.
236-6886
Open Mon.-Fri. 8 a.m.-5:45 p.m., Sat. 8 a.m.-4:30 p.m.

Fraerman's service is superlative, its selection of fine silks, velvets, woolens, linens, polyesters and draperies unending, and its prices thankfully reasonable. In addition, the first floor houses a vast line of printed fabrics in all materials, as well as bridal fabrics and intricately beaded appliqués, while the entire second floor is devoted to drapery, slipcovers and upholstery.

Jerome Fabrics

129 E. Chestnut St.
649-0770
Open Mon. & Thurs.
9:30 a.m.-7 p.m., Tues.-
Wed. & Fri.-Sat. 9:30 a.m.-
6 p.m., Sun. noon-5 p.m.

Jerome is one well-stocked shop, with virtually every fabric imaginable; one room is devoted entirely to bridal materials and another to patterns. Prices are reasonable. There's a large selection of lace and sequined and beaded trims to complement the finer fabrics. Be prepared to wait, however—the staff is small and often quite harried.

Vogue Fabrics

835 N. Michigan Ave.
(Water Tower Place)
787-2521
Open Mon. & Thurs.
10 a.m.-7 p.m., Tues.-
Wed. & Fri.-Sat. 10 a.m.-
6 p.m., Sun. noon-5 p.m.

Vogue's main shop in suburban Evanston is allegedly the second-largest fabric shop in the country. Although the Water Tower branch is obviously much smaller, it is thoroughly stocked and well serviced by a knowledgeable staff. And there are some stunning fabrics here—gabardines in silk and wool, raw and refined silks, lovely linens. Trims come in an array of designs and colors, and most everything is fairly priced.

FURNISHINGS

Asian House of Chicago

159 W. Kinzie St.
527-4848
Open Mon.-Sat. 10 a.m.-
6 p.m.

Perhaps the largest dealer of new Chinese imports in the Midwest, the Asian House sells superlative furnishings, painted screens, vases and urns of porcelain and bronze, most of which are reproductions from various Chinese dynasties. We suggest you take your time absorbing it all. Prices are moderately high, particularly for some of the cast-bronze pieces.

City

361 W. Chestnut St.
664-9581
Open Mon.-Sat. 10 a.m.-
6 p.m., Sun. noon-5 p.m.

Sleek, stark, streamlined—there is no better way to describe City, a hipper-than-thou furniture store done in a haute-warehouse style with gray cement walls and high ceilings. Most pieces are designer-made Europeans in black, white or gray (not in keeping with the recent trends toward color), constructed of leather and/or chrome. The Italian light fixtures are on the cutting edge, however, as are the high-tech gadgets, including ultra-cool bathwares, color-coordinated desk accessories, storage systems, dishes and table accessories. Upstairs, the boutique carries men's and women's clothing from Japanese designers. The clothes are chichi to the max, consistently black and/or white and substantially overpriced.

Euro 2000— Escapades

800 N. Clark St.
664-7766
Open Mon.-Fri. 11 a.m.-
9 p.m., Sat. 11 a.m.-6 p.m.,
Sun. noon-5 p.m.

The European, high-tech furniture here is, for lack of a better word, the coolest. Where else would you find a coat rack that transforms into a ladder? Or a couch that conceals swivel-out cocktail tables? Euro 2000 also specializes in futons and carries exciting futuristic-looking beds and beautiful polished-cotton futon covers. The staff is extremely friendly and gets a kick out of seeing you get a kick out of the innovative furniture.

Expressions

435 N. LaSalle St.
744-1480
Open Mon.-Fri. 10 a.m.-
6 p.m., Sat. 10 a.m.-5 p.m.,
Sun. noon-5 p.m.

Expressions believes you should get exactly what you want in life. So they aim to please, with 150 sofa, sleeper, sectional and chair styles and more than 600 designer fabrics to choose from. The selection is not as state-of-the-art as elsewhere in town, but this franchise does offer tasteful, affordable and up-to-date furnishings for the upwardly mobile. Some of the fabrics—cotton prints, solids, woolens and velvets—are absolutely breathtaking. Expressions delivers your custom-made sofa or chair within 45 days of your order.

Manifesto

200 W. Superior St.
664-0733
Open Tues.-Fri. 10 a.m.-
6:30 p.m., Sat. 10 a.m.-
5 p.m.

Don't be surprised if you feel like you've seen all this before—you have, in museums and in books on the great masters of furniture design. Manifesto sells exquisite reproductions of classic and modern furniture designed between 1890 and 1940 by the most prominent names in architecture and design: Alvar Aalto, Pierre Chareau, Le Corbusier, Antonio Gaudi, Eilleen Gray, Josef Hoffmann, C. R. Mackintosh, Gyula Pap, Eliel and Eero Saarinen, Guiseppe Terragni, Ludwig Mies van der Rohe and Frank Lloyd Wright. Other contemporary work in accessories, jewelry and silver are crafted after originals by, among others, Mario Botta, Vittorio Gregotti, Hans Hollein, Arata Isozaki, Carlo Scarpa and Ettore Sottsass. The furniture is made from the finest woods, and details and inlaid work are true to the original designs. If you're interested in a reproduction of a piece not displayed, the friendly staff will consult with its large stable of artisans and let you know the feasibility of creating the piece.

Phoenix Design

368 W. Huron St.
440-9590
Open Mon., Wed. & Fri.
noon-6 p.m., Sat. noon-
5 p.m., Sun. noon-4 p.m.

The goal of Phoenix Design's Larry Bowman is to present designer furniture at palatable prices. And he's pretty successful at it, selling precise reproductions of Mies van der Rohe, Le Corbusier and Mackintosh pieces, to name a few, at prices much lower than his competitors'. Bowman also designs his own furniture, mostly of leather but sometimes of vibrantly colored fabrics. Another Phoenix Design, at 733 N. Wells Street, specializes in Southwestern furniture.

Roche-Bobois

333 N. Wells St.
951-9080
Open Mon.-Fri. 9:30 a.m.-
5:30 p.m., Sat. 10 a.m.-
5 p.m.

We credit Roche-Bobois for being one of the few highly stylized, contemporary, imaginative furniture stores that is also accessible and comforting to the mind's eye when redecorating. Pieces are European, primarily Italian with a smattering of French. You can buy a single piece—a travertine-marble dining table, a three-bay sideboard, an asymmetrically shaped, subtly colored couch—without feeling as if you must replace all your other furnishings to match. Prices are high but, for the impeccable level of quality, worthwhile.

Roman Marble Company
120 W. Kinzie St.
337-2217
Open Mon.-Fri. 9 a.m.-5:30 p.m., Sat. 10 a.m.-2 p.m.

Not everyone wants to warm up in front of a Louis XIV marble fireplace, but those who do should check out Roman Marble Company, which sells the Midwest's largest selection of antique and reproduction marble fireplaces, pedestals, tabletops and statuary. Paul and Donna Pagett buy the majority of the pieces in France and Italy, and the marbles come in a surprising variety of colors—pink, green, white, black, beige. Prices range from $1,000 to $25,000. Replicas are handmade by French and Portuguese artisans, and Roman Marble will customize tables and mantles on the premises.

Skyline
232 W. Chicago Ave.
337-4899
Open Mon.-Sat. 10 a.m.-6 p.m.

Skyline sells some of the most unique and tasteful glass furnishings we've had the pleasure to discover. If floating glass tables, blasted-glass fireplace screens or faux-marble vanities and tabletops supported by Corinthian, Doric or Ionic fiberglass plaster columns aren't what you're in the market for, Skyline will custom build to your taste.

Studio 702
702 N. Wells St.
337-0452
Open Mon.-Fri. 9 a.m.-5 p.m., Sat. hours vary.

Another store specializing in glass design, Studio 702 also does a big business in acrylics, particularly frames and table bases. With the proper lighting, these creative designs, some seriously offbeat, can look great.

Tech Lighting
300 W. Superior St.
642-1586
Open Mon.-Fri. 9 a.m.-6 p.m., Sat. 10 a.m.-5 p.m.

The best selection of high-tech, state-of-the-art Italian lighting usually available only to architects and designers is sold to ordinary folks here. In addition to a wondrous array of track lighting, neon, torchières, pendants and halogen lamps, Tech Lighting has a particularly worthy line of low-voltage lighting (at, alas, rather high-voltage prices, but you won't find this type of quality and design elsewhere for any less).

HOUSEWARES & KITCHEN

Chiaroscuro
750 N. Orleans St.
988-9253
Open Mon. & Sat. 10 a.m.-5:30 p.m., Tues.-Fri. 10 a.m.-7 p.m.

Chiaroscuro is a wonderfully whimsical world of the absurd—wooden chairs with brightly painted faces, multicolored papier-mâché bowls, timepieces made from oversized colored springs and plastic and wood pieces and hand-painted tea and coffee sets. The jewelry is some of the most imaginative we've seen, created by local and nationally known designers. It all commands high prices, and though most intriguing to look at, none of it seems particularly functional. There's a gallery of paintings and pop art in back.

Chiasso

13 E. Chestnut St.
642-2808

303 W. Madison St.
419-1121
Open Mon.-Wed. & Fri.
10 a.m.-7 p.m., Thurs.
10 a.m.-8 p.m., Sat.
10 a.m.-6 p.m., Sun. noon-
5 p.m.

Postmodernism runs rampant at Chiasso, an accessory store for the home and office. Greek temple facades here are made of Washington State sandstone (ever so useful for making just the right interior statement). Of course, Chiasso is not without high-tech goods, such as the Sabattini silver-plated salad servers or the Saper tea kettle that toots like a choo-choo train. Other fun items include coloring place mats complete with crayons and an upright row of brightly painted cancan girls connected at the elbow.

Cooks Cupboard

3003 N. Clark St.
549-4651

1201 N. Clark St.
988-4651
Open Mon.-Sat. 10 a.m.-
9 p.m.

Cooks Cupboard is a quite comprehensive kitchenware store that stocks reasonably priced state-of-the-art cooking gadgetry—from the Scanpan 2001, the extremely effective nonstick cookware from Denmark, to Vacu-Vin, a repressurizer for wine bottles. Yet if all you need is a wooden spoon, carrot peeler or egg slicer, Cooks Cupboard will be happy to oblige. It carries a complete line of cookbooks as well. On Saturday afternoons, chefs from local restaurants give cooking demonstrations.

Crate & Barrel

850 N. Michigan Ave.
787-5900
Open Mon.-Fri. noon-
7 p.m., Sat. noon-6 p.m.,
Sun. noon-5 p.m.

No store stays in such seasonal step as Crate & Barrel, the last word in tasteful, innovative and affordable home and entertainment merchandise. Crate & Barrel sells everything from wooden lawn furniture and wall fabrics to glassware and china. Kitchenware comes in all materials—clay, brass, porcelain—and glasses and tableware are found in a tremendous array of colors and styles. It also sells elegant linens and fabrics by top designers. Call the above number for other locations, and don't miss Crate & Barrel's outlet store, 1510 N. Wells Street (787-4775), for discontinued lines at heavily discounted prices.

Elements

738 N. Wells St.
642-6574
Open Mon.-Sat. 10 a.m.-
6 p.m.

Come here for a rare, absolutely out-of-this-world item. Splendid dishes, home accessories and jewelry demand inspection, and if some of it doesn't make sense, it's only because you haven't seen it before. The $700 rough-cement block phone with two lines is an extreme example. Asymmetrically shaped tableware is made by artisans, as is the unique and abundant selection of jewelry. Vintage sunglasses from Japan and Europe run about $150. Our only complaint regards the staff; they can be snooty to new customers.

Material Possessions

54 E. Chestnut St.
280-4885
Open Mon.-Sat. 10 a.m.-
6 p.m., Sun. noon-5 p.m.

These material possessions will ensure that your house stays au courant with the latest design trends. Japanese-styled stainless-steel and brass place settings that sell for between $65 and $75 are worth a look, as are the oxidized stainless-steel salad servers. Mother-of-pearl butter knives ($14) are a special find. Hand-painted dishes in the most cheery colors sell for about $60 a place setting; there are equally cheery Matisse-like tiles. And the copper-and-mirror kaleidoscope ($215) will come in handy when conversation around the coffee table lags.

Pier I Imports
25 E. Washington St.
263-2112
*Open Mon.-Sat. 9:30 a.m.-
7 p.m., Sun. 11 a.m.-5 p.m.*

We know you can find one in every city, but Pier I is worth a mention because it always carries something perfect and inexpensive to accent a newly decorated home, even a posh one. Wicker, rattan and fabric furniture is consistently available in the brightest colors, and the brassware is charming. Paper lamp shades and large, fabric-covered fans will cheer any room. Pier I also carries some attractive, boxy cotton clothes and campy jewelry made from beads and wood. It's not as cheap as it once was, but prices are still excellent. Call the above number for other locations.

Table of Contents
448 N. Wells St.
644-9004
*Open Mon.-Fri. 10 a.m.-
5:30 p.m., Sat. 10 a.m.-
5 p.m.*

We've seen more imaginative tableware elsewhere, but Table of Contents does boast some elegant silver-plated sets. French designs by Christofle can run as high as $300 per place setting. And Table of Contents sells the work of Swid Powell Collaborations, the New York–based architectural group that designs superbly crafted silver-plated bowls and table settings.

Williams-Sonoma
17 E. Chestnut St.
642-1593
*Open Mon.-Wed. & Fri.
10 a.m.-6 p.m., Thurs.
10 a.m.-7 p.m., Sat.
10 a.m.-5:30 p.m., Sun.
noon-4 p.m.*

Enjoy a freshly brewed cup of Williams-Sonoma's house-blend coffee while inspecting the merchandise at this successful mail-order-catalog-turned-national-retailer. White floors and bright lighting are the trademark of this high-end kitchen-oriented shop, which will satisfy any cook's addiction to equipment, which ranges from French copperware to Calphalon and Chantal. The collections of linens and everyday dishes are especially notable. Regular prices are high, but periodic sales make purchases more than reasonable. Some novelties include Brinkmann's Smoke 'n' Pit and a little book called *47 Best Chocolate Chip Recipes*. Don't forget to check out the handsome blue-and-white Chinese porcelain.

LINENS

Polo
960 N. Michigan Ave.
280-1655
*Open Mon. & Thurs.
10 a.m.-7 p.m., Tues.-Wed.
& Fri.-Sat. 10 a.m.-6 p.m.,
Sun. noon-5 p.m.*

Those who can't bear taking off their oxford-cloth shirts at day's end to sleep on ordinary sheets need not fret. With Ralph Lauren's Home Collection, preppy dreams can come true—even dreams of oxford-cloth sheets. This handsome, conservative, frighteningly expensive bed-and-bath collection is patterned in solids, florals, stripes and paisleys. It's ideal for an English country cottage or for an American suburban household that wishes to emulate one. Sheets run about $50 each, and comforters about $300. The Home

Collection also features wicker and upholstered furniture, and fabrics that sell for an average of $47 a yard.

Private Lives
2725 N. Clark St.
525-6464
Open Mon.-Fri. 11 a.m.-
7 p.m., Sat. 10 a.m.-
5:30 p.m., Sun. noon-5 p.m.

When decorating bed or bath, our first stop is always Private Lives, which discounts fine linens by Ralph Lauren, Laura Ashley, Liberty of London and Esprit. It also has a healthy supply of shower curtains and bath accessories. A second store, at 3011 N. Clark Street, sells similar lines at retail prices.

Sassparella Ltd.
1551 N. Wells St.
642-7340
Open Mon.-Thurs. 10 a.m.-
7 p.m., Fri.-Sat. 10 a.m.-
6 p.m., Sun. noon-5 p.m.

Despite the spaciousness of this boutique, which specializes in fashions for bed, bath and table, the selection is limited to products by Laura Ashley, Cannon Royal Family and Fieldcrest. Why pay top dollar here, when the same merchandise can be had for less at other bath stores, such as Private Lives? Still, if you're looking for hand-embroidered pillows, Sassparella has them for about $100.

Scandia Down
702 N. Wells St.
787-6720
Open Mon.-Fri. 10 a.m.-
5:45 p.m., Sat. 10:30 a.m.-
4:30 p.m.

We can't think of a more comfortable store to be locked in overnight. If you're looking for down comforters, pillows and duvets, Scandia Down has a superb, albeit costly, selection. Luxurious eiderdown comforters can sell for $5,000, but a blend of gray duck down and small gray duck feathers is under $200. There are also some beautiful covers from France, Switzerland and West Germany, but also for hefty prices.

Shaxted
940 N. Michigan Ave.
337-0855
Open Mon.-Sat. 10 a.m.-
5:30 p.m.

You aren't likely to find these imported bed, bath and table linens anywhere else. Most are made in Italy and Madeira, the small island off the coast of Portugal. Shaxted does sell some French-made sheets, though most of the bed linens and towels are made exclusively for the store. If you bring in a wallpaper or paint swatch, Shaxted will custom-make matching linens for a price worthy of such personal service. The hand-embroidered tablecloths are some of the most beautiful we've ever laid eyes on.

IMAGE & SOUND

AUDIO/VIDEO EQUIPMENT

Paul Heath Stereo
2036 N. Clark St.
549-8100
Open Tues.-Thurs. 11 a.m.-
8 p.m., Fri.-Sat. 11 a.m.-
5:30 p.m.

Paul Heath is quite honest about its policies: It will not throw in even a nut or bolt for free. Systems start at $1,800 and go into the hundreds of thousands of dollars; in-home servicing is free for five years. If budget is a consideration, you won't be shopping here. Paul Heath sends its music consultants all around the country to install the finest sound systems known to the human ear. Its audiophile attitude may be a bit much, but we've yet to hear a complaint about the quality. It carries primarily American, Canadian and British equipment, with very little made in Japan; some of the names include Mark Levinson, Mirage, Magnepan, B & W and Celestion.

MusiCraft
48 E. Oak St.
337-4150
Open Mon. & Thurs.
10 a.m.-9 p.m., Tues.-Wed.
& Fri.-Sat. 10 a.m.-6 p.m.

MusiCraft has been at this location for 33 years, long outliving many other stereo chains. Its equipment isn't as high-end as at Paul Heath and ProMusica, but it sells respectable systems by Carver, AR, Vector Research, Sansui and others; and everything is serviced in-house. Most of the salespeople have been here for years and are very knowledgeable.

ProMusica
2236 N. Clark St.
883-9500
Open Mon. 11 a.m.-7 p.m.,
Wed.-Thurs. noon-7 p.m.,
Fri.-Sat. 11 a.m.-5:30 p.m.

ProMusica is for those who love music more than gadgetry. Not to say that these electronics aren't extremely expensive— systems run from $700 to $50,000—but priority is placed on reproducing music as honestly as possible. Though ProMusica sells equipment made in the United States and Canada, most of it comes from England; brands include Acoustat, Adcom, Aragon, Arcam, Arcici, Audiotech, Beyer, Creek, Dual, Energy, Goldring, Goodmans, Grado, Harman/Kardon, Janis, Linn, Quad, Rogers and Rotel, to name a few. It also provides custom-built oak and walnut cabinetry.

Saturday Audio Exchange
2919 N. Clark St.
935-8733
Open Thurs. 5:30 p.m.-
9 p.m., Sat. 10:30 a.m.-
5:30 p.m.

The Saturday Audio Exchange is one of the most popular audio-equipment stores in the city, quite a feat considering that it's open only ten and a half hours a week. If you're not into all that high-tech laser stereo stuff, Saturday Audio Exchange is the best place to go. It sells used equipment and new b-stock systems, which means they have some cosmetic flaws but carry a full manufacturers' warranty. The inventory is always changing, so we can't tell you exactly what you'll find. But we can tell you that Saturday Audio Exchange stands behind everything it sells, and its people are expert, friendly and honest. Expect to spend some time here—it's always crowded.

PHOTOGRAPHY

Helix
310 S. Racine Ave.
421-6000
Open Mon.-Wed. & Fri.
9 a.m.-5:30 p.m., Thurs.
9 a.m.-7 p.m., Sat. 9 a.m.-
5 p.m.

Helix purports to be the largest photography store in the United States, and it stocks the most comprehensive selection of underwater-photography gear in the country. The other specialty is eight-millimeter video equipment, including editing consoles, special-effects processors and postproduction equipment. All items are competitively priced, and

Helix rents to photography and industry professionals (only). Call the above number for other locations.

Photo World
20 N. Franklin St.
782-9726
Open Mon.-Fri. 8:30 a.m.-5:30 p.m., Sat. 9 a.m.-5 p.m.

Laid-back camera buffs love Photo World, as much for its excellent selection of new and used equipment as for the funky music and amiable staff. Photo World sells all major camera brands at considerable discounts and offers a six-month warranty on parts and labor for most of its used equipment. The shop is best known for its large selection of gadget bags—perhaps the largest in the city—and its outstanding darkroom department. It also carries audio-visual aids and some underwater gear.

Shutan's
312 W. Randolph St.
332-2000
Open Mon.-Fri. 8:30 a.m.-5:30 p.m., Sat. 9 a.m.-5 p.m.

What we have here is an extremely high-quality camera store with the best in camera, telescopic and underwater equipment; what we *don't* have here is a friendly atmosphere. Still, if you're seeking state-of-the art photo equipment (and price is of little concern) Shutan's is worth a visit. It also has a great array of binoculars, and you can even rent a deep-space telescope by Meade.

Standard Photo
43 E. Chicago Ave.
440-4920
Open Mon.-Fri. 8 a.m.-6 p.m., Sat. 10 a.m.-5 p.m.

About 75 percent of Standard's customers are professionals, which explains its somewhat holier-than-thou attitude toward amateurs who walk in looking a little lost. Nonetheless, it is the Midwest's largest photo-supply house, specializing in graphic arts, photography and audio-visual equipment. It's also the Midwest's sole distributor of Mole-Richardson lighting equipment. The many departments include one exclusively for professionals and another for amateurs, as well as photo-finishing, audio-visual, repair and a high-volume rental shop. Prices are competitive and student discounts are available.

RECORDED MUSIC

Dr. Wax
2529 N. Clark St.
549-3377
Open Mon.-Sat. noon-9 p.m., Sun. noon-6 p.m.

It's quite a scene at Dr. Wax—the guy behind the register with a cigarette dangling from his lips, a sign behind him reading, "All shoplifters will be terminated." Dr. Wax has a fine used-record collection, particularly in jazz, R & B and rockabilly. New is mixed in with used, so take a careful look at what you're buying. Prices are fairly reasonable for used discs but a little high for new ones.

Peaches
230 S. Wabash Ave.
939-7728
Open Mon.-Fri. 9 a.m.-8 p.m., Sat. 10 a.m.-6 p.m., Sun. noon- 6 p.m.

Peaches is probably Chicago's most ubiquitous record chain, with stores popping up on corners throughout the city. The selection is satisfyingly broad on most popular music, with good choices in jazz, soul and blues. Prices are fairly competitive; check the wooden crates for some fine deals on cassettes. Peaches also rents videos. Call the above number for other locations.

Rose Records
214 S. Wabash Ave.
987-9044
*Open Mon.-Sat. 9 a.m.-
5:30 p.m.*

Established in 1931, Rose Records is the largest regional record retailer in Chicago, and it appears to be better supplied than some of the larger, nationally known chains. Selections are extensive in rock, pop, folk, classical, jazz and blues. What it doesn't carry, it will order gladly. Watch the newspapers for sales—Rose has some of the best around. Call the above number for several other locations.

2nd Hand Tunes
2550 N. Clark St.
929-6325
*Open Mon.-Fri. 11 a.m.-
8 p.m., Sat. 11 a.m.-7 p.m.,
Sun. noon-6 p.m.*

This well-stocked used-record shop does its best in rock and ethnic music, though all tastes are accounted for. Easy browsing (records are clearly arranged by artist) and okay quality, but check before buying—there's no return policy.

See Hear Inc.
217 North Ave.
664-6285

1013 W. Armitage Ave.
327-6633
*Open Mon.-Sat. 10 a.m.-
9 p.m., Sun. 11 a.m.-9 p.m.*

One of the more civilized record-and-video shops, See Hear Inc. sells records for about $2 under retail. CDs are the best buys, selling for about $3 less than in other stores. See Hear's two Lincoln Park locations give it clout as a strong purveyor of new-age music. And its 5,000 video titles make it popular among the city's couch potatoes.

Sound Warehouse
1011 N. Rush St.
337-5595
*Open Mon.-Thurs. & Sun.
10 a.m.-10 p.m., Fri.-Sat.
10 a.m.- midnight.*

There are five floors of goods here, enough to keep any audiophile busy for quite a while. Videos are rented and sold in the basement; blank tapes and cassettes are found on the first floor, CDs on the second and tapes and LPs on the third; the fourth floor is reserved for classical. The immense inventory keeps prices fairly reasonable, and sales are frequent. Call the above number for other locations.

Wax Trax
2449 N. Lincoln Ave.
929-0221
*Open Mon.-Sat. 10:30 a.m.-
10 p.m., Sun. 11 a.m.-
8 p.m.*

There's nothing like knowing where to find the latest Jesus and Mary Chain or Cramps album. And there's nothing like Wax Trax, a veritable punk-rock gold mine for the city's Vaselineheads. Despite an inordinately large display of discs from bands named after every imaginable body part, some civility is found in the used-record collection, which abounds with jazz, blues and rock classics. Lots of overpriced black-and-white gear for the fashion-conscious sadomasochist.

DON'T FORGET: Gault Millau introduces you to the Best of New York, the Best of Washington D.C., the Best of Los Angeles, the Best of San Francisco, the Best of New England, the Best of France, the Best of Paris, the Best of Italy, the Best of London.

JEWELRY

J. Russel Andrews
3519 N. Halsted St.
525-8888
Open Tues.-Fri. noon-
6:15 p.m., Sat.-Sun.
noon-5:45 p.m.

These impeccably well-preserved sets of vintage art deco jewelry are well worth their fairly high prices. Andrews has both a sparkling collection of rhinestone pieces and some beautiful work in semiprecious stones: amethyst, lapis lazuli, topaz and turquoise. A small section of the store is devoted to European, Oriental and American antiques from the seventeenth century through the 1950s, including small furnishings, figurines, decorative mirrors, porcelain vases and glass lamps.

Christian Bernard
835 N. Michigan Ave.
(Water Tower Place)
664-7562
Open Mon. & Thurs.
10 a.m.-7 p.m., Tues.-Wed.
& Fri.-Sat. 10 a.m.-6 p.m.,
Sun. noon-5 p.m.

Christian Bernard is Water Tower's most innovative jewelry shop, selling mostly colored precious-stone pieces designed by the famous French jeweler. All pieces are imported, primarily from Paris, and are fashioned in fourteen-carat settings. Emphasis is on the simple and the small. You won't find a lot of gaudy glitz, just the elegant and the uncomplicated. And the prices aren't hard to take.

Cartier
630 N. Michigan Ave.
266-7440
Open Mon.-Sat. 10 a.m.-
5:30 p.m.

There is no finer jewelry store in town. Cartier is a vision of sparkle and shine, a dazzling display of the classic pieces that have made the store a mainstay of new- and old-money crowds who share one thing: good taste. The staff is extraordinarily friendly and attentive; the gems are impeccable, the china astonishingly beautiful, the watches exquisitely timeless and the stationery of superb quality. But it's the gold that strikes our fancy the most. Splendidly crafted in classic designs that transcend any fad, the French-made rings, bracelets and necklaces from the finest eighteen-carat gold are supremely elegant.

Feinstein
415 N. LaSalle St.
828-0012
Open Mon.-Thurs.
9:30 a.m.-6 p.m., Fri.
9:30 a.m.-7:30 p.m., Sat.
10 a.m.-3 p.m.

In 1987 Steven Feinstein decided to move his grandfather's wholesale jewelry business to River North's retail area, but still keep prices low. His venture is a complete success. Feinstein sells some of the most elegant and tasteful custom-jewelry designs around at about 50 percent less than other high-end boutiques. And his styles are a step ahead as well. Feinstein's best work is in fourteen- and eighteen-carat gold and in diamonds. Most pieces are made in the shop or imported from Italy or Bangkok. Despite the fine quality, the staff is unpretentious and helpful.

Great Lakes Jewelry
104 E. Oak St.
266-2211
Open Mon.-Sat. 10:30 a.m.-
5:30 p.m.

Considering its high-rent neighborhood, Great Lakes Jewelry has some spectacular bargains on ivory and fourteen-carat-gold pieces. But its forte is silver, which it makes in an out-of-town factory to keep costs down. (Some of the silver is imported from Italy, but the transatlantic flight is not reflected in the prices.) You'll also find some lovely antique-reproduction jewelry. Ongoing half-off sales make this Oak Street nook even more likable, as does as its friendly staff.

Matthew C. Hoffmann
970 N. Michigan Ave.
664-6373
Open Mon.-Sat. 10 a.m.-6 p.m.

Matthew C. Hoffmann is a small, dark, achingly ultra-elegant shop for people who express themselves through their jewelry. Hoffmann designs every single piece, all of which are made at his flagship boutique in Ann Arbor, Michigan. Though he does work with precious stones, Hoffmann is given more to using such unusual materials as tanzanite and tourmaline, unique and colorful minerals that he blends creatively with fourteen- and eighteen-carat gold. The clientele is young and affluent, the types who are ready to invest in jewelry. But they tend to be surprised at the reasonableness of Hoffmann's prices—usually between $250 and $1,500 per piece.

Jan Dee Jewelry
2304 N. Clark St.
871-2222
Open Tues.-Fri. noon-7 p.m., Sat. 11 a.m.-5 p.m., Sun. noon- 5 p.m.

You'll find contemporary gold and silver custom designs at great prices here, despite the highfalutin Lincoln Park address. Jan Dee is manned by its owners, who are incredibly patient with indecisive customers, sometimes to the chagrin of those awaiting their turn. There's a generous selection of wedding bands, men's jewelry and women's gold and silver; and it's a wonderful place to buy funky, original earrings.

The Jewel Box
835 N. Michigan Ave.
(Water Tower Place)
943-2226
Open Mon. & Thurs. 10 a.m.-7 p.m., Tues.-Wed. & Fri.-Sat. 10 a.m.-6 p.m., Sun. noon-5 p.m.

Not the sort of stuff you'd wear to a coronation, but certainly adequate as casual accessories for the office or lunch with the girls. Rhinestone necklace-and-earring sets go for $100 or less; separate pieces range from $20 to $80. The small selection of silver necklaces, bangles, earrings and rings are priced higher than you might expect from a large costume-jewelry chain, but frequent sales make purchases more palatable. Some reasonably priced but unimaginatively designed gold is also available. Other Jewel Box locations appear at seemingly every turn, including Michigan Avenue (337-5160) and Sears Tower (876-0604).

Lester Lampert
701 N. Michigan Ave.
944-6888
Open Mon.-Sat. 10 a.m.-5:30 p.m.

Recent recipients of the Morris B. Zale Award for excellence in jewelry retailing (awarded the year prior to Cartier of New York), Lester Lampert has been a well-known jeweler for four generations. Lester and son David custom-design about half of the store's pieces on the premises, and the entire sales staff has been trained in design. If you have a family heirloom that needs an update, a Lampert craftsperson will refashion the piece without sacrificing its sentimental essence. The people here are also skilled in matching antique pieces. Lampert imports diamonds directly from Antwerp and Israel and colored stones from all over the world. Prices are high and can reach into the many hundreds of thousands of dollars, though smaller pieces sometimes sell in the $150 range.

The Larc
3517 N. Halsted St.
528-5555
Open Tues.-Sun. noon-6 p.m.

Some of the best-kept and most unusual vintage jewelry we've seen. Because The Larc's people are experts in repairs, the art deco rhinestone pieces are in near-perfect condition. And the prices are as spectacular as the jewels. Some work in pearl and silver is also available, along with a small selection of antique glassware. And if you need stones replaced, dyed or cleaned, this is the place.

B. Leader & Sons
2042 N. Halsted St.
549-2224
Open Mon. 10 a.m.-4:30 p.m., Tues.-Thurs. 10 a.m.-5:30 p.m., Fri. 10 a.m.-5:45 p.m., Sat. noon-5:30 p.m.

The people at this family-run gem of a jewelry store handcraft fourteen-carat antique replicas in the back of the store—and they do a fine job. You'll find some beautiful diamond-inlaid wedding bands, as well as delicate, finely crafted bracelets and necklaces. Beautiful silver earrings sparkle in one case; another is stocked with silver-plated pizza cutters, ice cream scoopers and razors. There's a small selection of antique watches as well. We suggest a trip here if you're looking for a special piece that can't be found anywhere else.

McCaffrey & Company
2210 N. Clark St.
871-0288
Open Tues.-Fri. 11 a.m.-7 p.m., Sat. 11 a.m.-5 p.m.

A delightful neighborhood jewelry shop, McCaffrey is full of sophisticated, elegant treasures, including antiques from the Georgian, Victorian, art nouveau and art deco periods, though it is best known for its unusual mountings of diamonds in gold and its exceptionally fair prices. Thus, McCaffrey has many loyal customers. Tom McCaffrey, who learned the trade in Ireland, is as skilled at repairing new and antique pieces as he is at creating innovative designs with a European flair. Gold is well priced here.

C. D. Peacock's
101 S. State St.
630-5700
Open Mon.-Fri. 10 a.m.-5:30 p.m., Sat. 10 a.m.-5 p.m.

Peacock's, the city's oldest store, was established in 1837, before Chicago was even chartered. It's truly the grand ballroom of Chicago's jewelry shops: Bronze peacock doors open to quintessential old-world elegance, with green-marble ceilings, crystal chandeliers and stately wood cabinets lined with exquisite china, crystal and sterling. Peacock's deserves its reputation for fastidious service. The jewelry, watches, clocks and stationery are all of majestic quality, and the prices are worthy of the Queen Mother herself. The repair shop is one of the finest—and quickest—in town and is particularly skilled at hand engraving.

Tiffany & Co.
715 N. Michigan Ave.
944-7500
Open Mon.-Sat. 10 a.m.-5:30 p.m.

Always imitated but never duplicated, Tiffany has maintained its reputation for jewels and gifts of the finest quality and design. Although barely a dent in the wall compared to its New York parent, Tiffany Chicago sells the same merchandise in more limited selection: jewelry by Elsa Peretti, Paloma Picasso and Jean Schlumberger; Laurelton Hall crystal; exclusively made fine porcelain; and a handsome selection of clocks and watches.

Trabert & Hoeffer
738 N. Michigan Ave.
787-1654
Open Mon.-Sat. 9:30 a.m.-5:15 p.m.

The marble exterior may be rather foreboding, but inside the people are exceptionally friendly and personal, which is one of the many reasons Trabert & Hoeffer has supplied three generations of Chicagoans with jewels. Trabert & Hoeffer is a jewelry salon; there are no crass counters over which one is forced to make showy transactions, only discreet sitting rooms in back where one can choose one's jewels in well-heeled privacy. About half the pieces are custom-designed, made by Susan Berman, who works with only one elite shop per city; most of the other pieces are imported from Europe. As you may have guessed by now, the specialty here is precious gems: diamonds, rubies, emeralds and sapphires.

LUGGAGE

Chicago Trunk & Leather Works
12 S. Wabash Ave.
372-0845
Open Mon.-Fri. 9 a.m.-5:45 p.m., Sat. 9 a.m.-5 p.m.

If it's luggage or leather and you can't find it here, it may not exist. Chicago Trunk & Leather has been in business since 1916 and carries the widest selection of fine luggage, trunks, business cases, handbags, personal leather goods and travel accessories in the city. Among the more than 40 household names: Scully Italia, Members Only, Dilana Design, Bond Street and Anvil Specialty Cases.

Deutsch Luggage
111 E. Oak St.
337-2937
Open daily 9:30 a.m.-6 p.m.

This is another one of Oak Street's many surprises. The atmosphere in Deutsch Luggage is friendly and fun, the staff loves to show off the latest gadgets, like the motorized cocktail butler for $10.99 or the nose holder for eye glasses at $4.49. Of course this store's specialty is luggage, which tends to be a heck of a lot more expensive than the novelties, and there's a lot to choose from: Hartmann, Boyt, Samsonite, Bally, Coach and Atlantic, to name a few. Other travel needs are taken care of with portable tie and belt racks, knit shoe savers, toiletry and jewelry organizers, mini-irons and travel pillows.

Greene's Luggage
835 N. Michigan Ave.
(Water Tower Place)
337-3774
Open Mon. & Thurs. 10 a.m.-7 p.m., Tues.-Wed. & Fri.-Sat. 10 a.m.-6 p.m., Sun. noon-5 p.m.

You can smell the quality of Greene's the moment you enter. Most everything is made of leather, and the selection is endless. Some brand names include: Schlesinger, Bond Street, Pegasus, Andiamo, Tumi, Hartmann and Boyt. Greene's has some sophisticated choices in attaché cases, as well as smaller leather goods like notebooks, address books and wallets.

The Leather Shop

190 W. Madison
782-5448
*Open Mon.-Fri. 8 a.m.-
6 p.m., Sat. 9 a.m.-4 p.m.*

Another well-stocked leather luggage store for Loop shoppers. Some brands of note: Mark Cross, Ghurka, Hugo Bosca and Coach. The Leather Shop throws in free monogramming with each purchase and is skilled in attaché and luggage repair. It also has a nice selection of leather handbags and personal goods.

MCM

50 E. Oak St.
944-7250
*Open Mon.-Sat. 10 a.m.-
6 p.m.*

A German adaptation of the canvas-coated cotton that makes Louis Vuitton so durable, MCM's luggage gives the wealthy traveler a chance to display his financial status without looking like every other rich kid on the block. At least not yet. It's hard to say whether this well-crafted luggage voraciously tattooed with the MCM insignia will meet rank with its French counterpart. If the decision were based on price, MCM shouldn't have too far to go. There's also a large selection of handbags and shoes.

Louis Vuitton

835 N. Michigan Ave.
(Water Tower Place)
944-2010
*Open Mon. & Thurs.
10 a.m.-7 p.m., Tues.-Wed.
& Fri.-Sat. 10 a.m.-6 p.m.,
Sun. noon-5 p.m.*

There aren't a lot of people who will pay between $8,000 and $12,000 for a steamer trunk, but whoever they are, you'll find them at Louis Vuitton. Considering the substantial investment one makes in these well-made, forever-in-vogue goods, we're a bit put off by the "Don't touch the display" signs perched above every shelf in this small snobbery. Still, Louis Vuitton is a popular spot with the Michigan Avenue set that has kept it in business here and at Marshall Field's and I. Magnin's. Despite the Midwestern location, the staff seems to take more kindly to those who speak French.

SPORTING GOODS

Active Life Styles

47 E. Oak St.
787-3772
*Open Mon.-Sat. 10 a.m.-
6 p.m., Sun. noon 4 p.m.*

Considering the chichi Oak Street address, we expected a better selection and layout. But the women's workout wear is clumped together on shelves, and specific styles are difficult to find without wading through the piles of color-clashing clothes. Still, some attractive swimsuits are a good buy, though they're few in number.

Athlete's Foot

2140 N. Halsted St.
477-1200

2828 N. Clark St.
327-7333
*Open Mon.-Fri 10 a.m.-
9 p.m., Sat. 10 a.m.-6 p.m.,
Sun. 11 a.m.-5 p.m.*

Nike, Adidas, New Balance, Reebok, Avia, Puma... Athlete's Foot sells all these brands, along with some sport togs for running, tennis, basketball and aerobics. The staff is extremely friendly and will bend over backward to help you find what you need. If they don't have it in stock, they often give a ten percent discount for waiting.

Body Electric
857 W. Armitage Ave.
883-1700
Open Tues.-Thurs. 11 a.m.-
7 p.m., Fri. 11 a.m.-
5:30 p.m., Sat. 11 a.m.-
5 p.m., Sun. noon-5 p.m.

Body Electric has the city's best selection in women's workout clothing. Bodysuits in every conceivable cut, shape and color fill three floors in this shop dedicated to women who care about their bodies. The top floor boasts a limited but extremely varied line of swimsuits, many of which seem to cater to the bigger bust. Some trendy and moderately priced casualwear as well.

M. C. Mages
620 N. LaSalle St.
337-6151
Open Mon.-Wed. 10 a.m.-
9 p.m., Thurs.-Fri. 9 a.m.-
9 p.m., Sat. 9 a.m.-6 p.m.,
Sun. 10 a.m.-5 p.m.

Six floors of jock nirvana, M. C. Mages touts itself as Chicago's sporting-goods department store. And for good reason. From golf clubs and weight equipment to bicycles and basketball, running and tennis duds, M. C. Mages promises the best price in town, or it'll refund the difference. You'll find all the big names in sporting equipment and clothes, and you can park for free in the Ontario Street lot.

Murphy's Fit
2843 N. Clark St.
327-3020
Open Mon.-Thurs. 11 a.m.-
7 p.m., Fri.-Sat. 10 a.m.-
6 p.m., Sun. 12:30 p.m.-
5:30 p.m.

Specializing in biking and running shoes and apparel, Murphy's has a selection that is small but extremely high in quality. It doesn't sell all the big-name brands, stocking only what they believe to be quality workmanship. All prices are a few dollars below retail, and it has some terrific sales. The staff is friendly and knowledgeable.

Orvis
142 E. Ontario St.
440-0662
Open Mon.-Wed. & Fri.
10 a.m.-6 p.m., Thurs.
10 a.m.-7 p.m., Sat.
10 a.m.-5 p.m.

Although you can't fly-fish in Lake Michigan, Orvis's proximity to the largest Great Lake may be enough to lure you into taking one of its many fly-fishing or hunting expeditions. In addition to stocking a complete inventory for both sports, Orvis outfits men and women in the most preppy mode imaginable for the great outdoors. It also sells a strong line of gifts for outdoorsy types—wooden-duck decoys, brass lanterns, geese-embellished highball glasses and the like.

Sportmart
3143 N. Clark St.
871-8500
Open Mon.-Sat. 9:30 a.m.-
9:30 p.m., Sun. 10 a.m.-
6 p.m.

This growing chain of discount sporting-goods stores compensates in price for what it lacks in selection, particularly in clothes and athletic shoes. Although large and usually well stocked, Sportmart does a staggering volume of business, which often depletes shelves and racks of the most popular sizes. But if you find what you're looking for, you won't get a better price in town. Check local newspapers for sales.

Vertel's
1818 N. Wells St.
664-4903

1628 N. Wells St.
266-0877
Open Mon.-Fri. 10 a.m.-
8 p.m., Sat. 10 a.m.-6 p.m.,
Sun. noon-5 p.m.

Located smack between Lincoln Park and Old Town, Vertel's serves these yuppified neighborhoods with high-quality, friendly service and jacked-up prices. The charter store specializes in running and racquet sports and does a big business in stringing. The newer Vertel's, located south a couple of blocks on Wells, is geared toward sleek-yet-practical swimwear and aerobic fashions.

Windward Sports

3317 N. Clark St.
472-6868
Open Mon.-Fri. 10 a.m.-8 p.m., Sat.-Sun. 10 a.m.-5 p.m.

Windward caters to windsurfing, Chicago's favorite water sport and offers plenty of friendly expertise. In addition to a heady selection of Mistral boards, Windward carries O'Neill wetsuits and beachwear by Gotcha and Maui & Sons, and it's one of the only stores in the city that sells Quicksilver clothing. If windsurfing's not your sport, the folks here will do their best to win you over with classes and clinics.

TOBACCONISTS

Dunhill

835 N. Michigan Ave.
(Water Tower Place)
467-4455
Open Mon. & Thurs. 10 a.m.-7 p.m., Tues.-Wed. & Fri.-Sat. 10 a.m.-6 p.m., Sun. noon-5 p.m.

Dunhill's walk-in, sit-down humidor feels more like an exclusive men's club than a Water Tower retail establishment. Here, customers are seated on a large velvet sofa and invited to sample various Dunhill blends while Vivaldi plays in the background. In addition to the house blend, which is made in the Canary Islands, Dunhill carries exclusive mixtures by Monte Cruz, Don Diego, H. Upmann, Temple Hall, Macanudo and Partagas. A box of 25 cigars sells for an average of $50; a box of 20 aged cigars can sell for $135.

Iwan Ries & Co.

19 S. Wabash Ave.
372-1306
Open Mon.-Fri. 9 a.m.-5:30 p.m., Sat. 9 a.m.-5 p.m.

The aroma of tobacco wafts through the lobby of the Iwan Ries building, even though Chicago's oldest tobacco store (established in 1857) is on the second floor. Once the highest-volume tobacco merchant in the world, Iwan Ries still sells more pipes than anyone we know—it stocks about 25,000, ranging in price from $1.25 to $500. It's also known for its private-label Three-Star tobacco and its considerable mail-order business in pipes, cigars, tobaccos and smoking accessories. A refrigerated, walk-in humidor houses the finest cigars available in this country, and the pipe museum is a treasure of antique pipes, many elaborately carved from solid ivory. But the shop's greatest coup is a stick of tobacco found in the bottom of George Washington's personal trunk at the turn of the century. Once used as currency in Washington's home state of Virginia, as well as throughout the South in pre–Civil War days, this "tobacco coin" is the only entire stick known to have survived the last two centuries.

Old Chicago Smoke Shop

169 N. Clark St.
236-9771
Open Mon.-Fri. 8 a.m.-5:30 p.m., Sat. 9 a.m.-4 p.m.

The second-largest cigar retailer in the country, the Old Chicago Smoke Shop claims to provide three out of five Chicago-area smokers with tobacco, cigars, pipes and imported cigarettes through its Clark Street store and its four suburban locations under different names. Most cigars are handmade and imported from the Canary Islands, Jamaica, Mexico and Honduras. High-volume sales enable the store to sell tobacco products for 20 to 30 percent below retail.

The Up Down Tobacco Shop
1550 N. Wells St.
337-8025
Open Mon.-Thurs. & Sun. 11 a.m.-11 p.m., Fri.-Sat. 11 a.m.- midnight.

One of Chicago's smaller, more expensive tobacco shops, The Up Down is popular among late-nighters. Its hours allow them to get a late-night fix of high-quality tobacco, including a large selection of cigars from the Dominican Republic, Canary Islands, Jamaica and Honduras, as well as snuffs and some exquisite smoking accessories. The Up Down recently added high-priced quality coffee beans to its inventory.

WHERE TO FIND...

A BABYSITTER

American Registry for Nurses & Sitters
3921 N. Lincoln Ave.
248-8100

Established in 1950 and licensed by the Illinois State Department of Labor, the American Registry takes great care in finding sitters with good references. Over the last six years, in fact, it has turned away more applicants than it has hired, for lack of credentials. Its sitters, who average in age from mid-30s to mid-60s and charge $5 an hour, must have three recommendations from families or child-care establishments. If you're out after 9 p.m., you must drive the sitter home or pay for a cab, which the American Registry ensures will not exceed $7.

BARNYARD ANIMALS

Friendly Farms
32W 451 Smith Rd.,
West Chicago
584-3401
Open any reasonable hour.

Here's a great idea for a kids' party—rent a petting zoo stocked with 35 animals, including goats, sheep, ducks, chickens, geese and a calf. Or what about pony rides? Is your Christmas nativity scene missing a donkey? Friendly Farms will rent you one for $400 a day, the going price for all the animals owner Steve Vidmar keeps on his suburban farm. When nothing else will do, Vidmar will provide you with an elephant (through a locator service). Horse-drawn wagons are available in the spring, sleighs in the winter.

Whispering Winds
32W 451 Smith Rd.,
West Chicago - 377-2852
Open any reasonable hour.

Owned by Barbara Vidmar, mom to Steve of Friendly Farms, Whispering Winds provides Western-style horses for trail rides in this lovely suburban setting for $12 an hour.

A CLEANERS

Downtown Cleaners
318 S. Wells St.
939-7504
*Open Mon.-Fri. 7 a.m.-
6 p.m., Sat. 7 a.m.-4 p.m.*

It doesn't deliver, but if you need marinara sauce rinsed out of your shirt or a tear in the seat of your pants repaired before a four o'clock meeting, Downtown Cleaners's same-day service will come to the rescue. Also, it specializes in costumes and theatrical wardrobes. Three other downtown locations include 1011 S. State Street (922-1011), 407 S. Peoria Street (733-8174) and 331 S. LaSalle Street (939-3718).

Stitt Reed Cleaners
414 N. Orleans St.
661-0555
*Open Mon.-Fri. 7:30 a.m.-
6 p.m., Sat. 10 a.m.-2 p.m.*

Around the corner from the Apparel Center, Stitt Reed has a long-standing reputation for cleaning fine clothes, including leather and furs. Other services include tailoring, leather and suede repairs, reweaving and cleaning of all down products. Complimentary pickup and delivery service is available.

A DATE

Great Expectations
708 N. Dearborn St.
943-1760
*Open by appt. only Tues.-
Fri. 9:30 a.m.-7 p.m., Sat.
9:30 a.m.-2 p.m., Sun.
noon-4 p.m.*

This nationally known dating chain insists on upholding its 23-year-old reputation by accepting only "quality" applicants. And the program seems to work in the least-humiliating way possible. Interested parties undergo a preliminary telephone interview and then are asked to make a personal visit. If you pass that test, another appointment is made to immortalize you on your own videotape, which is filed among 2,500 others. The fee is between $800 and $2,000, depending on how frequently you use the service. A word of advice, however: In love, the greatest expectations are to have none at all. Happy hunting!

A DRUGSTORE

Walgreens
757 N. Michigan Ave.
664-8686
Open daily 24 hours.

With 94 branches throughout the city, 12 of which are open 24 hours, you can get a prescription filled anytime without having to go too far. But these vast warehouse-like stores fill many more needs than just prescriptions: They are chock-full of hair products, makeup, garden tools, kitchen appliances, photography supplies and food, just for starters. Call directory information for the nearest location.

A FIVE-AND-DIME

F. W. Woolworth
2354 N. Clark St.
477-0355
*Open Mon.-Fri. 9:30 a.m.-
7:30 p.m., Sat. 9:30 a.m.-
6 p.m., Sun. 11 a.m.-5 p.m.*

Like Walgreens, Woolworth is everywhere in Chicago, accommodating both those who have little money and those who have lots but don't like to fritter it away. The plants and kitchen supplies are especially good buys. We're not embarrassed to admit discovering some great costume jewelry here.

A HARDWARE STORE

Ace Hardware
2817 N. Clark St.
348-0705
*Open Mon.-Fri. 9:30 a.m.-
9 p.m., Sat. 9 a.m.-8 p.m.,
Sun. 10 a.m.-7 p.m.*

"Ace is the place with the helpful hardware man." That's the motto, and they're not kidding. This ubiquitous hardware chain can satisfy anyone's fix-it fetish; those who aren't terribly handy head upstairs to the housewares and bath departments. Ace is also a great place for lawn furniture, radios and TVs. The staff here is most helpful, though a bit beleaguered by all the would-be handypersons who don't really know what they're doing.

A LIMOUSINE

Chicago Limousine Service
188 W. Randolph St.
726-1035
Open daily 24 hours.

Go in style in a brand-new black Cadillac stretch limo for $52 an hour (including tax), with a two-hour minimum. All cars have a color TV, stereo, wet bar and phone.

Creative Auto
1830 S. Clinton St.
942-1874
Open daily 8 a.m.-6 p.m.

Why rent a limo when you can transport your date in a three-wheel police scooter? Or better yet, how about a '57 Chevy or '58 Cadillac? All these fun, finely maintained autos are available for between $50 and $200 a day at Creative Auto. It also has a locator service for just about any car imaginable, including vintage motorcycles, old Ferraris, Mercedeses and even Rolls-Royces.

Gold Coast Limousine Service
2430 W. Belden St.
227-1000
Open daily 24 hours.

Chicago's oldest limousine service offers a choice of color, but for a price. Black stretch Cadillacs and Lincolns are $50 an hour; white or gold cars go for $60. The interiors provide all the modern-day necessities: stereos, TVs, wet bars and phones ($1 a minute).

A MESSENGER

Cannonball
875 W. Huron St.
829-1234
Open daily 24 hours.

Although there are literally hundreds of messenger services in Chicago, we've found Cannonball to be the most reliable. Packages are expeditiously delivered throughout the city and suburbs through radio dispatch. Deliveries within the downtown area average $3 to $5.

A NEWSSTAND

Eastern Newsstand
940 N. Michigan Ave.
787-2188
*Open daily 7:30 a.m.-
10 p.m.*

Located in the lobby of the One Magnificent Mile building, this newsstand sells every conceivable magazine and newspaper, both national and international. Cards, cigarettes, small gifts and foodstuffs are also available. Other locations can be found throughout the city, including Water Tower Place.

A PET HOTEL

Collar & Leash
1433 N. Wells St.
787-1751
*Open Mon.-Fri. 8 a.m.-
5:30 p.m., Sat. 10 a.m.-
4 p.m.*

Collar & Leash may be the only place in Chicago (other than the many animal hospitals) that boards both cats and dogs. And it does it in style, with five-foot pens for each animal and use of an outdoor runway when weather permits. The drop-off is in Old Town; pets are then transported to more spacious surroundings at 3541 W. Columbus Avenue on the southwest side of town (737-1323). The daily fee for dogs is $8 for small to medium sized; $9 for large and $10 for extra large (Dobermans, German shepherds, St. Bernards). Cats are $6 a day. Make reservations at least two weeks in advance during summer months and holidays.

A PHOTO LAB

Gamma Photo Labs
314 W. Superior St.
337-0022
*Open Mon.-Fri. 8:30 a.m.-
6 p.m., Sat. 9 a.m.-1 p.m.*

Professionals come here for magazine- and portfolio-quality developing. Service is friendly and efficient, and jobs can be rushed (for a price). The cost depends on how you want your shots developed—by hand or machine.

**Magic 30
Minute Photo**
320 W. Madison St.
630-0154
*Open Mon.-Fri. 7:30 a.m.-
6 p.m.*

Loads of photo shops throughout the city will develop pictures in an hour, but Magic is the only one that will do it in half the time. Prints are developed on Kodak paper. Passport photos, frames and albums are also available.

A SECRETARY

Kelly Services
55 W. Monroe St.
853-3434
Open Mon.-Fri. 7:30 a.m.-
5:30 p.m.

Founded in 1946, Kelly Services has earned its stellar reputation with bright, clean-cut temporaries who get the job done. Fees vary for services, which include secretarial, clerical, accounting, marketing, technical and light industrial. Temps are available for all three work shifts.

SHOE REPAIR

Brooks Shoe Service
111 N. Wabash Ave.
372-2504
Open Mon.-Fri. 8 a.m.-
6 p.m., Sat. 9 a.m.-4 p.m.

Brooks is far and away the best shoe-repair service in the city; those who insist upon keeping their feet expensively wrapped swear by the place. No one does a better job of restoring worn leather or resoling shoes. A women's half sole costs $14.50, a men's, $17.75; $22.50 buys a whole sole.

A TAILOR

Frank's Alterations
& Tailoring
555 W. Roosevelt Rd.
733-9121
Open Mon.-Sat. 9 a.m.-
5:30 p.m.

Frank's old-fashioned tailor shop is a little out of the way, but it's the best around for fine work, including leather. Prices are more than reasonable, which makes up for the sometimes-unfriendly attitude.

Stitt Reed
414 N. Orleans St.
661-0555

See "Cleaners."

A TRANSLATOR

Berlitz Translation
Services
2 N. LaSalle St.
782-7778
Open Mon.-Fri. 8:30 a.m.-
5:30 p.m.

If somebody wrote it, Berlitz should be able to translate it: Spanish, French, Japanese, you name it. This internationally known language house supplies experts in all languages to interpret legal documents, technical manuals and advertising copy. Consecutive and simultaneous translation services are available. Berlitz also has an office in Water Tower Place (943-4262).

Some establishments change their closing times without warning. It is always wise to call ahead.

A TUXEDO

**Gingiss
Formal Wear**
185 N. Wabash Ave.
263-7071
*Open Mon.-Wed. & Fri.
9 a.m.-6 p.m., Thurs.
9 a.m.-7 p.m., Sat. 9 a.m.-
5 p.m., Sun. noon-5 p.m.*

Tuxedos by Christian Dior, Pierre Cardin, Bill Blass and Robert Stock rent for between $57 and $75 at this reputable chain, which has 22 Chicago-area locations.

Seno Formal Wear
6 E. Randolph St.
782-1115

See "Menswear."

A VETERINARIAN

**Chicago Veterinary
Emergency Services**
3123 N. Clybourn Ave.
281-7110
*Open Mon.-Tues. & Thurs.-
Fri. 7 p.m.-8 a.m., Wed.
& Sat.-Sun. noon-8 a.m.*

Chicago Veterinary Emergency Services opens when the city's other animal hospitals close. Three full-time vets man the graveyard shift, and part-time practitioners are called in as needed. If your pet needs prolonged medical attention, Chicago Vet will keep it overnight and defer to your regular veterinarian come morning. The emergency fee is $35, plus any additional services.

**Lake Shore
Animal Hospital**
960 W. Chicago Ave.
738-3322
*Open Mon.-Sat. 9 a.m.-
6 p.m.*

Strongly recommended by many of the city's pet shops, Lake Shore is staffed by three full-time vets and one part-time. The friendly staff can be cajoled into seeing your pet, even if the appointment schedule is tight. The hospital boards animals for clients.

SIGHTS

EXPLORING THE CITY

The best time by far to be in Chicago is May through October. When the weather is rotten it's no fun chasing down all the city's sights; but during the mild seasons, it's great. Chicago is uncompact enough that a car comes in handy for serious sightseers, since some of the major attractions are in the boonies and as much as twenty miles apart. But a first-time visitor with only a few days in town has plenty to check out in the Loop and environs, much of which can be done either on foot or via public transportation.

The city can be sliced many ways: the high-rise architecture—a form invented in Chicago and then elaborated on by such sometime Chicagoans as Mies van der Rohe (his glass box at 888 N. Michigan Avenue was, like it or not, the first of these in 1954); the opulent shopping emporiums on N. Michigan Avenue's so-called Magnificent Mile; the great (urban) outdoors; the many public sculptures; the ethnic neighborhoods; the restaurants; the *real* food (the Italian beef, the ribs, the pizza); the historic saloons (The Berghoff Cafe, the Billy Goat, O'Rourke's). No matter how obvious and corny, if you haven't seen it, you haven't seen it. Besides, these things become corny for a reason: They're fun to do. The food, the grog and the shops can be explored elsewhere in these pages; herewith, a look at Chicago's most worthwhile sights.

AMUSEMENTS

Brookfield Zoo
1st Ave. & 31st St.,
Brookfield
242-2630
Open daily 9:30 a.m.-6 p.m.

Fourteen miles west of downtown, covering 200 acres, Brookfield Zoo is far more spacious than the zoo in Lincoln Park, but its collection is about the same size. A pioneer of natural-seeming environments surrounded by moats, the zoo is known for its Bear Row promenade (on hot days, the shady beer garden is also a popular spot). The new indoor Tropic World replicates three different rain forests from Africa, Asia and South America—with representative birds and animals from each carrying on in naturalistic settings, right down to the thunder-and-lightning rainstorms that break out every so often. It's supposedly the world's largest such mixed-species exhibit, and it's especially pleasing on gray winter days.

Adults $2.50, seniors & children 3-11 $1, children under 3 free; admission free on Tues. Parking $2.50 Wed.-Mon., $3 Tues.

Lincoln Park
North Side Lakefront

A bacon strip of park stretching along the lakefront more than five miles from its North Avenue end, Lincoln Park is primarily landfill, a sculpted slice of greenery, beaches and lagoons created where there had been low sand dunes and swamp. In the 1860s, Frederick Law Olmsted, Central Park's creator, had a hand in designing part of it; the northernmost sections weren't finished until the 1920s. Lincoln Park offers all sorts of recreational possibilities—public swimming beaches (the water is clean), fishing, rowboating, a lakeside chess pavilion, tennis courts, a nine-hole golf course, a skeet-shooting range, a driving range, roller skating, bike rentals, kiddie playgrounds, a bird sanctuary, a yacht club, soccer fields, baseball diamonds, even a basketball court or two. And that's not counting the Historical Society, Lincoln Park Zoo, the Academy of Sciences or the Lincoln Park Conservatory. It also has what is arguably the best urban running trail in the country. An equestrian trail in grander times, it's a soft, cinder track that weaves the length of the park and is marked at half-mile increments. The less driven also enjoy walking along it.

The section of the park around Montrose Beach (the 4200 block of N. Lake Shore Drive) is especially lively on summer weekends; it's due east of Uptown, a neighborhood Studs Terkel described as "the UN of the disadvantaged." The sights and scents and sounds suggest Latin America and Asia far more than cornfield Midwest. Montrose also has the only hill in Chicago—a manmade one, to be sure—which in winter attracts kids with sleds. Birdwatchers love a line of bushes out on the point, which they call "the magic hedge," because so many unusual birds turn up in it—this because Montrose pokes far out into the lake and looks just great to weary migrating birds faced with all those miles of concrete and bus exhaust known as Chicago.

Lincoln Park Conservatory
2400 N. Stockton Dr.
294-4770

Garfield Park Conservatory
300 N. Central Park Blvd.
533-1281

It's always a treat (especially in the dead of winter) to experience the rain-forest atmosphere hidden inside these great, graceful Victorian greenhouses, whose earliest sections date from 1891–1892. Garfield Park's is bigger, and famous for its fern and desert gardens; but Lincoln Park's is more convenient for visitors staying downtown (it's also nestled against Lincoln Park Zoo), and it has great charm. Both have seasonal flower shows (see "Goings-On" in the Basics chapter) and permanent plant collections. Among them are some happy, gigantic specimens of the same sad, stunted, withering things on your window sill at home. Be sure to check out the fiddle-leaf fig in the jungle section of the Lincoln Park Conservatory—it's been working there since the building opened.

Lincoln Park Zoo
2200 N. Cannon Dr.
935-6700
Open daily 9 a.m.-5 p.m.

Lincoln Park Zoo is the wild, beating heart of Lincoln Park, its center. It's the coziest zoo in America, and it's free. More than 2,000 animals, birds and reptiles call its 35 acres home. Trivia pursuers know it as home of the '50s TV show *Zoo Parade*, hosted by Marlin Perkins, the zoo's director for many years. The Farm in the Zoo is home to cow barns, pigpens, horse stalls and chicken shacks—a replica farm for city dwellers long removed from country origins, where kids can let a lamb nibble their fingers, feed hay to a cow and watch eggs hatch. The puffins in the new Penguin/Seabird House are cute, and the polar bears swimming laps in their chilly 260,000-gallon pool aren't to be missed. (They make their turns underwater in front of the viewing windows, putting you about eighteen inches from these huge, swimming bears.) In the winter, the Siberian tigers snooze outside on the snow, catch some below-freezing rays and are pretty cool, as is the early-morning howling chorus of the wolf pack.
Admission free.

Maxwell Street Sunday Morning Market
Halsted St. & Roosevelt Rd.

South of the University of Illinois Circle Campus, just beyond Roosevelt Road and west of Halsted Street, is a bombed-out-looking area of urban blight—weedy vacant lots, crumbled sidewalks and just a few rickety, old buildings still standing. At the turn of the century this was the center of a prosperous Jewish community. And for a hundred years on Sunday mornings, the Maxwell Street area has turned into a permanent, floating flea market and street fair, the now-vacant lots fill up at dawn with vendors hawking practically anything that can be lugged there: vegetables, used truck tires and hubcaps, antique and merely old furniture, plumbing fixtures, puppies, hot typewriters, cases of cold cream, you name it. It's wonderful, unique in America as far as we know, and while it's smaller than it used to be, Sunday morning on Maxwell Street has thusfar refused to die. Impromptu blues bands often set up and plug into car batteries, filling the morning air with "da blooz" for change in a passed hat. Old hands insist that all the really good stuff's gone by 7 a.m., and most everybody's packing up to go home by noon.

Oak Street Beach
Oak St. & Lake Shore Dr.

It's a true miracle at the north end of the Magnificent Mile: a crescent of sandy beach snuggled elegantly among the high-rises, and clean, fresh water in which to swim—right there in the middle of the city. It's the most urbane and urban public swimming beach imaginable. The concrete promenade along the water, which extends a mile north and is overlooked by high-rise apartments, is reminiscent of Copacabana Beach in Rio de Janeiro—except instead of green mountains rising in the background, Chicago's factories lurk. On a good, hot Sunday, the beach population can be nearly 50,000—bigger than most towns in Illinois. And during the week in mild seasons it's a favorite of nearby office workers on their lunch breaks, as well as high-rise moms or their nannies wheeling their designer strollers.

John G. Shedd Aquarium
1200 S. Lake Shore Dr.
939-2438
March-Oct.: open daily 9 a.m.-5 p.m.; Nov.-Feb.: open daily 10 a.m.-5 p.m.

Glub, glub, glub! This is the world's largest indoor aquarium, with hundreds of species of undersea creatures, many in psychedelic hues and configurations, as if designed by Timothy Leary or the Merry Pranksters. The big hit is the 90,000-gallon coral reef, with its various inhabitants, which are joined thrice daily (11 a.m., 2 p.m. and 3 p.m.) by a diver who hand-feeds them.

Adults $2, children 6-17 $1, seniors 50 cents, children under 6 free; admission free on Thurs.

LANDMARKS

Auditorium Theater
70 E. Congress Pkwy.
922-2110

The 1889 Auditorium Building was perhaps Louis Sullivan's masterpiece—and a distinctly American one. Rejecting various old-world neoclassicisms, he gained his inspiration from natural forms, most ornately displayed in the liquid form of the Auditorium Theater. Its swirling, plant-like lines have led certain writers to credit Sullivan with inventing art nouveau in creating this space. It is American, too, in its democratic acoustics, which are perfect—the music sounds as good in the top row of the top balcony as it does down front. Pick your favorite band or ballet and spend an evening here; these days it's used primarily for concerts.

Baha'i House of Worship
100 Linden Ave., Wilmette
256-4400

It looks like an airy three-layer confection of intricate design, rising almost 200 feet near Lake Michigan in the northern suburb of Wilmette. Usually called the Baha'i temple, its thousands of concrete swirls and arabesques took more than 30 years to complete. The soaring 135-foot auditorium is one of the highest unobstructed interiors anywhere. There is only one of these per continent, and they are dedicated to the Oneness of Mankind by the people of the Baha'i faith, which originated in Persia during the mid-nineteenth century. All are welcome to worship, meditate or simply sightsee. During the '60s, it was a favorite place for tripping hippies to visit at dawn to watch the sun come up while the temple and all its squiggles pulsed and throbbed. It's still fairly trippy—*without* any help from your chemical friends.

Billy Goat Tavern

430 N. Michigan Ave.
222-1525
Open daily 7 a.m.-2 a.m.

Truly more of a "landmark" than a restaurant/lounge, this place was the inspiration for John Belushi's famous *"Cheesebugah! Cheesebugah! Cheesebugah!"* bit on *Saturday Night Live*. Located beneath the Magnificent Mile on the lower level of Michigan Avenue at Grand just north of the river, the scruffy Billy Goat is a hangout for print and TV journalists. So keep an eye out for folks like Mike Royko while standing in line for that cheesebugah. Actually, the food is perfectly acceptable true grease, and the generations of celeb photographs that cover the walls are worth a little indigestion in any case. Its Greek former owner was responsible for the "Cubs Curse": He used to take his goat to the games, but they threw him out of the '45 World Series—the last one the Cubs played in. There's just something quintessentially *Chicaga* about the joint.

Buckingham Fountain

Grant Park near
Congress Pl.

A 1927 pink marble extravaganza of water and light, its changing sculpture-like jets of water shoot as high as 135 feet in the air, and the seasonal 9-to-10-p.m. light show is far out, man. Actually, it wears thin pretty quickly and is best seen while doing something else entirely at Grant Park, such as attending the free blues festival or Taste of Chicago.

Chicago Tribune Building

435 N. Michigan Ave.
222-3232

In 1923 the *Chicago Tribune* held a contest for the design of its new skyscraper, which was to be built on newly developing N. Michigan Avenue (the bridge across the Chicago River had opened in 1920). This impressive (if somewhat zany) 46-story Gothic tower was the winner. That the top looks like a great stone crown probably wasn't lost on the judges, since the *Trib* modestly bills itself as "The World's Greatest Newspaper." Weirdest is that embedded in the building at street level are chunks of other great buildings from antiquity—a glob of the Parthenon, a rock from some Roman ruin and so on. How did they get these little souvenirs, one might wonder? And, as our teachers used to say, what if everybody did this?

Fourth Presbyterian Church

126 E. Chestnut St.
787-4570

When it was completed in 1914, this harmonious Gothic-revival church was in a largely residential outpost of downtown. Then the area comprised mostly mansions and vacant lots. Today the church is tucked in near the end of the Magnificent Mile, surrounded by skyscrapers, among them the humongous cross-hatched John Hancock Building right across the street—making its courtyard patch of greensward framed by Gothic arches a special haven amid all the big-shoulders stuff around it.

Graceland Cemetery

4001 N. Clark St.
525-1105

No, Elvis isn't buried here, but Chicagoans of note have been since it opened in the 1860s. Originally six miles out in the country in Irving Park, and a day trip on the "dummy railroad" from the city, it was one of the first graveyards to reflect new transcendental ideas. And instead of being a drab boneyard as cemeteries had been until then, it had—and has—lovely landscaped grounds with ponds and gardens. They're now pretty much filled with Thanatotic sculpture of many different kinds: art deco crypts, neoclassic mausoleums, a Laredo Taft sculpture called *Death* that's nice and eerie, and so on. Among the great and the near-great buried here are Charles Dickens's youngest brother; the founder of the Pinkerton Detective Agency; boxer Jack Johnson; the inventor of the Pullman car; and architect Louis Sullivan, who designed many important downtown buildings as well as some of the monuments here. Free maps are available at the main building.

John Hancock Center
875 N. Michigan Ave.
751-3681

Before Big John came along in the late 1960s, the 1934 Palmolive Building a block away had been—at 36 stories—the cock of the rock in this part of town. The Lindbergh Beacon on top of it was a Midwest landmark. The Palmolive is now the Playboy Building (the art deco elevators are worth a look), and the beacon is gone—because there are so many bigger buildings nearby now, a trend initiated by the Hancock Building. Its great, black, superhuman crisscrossing girders suggest a giant tick-tack-toe game in the sky, and at 100 stories—a quarter of a mile—it's the world's tallest combination residential/commercial skyscraper. The Sears Tower is higher, the world's tallest high-rise, in fact, but the Hancock's lakefront vantage makes its building-top observatory arguably better than Sears'. On a clear day you can see... Indiana? Oh, well, you're still way up there. For fans of flatness, the view extends across 50 miles and four states. It's like landing at O'Hare without having to get into an airplane. The view at night from the 95th Restaurant will almost make you forget the prices and underwhelming food. Order lightly and devour the city instead.

Picasso Sculpture
Dearborn St. & Randolph St. (Daley Plaza)

It's a woman's face! It's a cubist poodle! It's Big Bird! Interpretations vary. Many Chicagoans set up a howl when the Picasso sculpture was first unveiled in 1967. What was it? Why was it so big? Was this some kind of joke? But in twenty-plus years, it's become one of Chicago's most prized sights. And it has led the way for other important public sculptures in the Loop, including works by Alexander Calder, Marc Chagall, Joan Miró, Henry Moore and Claes Oldenburg. The Chicago Tourism Council has an excellent Loop Sculpture Guide with a map and detailed notes on more than 30 major pieces. It's available free at the Water Tower, which is at Chicago Avenue and Michigan Avenue (467-7114); or by mail from the Chicago Office of Fine Arts, Department of Cultural Affairs, 174 W. Randolph Street, Chicago, IL 60601.

Prairie Avenue Historic District

1800-1900 S. Prairie Ave.
326-1393

Looking like the block that time forgot, this small but impressive historic district consists of several restored nineteenth-century mansions on a period cobblestone street with gaslights—all the more striking for the decay and bleak lunar poverty now so close by. But in the 1880s and '90s, Prairie Avenue was Chicago's undisputed Millionaires' Row, where George Pullman, Marshall Field and Philip Armour all lived in $200,000 mansions. Of the restored buildings, the Romanesque Glessner House at 1800 S. Prairie is the most striking. Completed in 1886, its 35 rooms and interior courtyard were designed by architect Henry Hobson Richardson—this is his only remaining building in Chicago. (One- and two-hour tours are given Thursday through Sunday; call 326-1393.) And not far away on S. Indiana is the Henry B. Clarke House, the city's oldest building. It was built in 1836 as a suburban getaway from the city's bustle, a solid but graceful Greek-revival house with an imposing four-column portico and a widow's walk. It originally stood near what is now 16th Street and Michigan Avenue, not far from the site of the Fort Dearborn Massacre. After the 1871 fire it was moved to S. Wabash, where for many years it served, without its fancy porch, as St. Paul's Church of God and Christ. In 1977 It was moved—presumably a final time—to its present site close to where it began, at 1855 S. Indiana. It has been restored (the fancy porch is back) and turned into a museum. Two-hour guided tours begin at Glessner House and include Clarke House; call 326-1393 for times and details.

Robie House

5757 S. Woodlawn Ave., Hyde Park

At first glance, this handsome, low-slung former private residence looks like the height of modernity circa 1935 or so. But it was built in 1909 by Frank Lloyd Wright and is probably the finest example of the "prairie school" homes he built around the Chicago area—most of them concentrated in Oak Park. In its use of long, low lines, wood and brick, this Hyde Park house, unfortunately not open to the public at this writing, epitomizes Wright's aesthetic, inspired by the Midwest landscape.

Sears Tower

233 S. Wacker Dr.
875-9696
Skydeck open daily 9 a.m.-midnight.

What started with the Great Pyramids—man's unquenchable thirst to build a bigger house than his neighbor—has resulted in this 1,454-foot-high skyscraper, the world's tallest building (at least for the moment; we're waiting, Mr. Trump!). Two nonstop elevators whisk a steady stream of tourists to the 103rd-floor observation deck (the building continues to rise seven more stories), which, when the weather cooperates, affords views of seemingly the entire Midwest. Designed by Skidmore, Owings and Merrill and built in 1973, the sleek, black-glass, Bauhaus-influenced office building also amuses visitors with a marvelous Calder mobile, a seven-minute multimedia show called *The Chicago Experience* and an impressive model of the building. Take that, New York!

Adults $3.75, children 4-15 $2.25, children under 4 free.

Soldier Field
McFetridge Dr.
& S. Lake Shore Dr.
663-5100

This current home of the Chicago Bears looks at first glance like the result of a time warp from ancient Greece or Rome, the well-kept ruins of some classical sports stadium—but constructed of concrete and somehow deposited on Chicago's lakefront. Opened in 1924, Soldier Field has a row of two dozen paired 100-foot columns, which, in their long parade above the field, have a certain majesty in their superfluity. But the place is too big. It once accommodated 250,000 fans, most of whom were too far away from the action to see anything; so a few years ago bleachers were put in to cut off about one-third of the seating, which is now a more modest 60,000. Soldier Field was the site of the famous Gene Tunney–Jack Dempsey "long count" fight in 1927.

Water Tower
Chicago Ave.
& Michigan Ave.
467-7114

The rain of time, with some help from bus exhaust, is slowly melting this 130-foot soft-sandstone survivor of the 1871 Great Fire, along with its companion waterworks building across the street. The effect further heightens their already medieval aspect—a hybrid prairie Gothic caught somewhere between cathedral and fortified castle. Both were completed just two years before the fire, the tower built to cover the system's standpipe. Their complex machinery was considered by many as so much newfangled tomfoolery and a waste of taxpayers' money. They were close to the lake when they were built, but a century of landfill has changed that. The old waterworks building now houses a visitor's center that offers a useful free 45-minute get-acquainted film about Chicago, as well as a shop with all sorts of Chicago memorabilia for sale.

Wrigley Field
Clark St. & Addison St.
281-5050

The most beloved park in professional baseball and the last place where the game was played only in sunlight, Wrigley Field has finally succumbed to lights and night games. But these can be avoided; most of the games still take place in sunshine, as God intended. And Wrigley Field is still "the friendly confines," whose ivy-covered walls and comfortable proportions make it the country's most enjoyable stadium in which to watch a baseball game. It was built in 1914, its upper deck added in 1927, and there's an easy complacency to the look of it that somehow embodies those confident pre-Crash times. An essential Chicago experience is going there to watch the Cubs lose.

SPECIALTIES

ARCHITECTURE

In the 1880s and '90s, Chicago basically invented the world's high-rise architecture, for better or worse. It remains the home of the world's tallest building—the Sears Tower—along with several world-class contenders, led by the John Hancock Building. Frank Lloyd Wright learned his chops here from Louis Sullivan, and many of his World War I–era "prairie school" homes can still be seen in Oak Park and elsewhere around the city. (Incidentally, Sullivan, in creating the 1889 Auditorium Building, has been credited with creating art nouveau as well.) But Wright's ideas, however true to their school, did not become the national architecture. They lost out, in part, to modernist European thinking, such as that expressed by Mies van der Rohe, a Bauhaus German architect who ended up in Chicago in flight from Hitler. Mies van der Rohe's 1954 high-rise "glass box" apartment at 888 N. Lake Shore Drive once again invented a new form in Chicago. Some of us wish he hadn't thought of it, but what can you do? And now there are such recent postmodernist puzzles as Helmut Jahn's State of Illinois Building to smile at and scratch our heads over. Chicago is an architectural bonanza, attracting building freaks the world over—downtown is virtually a great museum of innovative city architecture from the last 100 years.

The Chicago Architecture Foundation holds more than 50 different tours during the warm summer months, from "Birth of a Metropolis" (important early Loop buildings) to "Wicker Park" (an old, now primarily Hispanic neighborhood on the West Side with gobs of charming Victorian residences) and much in between. Call 782-1776 for tour information, or write the Chicago Architecture Foundation, 1800 S. Prairie Avenue, Chicago, IL 60616 for a free brochure (it's also available at the Water Tower Visitors Center).

Frank Lloyd Wright is probably Chicago's best-known architect, and many of the residences (along with one temple) he built in the west suburb of Oak Park are still standing and in splendid shape—including his own 1889 home and 1898 studio. Quite a few tours, mostly in the warmer months, originate at the Oak Park Tour Center at Forest and Lake streets. The Frank Lloyd Wright Home and Studio Foundation, which operates the tour center, also hosts an annual tour that takes place in late May. Called "Wright Plus," it's a look at the interiors of ten historic houses, half of them designed by Wright. Call 848-1500 for information on all Wright tours. Oak Park, just ten miles west of downtown, was the birthplace of Ernest Hemingway.

BANKS

First National Bank of Chicago
1 First National Plaza
732-6037
Tour times vary.

For those intrigued by the wonderful world of money, the 57-story First National Building is home to Chicago's largest bank. Tours are available if you call in advance. Admission free.

NEWSPAPERS

Chicago Sun-Times
401 N. Wabash Ave.
321-2035
Tours Mon.-Fri. 10:30 a.m.

The *Chicago Sun-Times* building, overlooking the Chicago River, might be described as Dumpy Modern—but inside it's a space-age daily newspaper plant, and guided tours of the newsroom, pressroom and composing room are held every weekday morning. Advance reservations required. Admission free.

Chicago Tribune
435 N. Michigan Ave. (newsroom), 777 W. Chicago Ave. (printing facility)
222-3232
Tour times vary.

These days the *Trib* is split in two. The editorial stuff still comes out of the Tribune Building, but it's printed over near the river on W. Chicago Avenue. Regular tours of the fairly amazing printing facility, which last about 45 minutes, are available if advance arrangements are made. Admission free.

PYRAMIDS

The Gold Pyramid House
Near the intersection of Rte. 41 & Rte. 132, Gurnee
no phone
June-Labor Day: tours Sundays, times vary.

Sure, it's only ten miles from the Wisconsin border, more than an hour from Chicago, but we're talking deeply wacky here. Yes, it's a pyramid-shaped private residence that's been gold-plated. It's oriented toward true north just as its model, the Great Pyramid of Cheops, was, and a twenty-foot-deep moat surrounds it. Like Jack Paar, we kid you not. As the brochure puts it: "This unique structure exists because of Jim Onan, the builder, and his love affair with the mysteries of ancient Egypt. It is now the luxurious home of the Onan family... The Gold Pyramid is aptly named. Its 12,000 square feet of exterior walls are completely covered with 24-carat gold plate, making it one of the largest gold-plated structures in existence. It is the only known authentic pyramid to be built in over 4,500 years. Its apex rises 55 feet above the suburban countryside..." Sounds fabulous, eh? This is a *lot* of money and effort just to get your razor blades to sharpen themselves. It's number one on the All-Kitsch Tour of greater Chicago.

Adults $7, children under 12 $4.

TOURS

BOAT

Mercury Cruise Lines
Michigan Ave. Bridge
& Wacker Dr.
332-1353

Wendella on the north side of the Michigan Avenue Bridge, and Mercury on the south, are both Chicago traditions. Several different tours of the Chicago River and Lake Michigan are offered, ranging in duration from one to about three hours. On soft summer evenings, the Lake Michigan tour is a favorite with new lovers, young or old. And the Wendella rush-hour commuter boat between the Michigan Avenue Bridge and Northwestern Station is at once cheap, quick and scenic. It ain't the *Staten Island Ferry*, or the *Star Ferry* in Hong Kong, but it has some of the same appeal.

Hours and prices vary.

Wendella Sightseeing Boats
Michigan Ave. Bridge at the
Wrigley Building
337-1446
May-Sept.: tours daily.

Shoreline Marine Sightseeing Boat
Docks at Shedd Aquarium
days, Buckingham Fountain
days & evenings, Adler
Planetarium days
& evenings
673-3399
May-Sept.: tour times vary.

These 30-minute lake excursions are available from May through September. If you don't have lots of time, they're perfect, and the part of the lakefront they poot around in is due east of the Loop and Grant Park and the Field Museum—a snazzy part of town.

Adults $4, children under 10 $1.50.

Star of Chicago
Navy Pier
644-5914
Mid May-mid Oct.: dinner cruise times vary.

This three-hour lake cruise includes brunch, lunch or dinner. Perhaps Chicago's only floating restaurant, the *Star of Chicago* leaves Navy Pier, heads south to McCormick Place, then north all the way to Evanston and back. The budget-conscious can join in the two-hour cocktails and hors d'oeuvres TGIF special on Fridays from 5:30 to 7:30; it's the cheapest cruise at $15.95 per person. Most expensive are the weekend dinner cruises at $45 per person.

BUS

Adelei Chicago Tours
8 S. Michigan Ave.,
Ste. 1120 - 781-0081

American Sightseeing Tours
530 S. Michigan Ave.
427-3100

Gray Line of Chicago Sightseeing Tours
730 W. Lake St.
454-0322
Tour times & prices vary.

These companies have guided tours of Chicago in comfy air-conditioned buses. Bilingual guides are available. Choose from standard landmark tours as well as more specialized stuff.

CTA Culture Bus
(800) 972-7000
(outside Chicago),
836-7000 (in Chicago)
May-Sept.: tours Sun. & holidays; times vary.

It's the *people's* bus tour of Chicago! As guided tours go, the prices are rock-bottom—and you get to ride on an actual CTA bus! There are three different routes—North Side, West Side and South Side—that stop at major points of interest, so you can get off to check out those that appeal to you, and then get back on the next Culture Bus that comes along (about every half hour). If you do, there's the additional price of a Supertransfer, which costs 75 cents for adults and 40 cents for seniors and kids. It's not the quickest bus tour of the city, but it is the biggest bargain. The buses leave from the Art Institute at Michigan and Adams, but can be boarded at any point along their routes.
Adults $2.50, seniors, the disabled & children 7-11 $1.25, children 6 and under free.

Chicago Motor Coach Company
5601 N. Sheridan Rd.
989-8919
Tours daily. Times vary.

Daily tours no matter the weather for those who want to do it in an old-fashioned open-air double-decker bus. Admission vary.

TRAIN

Ravenswood El Train
836-7000

This El train loops the Loop, and then zigzags northwest through the city out to Kimball and Lawrence, for many years a predominantly Jewish residential neighborhood and now home to many Korean and Thai families. Between the Loop and Kimball lie many changing neighborhoods—the factory/art SuHu district (named for Superior and Huron streets), semibombed sections around North Avenue, bungalows galore. The Ravenswood's backyard view is like peeking in their windows. Actually, "like" is too mild a word—you *can* peek through their windows on the Ravenswood El. A bargain at $1. A round trip from the Loop takes about an hour.

Admission $1.

BY HORSE

Carriage Company
Stand on Pearson St. east of Michigan Ave. next to Water Tower Place
280-8535

Coach Horse Livery
Stand a block west of Michigan Ave. at the Water Tower - 266-7878

For $25 per half hour, you can clip-clop around the northern end of the Magnificent Mile in an old-fashioned horse-drawn carriage.

ARTS

GALLERIES

It's easy to be an art enthusiast in Chicago, because virtually all of the city's galleries are located in two adjacent Near North Side districts. For years most of them were huddled like hunter-gatherers around the fire of the Museum of Contemporary Art at 237 E. Ontario Street; and a half dozen or more remain in the area, which is bounded by Michigan Avenue, Erie and Grand streets. But as area rents continued to climb, one gallery after another began bailing out to an old factory district less than a mile west, where vast spaces were renting for relative pittances (seven or eight years ago, anyway). Centering on Superior and Huron streets between Wells and Sedgwick, this new gallery district is generally called, in typical Second City fashion, SuHu (although one dealer who shall remain nameless is trying to popularize another nickname: Wee-Wee, for West of Wells). Today *most* of Chicago's interesting galleries are congregated here. But since the rents began to soar in SuHu, some galleries have begun moving on to cheaper digs farther northwest—so it's possible that one or two of the galleries listed below will have new addresses in the near future.

For a complete, up-to-date listing of what is being shown where, pick up a free copy of *Chicago Gallery News*, published three times a year and available at all the galleries and in some hotels; also by mail from *Chicago Gallery News*, 107A W. Delaware Place, Chicago IL 60610.

A number of the galleries, naturally, feature local artists in every medium you can think of and a few you can't. If it's possible to generalize about such diverse work—whether wonderfully wacky Hairy Who constructions, Roger Brown paintings, Robert Lostutter's meticulous bird people or former Chicagoan Ruth Thorne-Thomsen's primitive-looking surreal photography—it can be said that much of it has a sense of humor. Which, in turn, makes it fun to look at. So don't pass up the galleries that feature local artists to concentrate only on those showing blue-chip stuff.

The following is a selection of galleries that consistently have shows of interest, with some brief comments about their general focus and direction. In the summer, call first before visiting; many galleries have abbreviated hours during the hot months.

Roy Boyd Gallery
739 N. Wells St.
642-1606
*Open Mon.-Sat. 10 a.m.-
5:30 p.m.; summer hours
vary.*

Contemporary abstract artists are shown in a split-level space designed in a cool, constructivist style that echoes many of the artists' works. Also, unique among Chicago's galleries, there's a small, pleasant, outdoor sculpture garden out back.

CompassRose
325 W. Huron St.
266-0434
*Open Tues.-Sat. 10 a.m.-
5:30 p.m.; summer hours
vary.*

A relative newcomer to the Chicago scene, CompassRose shows works by the city's well-known artists, such as Alice Neal, as well as by its lesser-knowns.

Dart Gallery
750 N. Orleans St., 3rd Fl.
787-6366
*Open Tues.-Fri. 10 a.m.-
5:30 p.m., Sat. 11 a.m.-
5:30 p.m.*

Dart tends to specialize in the avant of the avant-garde, New York and Chicago style; it has just moved into this new space upstairs from Marianne Deson.

Marianne Deson Gallery
750 N. Orleans St., 2nd Fl.
787-0005
*Open Tues.-Sat. 10:30 a.m.-
5:30 p.m.*

A great place to see up-and-coming—and experimental—European artists and, occasionally, their spiritual cousins from Chicago. They like it a little hard-edged here.

Richard Gray Gallery
620 N. Michigan Ave.
642-8877
*Open Tues.-Fri. 10 a.m.-
5:30 p.m.*

Chicago's classic blue-chip gallery, Richard Gray features such class acts as lovely Matisse drawings and cubist photo collages by Hockney, as well as many more big-bucks, museum-quality pieces by twentieth-century heavyweights.

Richard Gray/ Superior Street
301 W. Superior St.
642-8865
*Open Tues.-Sat. 11 a.m.-
5 p.m.; summer by appt.
only.*

You'll find the same blue-chip slant—but with a more contemporary eye—as at the original gallery on Michigan Avenue.

Carl Hammer Gallery
200 W. Superior St.
266-8512
*Open Tues.-Sat. 10:30 a.m.-
5:30 p.m.; summer hours
vary.*

Get thee behind me, art school! This gallery is devoted to paintings, drawings, sculpture and objects created by self-taught artists—so-called "outsider art." Much of it is by no means "folksy" or "primitive"—just done without *Art Forum* in mind, which is what makes it so refreshing.

Rhona Hoffman Gallery
215 W. Superior St.
951-8828
Open Tues.-Fri. 10 a.m.-5:30 p.m., Sat. 11 a.m.-5:30 p.m.; summer hours vary.

One of the best Chicago galleries, Hoffman is also one of the oldest in the SuHu area. It has been a leader in showing such conceptual artists as Vito Acconci and Barbara Kruger.

Edwynn Houk Gallery
200 W. Superior St.
943-0698
Open Tues.-Sat. 10 a.m.-5 p.m.

At the time of this writing, this is the only Chicago gallery devoted exclusively to top-of-the-line twentieth-century photography: Stieglitz, Weston, Man Ray, Walker Evans, Robert Frank.

R. S. Johnson Fine Art
645 N. Michigan Ave., 2nd Fl. - 943-1661
Open Mon.-Sat. 9 a.m.-5:30 p.m.

This is another blue-chipper, with European and American paintings and prints by masters old and new; also drawings, other graphics and sculpture.

Phyllis Kind Gallery
313 W. Superior St.
642-6302
Open Tues.-Wed. & Fri.-Sat. 10 a.m.-5:30 p.m., Thurs. 10 a.m.-8 p.m.; summer hours vary.

The premier showcase for Chicago artists, especially such Hairy Who or Chicago Imagist members as Jim Nutt, Ed Pashke and Roger Brown.

Klein Gallery
356 W. Huron St.
787-0400
Open Tues.-Sat. 11 a.m.-5:30 p.m.

"We're interested in aggressive abstraction," said the young man tending things the last time we were there. "I'm not sure what that means, but... actually, the big focus is the line between painting and sculpture. Like this stuff"—gesturing to the current show—"it's up on the walls, but it's very sculptural."

Objects
341 W. Superior St.
664-6622
Open Tues.-Sat. 10 a.m.-5 p.m.

As the name implies, owner Anne Nathan shows *things*, whether folk art, minimalist sculpture or furniture (made by artists, natch).

Randolph Street Gallery
756 N. Milwaukee Ave.
666-7737
Open Tues.-Sat. noon-6 p.m.; summer hours vary.

Get it while it's new and uncompromising! This one's out in the boonies, and it's also out there on the cutting edge—or trying to be, anyway, sometimes successfully. It shows all media, sometimes previously unknown to man, along with performance art on weekends. An admirable avant enterprise.

Struve

309 W. Superior St.
787-0563
*Open Mon.-Fri. 10 a.m.-
5:30 p.m., Sat. 10 a.m.-
5 p.m.*

Struve's long suits are contemporary American art by younger artists, architectural drawings and Frank Lloyd Wright furniture, but it also has branched off into contemporary Soviet art in the last few years.

Van Straaten Gallery

361 W. Superior St.,
2nd Fl. - 642-2900
*Open Tues.-Sat. 10 a.m.-
5 p.m.*

Two floors of contemporary drawings, prints and paintings, arranged so it's possible to examine several hundred if your eyes can hold out. A good place for first-time art buyers to get their feet wet—there's lots to choose from.

Gallery Vienna

750 N. Orleans St.
951-0300
*Tues.-Fri. 10 a.m.-5 p.m.,
Sat. 11 a.m.-5 p.m.*

Austrian dining room sets *uber alles!* This gallery specializes in art objects, especially furniture, from Austria, particularly from "the Biedermeir and secession movements," according to *Gallery News.* If you know what that means, this is the place for you.

Worthington Gallery

620 N. Michigan Ave.
266-2424
*Tues.-Sat. 10 a.m.-5:30
p.m.; summer hours vary.*

This one majors in German Expressionists and "Blauer Reiter." If you know what that means...

Donald Young Gallery

325 W. Huron St.
664-2151
*Open Tues.-Fri. 10 a.m.-
5:30 p.m., Sat. 11 a.m.-
5:30 p.m.; closed Aug.
20-Sept. 6.*

This is one of our favorite galleries, often showing what we've read about in *Art Forum.* Young is especially big on the hot contemporary names in sculpture.

Zolla/Lieberman Gallery

356 W. Huron St.
944-1990
*Tues.-Fri. 10 a.m.-5:30
p.m.; summer hours vary.*

This cavernous gallery, one of the city's best, was the first in the SuHu area. Contemporary painting and sculpture are the mainstays. Among its regular artists is John Buck; his large neo-expressionist sculptures—of late, variations on a man's body with an inner man's body within, and some barbed wire in there, too—are something else.

DON'T FORGET: Gault Millau introduces you to the Best of New York, the Best of Washington D.C., the Best of Los Angeles, the Best of San Francisco, the Best of New England, the Best of France, the Best of Paris, the Best of Italy, the Best of London.

MUSEUMS

ART MUSEUMS

The Art Institute of Chicago

S. Michigan Ave.
& Adams St.
443-3600
*Open Mon. & Wed.-Thurs.
10:30 a.m.-4:30 p.m., Tues.
10:30 a.m.-8 p.m., Sat.
10 a.m.-5 p.m., Sun. &
holidays noon-5 p.m.*

If we had to pick the single most wonderful thing about Chicago, our vote would go to the Art Institute. The French Impressionist rooms are the showpieces, the most popular and rightly so. They are special favorites of sensitive, romantic undergraduates in love (and away from home) for the first time. They hold hands and sigh over Picasso's *Old Guitarist*, a print of which, along with a Spanish bullfighting poster, used to hang on the wall of every beatnik's spartan pad in the '50s. And they swoon over Seurat's huge pointillist *Sunday Afternoon on the Island of La Grande Jatte*, that placidly formal Sunday in the park that is so inviting, you want to walk into it and stretch out under a tree. And there are a couple of diaphanous lily-pad marsh scenes by Monet, who clearly wasn't wearing his glasses when he painted those lyrical violet fogs. The photography collection is superb—there's always an interesting show in the downstairs gallery. The room of Chinese buddhas and bhodisattvas (the ones who decided to stay on the wheel of existence to help others, even though they could have opted for the white-light bliss of nonexistence and nirvana) is a place to gain a bit of strength, their eternal smiles at nothingness and oblivion somehow soothing. And the original (which is surprisingly small) of Grant Wood's *American Gothic* is always good for a laugh of a different sort—as is the room devoted to Chicago real estate magnate and benefactor Arthur J. Rubloff's exotic *paperweight* collection, proof of the power of benefactors.

Suggested donation: adults $5, students $2, children $2.50.

The Museum of Contemporary Art

237 E. Ontario St.
280-2660
*Open Tues.-Sat. 10 a.m.-
5 p.m., Sun. noon-5 p.m.*

Created in 1967 as a protest against the conservative stranglehold the Art Institute had on the Chicago art scene, the MCA is avant-garde heaven, with changing shows in media ranging from minimalist sculpture to performance art, with paintings, photography, computer graphics and installations in between. There's a small permanent collection, but it's on display only sporadically, so call to find out where the frontier of art has been advanced to this week. The building seems almost deliberately bland and neutral, which allows it to change, chameleon-like, with every show.

Adults $3, students & seniors $2; admission free on Tues.

Oriental Institute

1155 E. 58th St.
702-9520
Open Tues.-Sat. 10 a.m.-4 p.m., Sun. noon-4 p.m.

According to *current* usage, anyway, the Oriental Institute is somewhat misnamed, since its collections are all objects of Near Eastern art and archaeology from Egypt, Mesopotamia (encompassing Sumer, Babylonia and Assyria), Anatolia (present-day Turkey), Persia (present-day Iran) and Syria/Palestine. Established in 1894 as part of the University of Chicago campus in Hyde Park, the Oriental Institute is incongruously housed in one of the university's ersatz-ancient-Gothic buildings. Like the Field Museum, which is about the same age, it was begun in a time when it was still easy to dig up and take home ancient treasures—grand national theft in the name of science. And, boy, did they get some good stuff. This is truly a tasty small collection, although some individual pieces are pretty big—like the fifteen-foot-tall, twenty-foot-long Assyrian human-headed bull from 700 B.C. that weighs in at about 40 tons and occupies most of one wall. There's also a twice-life-size statue of King Tut and a huge, gray stone head of a guardian bull taken from the entrance to the Throne Room of Xerxes at Persepolis, made around 450 B.C. In a city where the oldest standing building was constructed in 1837, these things have even greater resonance. Among smaller objects of interest (we're really getting back in time now: 3500 B.C. is an Egyptian stone jar shaped like a duck; a Dead Sea Scroll fragment from the time of Christ; and, for fans of early writing, an extensive collection of Mesopotamian signature stamps and cylinder seals, each one different, along with early clay tablets recording not poetry but important stuff like lawsuits and inventories (first things first). Parking around the University of Chicago is always annoying, so going by taxi is a good idea.
Admission free; donation requested.

David and Alfred Smart Gallery

5500 S. Greenwood St.
702-0200
Open Tues.-Wed. & Fri.-Sat. 10:30 a.m.-4 p.m., Thurs. 10 a.m.-7:45 p.m., Sun. noon-4 p.m.

Part of the University of Chicago, this "gallery" is really more like a small museum, located in an attractive modernist space on campus. As someone who works there once put it, "The collection is a little bit of everything. There are a few ancient and Eastern art objects (most of these are nearby at the U. of C.'s Oriental Institute), but it's mostly from medieval and Renaissance through to modernist and contemporary." Some of the standout pieces are Monet's *The Poplars,* several Henry Moore sculptures, some Rodin sculptures, Frank Lloyd Wright furniture and several famous pieces by the Chicago Imagists.

Terra Museum

664 N. Michigan Ave.
664-3939
Open Tues. noon-8 p.m., Wed.-Sat. 10 a.m.-5 p.m., Sun. noon-5 p.m.

On the trendy section of Michigan Avenue, the privately owned Terra Museum is arranged like an imperfect Guggenheim, with a rectangular room and stairways intruding here and there. A monstrous elevator takes you up to the fourth floor, and then you walk down (with a couple of upward side excursions) through the exhibits, all of it American art from the eighteenth century to the present. The display from the permanent collection always varies. The museum is strong on American impressionists, most of whose names only an art-history major would know, and some of whose paintings only a mother could love—muddy, derivative takes on French impressionist splendors (no matter how boosterish your cultural attitudes). But some are quite nice. And they are, after all, our past, which makes them interesting for their historical content even when they're not so successful as art. And there's plenty more: Among the Maurice Brazil Prendergasts and Charles Courtney Currans and others most people have never heard of are Audubons, Homers, Whistlers, Sergeants, Sheelers and Hoppers—so the Terra is definitely worth a look, bad American impressionists notwithstanding.

OTHER MUSEUMS

The Adler Planetarium
1300 S. Lake Shore Dr.
322-0300
Open Mon.-Thurs., Sat.-Sun. & holidays 9:30 a.m.-5 p.m., Fri. 9:30 a.m.-9 p.m.

Beam me up, Scotty! Lying on a point just east of the Field Museum, the Adler Planetarium is a handsome, twelve-sided structure made of pink marble, which, when it opened in 1930, was the first such planetarium in the United States. It has kept pace with technology, and its Zeiss Mark VI projector provides stunning shows featuring our friend the universe, in the dome-shaped Sky Theater—the best starry nights you'll ever hope to see. These are no mere constellations waltzing sedately overhead, with the intrusion of an occasional comet. Instead, the shows are more on the order of the special effects from *Star Wars*, taking the viewer from this earth into outer space, then back through time to the *beginning* of time—the Big Bang—fifteen billion years ago. And if the weather allows in often-cloudy Chicago, the evening Sky Shows end with a tour of Doane Observatory and "live" video views of various celestial objects through the twenty-inch telescope. There's also an extensive collection of astronomical tools of the trade, particularly scientific instruments of historic interest—altogether three floors of exhibits about various aspects of the universe, along with the history of man's attempts to get just the faintest glimmer of what's going on out there.
Admission to museum free; admission to shows varies.

The Chicago Academy of Sciences
2001 N. Clark St.
549-0606
Open daily 9 a.m.-9 p.m.

A jewel box (as natural-history museums go), this modest brick building on the west edge of Lincoln Park at Armitage is like the Field Museum trash-compacted down to a few small exhibit galleries on two floors. But every square inch is put to good use—so maybe the proper analogy is not jewel box but Manhattan apartment. Anyway, it's pretty amazing in its quiet way, and it's a great museum for kids (they especially love the dinosaur exhibits; call the Dino Hotline, 871-3466, for information). The second floor chiefly comprises the work of Dr. William Beecher, the former director, who personally built many of the dioramas artificial leaf by artificial snowflake. The museum's emphasis is on the natural history of the Midwest as shown in Beecher's dioramic scenes—a prairie, a marsh, wolves in winter. The second-floor ceiling is a view of nighttime stars before the streetlights blew them away for city dwellers. On the first floor is a walk-in replica of Chicago some 300 million years ago, during the Carboniferous Period—it was basically a marsh, supporting tree-size ferns and other prehistoric-strength plants. Though the display is only the size of a big closet, standing in there for a few moments can be a time-travel trip. Don't neglect the landing on the stairway to the second floor—in two cases tucked into the landing's wall is a comparison, using trophy-like models, of the number of species of fish in Lake Michigan before and after we all got here; naturally, a number of pre-Chicago species have bitten the big one. Then look up at the ceiling of the landing— now *you're* a fish, in this underwater view of an Indian canoe passing overhead, with a paddle dipping into the water. Like we said, they've used every nook and surface.

Adults $4, children & seniors $2.50; Mon. adults $3, children & seniors $2.

The Chicago Historical Society
Clark St. & North Ave.
642-4600
Open Mon.-Sat. 9:30 a.m.-9:30 p.m., Sun. noon-5 p.m.

The Historical Society building was recently refurbished and expanded, with added exhibit rooms and more wonderfully odd old stuff on display. Its focus is on general American as much as Chicago history, so there's everything from a famous Turner portrait of Washington to the (putative) anchors from a couple of Columbus's ships—plus the wooden shutters, or so they claim, from the house Columbus lived in on the island of Madeira (certainly a major historical relic). There's also a two-room peer-in log house of a typical eighteenth-century French settler in Illinois, including a little four-poster canopied bed that seems sadly out of place, an emblem of a natural yearning for home that shows itself in many of the frontier-French details. Another gallery offers other life-size peeks into 1840s frontier life—a stable, a printshop, candlery and so on, where the tools and everyday skills of the time are demonstrated daily. The Chicago Dioramas room encapsulates Chicago history into eight dramatic, miniature 3-D scenes that are both silly and informative. These include one of General "Mad Anthony" Wayne, after the 1795 Battle of Fallen Timbers, forcing the defeated Indians to sign over prime real estate that included Chicago-to-be. In a horseshoe around the dioramas are five rooms also devoted to Chicago history, arranged chronologically, with terrific odds and ends of the city's past. The antiques dealers would start hyperventilating if they got their hands on this stuff: seventeenth-century French maps that spell it "Checagau," so named for the wild onions that grew along the Chicago River; the first newspaper, from 1833, detailing big plans to build canals; a poster of John Wilkes Booth playing Chicago in *Hamlet* a week before he shot Lincoln; a pictoral history of how the modern high-rise first evolved in Chicago; a copy of the first *Playboy*, a six-pack of now-defunct Old Chicago beer; a mannequin of Walter Payton in full number-34 Bears uniform; and Chicago's first locomotive, retired in 1874 (a hole was ripped in the building to get it in). Special shows, often on non-Chicago subjects, are sometimes mounted; a typical recent one was "William Wordsworth and the Age of English Romanticism," with lots of original Wordsworth manuscripts, drawings by Blake, Constable and J.M.W. Turner paintings and so on. The Society's giftshop/bookstore has a better selection of books about the Chicago area than does anywhere else in town.

Adults $1.50, children & seniors 50 cents; admission free on Mon.

Du Sable Museum of African-American History
740 E. 56th Pl.
947-0600
Open Mon.-Wed. & Fri.-Sat. 9 a.m.-5 p.m., Thurs. & Sun. noon- 5 p.m.

This small museum on the edge of Washington Park, facing a formal sunken garden, is devoted to exhibits tracing African-American history. It is named for Jean Baptiste-Pointe Du Sable, a Haitian of mixed African and European parentage. In 1779 he became the first non-Indian settler in the area that was to become Chicago (his cabin was located near the mouth of the Chicago River). He became a prosperous trader and married the daughter of a Potawatomi chief, which improved his standing with the local Indians, who weren't exactly thrilled by the appearance of the Europeans. He sold out in 1800 and kept moving west until his death in 1818 in St. Charles, Missouri. The nose of a bronze bust of Du Sable just inside the main entrance shines from the many friendly rubs it has received over the years since the museum's opening in 1961. The exhibits are drawn from a permanent collection of 800 works of art, mainly from the W.P.A. period through the present, and a library of more than 10,000 volumes. There's also much miscellaneous material of interest among the displays on important African-Americans, including Muddy Waters's electric guitar and 1971 Grammy Award, the now-cracked and ancient-looking boxing gloves Joe Louis wore when he won the Golden Gloves in 1934, and the christening dress of poet Langston Hughes. Among those honored is one Bessie Coleman, the world's first black female pilot, whose first 1921 license is displayed alongside photos of her exploits.

Adults $2, students & seniors $1, children 50 cents.

Field Museum of Natural History

Roosevelt Rd.
& Lake Shore Dr.
922-9410
Open daily 9 a.m.-5 p.m.

Begun by a department-store magnate in the 1890s, back when it was still possible to plunder the world's archaeological, anthropological and natural treasures with impunity, the Field Museum has the third best such collection in the country—and is in many ways one of our own favorite Chicago museums. It's somehow soothing simply to walk inside, into the vaulting main hall and its greeting committee of dinosaurs. With enough time and attention, it's possible to educate yourself here in many areas. Its incredibly diverse collections are like the world's attic, with explanatory notes. The new "Plants of the World" hall has splendid life-like dioramas (don't miss the jaçana birds perched on giant Amazonian water lilies, whose leaves look like green, eighteen-inch deep-dish pizza pans) and plant models so real-looking that it's hard to believe they aren't. The North American bird collection is nearly complete and presents the opportunity to see confusing fall warblers and usually distant ducks up close, if sometimes a bit faded and dusty. The Orientalia is also heavy duty, and the Northwest Coast Indian totem-pole room is absolutely transporting.

Adults $2, children $1, seniors 50 cents; admission free on Thurs.

The Museum of Broadcast Communications

800 S. Wells St.
(River City)
987-1500
Open Wed.-Fri. & Sun. noon-5 p.m., Sat. 10 a.m.-5 p.m.

This new museum is located in the also-new River City complex—what real estate types call an "anchor" in the redevelopment of this area south of the Loop, a sleek, gray, postmodernist high-rise barnacle colony on the south branch of the river. There are a number of marginally interesting artifacts in one large room—among them Edgar Bergen's actual Charlie McCarthy and Mortimer Snerd puppets and a good selection of old radios and TVs, probably including the ones your parents and grandparents had. But the museum is primarily a tape library, with viewing/listening booths (the collection includes vintage radio as well as TV shows) available for the price of admission. It's not really worth the trip if you don't plan to watch anything from the video library, which is both a useful archive and lots of fun on days when the weather's rotten—like having the ultimate cable service. The top-five most-requested hits recently were, in order: *The Funniest Commercials of All Time, The Best of Ernie Kovacs, The Bullwinkle Show, The 100 Greatest Commercials* and *The Joe Sedelmeier Demo Reel*, a tribute to the man behind all those strange wide-angle commercials (Madison Avenue must love this museum). In the radio division it was *Vic and Sade,Fibber McGee and Molly, The Last Flight of the Hindenberg, Tom Mix* and *Chase & Sanborn*. The Kraft Video Theater auditorium regularly shows selections from the collection in state-of-the-art circumstances, and on Saturday afternoons a popular nostalgia radio show called *Those Were the Days* is broadcast from the museum.

Adults $3, students $2, seniors & children under 13 $1.

Museum of Science and Industry

57th St. & Lake Shore Dr.
684-1414
Memorial Day-Labor Day: open daily 9:30 a.m.- 5:30 p.m. Other months: open Mon.-Fri. 9:30 a.m.- 4 p.m., Sat.-Sun. & holidays 9:30 a.m.-5:30 p.m.

Since its opening as part of the Century of Progress in 1933, this has been one of the world's best hands-on museums. It can be played with like some vast toy—which is probably why the Museum of Science and Industry is the single most popular tourist attraction in the entire Midwest. There are more than 2,000 exhibits in 75 major halls. You can descend into a remarkable life-size coal mine; get an idea of what life was like on an actual captured German U-boat from World War II; trade whispers in the echo gallery; walk through a fifteen-foot human heart; and punch buttons and turn cranks to your heart's content. The real human body displayed in twenty or so cross sections from head to foot is both gruesome and informative, a favorite of the preteen set. There are eighteenth-century stagecoaches, historic aircraft hanging from the ceiling, antique automobiles, a model Santa Fe railroad the size of a basketball court and the new Space Center with an advanced-optics Omnimax Theater, which takes you on a beyond-2001 ride in space. The prosaic turn-of-the-century Main Street seems uncannily authentic, and its old-fashioned ice cream shop is a great place to take a breather before pressing on to the 22,000-piece miniature circus or *Ships Through the Ages*. There's no better place to take the kids when the weather's rotten.

Admission free.

The Peace Museum

430 W. Erie St.
440-1860
Open Tues.-Wed. & Fri.- Sun. noon-5 p.m., Thurs. noon-8 p.m.

This modest museum with high aims attempts to educate people about peace and war, and why the former is preferable, through changing, well-mounted exhibits, videos and live performances. The permanent collection includes a variety of unusual objects, among them a guitar that once belonged to John Lennon.

Adults $2, students, children & seniors 50 cents.

Spertus Museum

618 S. Michigan Ave.
922-9012
Open Mon.-Thurs. & Sun. 10 a.m.-5 p.m., Fri. 10 a.m.-3 p.m.

Spertus has the largest collection of Judaica in the Midwest, with changing exhibits from the permanent collection plus shows in the Ann C. Field Gallery. A recent special exhibit in several rooms focused on the trial of Adolph Eichmann, including television footage of the war criminal testifying from his bulletproof acrylic box. In a nearby Zell Holocaust Memorial room are heartbreaking objects retrieved from Auschwitz (wedding rings fused together by heat, a muddy, crumpled child's leg brace attached to a destroyed little shoe...), along with a window of Nazi memorabilia: SS Trooper hats, arm bands and swastika buttons, all the more chilling given where they are sitting.

On happier notes, many of the exhibits showcase objects related to religious observance. These include ancient Torahs in beautifully embellished cases; silver yads (Torah pointers) and rimmonim (Torah finials) from the 1890s; silver Passover plates; Hannukah lamps from various times and places; and hadas, the silver spice boxes made in a variety of forms (one a fish, another a miniature Gothic tower) and used for Havdalah, the service marking the ending of the Sabbath, the start of the new week and the return to the mundane everyday world. There are also objects associated with bar mitzvah and traditional circumcision—an elegantly made but still basically chisel-shaped knife, little silver scissors, a "circumcision leg tie," two little silver bowls and what looks to a noninitiate like a saltshaker. Adults $3.50, children, students & seniors $2.

MUSIC & DANCE

Chicago has several national treasures, chief among them the Chicago Symphony Orchestra directed by Sir George Solti. It is by consensus currently one of the world's best, and its home, Orchestra Hall, is an architectural treasure. The season runs through autumn and winter. But the CSO isn't the only classical music act in town (or environs). The Lyric Opera season goes full force at the same time as the CSO's, and The Chicago Chamber Music Alliance performs regular concerts. In summer, the classical music at Ravinnia (much of it provided by members of the CSO in various configurations) is literally a picnic, since you're encouraged to bring a basket and spread a quilt on the ground. The city offers free classical music concerts all summer long in Grant Park, and there are always once-only concerts around town, as well as such short summertime festivals as the Woodstock Mozart Festival and the ever-popular Romantic Organ Festival in Evanston.

Dance offerings on a regular basis are somewhat more limited, but two companies—the jazz-dancing Hubbard Street Dance Company and the more modern/experimental MoMing Dance & Arts Center–generally have something happening. The MoMing space is fun, because it looks like a junior-high gym, sometimes taken over by dancers from outer space.

For information on these and other dance performances, call the Chicago Dance Arts Coalition, 419-8383.

THEATER

The Chicago theater scene is lively and varied. More than 50 theaters are sprinkled throughout the city, with another two dozen in the suburbs. And that's not counting the "floating" ensemble companies, such as American Blues Theater, whose productions don't have a regular home. The range is enormous: from corny suburban dinner-theater revivals starring faces from old TV shows to uncompromising neo-Brechtian cabarets (such as Lower Links) that are heavy on esoteric performance art—with plenty in between. Some of the more consistently interesting are the "Chicago-style" Steppenwolf (John Malkovich's home theater), the sometimes hippie-dippie Organic Theater, the Broadway-style Goodman Theater and satirical standby Second City.

Two good sources of information about performances are the *Chicago Reader*, a free weekly found in shops, libraries and such, mainly in lakefront neighborhoods, and the monthly *Chicago* magazine, available at all newsstands. Or telephone the 24-hour Curtain Call hotline, 977-1755.

Tickets are available through Theater Tix, a charge-by-phone service (853-3636), open daily from 10 a.m. to 8 p.m. except for major holidays.

For half-price, same-day tickets, try the Hot Tix Booth at 24 S. State Street. It's open Monday from noon to 6 p.m., Tuesday to Friday 10 a.m. to 6 p.m. and Saturday 10 a.m. to 5 p.m, with tickets for Sunday performances sold on Saturday. Other locations can be found in Evanston at the Sherman Avenue garage between Church and Davis streets (Tuesday to Saturday 10 a.m. to 3 p.m.) and in Oak Park at the Park Square Atrium, Lake and Marion (Tuesday to Saturday 10 a.m. to 3 p.m.). Be warned that cash is the only form of payment accepted.

BASICS

AT YOUR SERVICE

FOREIGN EXCHANGE

Most of the major down town banks will change money, slowly and grudgingly. That is, if they're open, which is rare.

To change most foreign currencies into dollars, or to obtain lire, sucres or yuan, Deak Illinois, Inc., 111 W. Washington Street, 236-0042, has a street-level office in the Loop that's handy. Open Monday to Friday 9 a.m. to 5 p.m.

World Money Exchange, 6 E. Randolph Street, 641-2151, also handles all major currencies. Open Monday to Friday 9 a.m. to 5 p.m.

Travelers wishing to change money at O'Hare will find First Chicago and Independence Bank outlets located in Terminal Four, the international terminal, on the ground floor between customs and the ticket counters. It's open Sunday to Thursday 10 a.m. to 8 pm., Friday and Saturday 8 a.m. to 8 p.m. Two mobile carts are available to meet many of the international flights. They handle 50 major currencies and on a good day change up to $60,000.

LATE NIGHT

BABYSITTER

American Registry for Nurses & Sitters, 3921 N. Lincoln Ave., 248-8100 or 348-8514. Overnight sitters are available, but call in advance, especially if it's a weekend. Rates are $5 an hour for one to two children of the same family, higher for more children, and there's a four-hour minimum. After 9 p.m., for nonovernight sitters, you must either take the sitter home or pay for cabfare.

CAR REPAIR

AAA Motor Club, 800-262-6327.

CHILDREN'S EMERGENCY SERVICES

Most emergency rooms serve adults primarily, even in trauma centers, and the quality of care for children is uneven. The safest place for a child to be accurately diagnosed and treated is the Children's Memorial Hospital Emergency Room, 2300 N. Children's Plaza, Fullerton and Lincoln, 880-4000.

DENTIST

Chicago Dental Society Referral Service, 726-4321. Three dentists are on call around the clock.

DOCTOR

Chicago Medical Society, 515 N. Dearborn St., 670-2550. Referrals daily 8:30 a.m. to 4:30 p.m. For after-hour problems, call a convenient hospital emergency room; they're all listed in the Yellow Pages.

LIMOUSINE

AMMS Limo Service, 733-0354, is the only one with 24-hour dispatching all over the city. Its 110 vehicles—Cadillacs, Olds and Lincolns—will go for pickups anytime, anywhere in the Chicago area.

LOCKSMITH

What's the biggest middle-of-the-night problem? "Lockouts," said the man from AAA Security, with the authoritative tone of one who's been there. It's not cheap to lose those keys in the middle of the night—most 24-hour locksmiths charge more than $50 just to say hello.

AAA Security & Communications Systems, 248-1411. Emergencies 24 hours, all over the city. You'll pay a $55 minimum for middle-of-the-night calls.

Amazing Lock Service, 935-8900. On call 24 hours to the North and West sides. Minimum $45.

Cleo's Lock & Keys, 6701 S. Ashland Ave., 434-2000. Also 24 hours. Located on the South Side but will go all over the city; charges a $40 minimum.

D & J Lock Surgeon, 4107 N. Kedzie St., 463-8373. A 24-hour emergency service covering a ten-mile radius from Irving and Kedzie. A $65 minimum for middle-of-the-nighters.

PHARMACY

Twelve Walgreens citywide have all-night pharmacies. Among them:
757 N. Michigan Ave. (corner of Chicago), 664-8686
7501 S. State St., 224-1211
3302 W. Belmont Ave., 267-2328
1554 E. 55th St., 947-8886.

PHOTOCOPY

Kinko's Copies, 2451 N. Lincoln Ave., 327-7770. Open 24 hours, seven days a week. Two other 24-hour Kinko's are at 444 N. Wells St. (670-4460) in Old Town and 1309 E. 57th St. (643-2424) in Hyde Park.
Assurance Graphic Services, 209 W. Jackson St., 786-9220. Open 24 hours Monday to Friday, and Saturday until 4:30 p.m.

PICKUP & DELIVERY

Choose from two round-the-clock messenger services: Cannonball, 829-1234, and U.S. Messenger, 326-6300.

RESTAURANTS

All-night restaurants, coffee shops and diners are found all over Chicago, but, naturally, some have more to offer than others, whether in character or chow or both. Here are a few essential stations of the late-night cross:
Belden Corned Beef Center, 2315 N. Clark St. at Belden, 935-2752. Here, 24 hours a day, you can get a blintz to kill for, as well as other European/Jewish treats—along with a great deal more from the six-page menu. A plain, well-lighted place that's a Sunday breakfast favorite, too.
The Busy Bee, 1546 N. Damen St., 772-4433. An all-nighter in Logan Square, serving good, solid coffee-shop food. The Hispanic neighborhood is currently under invasion by starving artists, so now it's sprinkled

with insomniac sculptors and intense-looking Brechtian directors.

Diner Grill, 1635 W. Irving Park Rd., 248-2030. Edward Hopper's "Nighthawks" lives! A 24-hour diner of the old school—lots of too-white fluorescent light, stainless steel and Formica. The best postparty, after-the-bars-close diner cheeseburger and fries around. The coffee is good and strong, and the ham for your eggs is cut from the bone before your very eyes. Also old-fashioned made-by-humans shakes and malts, unlike the cement that passes for the form today.

Jeff's Laugh-In Restaurant and Cocktail Lounge, 1800 N. Lincoln Ave., 751-0434. Kinda basic, foodwise, but a longtime after-hours hangout (open 24 hours) for the actors and musicians working in nearby Old Town clubs, ranging from Second City to The Bulls.

Lawrence's Fisheries, 2120 S. Canal St., 225-2113. A 24-hour stand-up, takeout-only, fried-seafood joint right on the canal. In an industrial-strength neighborhood, surrounded by factories, it's *the* place for 3 a.m. french-fried shrimp, catfish, frogs' legs, seafood gumbo and smoked chubs. Always busy, day or night.

McDonald's, 600 N. Clark St., 664-7940. A Mc-trendy, Mc-all-night McDonald's, done up in pop '50s and '60s memoro-trash... but it's the same old food.

Oak Tree, 25 E. Oak St., 751-1988. This 24-hour coffee shop at Oak and Rush streets offers standard-issue coffee-shop food, edible if forgettable. But it wins the all-night people-watching award hands down. Sailors on leave, transvestites in training, conventioneers, working girls and boys, you name it.

El Presidente, 2558 N. Ashland Ave., 525-7938. A round-the-clock Mexican restaurant whose regulars swear by the pozole, a spicy dish somewhere between soup and chili.

Scampi Restaurant, Hyatt Regency Hotel, 151 E. Wacker Dr., 565-1234. Part of a Jetsons-moderne lobby suggesting a 21st-century resort in the Asteroid Belt, with multilevel 3-D fountains and piano bars and curving stairways in a great vaulting glass-enclosed space, this all-nighter boasts a trendy upscale menu at trendy upscale prices.

Star Top Café, 2748 N. Lincoln Ave., 281-0997. This deceptively modest-looking storefront on N. Lincoln is one of the recent Pick Hit nouvelle restaurants in town, and on Fridays and Saturdays it's open from 5:30 p.m. until 5 a.m.; other nights it closes by 11 p.m. It's not cheap, but everybody seems to love it.

TELEPHONE NUMBERS

Ambulance, 911
Amtrak, 558-1075
Animal-bite Reporting, 911
Birdwatching Hotline, 671-1522
Camping, 917-2070
Chicago Tourism Council, 280-5740
Chicago Transit Authority (C.T.A.), 836-7000
Children's Emergency Services, 880-4000
Coast Guard, Search & Rescue, 353-0278
Concert/Theater Tickets: Ticketron, 853-3636; Ticket Exchange, 902-
    1888; Ticketmaster, 559-1212
Dial-a-Poem, 346-3478
Directory Information, 411
Fire & Rescue, 911
LaSalle Street Station (Metro R.T.A. commuter trains), 322-6505
Library Information, 269-2900
Lottery Information, 449-9110
Marriage Licenses, 443-5663
Meigs Field, 744-4787
Midway Airport, 767-0500
Northwestern Station (Chicago & Northwestern): Commuter Informa-
    tion, (800) 972-7000; General Information, 559-7000
O'Hare Airport, 686-2200
Paramedics, 911
Parks, 294-2493
Passports, 353-5426
Poison Control, 942-5969
Police Emergencies, 911; Nonemergencies, 744-4000
Postal Information, 765-3210; Zip Code Information, 765-3585
Randolph Street Station: Chicago South Shore Line, 782-0676; Illinois
    Central Railroad, 836-7000
Regional Transit Authority (R.T.A.), 836-7000
Taxis, 248-7600 (American United), 829-4222 (Checker and Yellow),
    561-1444 (Flash)
Time, 976-1616
Weather, 976-1212

GETTING AROUND

AIRPORT TRANSPORTATION

O'HARE INTERNATIONAL AIRPORT

Yes, it's one of the world's busiest airports, changing-planes central. One thing people love about *living* in Chicago is that they rarely have to change planes to fly anywhere in the United States—and, increasingly, worldwide. Recently O'Hare has also seemed like the world's latest-running airport, although the situation is supposedly improving. The handsome, new United Terminal, which looks like a 21st-century Victorian train station, claims to set new efficiency standards.

Unfortunately, getting between downtown Chicago and O'Hare can take as long as some of the shorter flights. Located seventeen miles northwest of the Loop on the Kennedy Expressway (I-90/94), O'Hare *can* be reached in about a half hour by car. But the Kennedy is the least predictable of expressways. The city is always fixing it, for one thing, and traffic jams congeal at the most unexpected times in both directions. Old hands always allow 90 minutes before flight time, minimum—and that's in a taxi or private car.

Continental Air Transport's bus line services O'Hare, with pickups and drop-offs at more than 30 downtown hotels. Call 454-7800 for locations and times (and estimates of when to leave to make your plane). One-way fare is $9, $16 round trip.

If you're traveling light, the cheapest and fastest way to go is the Chicago Transit Authority (C.T.A.), whose O'Hare trains reliably take about 35 minutes from the Dearborn Street subway station downtown, arriving beneath the main parking garage in a pleasant new station at O'Hare. This train may be boarded at stops all along its route as well, and it runs frequently 24 hours a day. The fare is an unbeatable $1, but be prepared to do some walking to reach your gate.

Arriving visitors *not* heading downtown can opt for small van and bus services to most towns and suburbs as far away as Milwaukee, Rockford and Gary, Indiana. Call O'Hare general information, 686-2200, for details.

Taxis are almost always abundant at O'Hare for arriving visitors. The drivers usually grumble if you're not going somewhere near downtown, and suburban destinations are prorated according to a fixed schedule. To get to O'Hare from the city by taxi, try Abernathy's Jiffy Cabs (487-9000), American United (248-7600), Flash (561-1444) and Yellow and Checker (829-4222); they take phone orders 24 hours a day. It's usually about $25, plus tip, to or from downtown. Batches of limo services (check your hotel's concierge or the Yellow Pages) will get you there in a Caddy or a Rolls for about $60.

CHICAGO MIDWAY AIRPORT

Named for the crucial Pacific-island battle that began turning things our way during World War II, Midway was the world's busiest before O'Hare took over in the '50s. It's not that much closer to downtown than O'Hare, and the chaotic holiday crunch at Midway can still be time-consuming and aggravating, but it's generally a breeze compared to the Big O. Seven airlines—America West, Chicago Air, Continental, Midway, Northwest, Southwest and United—currently land there. It's especially worth checking out for hops of 600 miles or less.

Midway is on the Southwest Side at 5500-6300 S. Cicero Avenue and is reached from downtown by taking the Stevenson Expressway (I-55) to Cicero and then going south three miles on Cicero to the airport. In a car or taxi, during nongridlock hours allow a minimum of 60 minutes before flight time, with 90 minutes during rush hours.

Continental Air Transport has Midway shuttle buses that stop at a dozen or so downtown hotels. One-way fares are $7.50, round trip $13. Call 454-7800 for locations and times.

Getting to Midway on public transportation is a little tougher. From downtown, take the Douglas B Train from Dearborn Street stations at Washington, Monroe or Jackson to the street-level station at Cicero Avenue, then transfer to a 54B bus southbound on Cicero. Call 836-7000 (Chicago Transit Authority) for specifics.

See the O'Hare section for information about taxis and limos. Roughly speaking, the cost from downtown is about the same to both airports.

MEIGS FIELD

Lear-jet heaven, right along the lakefront at 15th Street, Meigs Field is the small, downtown businessman's airport. Continental Express operates between here and Springfield, Illinois—but otherwise it's all private planes and charters. Open 6 a.m. until 10 p.m. Call 744-4787 for information.

CARS

Chicago is spread out enough (and the driving isn't so hideous) that having a rental car during a visit can be really helpful—if only for a drive along the splendid twenty miles of lakeshore from city limit to city limit.

Among the several rental-car companies are Avis (800-331-1212), Hertz (686-7272), Budget (968-6661), Dollar (671-5100), Thrifty (298-3383) and National (800-328-4567). Despite their names, who's cheapest depends on that week's special. A spot check of these six for a new four-door sedan rented out of O'Hare for a week proved Avis most expensive and—surprise!—old number-one Hertz the cheapest of the bunch, a full $60 lower than Avis. But it could be the other way around tomorrow, so it pays to check. It's also cheaper in most cases to rent from the airport than from offices downtown. For Midway travelers and others on the Southwest Side, Rent-A-Wreck (585-7300) has '85 and '86 Plymouths for about half what the others charge. And big spenders can find the perfect overpriced four-wheel personal statement at Atlantic Luxury Rentals (439- 9997).

PUBLIC TRANSPORTATION

CHICAGO TRANSIT AUTHORITY

Chicago's public transportation system is by far the best way to get around along certain major routes—and not so hot along others. Lifelong bus and El train riders rightly complain that the Chicago Transit Authority (C.T.A.: 836-7000) system has gone noticeably downhill in the last twenty years, with routes completely eliminated or cut back, less 24-hour service on some routes and fewer buses or trains per hour. And one lifetime rider, who times them for amusement, swears that El trains got you there faster back in the '50s—this due to what he regards as wimpy new safety regulations regarding train speed.

Nevertheless, the El trains remain a great way to get around—except maybe late at night. For many destinations around the city they're simply much faster than any other means of transportation. They're the best way to go to or from a baseball game at both Wrigley Field and Comiskey Park, for instance—no parking problems once when you get there. They're also the quickest and cheapest way to O'Hare—when the equipment's working (our regular rider says breakdowns aren't as infrequent as they should be). And some of the El trains are also swell for sightseeing, particularly a ride on the Ravenswood, which forms a loop around the Loop, and then zigzags above ground through neighborhoods to the Northwest Side, ending at Kimball Avenue. Most El routes operate 24 hours a day—*except* Evanston Express, Ravenswood and Skokie Swift. Service operates every 5 to 15 minutes all day and evening, and every 15 to 60 minutes overnight. The fare is $1, with 25-cent transfers, allowing two additional rides on C.T.A. buses and trains or PACE (suburban) buses.

The C.T.A. buses are often another story. You can wait 40 minutes for the number-22 Clark Street bus, and then three of them will show up one after another. In good weather and heavy traffic, walking is usually just as fast—and often faster downtown and along Michigan Avenue. But for the patient, the bus routes form a grid on the city and can get you within three or four blocks of wherever you want to go.

Call 836-7000 for El train and C.T.A. bus directions and schedules.

REGIONAL TRANSIT AUTHORITY

The Regional Transit Authority (R.T.A.) runs the PACE bus system, which covers the six counties surrounding Chicago, with frequent service stopping at many points. Call 836-7000 for specifics. Information regarding the half-dozen commuter rail systems serving the Chicago area is available at the same number. Including Amtrak, eight different rail lines fan out of the city to various suburbs and exurbs—a relic of the days when Chicago was the country's undisputed major railroad hub.

TAXIS

As in every big city, cab driving is an entry-level job for Chicago newcomers, so these days you'll ride with fewer grizzled 30-year veterans boiling over with philosophy. Instead you'll be transported by neophytes from all over—India, Africa, the Caribbean, South America. This can be fun and educational if you can get them to talk about home; it can be a pain if they're so new they don't know the city well. So when taking a cab, it pays to come armed with directions. Except during the thick of rush hour and during rotten weather, taxis are readily available for hailing downtown and north along the lakefront just about up to Irving Park (4000 N.). The light on top is lit when they're empty. Tip the good ones fifteen to twenty percent, and stiff the kamikaze jerks who blow through red lights and such. The flag fee at this writing is $1 for the first mile, 90 cents for each additional mile, plus 10 cents every 35 seconds you're stuck in traffic and 50 cents for each additional person. Yellow and Checker (829-4222) have 24-hour radio-dispatched cabs citywide. On the South Side, Abernathy's Jiffy Cab (487-9000) is good, as is Jimmy Morgan Taxicab Associates (684-1111). And North Siders have relied on Flash (561-1444) for years.

GOINGS-ON

Frank Sinatra didn't call Chicago "that toddlin' town" for nothing. There's always *something* cooking, day and night, whether you're a birdwatcher or a member of the dedicated party set.

The most extensive and up-to-the-minute events listings are in the *Chicago Reader*, an excellent weekly paper that comes out on Thursdays and is distributed free in drugstores, public libraries and, soon, in lakeshore neighborhoods from Evanston to Hyde Park.

And the Chicago Tourism Council publishes a detailed yearly calendar of a variety of onetime and annual events of all sorts. It's available—as is current information about these events—at the Historic Water Tower, 806 N. Michigan Avenue, Chicago, IL 60611, 280-5740.

Here's a sampler of some of the usual suspects:

JANUARY

Christmas Flower Show at Lincoln Park Conservatory, Fullerton and Stockton, 294-4770, and Garfield Park Conservatory, 300 N. Central Park Blvd., 533-1281. The Christmas shows last into January, but it's always a treat (especially in the dead of winter) to enter the rain-forest atmosphere inside these great Victorian greenhouses, whose earliest sections date from 1891-1892. Garfield Park is bigger, but Lincoln Park has great charm. Be sure to check out the fiddle-leaf fig in the jungle section of the latter; it's been there since the building opened.

Chicago Symphony Orchestra at Orchestra Hall, 220 S. Michigan Ave., 435-8122. By January, the season is in full swing. Hearing Solti conduct the C.S.O. for an evening of Mozart, say, is probably as close to heaven as you'll get in Chicago without the use of illegal stimulants.

Ice Skating, Daley Plaza, 337 E. Randolph St., 294-4790. Throughout the winter, ice skates are rented at Daley Plaza for skating among the high-rises, under the smile (isn't it?) of the Picasso sculpture.

Sport Fishing, Travel & Outdoors Show, O'Hare Exposition Center, Rosemont, 692-2220. Generally held in late January or early February, it's timed to be welcome proof to shivering, house-happy Chicagoans that life is not all snow, subzero cold and gray skies.

FEBRUARY

Midwest RV, Camping & Travel Show, O'Hare Exposition Center, Rosemont, 692-2220. This follows almost immediately after January's Outdoors Show, for those who can't get enough, and yearn to join the Winnebago set.

Blackfolk, Chicago Office of Fine Arts, Chicago Public Library Cultural Center, 78 E. Washington St., 744-6630. Various events celebrating Black History Month.

Black Achievers in Science, Museum of Science & Industry, 57th and Lake Shore, 684-1414. More Black History Month exhibits.

Azalea and Camellia Show, Lincoln and Garfield Park conservatories, 294-4770 or 533-1281. Take the chill off the wind-chill factor with a look at these blooms.

Chinese New Year Parade, starting at Wentworth and Cermak, the official gateway to Chinatown, 225-6198. The first of Chicago's many ethnic celebrations and parades held throughout the year.

Medinah Shrine Circus, Medinah Temple, 600 N. Wabash Ave., 266-5000. This small circus returns every year to Medinah Temple; it's another cheery way to hide from winter for an afternoon.

Midwest Boat Show, O'Hare Exposition Center, Rosemont, 692-2220. Continuing the adventure theme of the Outdoors and RV shows mentioned above.

MARCH

Annual Atrium Arts & Crafts Show, State of Illinois Center, Randolph St. and Clark St., 895-3710.

Women's Film & Video Festival, Facets Multimedia, 1517 W. Fullerton Ave., 281-4988. A weeklong presentation of videos and films by and for women (and their friends).

St. Patrick's Day Parade (March 17th), Dearborn St. and Wacker Dr., 744-3370. Easily Chicago's most raucous parade, and probably the year's biggest; along with the beer, the whole town turns green, and sane people don't drive after 6 p.m.

Maxwell Street Sunday Morning Flea Market (Sundays from dawn to noon), 1200 S. Roosevelt Rd. at Halsted. Technically, it's a year-round event, but no one goes until the spring thaw. Probably unique in the United States and an essential Chicago experience, this permanent floating flea market is held among the lunar remains of a semiflattened, poor, old neighborhood south of the University of Illinois's Circle Campus. Street-blues bands plug in to car batteries and fill the morning air with their sweet, gritty sounds, while impromptu street stands offer for sale everything imaginable that's portable enough to bring there—from new puppies to antique bedsteads and hot typewriters to cold drinks.

APRIL

International Kennel Club Dog Show (late March-early April), McCormick Place North, 23rd St. and Lake Shore Dr., 237-5100. *Do* the owners resemble their prize barkers? There's only one way to find out.

Cubs and White Sox seasons open, Wrigley Field, Addison St. and Clark St., 281-5050, and Comiskey Park, 35th St. and Dan Ryan Expressway, 924-1000. Often the other dogs in town are the Cubs and/or Sox, but it's always fun to watch the Cubs lose in the "friendly confines" of Wrigley Field, the most beloved park in professional baseball.

Spring and Easter Show, Lincoln Park and Garfield Park conservatories, 294-4770 and 533-1281. It may not *look* like spring outside just yet, but it's busting out all over in these conservatories.

Volvo Tennis Tournament, University of Illinois Circle Campus Pavilion, 413-5740.

International Theatre Festival of Chicago, various theaters, 664-3370. They *hope* it will be annual. Twenty productions.

MAY

Chicago International Art Exposition, Navy Pier, 787-6858. Art and photo galleries from the world over convene with their best goodies for sale at one of America's most prestigious (and largest) art expos.

Buckingham Fountain, Grant Park, 744-3370. This elaborate replica of the one from you-know-where is turned on May 1 and spouts until October 1, with nighttime light shows.

Polish Constitution Day Parade (May 7), on Clark St. from Wacker to Congress, 286-0500. The only city in the world where there are more Polish residents than in Chicago is Warsaw, Poland, so this is a big party.

Culture Bus Tours (Sundays and holidays, May 8-Sept.), 836-7000. Guided tours of the city on C.T.A. buses, leaving from the Art Institute every twenty minutes or so, covering three different routes—south, west and north. Approximately $3.

Greek American Parade (May 14), south on Michigan Ave. from Wacker to Congress. Chicago's Greeks aren't to be left out either.

Wright Plus Tour, 848-1978. A walk through the Frank Lloyd Wright home and studio in Oak Park. The tour begins at the nearby Wright center; call for information.

Chicago International Festival of Flowers and Gardens, Navy Pier, 787-6858. Yet another flower show. Perhaps this flower mania is the reason why Chicago once called itself the "Garden City."

JUNE

Asparagus Fest, Lincoln Ave., Lawrence Ave. and Western Ave., 878-7331. Get down with your little green buddies.

Park West Antiques Fair (first weekend in June), 600 W. Fullerton Ave., 477-5100. Antiques merchants gather to hawk their wares.

Body Politic Street Festival (first weekend in June), 2200 block of N. Lincoln Ave., 348-7901. Boogie with street bands and the artsy crowd.

Chicago Blues Festival, Petrillo Music Shell, Grant Park, 744-3315. A wonderful—and free—three days of music here in the home of the urban electric blues.

Old Town Art Fair (second weekend in June), 1800 N. Lincoln Ave., 337-1938. A street fair offering everything from sofa-size paintings to "real" art.

Puerto Rican Day Parade (June 11), on Clark from Wacker to Congress, 292-1414. Viva puertorriquenos!

Filipino American Council Parade, on Clark St. from Wacker to Congress, 281-1210. Chicago's Philippine community has also been growing quickly in recent years.

Chicago International Boat Show, Navy Pier, 787-6858. What more can one say?

Gospel Festival, Petrillo Music Shell, Grant Park, 744-3315. Even for nonbelievers, a moving battle of the bands, holy style.

Chicago Maritime Folk Festival, Navy Pier, 348-2017. The Sloop John B lives! A celebration of the sea—held, cleverly enough, at Navy Pier—featuring folk musicians and storytellers working out maritime themes. Also scrimshaw and tattoo artists, model ship exhibits and sea-related antiques.

Printers Row Book Fair, on Dearborn St. from Harrison to Polk, 663-1595. Used-book aficionados shouldn't miss this open-air book sale.

Grant Park Concerts, Petrillo Music Shell, Grant Park, 744-3315. Starting in late June and running through the end of August, free concerts are held Wednesday, Friday and Saturday at 8 p.m. and Sunday at 7 p.m.

Ravinia Festival, Ravinia Park, Highland Park, 728-4642. A summer of music, both classical and pop, on the lawn or under the shell, from late June through Labor Day.

Gay Parade (last Sun. in June), south from 3800 N. to 2800 N. Broadway, 348-8243. Yes, all of Chicago's minorities are proud. This annual parade, one of the first of its kind in the country, is ebullient and always colorful; and, as a bonus, it never fails to shock the neighborhood's high-rise matrons. A festival, featuring music, food and rallies, is held in Lincoln Park after the parade.

PGA Beatrice Western Open, Butler Golf Course, Oakbrook, 724-4600.

JULY

Taste of Chicago, Grant Park, 744-3370. For seven days centering on the Fourth of July weekend, nearly 100 restaurants set up bite-size booths to host a preferred Chicago way to celebrate the revolution—by eating enough for an entire regiment.

Fireworks Display and Concert (Fourth of July weekend), Petrillo Music Shell, Grant Park, 744-3370. A way to give your stomach a rest from all that Taste of Chicago food, for a while at least.

Air & Water Show, Chicago Ave. at Lake Michigan, 294-2200. Amazing stunts and gymnastics, aerial and aquatic, along the lakefront; featuring a flying convention of aircraft fierce, lovely and strange, doing their zooming tricks over the lake by the Gold Coast.

Chicago–Mackinac Island Boat Race, Chicago Yacht Club, Monroe Street Harbor, 861-7777. Considerable crowds gather to send off sailboats of all sizes on a 300-some-mile race that runs the length of Lake Michigan.

Chinatown Moon Festival, Cermak and Wentworth. Call the Chinatown Chamber of Commerce, 326-5320, or the Department of Human Services, 277-8000.

Taste of Lincoln Avenue, on Lincoln from Fullerton to Wrightwood, 477-5100. North Side eateries show off their stuff.

AUGUST

Irish Festival, Navy Pier, 775-1749. Yet another strong, proud Chicago ethnic community struts its stuff.

Medieval Faire in Oz Park, Webster, Larrabee and Lincoln, 880-5200. An urbanized version of the Renaissance Faire, with food, crafts and entertainment of the era.

Pan American Festival, Navy Pier, 772-2244. Three days of salsa—both musical and edible—with bands from Mexico, the Caribbean and South America, and corresponding *sabroso* food booths.

Gold Coast Art Fair, vicinity of Oak St. and Rush St., 744-3370. More tacky alleged art per block than all the others, and a laugh riot for the discerning collector.

Bud Billikin Day Parade, 31st St. and King Dr. to Washington Park, 225-2400. Events and festivities celebrating the *Chicago Defender*'s support of the black community.

Venetian Night, Chicago River from Monroe Harbor, 744-3315. A water parade of illuminated boats decorated according to ethnic and purely imaginative ideas, Venetian Night is a sailor's Halloween.

Festa Italiana, Navy Pier, 829-8888. *Mangia, mangia* to Mediterranean tunes.

Dancin' in the Streets: River North Festival of the Arts, River North, 643-1988. Primarily a dance festival; a street stage showcases performances ranging from ethnic folk dancing to avant-ballet. There's also a dance contest, a dance marathon and, for the uninitiated, dance lessons.

Chicago Triathlon, from Oak Street Beach south along the lake, 761-6311. Billed as "the world's largest." Would-be Supermen and Superwomen run, bike and swim their hearts out along the lakefront.

Chicago Jazz Festival, Petrillo Music Shell, Grant Park, 744-3315. This series of free jazz concerts featuring international legends claims to be the world's largest.

Rhythm & Blues Festival, Navy Pier, 663-3101. Top black artists and the best local blues bands boogie for three days.

Arlington Million, Arlington Park Race Track, 255-4300. Illinois' richest horse race takes place in late August.

SEPTEMBER

Chicago Federation of Labor Parade (Friday before Labor Day), on Dearborn St. from Wacker to Congress, 263-6642. Chicago's workingmen and -women unite.

Lyric Opera, Chicago Opera House, 20 N. Wacker Dr., 332-2244. The season opens midmonth.

Chicago Symphony Orchestra, Orchestra Hall, 435-8111. Its season also opens midmonth.

Berghoff Oktoberfest, Adams St. from State to Dearborn, 427-3170. Named for the landmark German restaurant, these four days of schnitzels and beer jump the gun a bit, but who's counting?

Chicago International New Art Forms Exposition, Navy Pier, 787-6858. "What the devil is *that*, Helen?" "You got me, George—I suppose it's art, but that artist is sure no Norman Rockwell." "You said it. But a lot of these people here seem to love this modern-art stuff."

OCTOBER

Columbus Day Parade, on Dearborn St. from Wacker to Congress, 828-0010. Now it's the Italians' turn to puff up their chests and walk proud.

Chicago International Antiques Show, Navy Pier, 787-6858. The old vies with the older, sort of like the Maxwell Street flea market for the museum set, as antiques dealers from the world over converge.

Chicago International Film Festival, various Chicago theaters, 644-3400. The selections are usually dutifully obscure, but there are happy surprises every year.

NOVEMBER

Chrysanthemum show, Lincoln Park and Garfield Park conservatories, 294-4770 and 533-1281. More flowers to brighten the approaching gloom of Chicago's winter.

Christmas Around the World, Museum of Science and Industry, 57th St. and Lake Shore Dr., 648-1414. Seasonal exhibits featuring crèches and decorated trees from almost everywhere Christmas is celebrated, from Thanksgiving to New Year's.

Christmas Tree Lighting, Daley Plaza, 744-3770. The lighting of the 75-foot (or so) city tree, accompanied by choirs and a few speeches, generally takes place the Friday after Thanksgiving.

Christmas Parade, on Michigan Ave. south of the Chicago River (location may vary), 744-3770. Leaving nothing to the last minute, it's right after Thanksgiving.

DECEMBER

The Nutcracker ballet, Arie Crown Theatre, McCormick Pl., 791-6000. Taking your kids, or borrowing some to take, is a longtime Chicago holiday tradition.

A Christmas Carol, Goodman Theater, 200 S. Columbus Dr., 443-3800. This production is also establishing itself as a holiday perennial.

Christmas Flower Show, Lincoln Park and Garfield Park conservatories, 294-4770 and 533-1281. And we're back to the beginning. See January entry.

MAPS

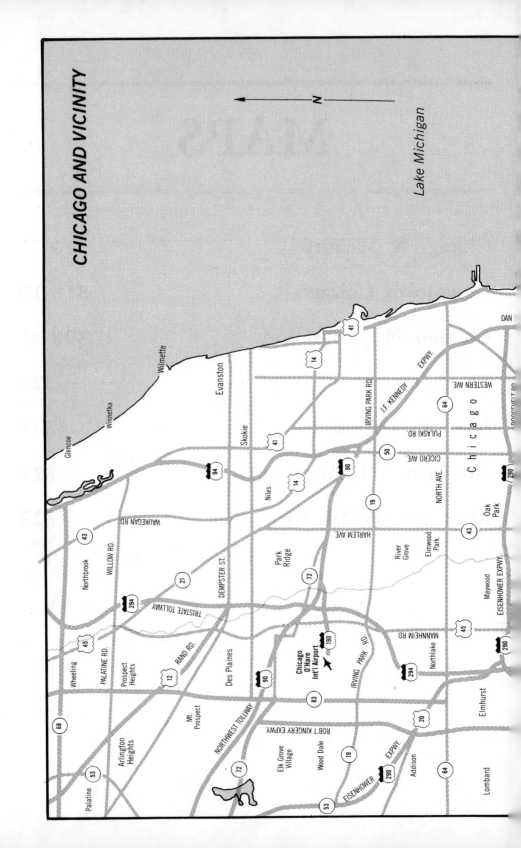

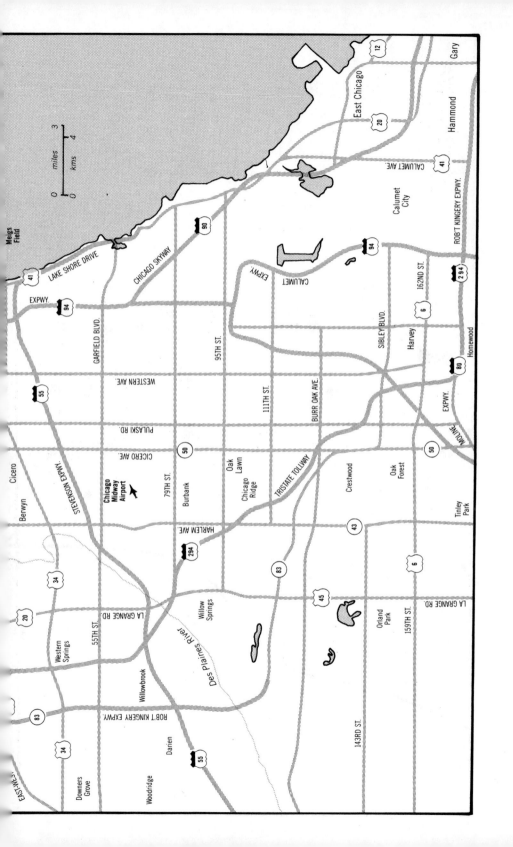

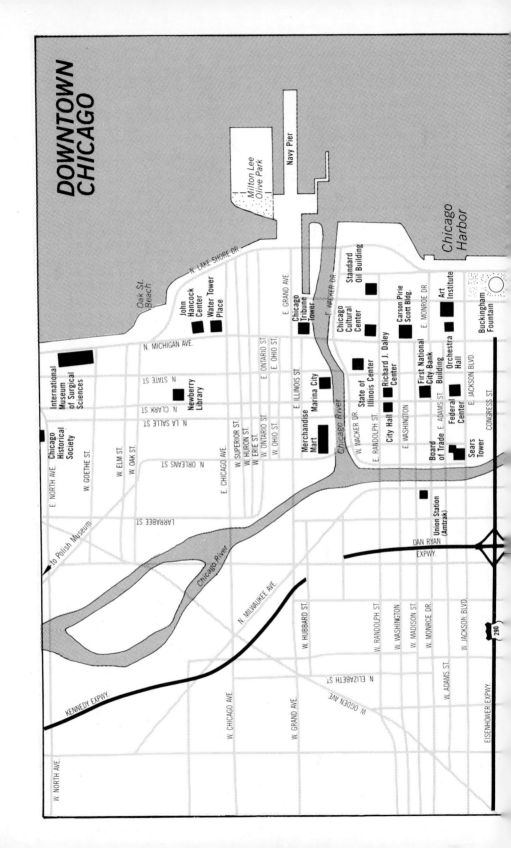

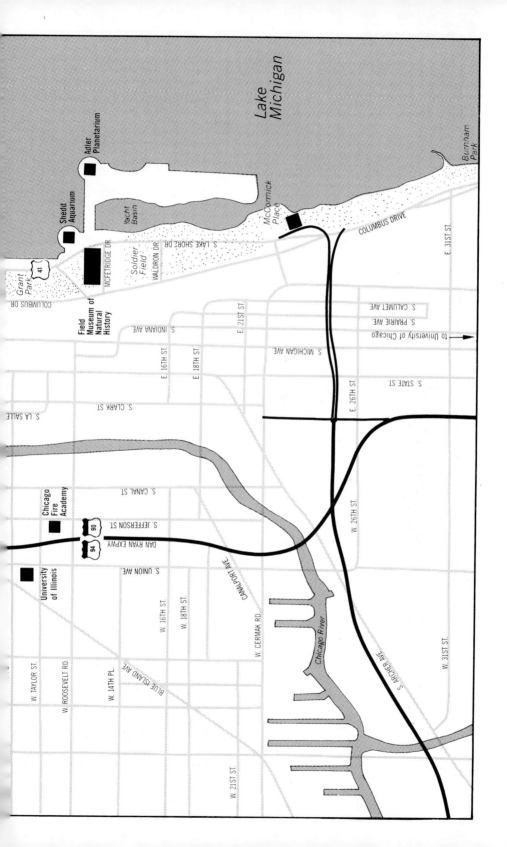

CHICAGO NEIGHBORHOODS

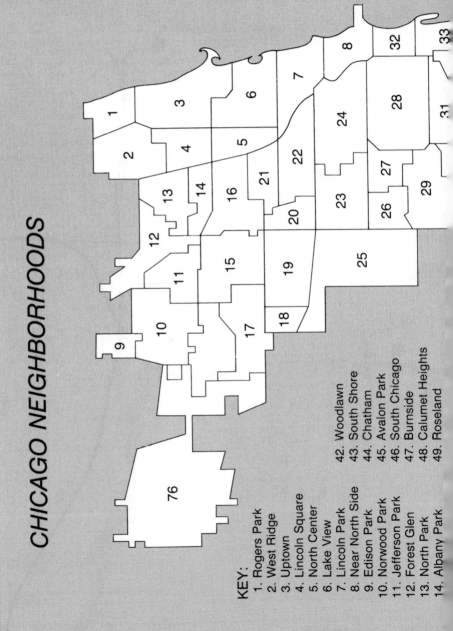

←—N—

KEY:
1. Rogers Park
2. West Ridge
3. Uptown
4. Lincoln Square
5. North Center
6. Lake View
7. Lincoln Park
8. Near North Side
9. Edison Park
10. Norwood Park
11. Jefferson Park
12. Forest Glen
13. North Park
14. Albany Park

42. Woodlawn
43. South Shore
44. Chatham
45. Avalon Park
46. South Chicago
47. Burnside
48. Calumet Heights
49. Roseland

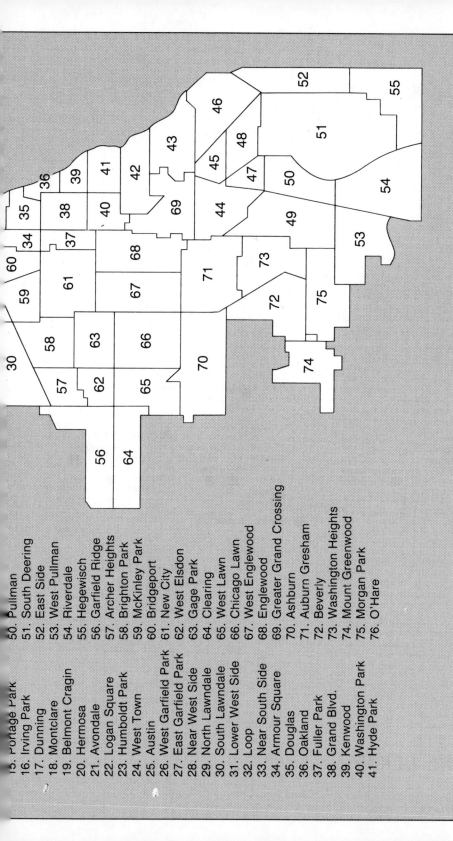

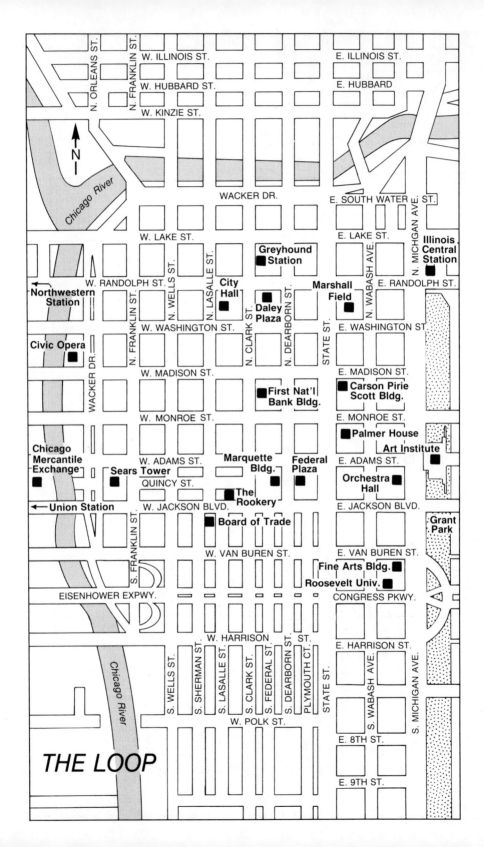

THE LOOP

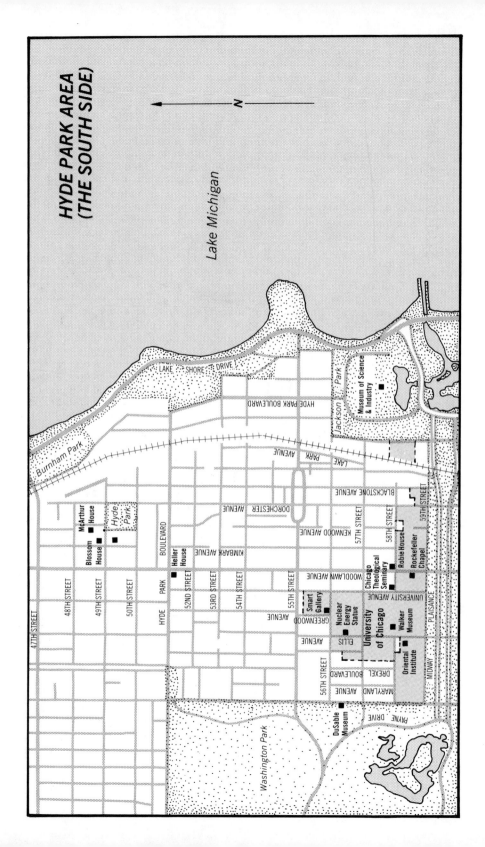

HYDE PARK AREA
(THE SOUTH SIDE)

N

Lake Michigan

LAKE SHORE DRIVE

HYDE PARK BOULEVARD

Burnham Park

Jackson Park

Museum of Science & Industry

LAKE PARK AVENUE

BLACKSTONE AVENUE

DORCHESTER AVENUE

KENWOOD AVENUE

57TH STREET

58TH STREET

59TH STREET

McArthur House

Hyde Park

Blossom House

HYDE PARK BOULEVARD

Heller House

KIMBARK AVENUE

52ND STREET

53RD STREET

54TH STREET

55TH STREET

WOODLAWN AVENUE

Robie House

Rockefeller Chapel

Chicago Theological Seminary

47TH STREET

48TH STREET

49TH STREET

50TH STREET

HYDE PARK BOULEVARD

GREENWOOD AVENUE

Smart Gallery

Nuclear Energy Statue

UNIVERSITY AVENUE

University of Chicago

Walker Museum

ELLIS AVENUE

56TH STREET

DREXEL BOULEVARD

MARYLAND AVENUE

Oriental Institute

MIDWAY PLAISANCE

Washington Park

DuSable Museum

PAYNE DRIVE

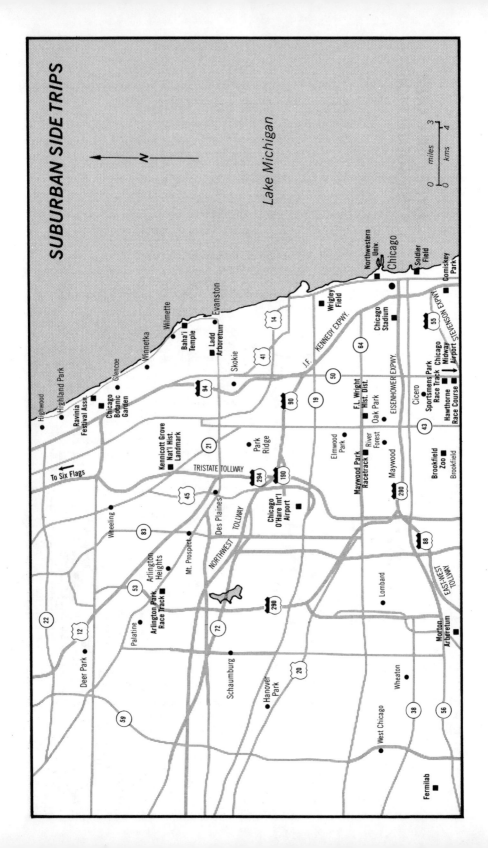

SUBURBAN SIDE TRIPS

N

Lake Michigan

0 miles 3
0 kms 4

Northwestern Univ.
Chicago
Soldier Field
Comiskey Park

Wrigley Field

Chicago Stadium

J.F. KENNEDY EXPWY.

Evanston

Baha'i Temple
Ladd Arboretum

Skokie

55

64

Midway Airport

F.L. Wright Hist. Dist.
Oak Park

EISENHOWER EXPWY.

Cicero

Sportsmens Park Race Track
Hawthorne Race Course

50

19

43

Highwood
Highland Park
Ravinia Festival Assn.

Winnetka
Glencoe

Wilmette

Chicago Botanic Garden

94

90

Elmwood Park

Maywood Park Racetrack
River Forest
Maywood

290

Brookfield Zoo
Brookfield

Park Ridge

Kennicott Grove Nat'l Hist. Landmark

TRISTATE TOLLWAY

21

To Six Flags

45

294

190

Des Plaines

Chicago O'Hare Int'l Airport

NORTHWEST TOLLWAY

88

EAST-WEST TOLLWAY

Wheeling

83

Mt. Prospect

Lombard

Arlington Heights

Arlington Park Race Track

53

Palatine

22

12

Deer Park

72

Schaumburg

Hanover Park

20

290

Morton Arboretum

Wheaton

38

56

West Chicago

59

Fermilab

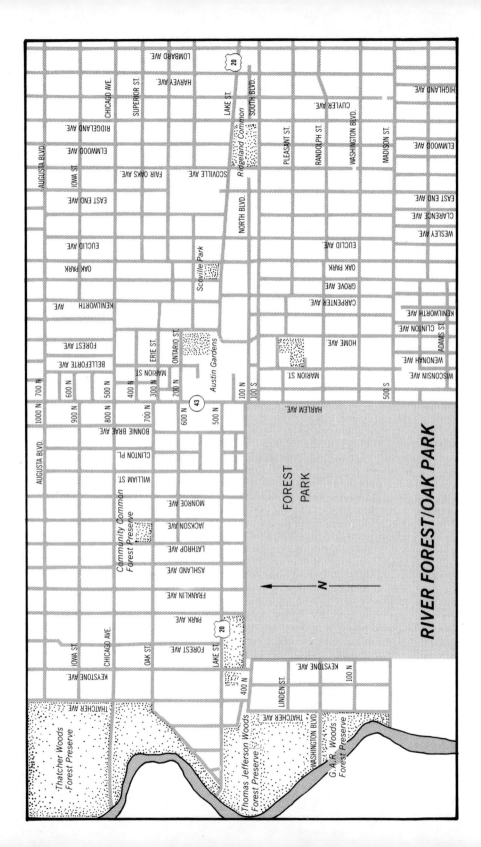

INDEX

D

E

H

T

The Gault Millau series of guidebooks reflects our readers' demand for insightful, incisive reporting on the best (and worst) that the world's most exciting destinations have to offer. To help us tailor our books even better to your needs, please take a moment to fill out this anonymous (if you wish) questionnaire, returning it to:

Gault Millau, Inc., P.O. Box 361144, Los Angeles, CA 90036.

1. How did you hear about the Gault Millau guides: newspaper, magazine, radio, friends, other (please specify)?

    ....

    ....

2. Please list in order of preference the cities (or countries) on which you would like to have a Gault Millau guide, aside from the already existing destinations.

    ....

    ....

3. Do you refer to the Gault Millau guides in your travels or for your own city?

    A. (Travels) .... B. (Own city) .... C. (Both) ....

4. Do you use any other guides than Gault Millau?

    If yes ....

5. Please list, starting with the most preferred, the three features that you like most about the Gault Millau guides.

    A. ....

    B. ....

    C. ....

6. What are the features, if any, you dislike about the Gault Millau guides?

....

....

7. Please list any features you would like to see added to the Gault Millau guides.

....

....

8. Please list the features you like most about your favorite guidebook series if it is not Gault Millau?

A. ....

B. ....

C. ....

9. How many trips do you make per year for business and for pleasure?

Business: International: .... Domestic: ....

Pleasure: International: .... Domestic: ....

10. Is your annual household income over (check appropriate choice)?

$ 20,000 .... $ 40,000 .... $ 60,000 ....

$ 80,000 .... $ 100,000 .... Other (please specify) ....

11. If you have any comments on the Gault Millau guides in general, please enclose them on a separate sheet of paper.

We thank you for your interest in the Gault Millau guides and we welcome your remarks and your recommendations about restaurants, hotels, shops, services.

CHI

MORE GAULT MILLAU "BEST" GUIDES

Now the series known throughout Europe for its wit and savvy reveals the best of major U.S. and European areas—New York, Washington, D.C., Los Angeles, San Francisco, Chicago, New England, France and Italy. Following the guidelines established by the world-class French food critics Henri Gault and Christian Millau, local teams of writers directed by André Gayot, partner of Gault Millau, have gathered inside information about where to stay, what to do, where to shop, and where to dine or catch a quick bite in these key locales. Each volume sparkles with the wit, wisdom, and panache that readers have come to expect from Gault Millau, whose distinctive style makes them favorites among travelers bored with the neutral, impersonal style of other guides. There are full details on the best of everything that makes these cities special places to visit, including restaurants, diversions, nightlife, hotels, shops, the arts—all the unique sights and sounds of each city. These guides also offer practical information on getting around and coping with each city. Filled with provocative, entertaining, and frank reviews, they are helpful as well as fun to read. Perfect for visitors and residents alike.

Please send me the books checked below

☐	The Best of Chicago	$15.95
☐	The Best of London	$16.95
☐	The Best of Los Angeles	$14.95
☐	The Best of New England	$15.95
☐	The Best of New York	$14.95
☐	The Best of Paris	$16.95
☐	The Best of San Francisco	$14.95
☐	The Best of Washington, D.C.	$14.95
☐	The Best of France	$16.95
☐	The Best of Italy	$16.95

PRENTICE HALL TRADE DIVISION
Order Department—Travel Books
200 Old Tappan Road
Old Tappan, New Jersey 07675

In U.S. include $2 shipping UPS for 1st book, $1 each additional book. Outside U.S., $3 and $1 respectively.

Enclosed is my check or money order for $ —————————————————

NAME ————————————————————————————————

ADDRESS ——————————————————————————————

CITY ———————————————— STATE ——————— ZIP ————————